CAPABILITY BROWN
DESIGNING THE ENGLISH LANDSCAPE

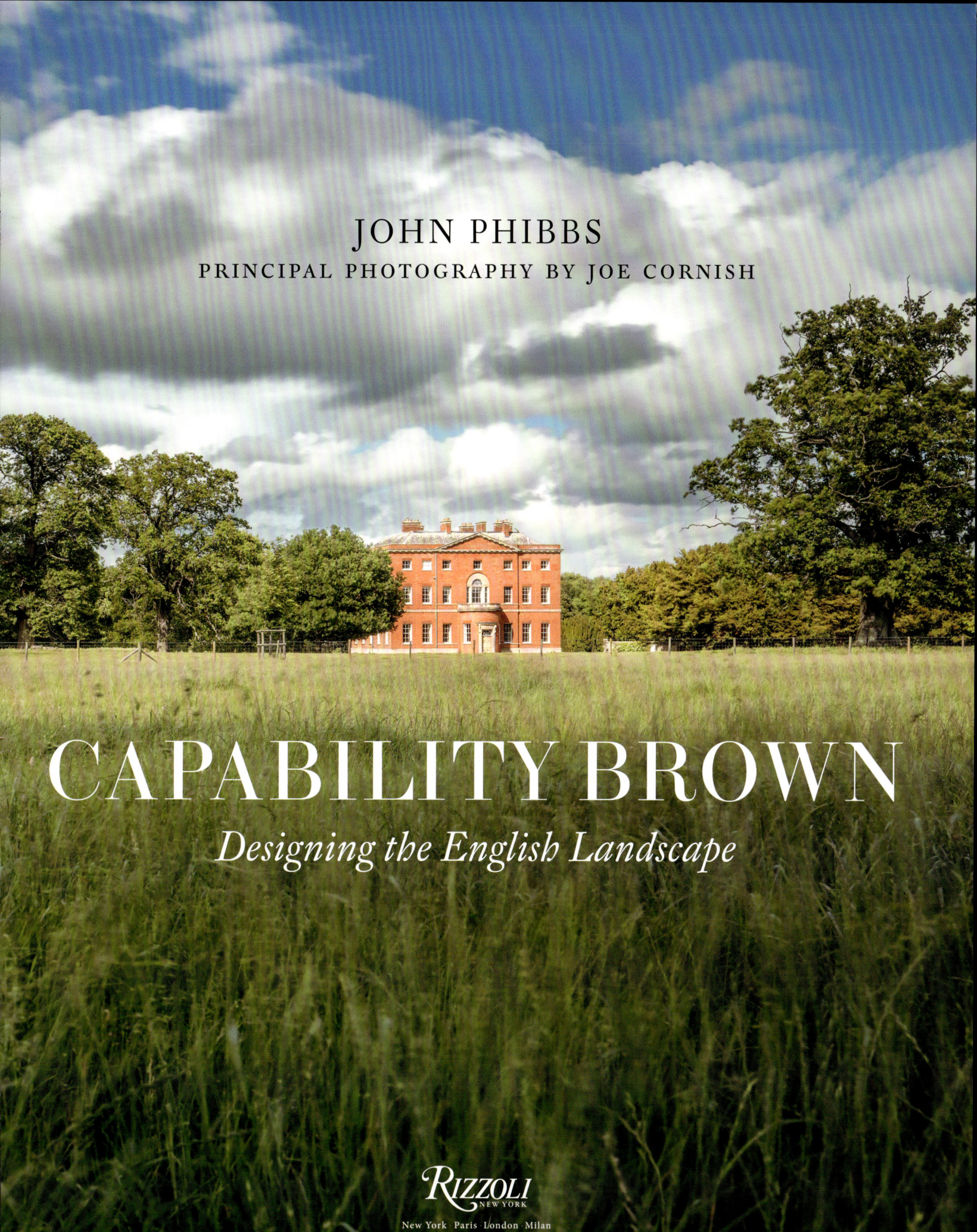

First published in the United States
of America in 2016 by
Rizzoli International Publications, Inc.
300 Park Avenue South
New York, NY 10010
www.rizzoliusa.com

Copyright © 2016 by John Phibbs
All photography copyright © 2016 by Joe Cornish
except as noted on page 280.

Picture research by Kate Hesketh-Harvey

Designed and typeset in Fleischman by Dalrymple

All rights reserved. No part of this may be reproduced, stored in a retrieval system, or transmitted in any form or by any means, electronic, mechanical, photocopying, recording, or otherwise, without prior consent of the publishers.

ISBN: 978-0-8478-4883-6
Library of Congress Catalog Control
Number: 2016944206

2017 2018 2019 / 10 9 8 7 6 5 4 3

Printed in China

Dust jacket front: The hunting tower on the wild hill of the old deer park rises above the polished gardens of Chatsworth House.

Dust jacket back: The formality of the avenue at Wotton does not detract from the fundamentally bucolic scene.

Case wrap: The oak avenue at Moccas was planted in 1841 to link the house with its ancient deer park.

Previous pages: A preamble in Brown's English landscape.

Page 1: The old farm gate at Himley is an inducement to explore.

Page 2: Brown's approach, as well as several of the drives that might be attributed to him at Milton Abbey, make long straight cuts through the hillside.

Pages 3 and 4: A series of ponds and water-courses collects the water from the higher ground of Baggeridge Woods and feeds it into the water system at Himley Hall.

Page 5: A woodland beech at Himley Hall. Brown frequently cut the top off every other beech when planting in plantations to get a better chance of success; he also recommended cutting unsuccessful saplings to the ground to allow them to reshoot.

Page 6: The park at Himley has reverted to agriculture, but still retains the stamp of Brown's work.

Page 7: The oaks around Pauncefoot Manor conceal it today in views from Broadlands.

Title pages: Moccas Court remains an agricultural landscape.

Introduction 13

THE EARLY DAYS
1 Kirkharle and Wallington 24
2 Stowe 38
3 Wotton House 54
4 Wakefield Lodge 68

THE MIDDLE PERIOD
5 Petworth House 90
6 Burghley House 104
7 Chatsworth 126
8 Blenheim Palace 142

THE PRIME YEARS
9 Broadlands 156
10 Weston Park 174
11 Milton Abbey 190

THE LATE WORK
12 Himley Hall 212
13 Dinefwr 228
14 Moccas Court 240
15 Berrington Hall 254

To Conclude 267
Notes 277
Acknowledgments 280

— CAPABILITY BROWN —

INTRODUCTION

WE DEFINE OURSELVES by the art we produce—fifth-century Athens, fourteenth-century Florence, seventeenth-century Paris. We remember these times and places not for the way people lived, but for what they left behind.

As with these peaks of European civilization, each nation also breaks up its history into centuries. So England has the sixteenth of Elizabeth and Shakespeare, the seventeenth of civil war, the nineteenth of Victoria and empire, the twentieth of war again. Its eighteenth century, though, presents a curious blank. The century in which England became a world power, driven by an astonishing array of engineers and inventors, soldiers and thinkers, is but modestly represented in school curricula. Perhaps this has happened because, despite all their achievements, these men and women left behind no equally potent tradition in the arts. There was no one in their ranks to match such sculptors as Donatello of the Italian Renaissance or Praxiteles at the Acropolis.

However plausible this explanation may sound, a very different story comes closer to the truth. The eighteenth century did produce a great artist, it did create a great art form, but this art, at its best, was consciously intended to go unnoticed. For a strange extravagance united the educated classes of eighteenth-century Britain, a fascination with the possibilities of refashioning the land itself to express a new kind of relationship with nature. In the words of the poet Thomas Gray, "It is not forty years since the art was born among us; and it is sure that there was nothing in Europe like it."[1] This was the English response to Florentine sculpture and Athenian temples. The English style of landscape gardening was a new art, its medium the country estate, and its Michelangelo—an original, self-taught genius, acknowledged in his own time as "the Shakespeare of Gardening"—was Capability Brown.

Lancelot Brown (1716–1783), also known as "Capability," liked to call himself a "place-maker," but was more often described as a magician. The Rev. William Gilpin, though he knew Brown as a man, was still driven to describe his work at Burghley as a piece of magic "so great it has given ye house a

opposite: Nathaniel Dance's portrait of Brown was painted in about 1769 and copied several times for his clients, as here at Burghley House.

new situation: from a bottom he has raised it upon a hill."[2] Brown had the uncanny ability to transform the countryside, and yet leave no mark of his presence upon it, and in consequence, as his obituarist observed, such "was the effect of his genius that when he was the happiest man, he will be least remembered; so closely did he copy nature that his works will be mistaken." That sense of magic and mystery persists as we try to understand Brown today. Not only are his interventions in nature generally imperceptible on the ground, but he also wrote very little about his work. At most of the places where he is known to have contributed we have no plans or correspondence, at many sites there are no accounts. Even Chatsworth has no plans by Brown and only a handful of references in the estate records.

While I have tried to make it clear when a piece of work is known to have been carried out by Brown, so often the judgement as to whether he himself was involved is one of connoisseurship—a detail of earth-working or tree-planting is judged to be Brownian because something like it crops up in a number of other places where he is known to have had a commission. I have not tried to conceal how little we know. So often all we are left with is an unverifiable sense that something great has happened to a place.

It would be understandable for anyone, given this degree of uncertainty, to dismiss Brown's work as too vague to be rated, but I would ask his critics to compare it with that done by his foremen when they were working independently. Samuel Lapidge, for example, worked closely with Brown for nearly twenty years and was the executor of his estate, but Lapidge's own plans, such as his designs for

right: The Grecian Valley from the Temple of Concord and Victory, Stowe.

14 · CAPABILITY BROWN

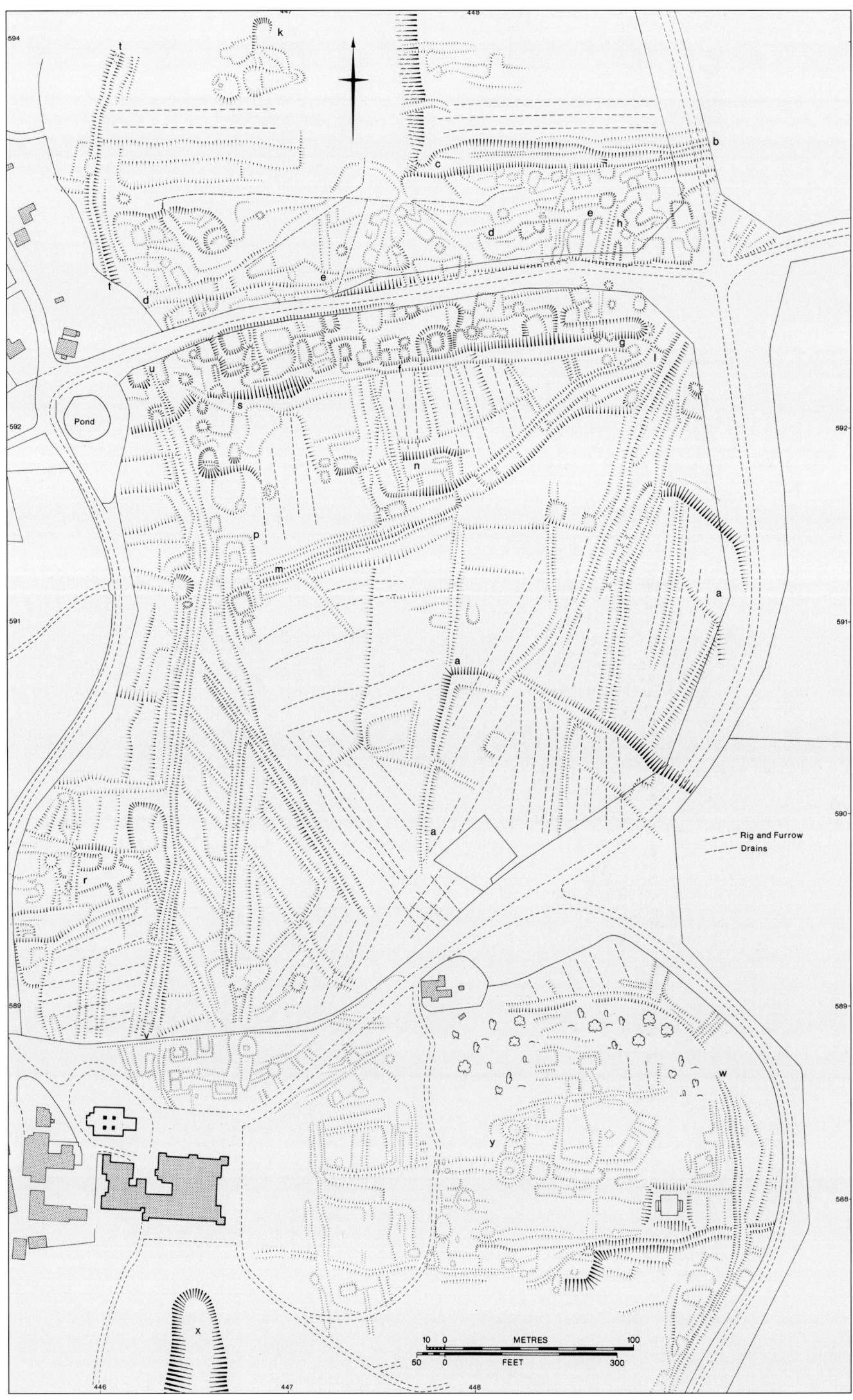

Milton Park, Peterborough, and Burley-on-the-Hill, Rutland, are embarrassingly weak and tentative. On the other hand, where Brown had set up a project, the contribution of his foremen is indistinguishable from his own. In short, there was something that Brown was able to provide as designer and leader of his organization that even his closest and most experienced colleagues could not match.

We must sympathize then with those tourists who come in the hundreds of thousands to Brown today—to Blenheim and to Chatsworth—what do they see? What do they make of all those trees? Of the water? Of the grass? The grass is the most mysterious thing, a perceptive Chinese visitor of the 1920s was amazed that any civilized person should want a "mown and bordered lawn" that "while no doubt pleasing to a cow, could hardly engage the intellect of human beings."[3] When I took my grandfather, a Sligo man, to see Blenheim, he said it was all very fine, but a waste of a good cabbage field, and I had to concede the point.

On the other hand, if we accept that Brown's idea was to explore the underlying character of the land rather than to impose upon it, then it follows that he, in concert with Edmund Burke and his contemporaries, might strive to reclaim an imagined golden age of pastoralism from England's deep Plantagenet past. For, despite the lack of clarity that surrounds his work, what we see in William Shenstone, Horace Walpole, Thomas Whately, and those who wrote about the English landscape movement in the eighteenth century, is not just the appropriation of a kind of gardening as English in origin, rather than French or Chinese, but a reaching back into the past to redefine what it was to be English in terms of the hitherto despised gothic, of organic growth, as Burke might have described it, that set itself up as anti-intellectual and irrational, in opposition to the conspicuously rational gardens and attitudes of the French, and that promoted Shakespeare above Racine and Corneille. These people, one might add, were fully aware of the importance of Britain and Britishness as a vehicle to strengthen the union between England and Scotland, but they were equally determined that this would be an English landscape movement, not a Scottish one.

I have also tried in this book to provide a narrative in which Brown's style developed continually from landscape to landscape throughout his career. It is easy to find apparent exceptions: a landscape such as Heveningham, from the end of his life, does not, on the face of it, differ greatly in ambition and technique from Coombe Abbey (1771–1772) or Burghley (from 1754), laid out ten and twenty years earlier. However, there are affinities between some of the landscapes he was involved with in his early days (Stowe and Wotton); there is a new understanding of order and gradation at Burghley (1754–1779) and Petworth (1752–1765), and equally there is something carefree and unconstrained about his work from the mid-1760s, as seen in Broadlands (1763–1779) and Milton (1763–1782). One would like to think that at the end of his career, at Moccas Court (1778–1781) and Dinefwr (1775), he had somehow brought about a new fusion between the parkland and the countryside beyond.

I might alternatively have used the degree of Brown's involvement with each landscape as a means of categorizing his work. His landscapes

opposite: The parkland immediately north of Highclere Castle still bears the imprint of the medieval village and ironworks. Its earthworks are perfectly preserved under the grass and were left as found in Brown's day.

can be divided into three classes on that account. There are those, like Stapleford and Highclere Castle, for which he simply provided a plan, usually submitted on a base provided by one of his surveyors, Samuel Lapidge or John Spyers. These tend to have had limited or no ground modeling—the medieval agricultural earthworks and the archaeological remains of older gardens often survive today under the turf. Then there are places where he worked as a contractor, with or without a foreman, or at least regularly visited the site as a consultant, and these places fall into two classes—those with extensive earthworks, such as Himley and Blenheim, where hills have been removed and ground levels changed by up to 4 meters (these can usually be singled out by the disappearance of medieval earthworks); and those where the earthworking was limited to slight modifications to create local effects, as at Broadlands and Dinefwr, embellishing the existing topography and scenery, rather than changing it.

One might also distinguish between those places where Brown had a short contract and those such as Burghley, Milton, and Himley, where he worked for a decade or more and may be said to be more deeply imbued with his character and ideas.

Because this is a book of photographs, its emphasis is inevitably visual, but one should always read landscape photographs with a degree of caution. The photograph captures one fleeting moment that happened to attract the photographer, while landscape

above: The parkland at Broadlands rises above the water-meadows, which Brown left largely untouched.

18 · CAPABILITY BROWN

is something in constant flux. In addition, although in his day landscape was primarily judged by what it looked like, Brown himself was not primarily a visual artist. It is true that there are landscapes whose form seems to be determined very largely by picture-book compositions, designed to be seen from fixed points. These sites include Brown's earliest work: Stowe, Croome, and Wotton, but there are many more, such as Dinefwr, in which his physical alterations were minimal and his contribution was to provide routes and particular points from which to enjoy the existing landscape—his work is closer to sculpture in that respect and, indeed, his materials are evidently as three-dimensional as sculpture. However, Brown's skills are architectural as well, not only because he designed so many buildings, as at Burghley, but also because so often his freedom to design was constrained by external factors such as the prior existence of buildings and trees, the sources of water, the demands of his client, and the needs of a country estate.

A NOTE ON LANDSCAPE TYPES

Brown's work is associated in the public mind with parks and gardens. However, he worked on a number of other types of landscape, which the selection in this book mostly covers. The term "park" is used for a deer park, while "parkland" is a more generic term, which might be defined as "land that looks like a deer park, but generally is not."

overleaf: The design of Wotton is relatively stiff and inflexible, but the landscape is animated by the farm animals that graze upon it.

INTRODUCTION · 19

1716–1751
THE EARLY DAYS

The english landscape style is made up of and formed by four distinct components, to which, as luck would have it, Brown had been exposed at an early stage in his career: at Wallington, Stowe, Wotton, and Wakefield Lodge.

opposite: Codger's Fort may have been built as a defense against another Jacobite rebellion from Scotland, but it also ornamented the Rothley Lakes near Wallington in Northumberland. To the south, the top of another folly, Rothley Castle, stands out above the trees.

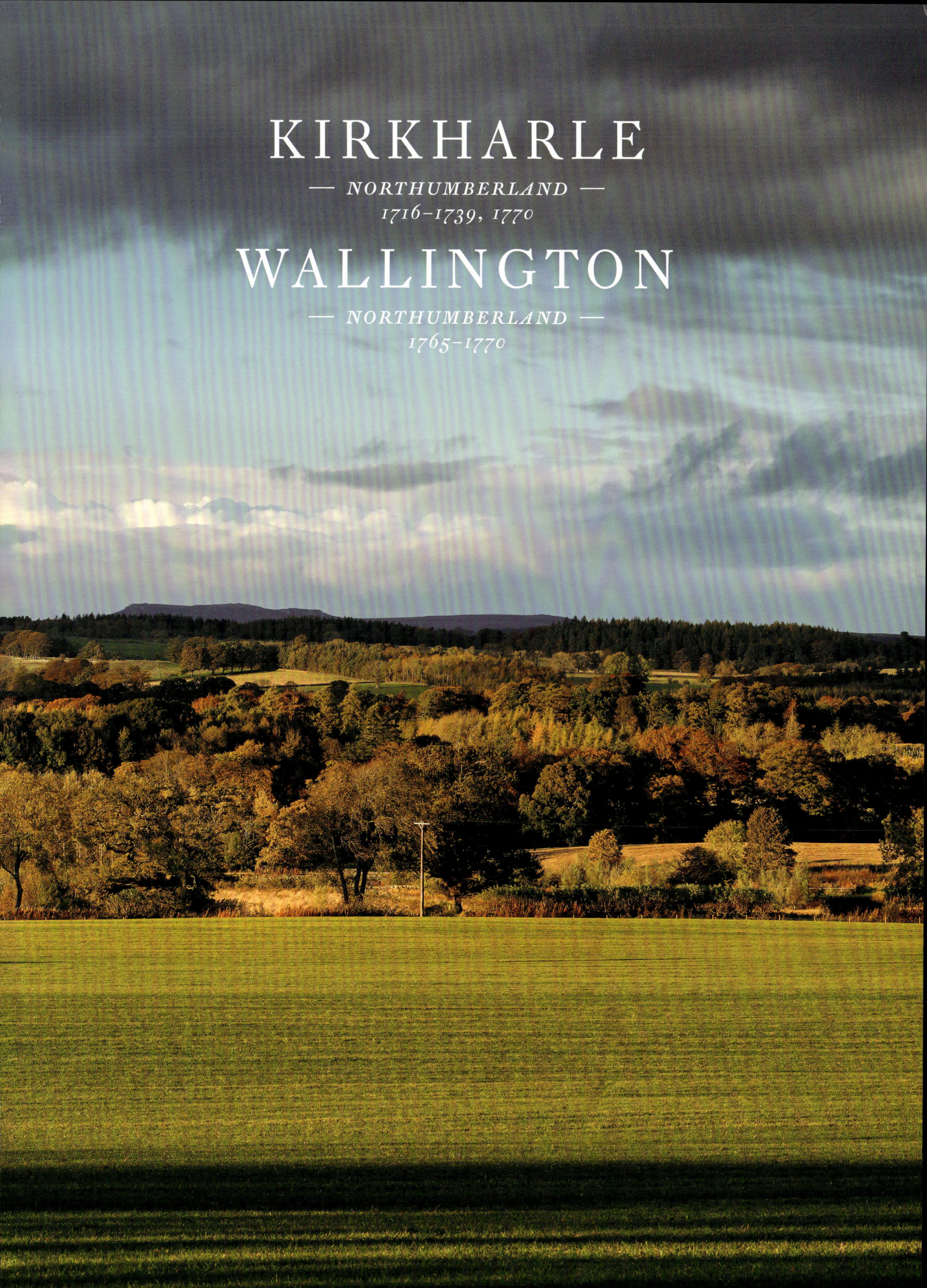

KIRKHARLE
— NORTHUMBERLAND —
1716–1739, 1770

WALLINGTON
— NORTHUMBERLAND —
1765–1770

— CHAPTER ONE —

KIRKHARLE
AND WALLINGTON

LANCELOT "CAPABILITY" BROWN was baptised on August 30, 1716, at Kirkharle, Northumberland, the fifth of six children of William Brown, a yeoman farmer, and his wife Ursula. The farmstead where young Brown spent his first years stood in the shadow of the great house of Kirkharle, and when Sir William Loraine had begun to improve the estate, after inheriting in 1719, Brown and his family were rehoused at a more polite distance. Brown was to begin work in the gardens at Kirkharle in about 1730, and thus one might say that his entire life, from his earliest years, was spent in the atmosphere of "improvement," or "alteration" as Brown himself preferred to call it.

Kirkharle was not a large estate by Northumbrian standards, but crucially for Brown's education, Loraine "divided his lands, erected new farmhouses and buildings, drained the morasses, and cleared the land of 'ponderous massy and hard stones' to prepare it for tillage"; he planted extensively and reshaped the gardens. Thus all the requisites for a business in landscape gardening were offered to the boy. In the 1770s, he was to return to Kirkharle and it was then that he provided a plan for the landscape, but it is for his physical contribution as a teenager that the Loraine family was pleased to regard this as his first work.[1]

Equally educational, however, may have been the improvements set in hand at the neighboring and altogether grander estate, Wallington Hall, which Sir Walter Blackett (1707–1777) had inherited in 1728 from his uncle. Brown went to school in Cambo, Wallington's estate village, and his daily walk would have taken him over the high ground on the south bank of the River Wansbeck, from which the whole estate of Wallington could be seen, and round the west side of the great house. Sir Walter was landscaping at an unprecedented scale, with a series of campaigns that stretched from the Wansbeck to the high point of the estate, Liniel Law, five miles to the north. It was a project that occupied his entire life, and it is impossible to say when or how the idea germinated, but from north to south his embellishments included the ornamental gateway at Liniel Law (1760s), Rothley lakes (1767–1770), Codgers Fort (1769), Rothley Park and Castle (1740–1746), James

previous pages: Kirkharle, eastern Northumberland, with the great bank of Simonside to the north.
opposite: The River Wansbeck effectively bounds the south end of the Wallington estate.
overleaf: Wallington Hall from the south side of the River Wansbeck.

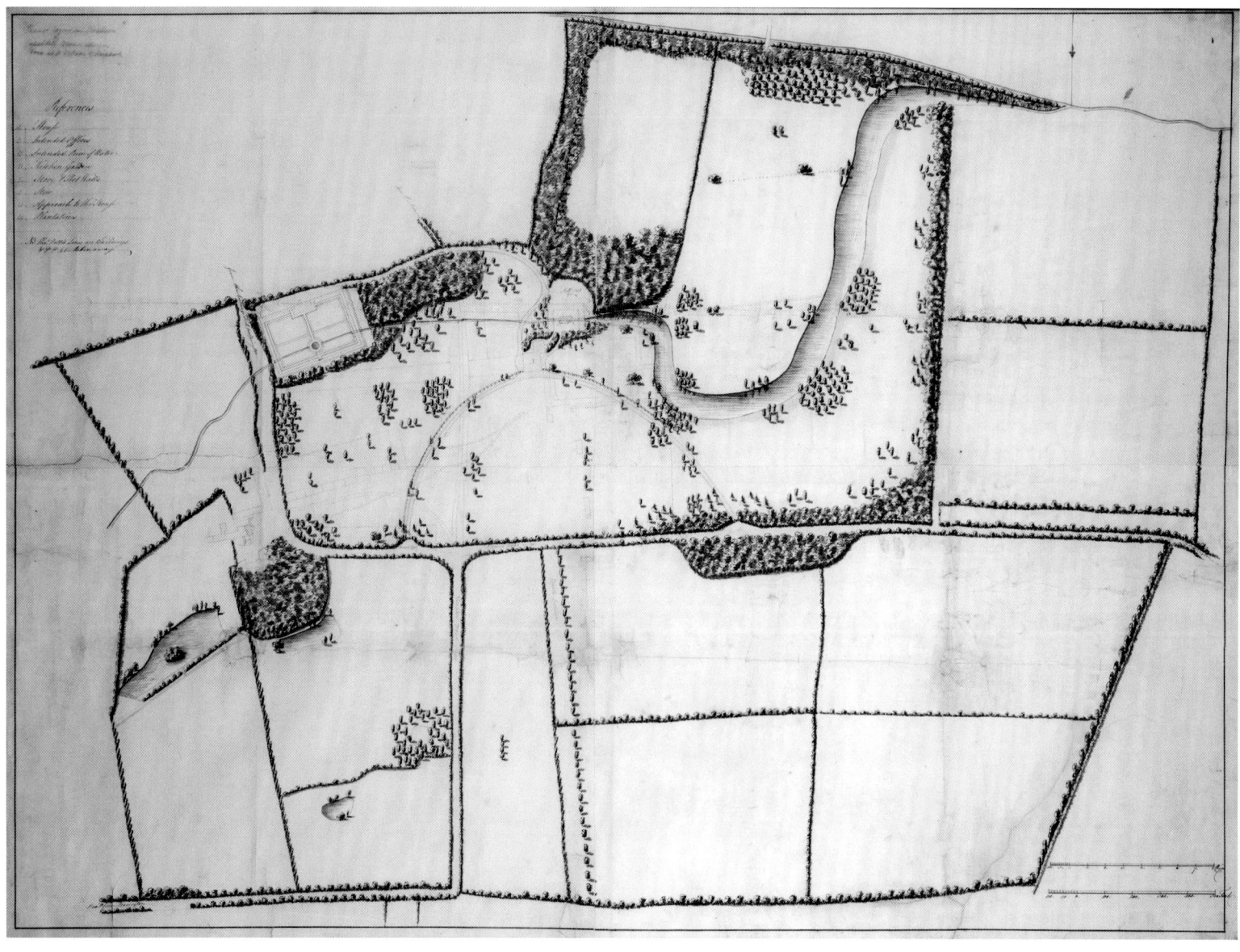

Paine's Bridge (1755) and the Arches (1740s), besides a transformation in the pleasure grounds and around the hall itself. In fact, at least one of the Rothley lakes was designed by Brown.

Although the landscape was designed to be enjoyed by the family and their guests at the hall, it reads best as a journey of the imagination, docking by ship at Alnmouth, traveling up from Rothbury onto the bleakest of moors and Harwood Forest, and then arriving at the sublime hilltop prospect of Liniel Law at the north edge of the estate, from which one drops down through increasingly polished countryside from the sinuous beauty of the Rothley lakes and the sporting ground of Rothley Park to the almost domesticated *ferme ornée* (ornamented farm) between Cambo and the hall itself, with belts of plantation surrounding a series of fields of more or less equal sizes; and, immediately beyond the hall, around the Wansbeck, to the busyness of the nascent mining industry.

Sir Walter also laid out a series of straight roads to connect his estate. These included the route most visitors take today, crossing the Wansbeck on Paine's Bridge. These roads were not the straight ridings that

above: Brown is reckoned to have drawn his plan for Kirkharle as a gift. His proposal was not acted on.
opposite: Evening calm, and the High Lake at Rothley takes on the sinuous character of a river.
overleaf: Wallington must have impressed Brown with the sheer scale of its horizon and the rugged intricacy of its detail.

30 · CAPABILITY BROWN

Brown would shortly discover at Wakefield Lodge and Stowe and that were designed for hunting. They may have been adapted from the needs of hunting but were a means of showing off the landscape and providing for the efficient carriage of goods. Indeed, Sir Walter built them to such a high standard that they were known as "turnpikes." More significant for Brown, however, is the series of private drives or "ridings" that linked the components of the estate. These drives were turfed for summer use by light carriages, and rather than riding roughshod over the terrain, they followed its contours, and took in scenic passages of natural landscape that might otherwise be missed. They were designed for pleasure—happiness, in Dr. Johnson's words, is "being swiftly drawn in a chaise over undulating turf in the company of a beautiful and witty woman."[2]

This use of ridings, by which a landowner might make "a pretty Landskip of his own Possessions,"[3] in the words of the early eighteenth-century journalist

above: The riding can be traced as a slight earthwork running from right to left across the rough grass.
left: The bridge over the Wansbeck, designed by James Paine in 1755.

KIRKHARLE AND WALLINGTON · 35

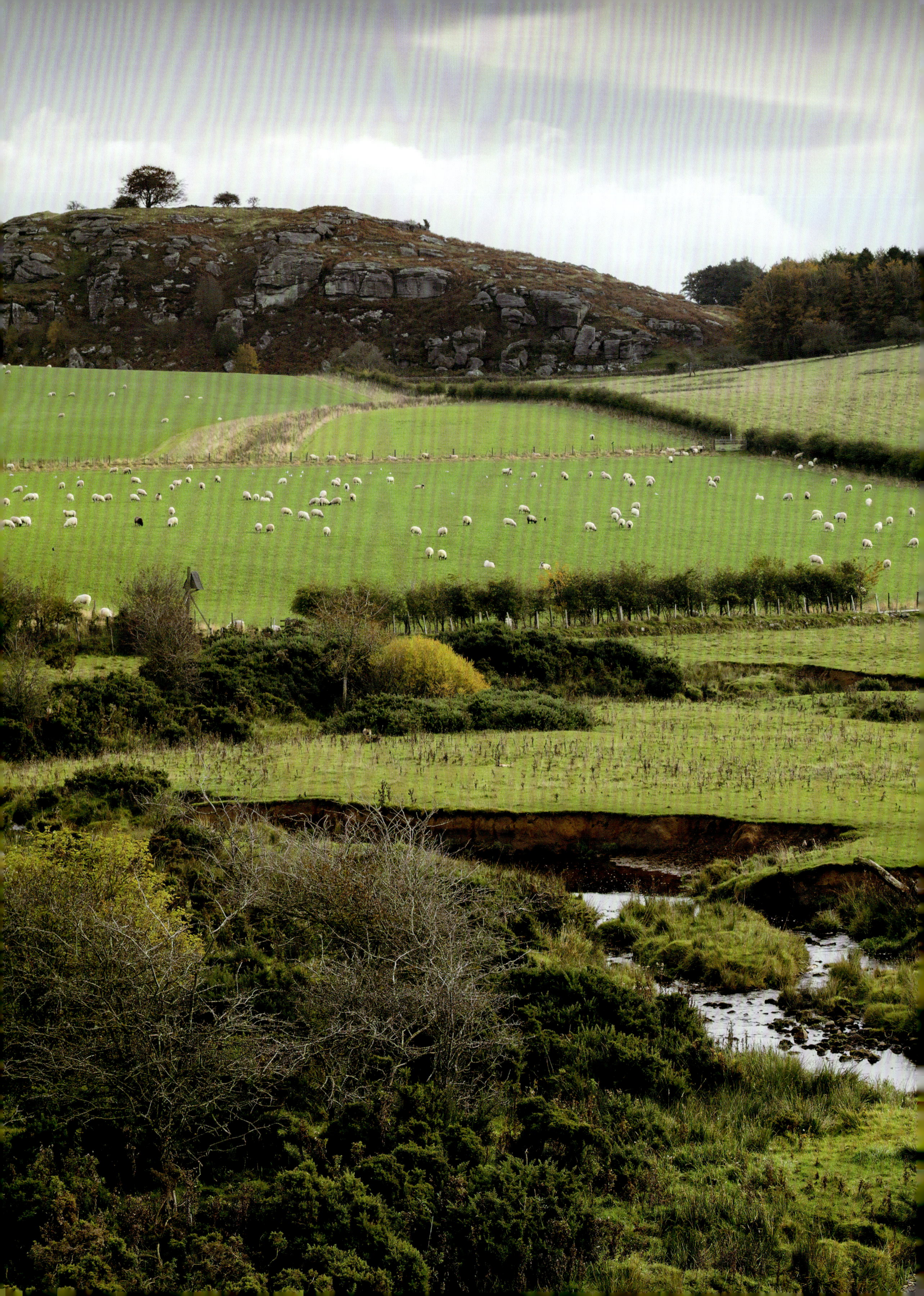

Joseph Addison, was to be a lasting characteristic of Brown's style. Indeed, it has been argued that the Wallington ridings were actually set out by him when he worked on Rothley lakes in the 1760s. As we shall discover he had been laying out extensive ridings since the 1750s, at the latest. Questions of authorship should not, however, take from the fact that by 1740 Blackett was designing at an exceptionally large scale on land that went well beyond the home park around his house. Neither Blackett, nor Brown after him, were ever defeated by the number of acres with which they had to work.

opposite: The riding winds down the burn, showing off the best of the scenery along its route.
above: Brown's Rothley Low Lake sets off Codger's Fort and provides a boundary to the grassland around it.
His walk around the lake can still be traced in the grass.

KIRKHARLE AND WALLINGTON · 37

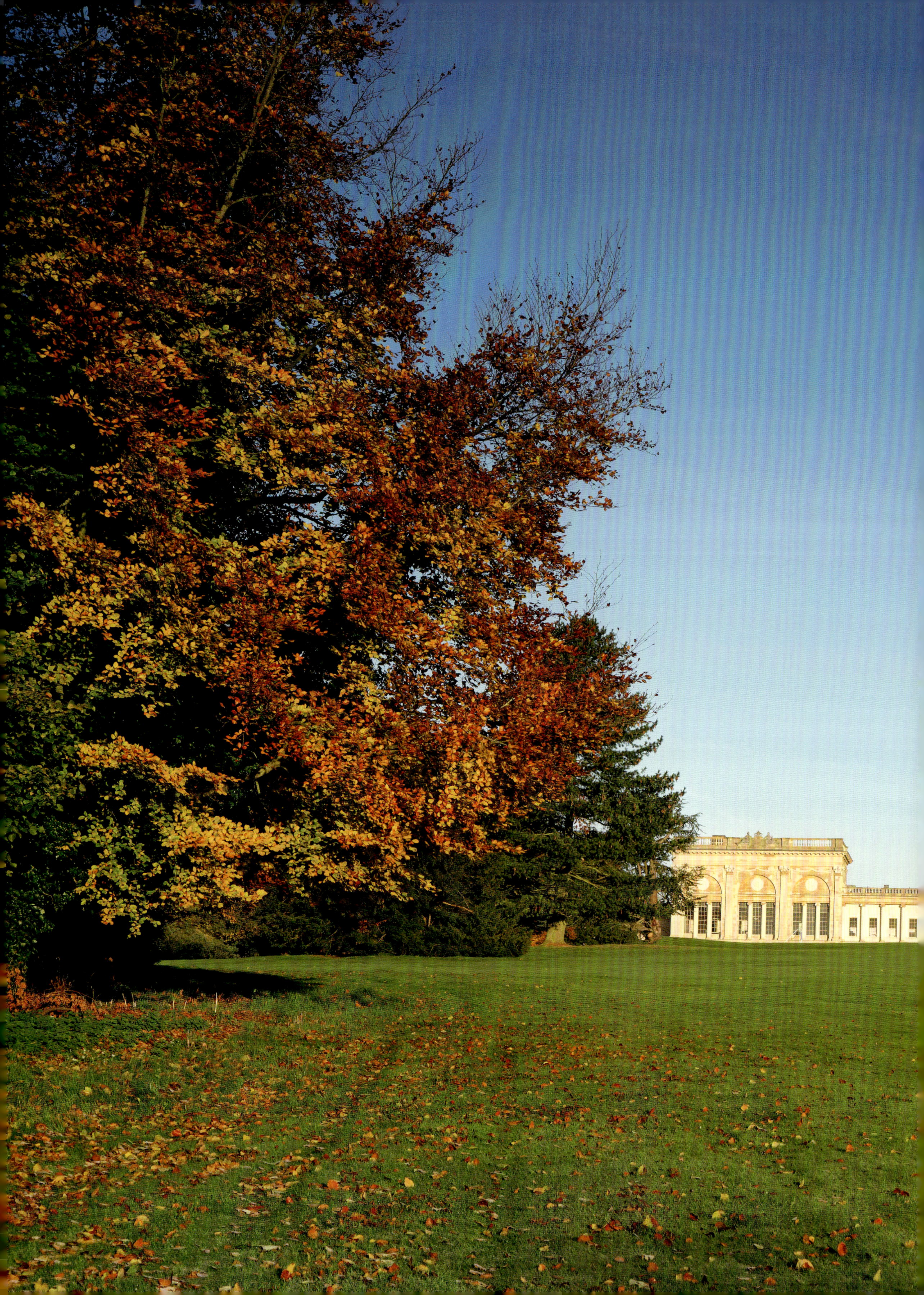

STOWE
— *BUCKINGHAMSHIRE* —
1741–1751

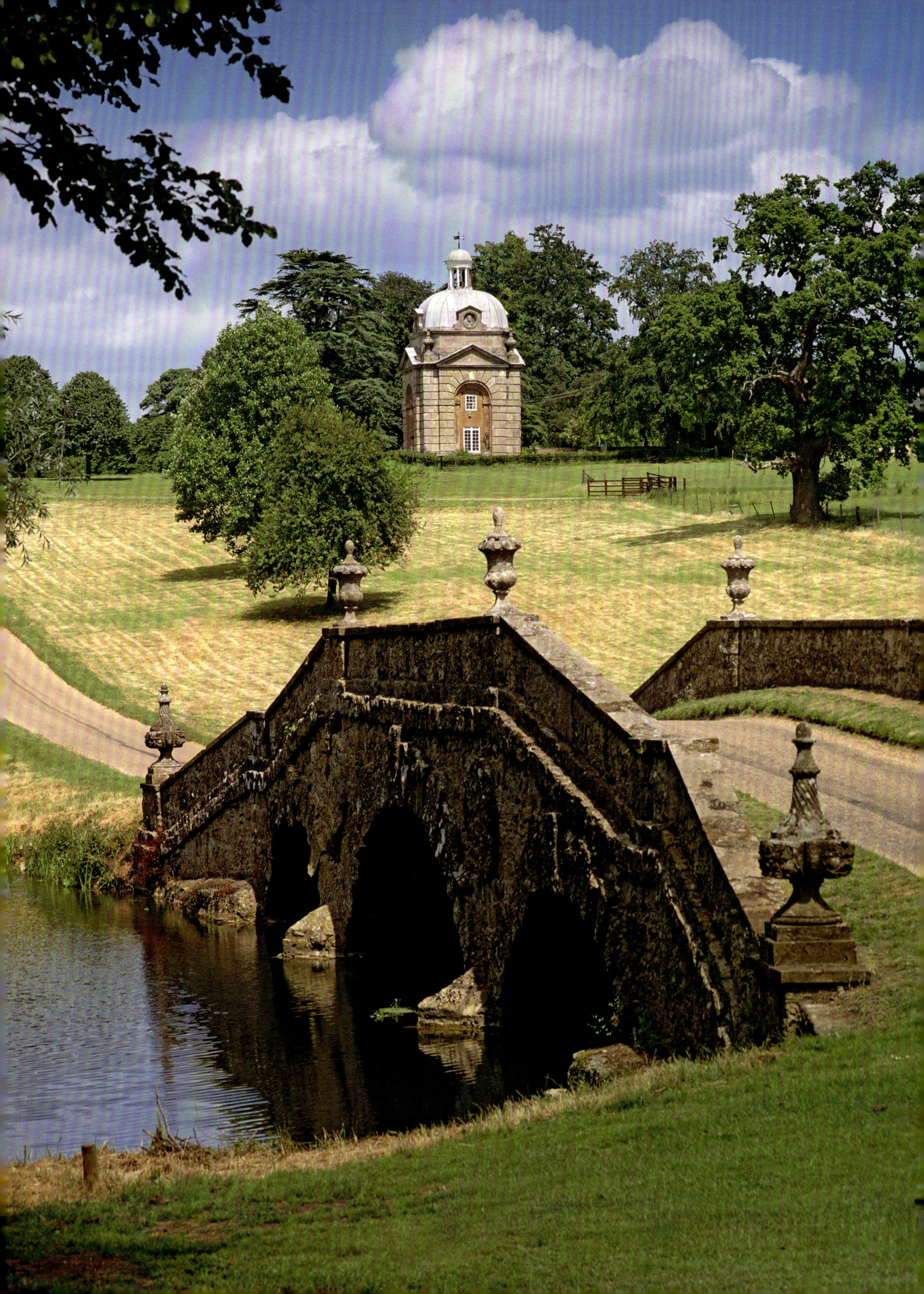

— CHAPTER TWO —

STOWE

It is not possible to overestimate the importance of Stowe to Brown and to the whole English landscape movement. It was the cradle of experiment for Sir John Vanbrugh (1664–1726), James Gibbs (1682–1754), William Kent (1685–1748), and Charles Bridgeman (1690–1738), as well as for Brown. He had left Northumberland in 1739 and found his way to Stowe where he worked from 1741 to 1751 as head gardener and clerk of the works. Here, if not at Wallington, he would have come across the "very beautiful Ridings" laid out for miles through the woods.[1] Here he learned to manage men and organize contracts, experimented with large-scale earthworking, learned architecture, theoretical and practical, and explored the role of buildings in landscape.

For Stowe is studded with buildings. They are in themselves a rebus on the Temple family's motto "Templa Quam Dilecta" (how delightful are thy temples). As a *ferme ornée* Stowe faced the same difficulties as at Wotton in creating buildings of a size suitable for small paddocks, while being sufficiently striking to take their place in the whole landscape. Here the designers experimented with numerous different devices. First, a building could be polymorphous, "like a Person acquainted with the World, who can suit his Behaviour to Time and Place"; it could "vary itself upon occasion into a more humble Shape, and when view'd thro' a retired Vista, [could] take upon it the lowly Form of a close Retreat."[2] Such were the Boycott Pavilions (1729, designed by Gibbs), and such the Gothic Temple (built 1741–1748, with Brown as clerk of the works to a design by Gibbs): "Immediately above the alder grove... the vast pile seems to be still larger than it is; for it is thrown into perspective, and between and above the heads of the trees, the upper story, the porticoes, the turrets, and balustrades, and all the slated roofs appear in a noble confusion...."[3]

Second, and more frequently adopted by Brown, buildings could be crowded together,[4] and this jumbled effect can be seen clearly today from the Temple of Friendship (designed by Gibbs in 1739, immediately before Brown's arrival), with its view to the house across the Temple of Ancient Virtue

*previous pages: The front of Stowe House, Buckinghamshire, was completed in 1779.
The design of the south lawn that runs up to the house is a good deal more complex than it looks.
opposite: Brown lived in the westernmost of the Boycott Pavilions from 1741 to 1751.*

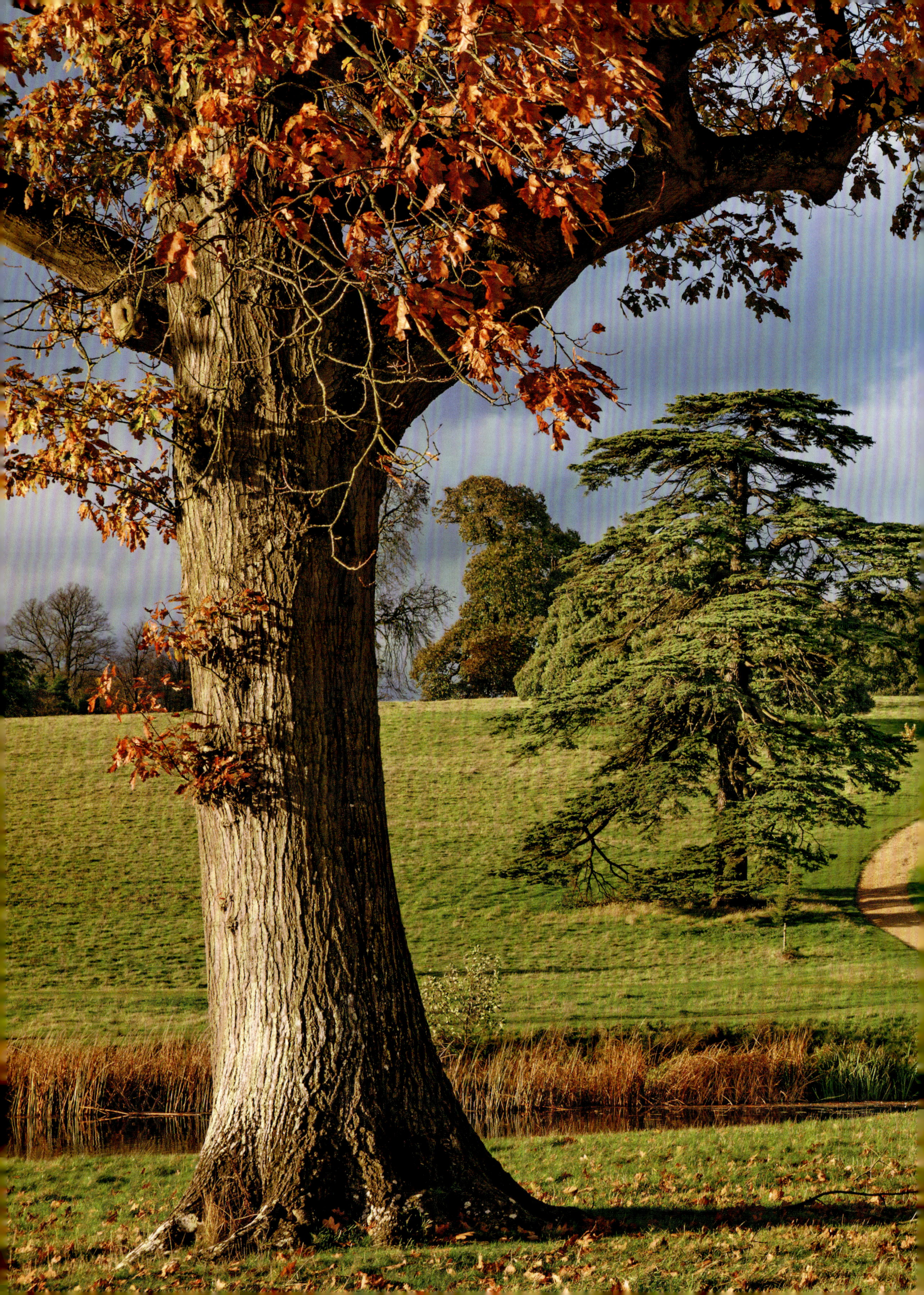

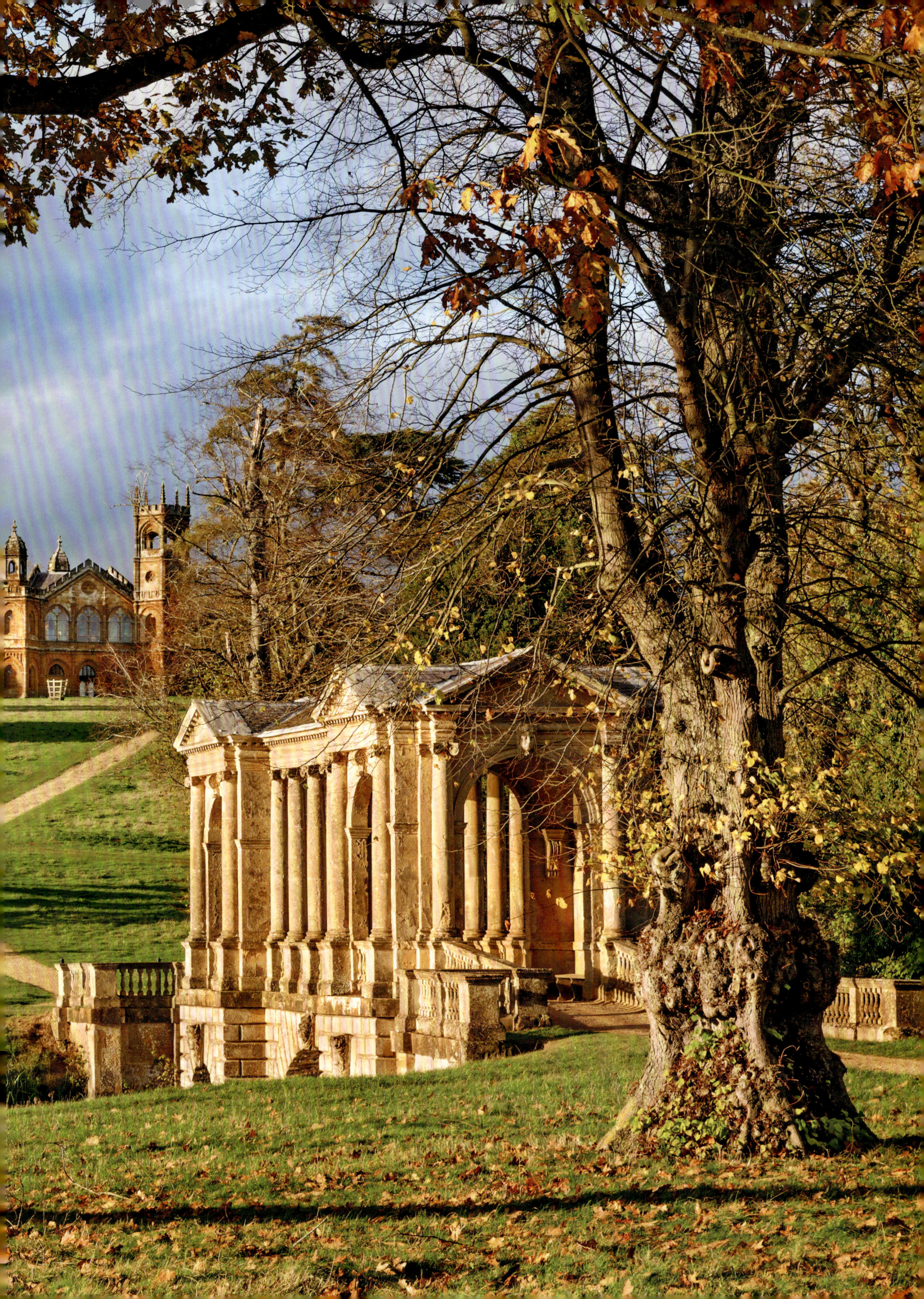

(1737, designed by Kent) and the fourteenth-century St. Mary's church (where Brown was married in 1744). The view survives intact despite the prediction of the traveler and agriculturist, Arthur Young, that it would be improved "when the wood is enough grown to hide the house."[5] These jumbles were very much regarded as a characteristic of Brown's style, "the system of modern gardening, in spite of fashion and Mr. *Brown*, is a very foolish one. The huddling together every species of building into a park or garden, is ridiculous."[6] Yet it was a way of combining a series of small buildings to create a single grand effect, and it was lighthearted, a *capriccio* in every sense of the word.

The Gothic Temple was known in Brown's day as the Temple of Liberty, for there was a close association between Liberty, the political virtue on which Great Britain most congratulated itself in the eighteenth century, and the country's imagined medieval Gothic past. This association was to encourage Brown to design for the medieval Blenheim and ancient Burghley in his preferred form of the more playful "Strawberry-Hill" Gothick.

A second building stands out for its influence on Brown's development. The New Inn (1717) lay at the crossroads of the Ratley Ridgeway and Hey Way, and announced the estate to travelers from the south, with its more regular and imposing front looking away

previous pages: From every angle, the Gothic Temple dominates the Hawkwell Field in which it sits.
above: The Temple of Friendship (designed by James Gibbs, 1739) was reduced to a shell after a fire in the early nineteenth century and has since been designedly left as a ruin.

44 · CAPABILITY BROWN

from the landscape to the southeast, while its back side, a farmyard, a smithy, and a jumble of walls and tiled roofs from the day when it was built, lay close to the axis of Warden Hill Walk, the west terrace of the garden, which runs back to the Boycott Pavilions a mile away, where Brown lived. Given the quality of the other buildings in the landscape, the New Inn seems to be the wrong way round, but in fact, when looking out from the gardens, it played the part of the village, regarded as a "beautiful Object within the Range of a Country" when it was seen from the west terrace in 1749,[7] as well as a signature of the generosity of the temples to their tenants and staff. As Thomas Whately remarked: "The farm-yard itself, if an advantageous situation be chosen for it... properly blended with trees; may be made a picturesque composition."[8] This was a radical invention that Brown was to redeploy at Chatsworth and Blenheim, Broadlands and Milton Abbey. Even if the New Inn were not an old building retained, it consciously brought the vernacular into the design and counters any argument that buildings were put into parkland solely to evoke the Arcadia of Virgil and Theocritus.

It is hard to say how far Brown was working to the designs of William Kent and his client, Lord Cobham, at Stowe. However, one piece of work that is generally regarded as originating with him is the Grecian Valley (1747–1749). Brown appeared

above: The south front of the New Inn was decidedly old-fashioned for its date and faced away from the landscape. The north front comprises a miscellaneous clutter of buildings and yards and yet was visible from the pleasure ground.

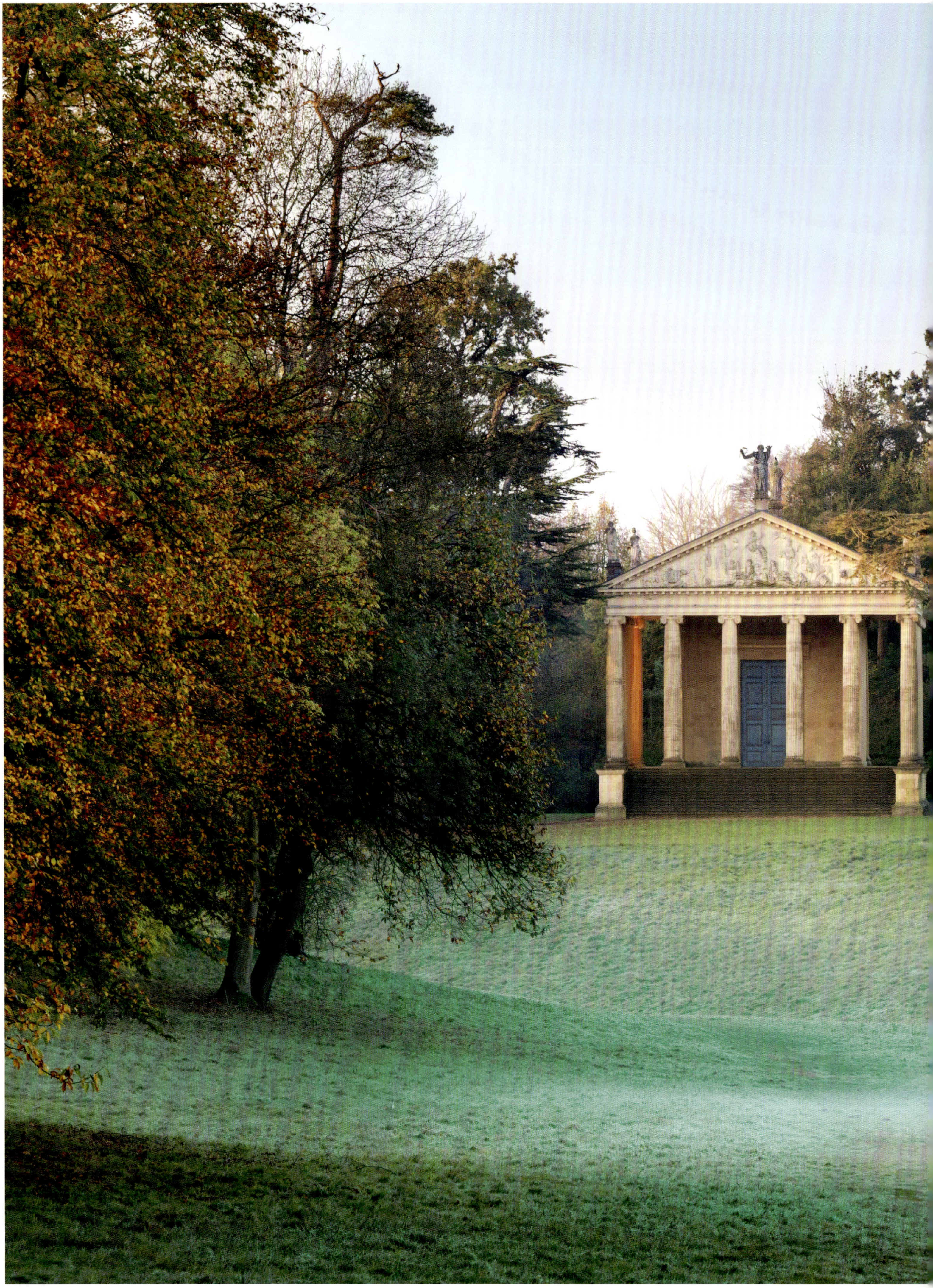

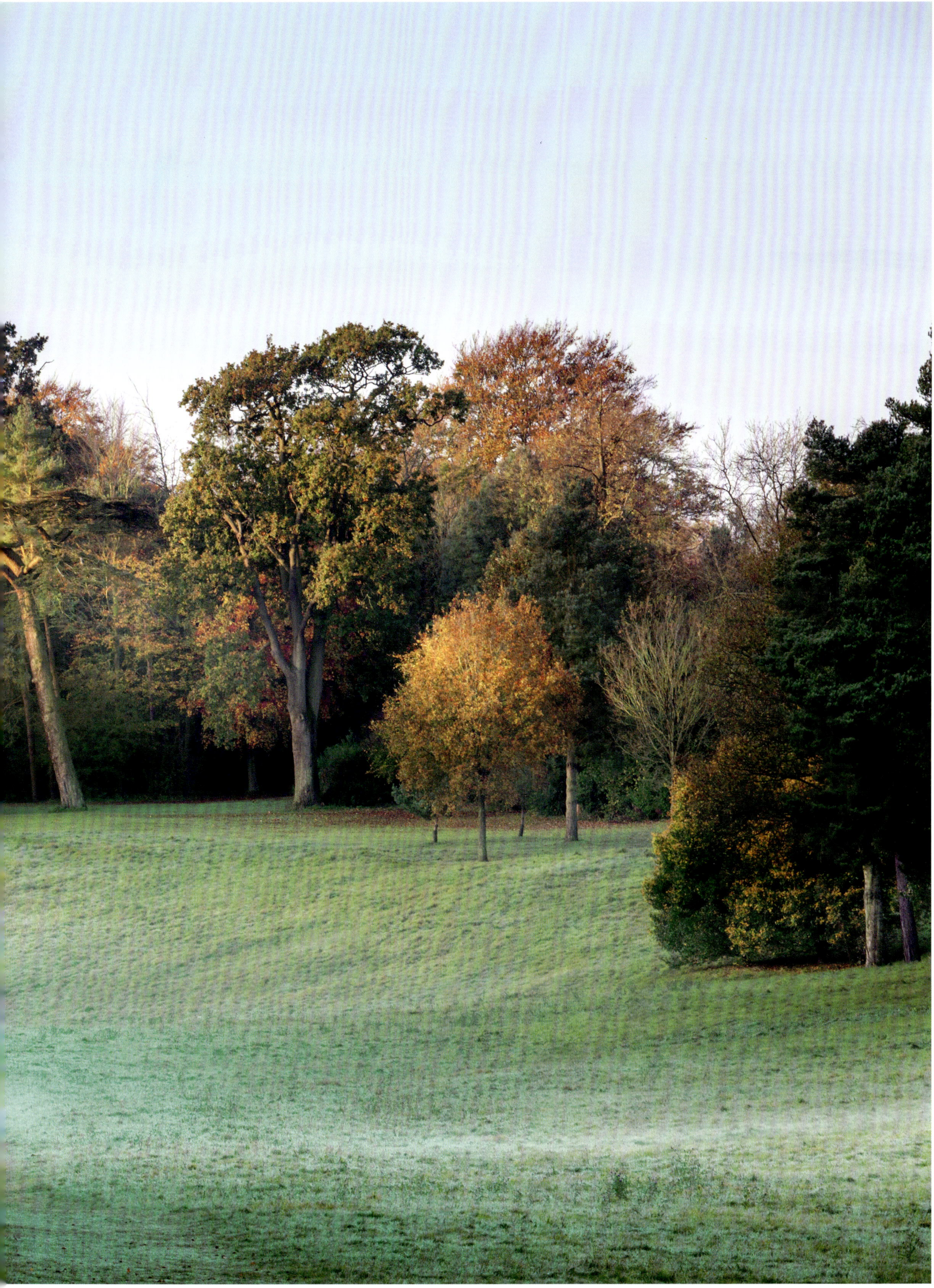

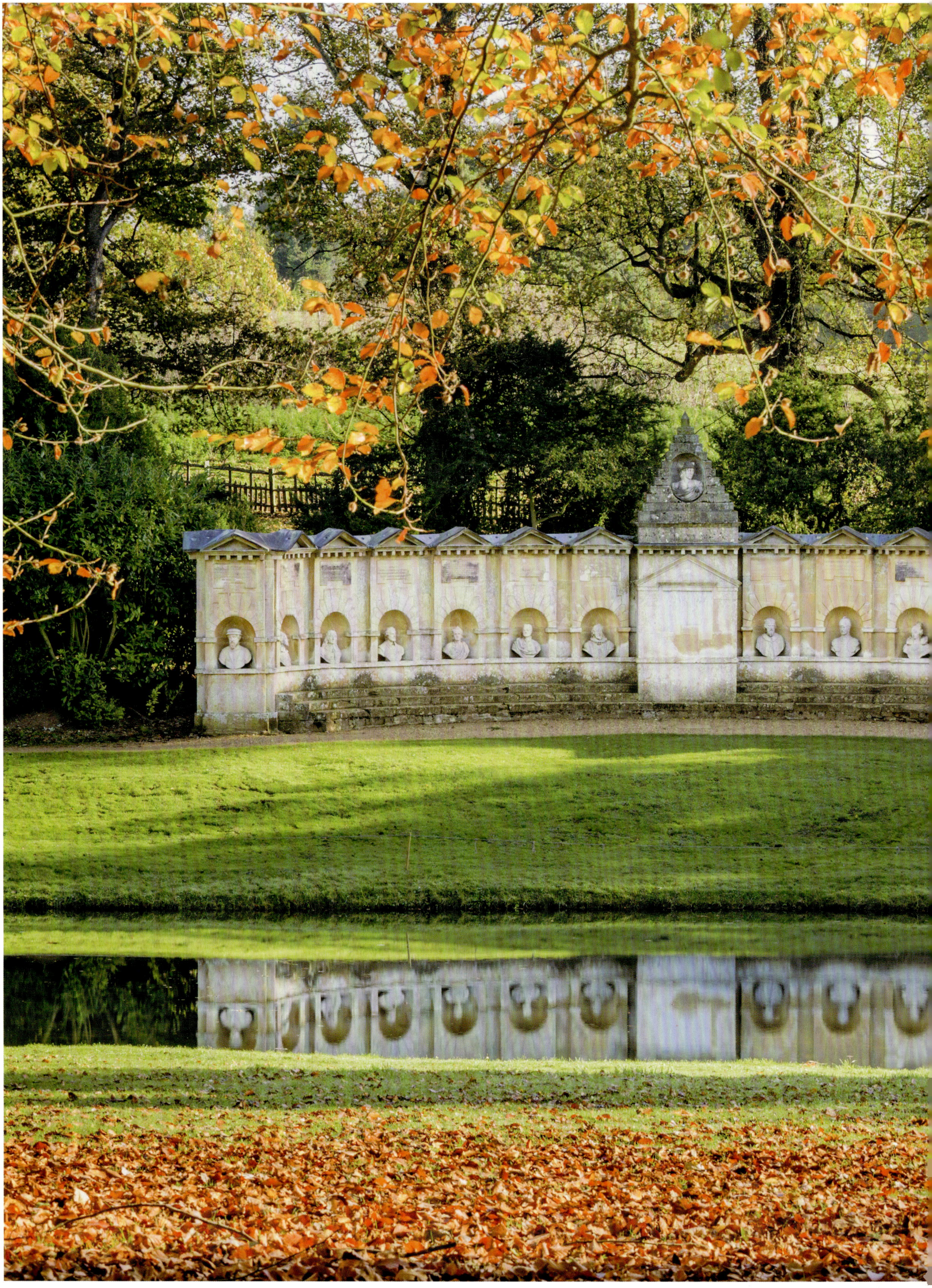

previous pages: A light frost shows off the care with which the slopes of the Grecian Valley were finished. Throughout his career, Brown was to revisit this idea.

to disclaim the work in an exchange with Lord Cobham in 1746:

> *As to finishing the head of the oval I had never formed any other idea on it than what your Lordship gave me which was to forme the laurell plantation with a sweep under it and concave to the oval that the slope of the head your Lordship thought might some time or other have statues put on it, but gave me no absolute orders to finish it and indeed I think it would be better not finished this season I thinking that a summer's talk and tryels about it may make it a very fine thing.*[9]

But Lord Cobham's suspicions must have had some foundation, and Brown's suggestion that they have further discussions before finishing the valley shows that at the very least the design was a collaboration. History rapidly attributed the design to Brown, however, because it was intended as a lake, and it failed. The story, which must have prompted much laughter amongst Brown's critics, is best told by William Marshall, a man who had worked with Brown and admired him:

> *This miscarriage is not brought forward, here, in detriment to the professional character of Mr. BROWN. Every novice, in every art, is liable to commit errors; and one mistake, in the course of an extensive practice, is but a single blot in writing a volume. We produce it as a lesson for young artists. Water can seldom be retained with advantage, in upland situations; even where the substratum is retentive. In places where this is absorbent, and where the neighbourhood affords no materials to correct the defect, it is in vain to attempt it.*

left: The Temple of British Worthies, designed by William Kent and built in 1734–5 for the Elysian Fields at Stowe.

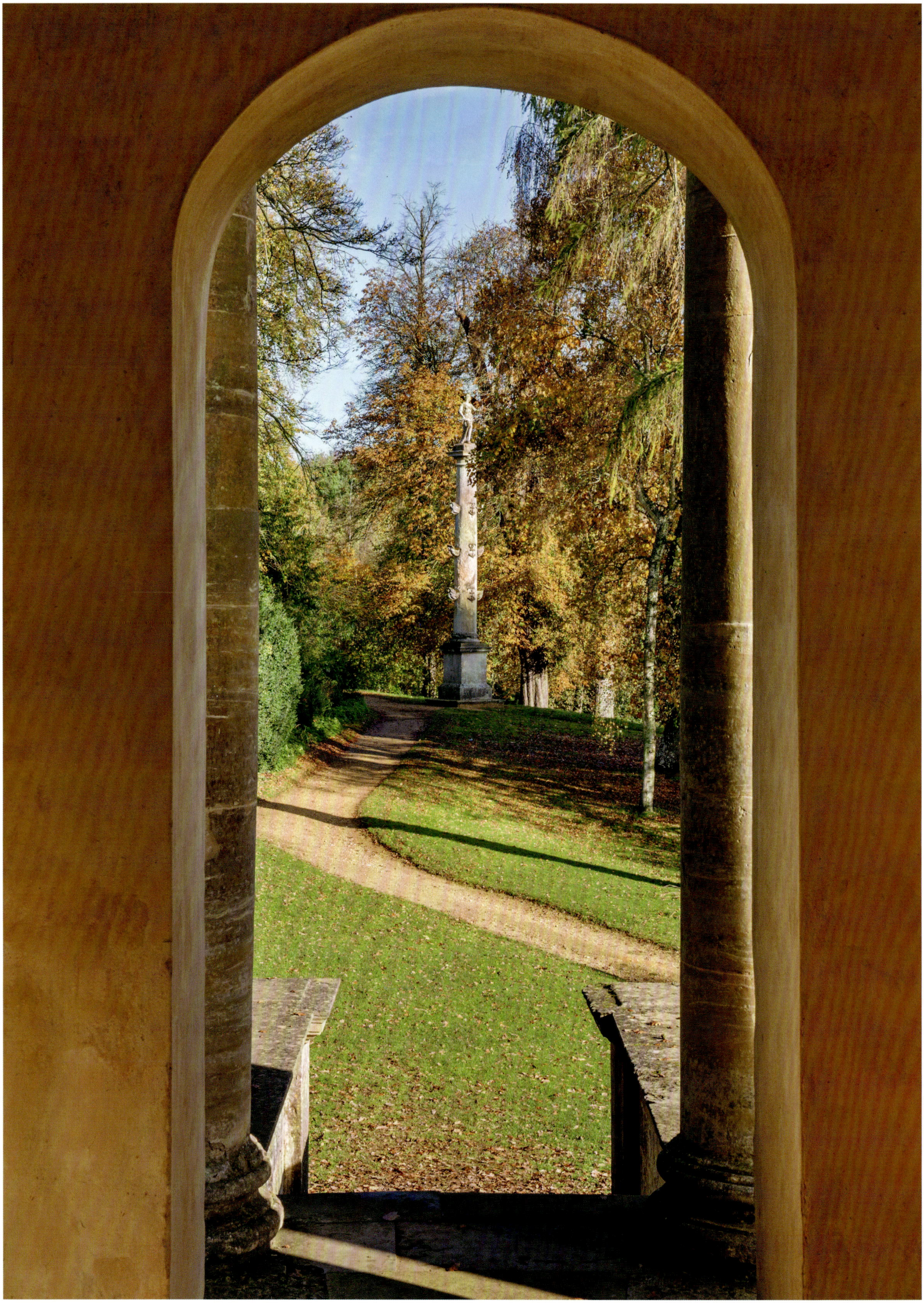

While the work was underway, it had already seemed a step too far to some: "The Laying-out seems to have no sort of Variety… a Piece of Water is to be in the Valley below, and vast Buildings larger and mightier than all the Others upon the sides:—Sure this is not Taste or Judgement!"[10] However, Marshall went on to show how Brown solved the problem, and thereby no doubt, secured his reputation as a problem-fixer:

MR. BROWN, however, on discovering his error, had great merit in the manner of correcting it. Sloping away the bank of the river, and thus forming a valley, instead of returning the excavated materials to their former state, shewed, in a favorable light, his talent for expedient.

In the case under notice, the effect of the grassy dell is infinitely better, than any which a weed-grown canal could ever have produced; beside the injury which water, pent up in that situation, must have done to the grounds that lie below. A man may discover as much talent, in making a retreat, as in gaining a victory.[11]

The result, the Grecian Valley, is an L-shaped dry valley—it seems likely that Brown's attempt to make a lake was at the foot of the L, at the lower end of this sloping bowl, where the water still collects in wet weather. The bowl tips up toward the northeast and the corner of the L is the triumphant Temple of Concord and Victory (1747–1749, the designer is unknown). The sides of the valley were decorated

above: The Temple of Concord and Victory commemorates the Seven Years' War.
opposite: The Grenville, or Rostral, Column was built by Brown in 1749, but moved to this position in 1756. It now stands in the view from the Temple of Ancient Virtue, designed by William Kent in 1737.

with shrubberies, walks, and statuary, and Thomas Whately described the effect of the building and its setting in a passage of transported prose:

> *The temple of concord and victory at Stowe has been mentioned as one of the noblest objects that ever adorned a garden; but there is a moment when it appears in singular beauty; the setting sun shines on the long colonade which faces the west; all the lower parts of the building are darkened by the neighbouring wood; the pillars rise at different heights out of the obscurity; some of them are nearly overspread with it; some are chequered with a variety of tints; and others are illuminated almost down to their bases. The light is gently softened off by the rotundity of the columns; but it spreads in broad gleams upon the wall within them; and pours full and without interruption on all the entablature, distinctly marking every dentil: on the statues which adorn the several points of the pediment, a deep shade is contrasted to splendor; the rays of the sun linger on the side of the temple long after the front is over-cast with the sober hue of evening and they tip the upper branches of the trees, or glow in the opening between them, while the shadows lengthen across the Grecian valley.*[12]

The story is that Brown used the spoil to bury the garden terraces on the south front of the house. In another clever maneuver he constructed this new south lawn in two planes, slightly pitched halfway down so that from the door of the house the Octagon Pool is visible, but from the bottom of the steps that run up to the door it is not—a perspective trick that he might have borrowed from the great French gardener, André Le Nôtre.

This huge earth-moving operation, reckoned to amount to around 35,000 barrow-loads of earth, allowed Brown to create a new effect on the east side of the vista. Here he had to drop the levels rapidly in order to accommodate the church, and this gave him the opportunity to turn the steep bank into a picturesque back lane, lined with yew, sycamore, and beech, whose roots swarm across the banks and rocks today and provide a concealed access to the church for parishioners. This was another expeditious piece of problem-solving, and it is one that Brown was successfully to repeat below the dams at Trentham and Bowood.

Brown's work at Stowe was sufficiently well-regarded for him to be lent out to friends of Lord Cobham, and two of these early works, Wotton and Wakefield Lodge, made a bridge between the style he was to develop for himself and other well-established traditions of design. The first was a *ferme ornée*, the second, Wakefield Lodge (from 1748), was set in a deer launde (that is to say an extensive open grass lawn) in the medieval Whittlewood Forest.

opposite: The Cobham Monument was designed by Brown and was much criticized by William Marshall, among others: "The fluted column, erected, if we recollect rightly, by Lady Cobham, to the merits of her husband, during his lifetime."

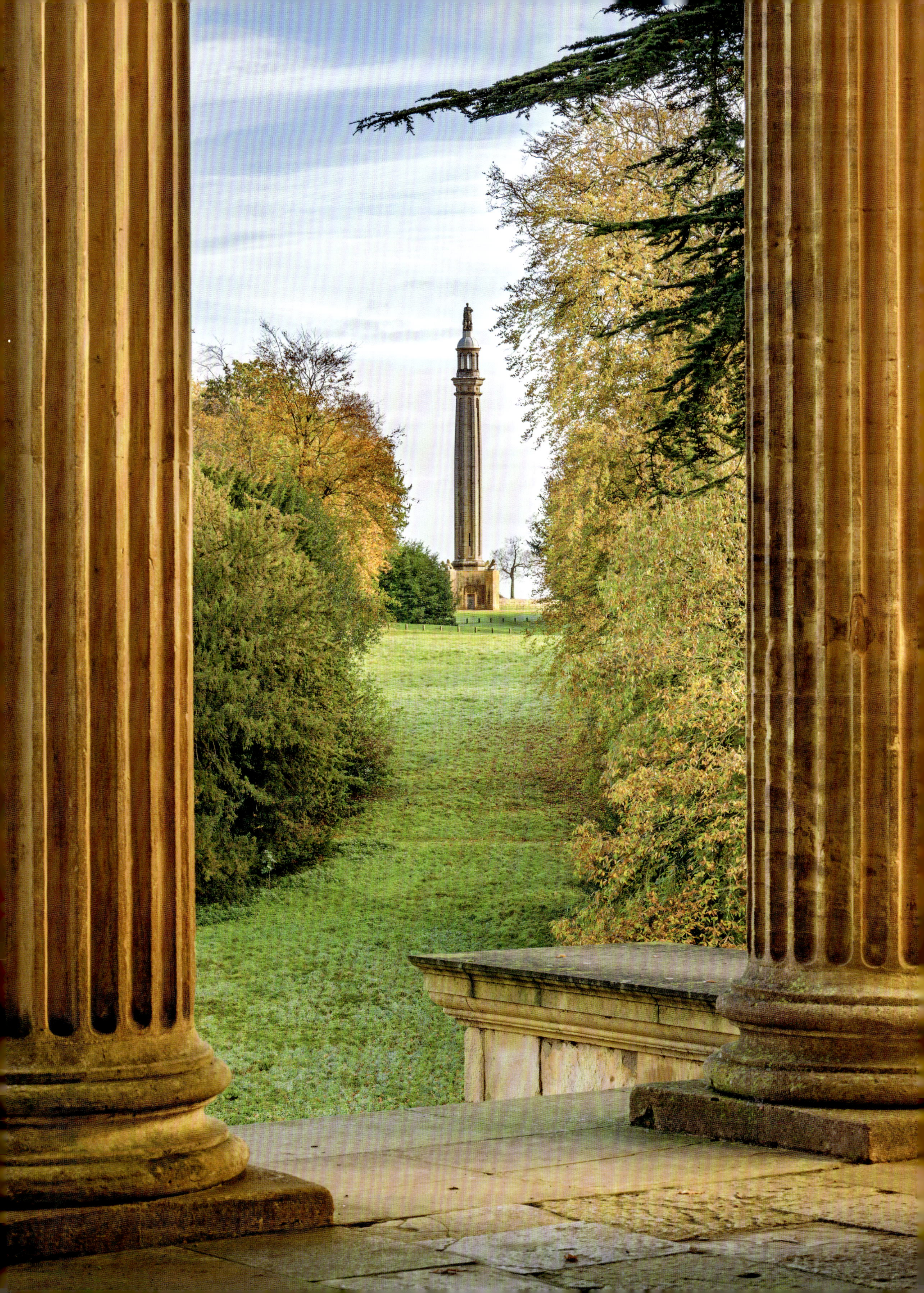

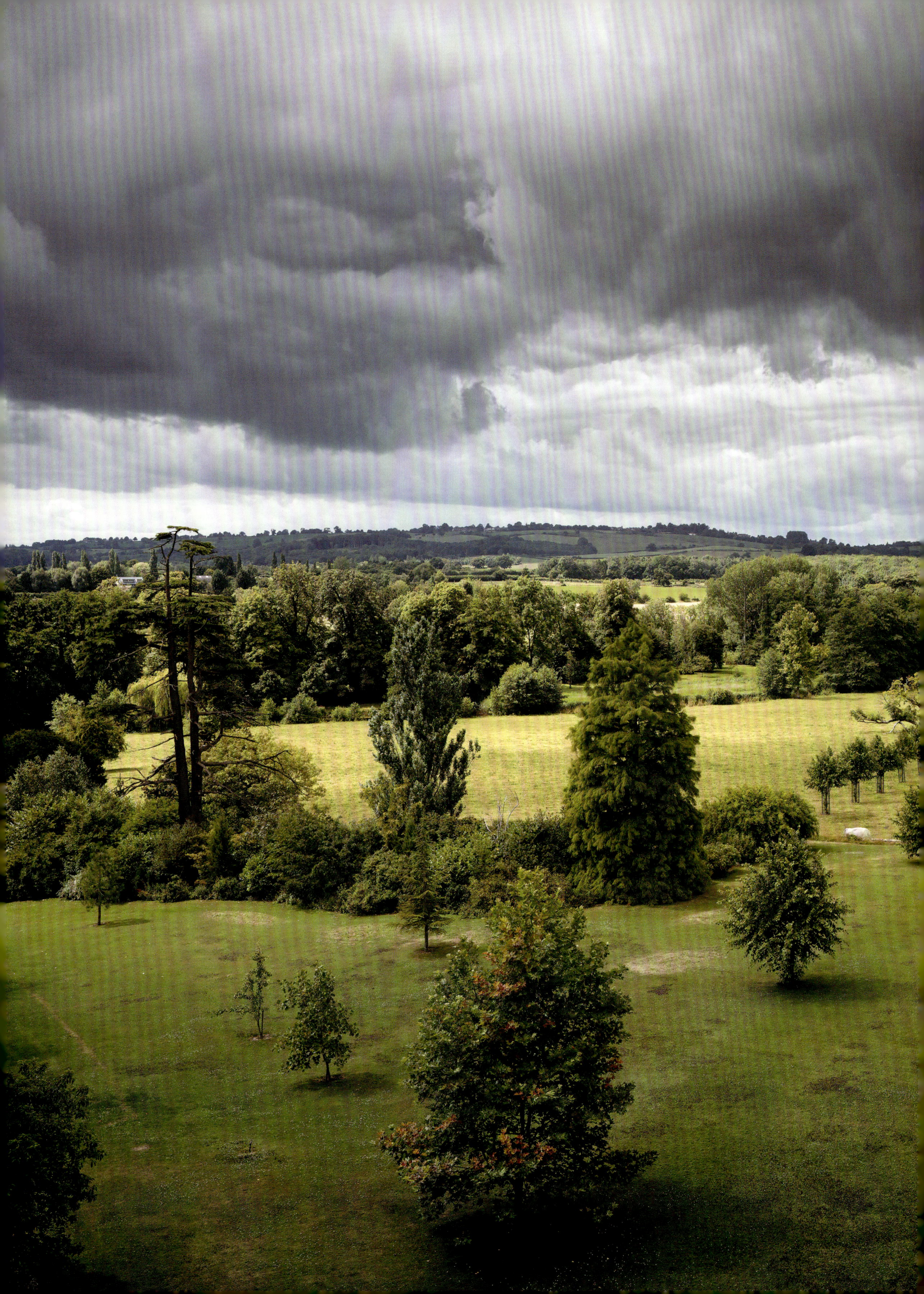

WOTTON HOUSE
— BUCKINGHAMSHIRE —
FROM 1742

A Plan of
The MARQUISS of BUCKINGHAM'S
Seat and Pleasure Ground
at
Wotton
in the County of
BUCKS
Surveyed 1749
by
Jno Beale

Scale of Two Chains to an Inch

— CHAPTER THREE —

WOTTON HOUSE

Wotton is often described as the sister to Stowe. Here one can see more clearly that the underlying character of the latter's design is a *ferme ornée*, a form made famous by one of Brown's mentors, Philip Southcote (1698–1758), at Wooburn Farm, Surrey. This carried with it the idea that the simple life of the farmer was bound to be beautiful and hence persuasively combined use and beauty. Thomas Whately defined its basic unit: "A field surrounded by a gravel walk is to a degree bordered by a garden."[1] So at Wotton, the pleasure grounds really consist of walks around paddocks and are not far off being 5 miles long and 20 yards wide. This system was also pleasingly adaptable—it had numerous small fields (seldom more than 20 acres), each set with at least one building to give variety and linked by walks, and it could be suited to any topography.

Although Wotton is the most complete example in his oeuvre, Brown experimented with this form throughout his life, leading to the criticism by Sir William Chambers that Brown's designs differed "very little from common fields, so clearly is vulgar nature copied in most of them."[2] There is some truth in what Chambers said, for the *ferme ornée* has at least three related faults, and Brown had trouble with all of them. First, it was felt that there should be an overriding geometry, binding the reticulated landscape of small fields and walks, so that from each building there should be a series of views of other buildings, each perfectly framed by its windows and columns. A revealing slip-up in the execution at Wotton proves the importance of this idea: the Octagon Seat (about 1758) has just such framed views to the Grotto (1755), the house, and a couple of vases on mounds, but it just missed the view to the boathouse on the Worrels. This made it necessary to create an additional mound less than 100 yards from the boathouse so as to rectify the layout. Too rigorous an attachment to geometry of this kind was bound to be a considerable constraint on design.

Second, there are the shortcomings of scale: a building that is small enough to suit being seen beside the walk is not going to be big enough to command attention in views from buildings in the more

previous pages: The landscape at Wotton is exemplary in accommodating natural curves
and forms to a rigid and essentially formal framework.
opposite: Within the naturalistic shapes of this design its antecedents of straight avenues can still be traced.

right: The river cut by Brown provides a relaxed foreground, while the sunk hedge beyond it enabled him to keep open the view. To him also are attributed the Tuscan temples, nestled at the foot of the slope below the house, and formally placed with respect to the axis of the house.

distant parts of the landscape. Earlier designers had tended to cluster their buildings (banqueting houses, dovecotes, orangeries, summerhouses) and gardens around the house, but the dispersal of buildings around the walks would always be problematic. To some extent this difficulty might be mitigated by the sort of architectural tricks that were tried successfully at Stowe.

Third, there is a problem with monotony: one might expect a reticulated landscape consisting of a series of fields separated by planting to provide variety because each field could be given its own character. However, the grandest variable available to landscape design is that of scale, and, given the similar size of its fields, Wotton has something of the look of a set of amorphous organic cells seen under a microscope: each different, but each so very much the same.

These shortcomings with the style were widely acknowledged in Brown's own day and by his greatest admirers. As Edmund Burke and Thomas Whately said, respectively, "The variation itself must be continually varied"[3] and "though the enclosures should furnish a succession of scenes, all beautiful, and even contrasted to each other, yet the walk will introduce a similarity between them."[4]

Wotton triumphs over these difficulties, but it was the last attempt in Brown's oeuvre to create a *ferme ornée* in its pure form. The scenes created by the design are many and varied and good, but its success is most completely expressed in the view from the Turkey Building, or "Turk." This structure is a triptych, its three principal sightlines being to the Grotto on the island, the Rotunda, and the so-called "Poplar Urn." These structures are spread

overleaf: The medieval Chilton Park Farm hangs above the landscape and serves as an "eye-catcher" at the end of one of the avenues from the house.

58 · CAPABILITY BROWN

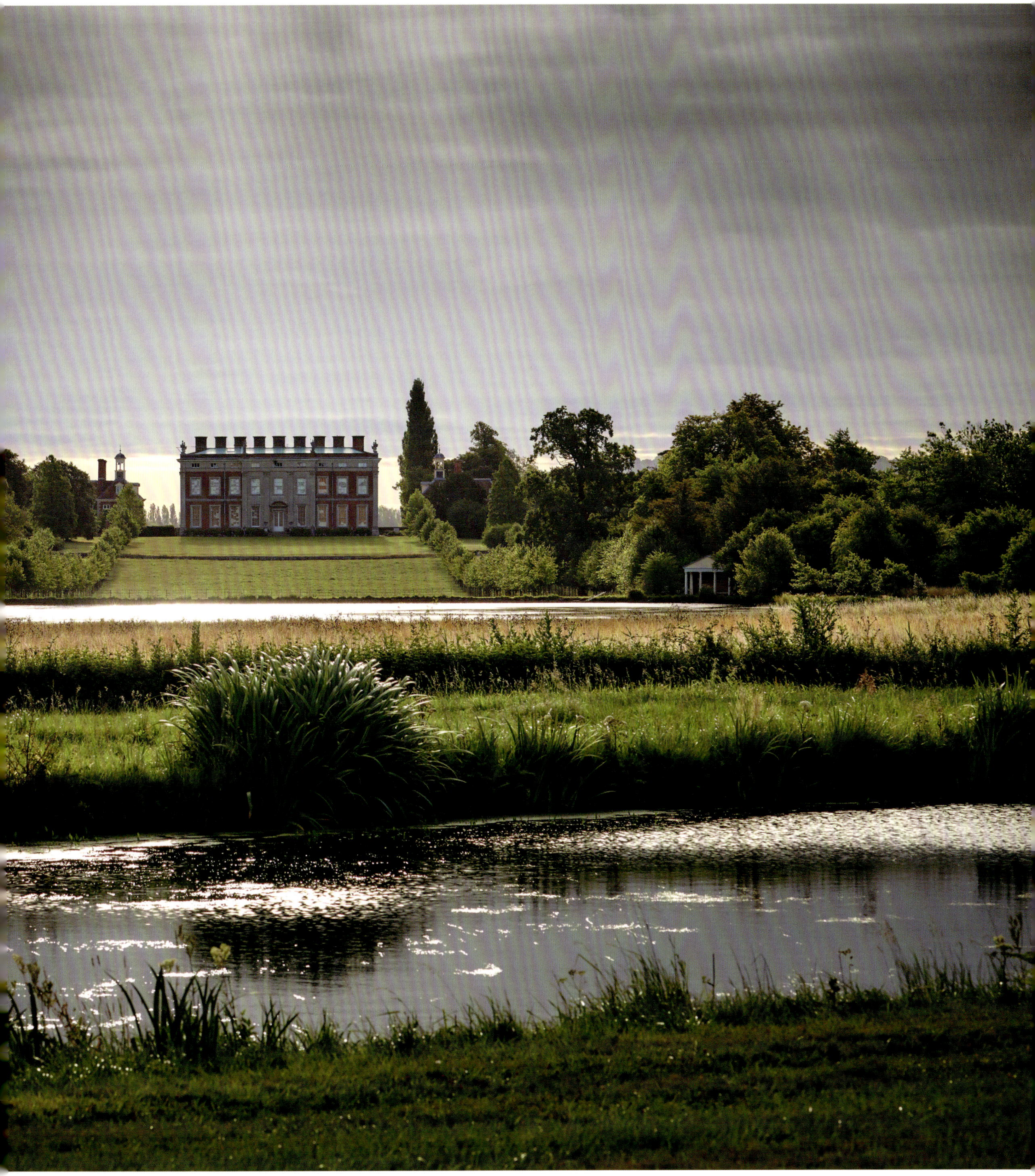

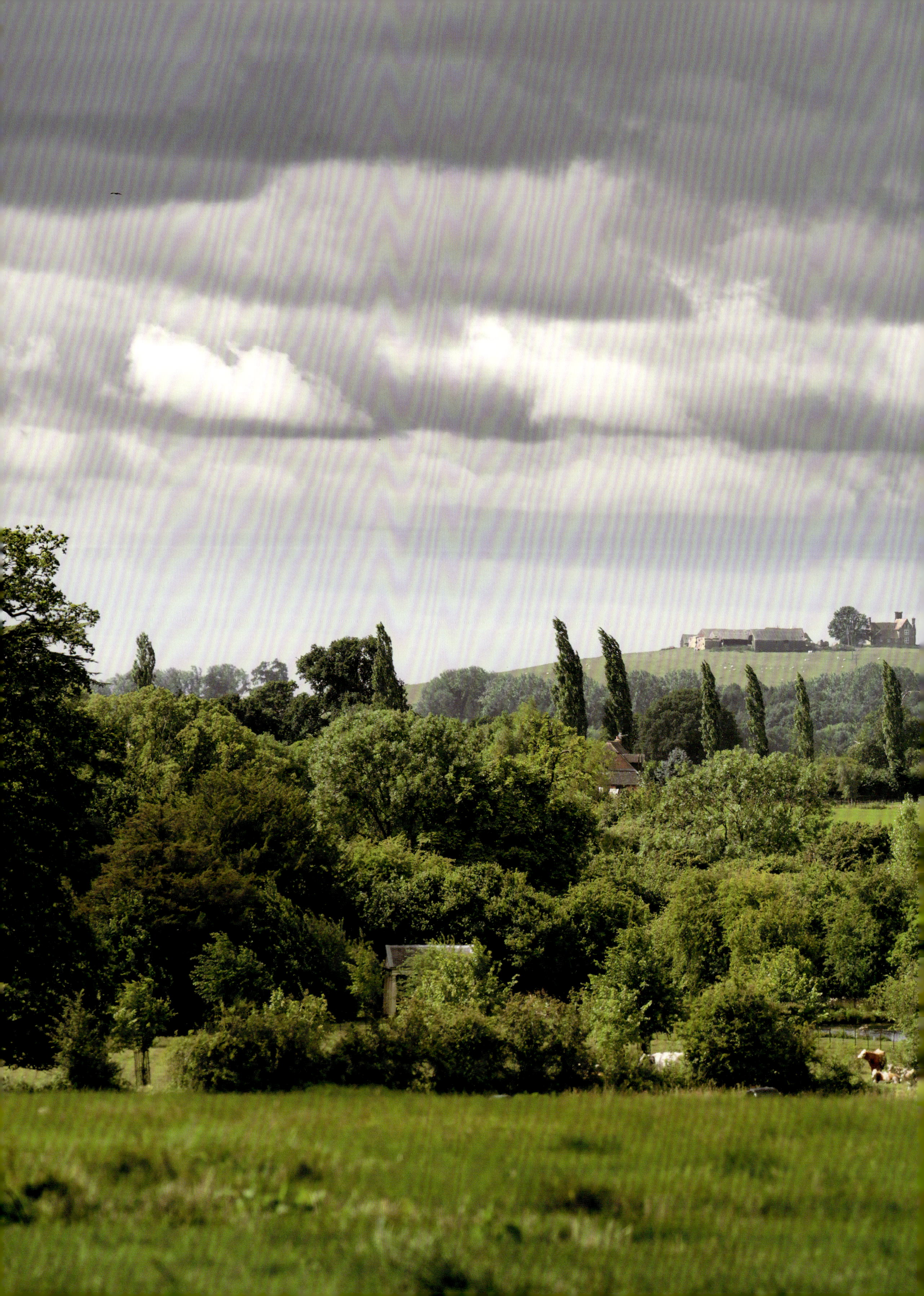

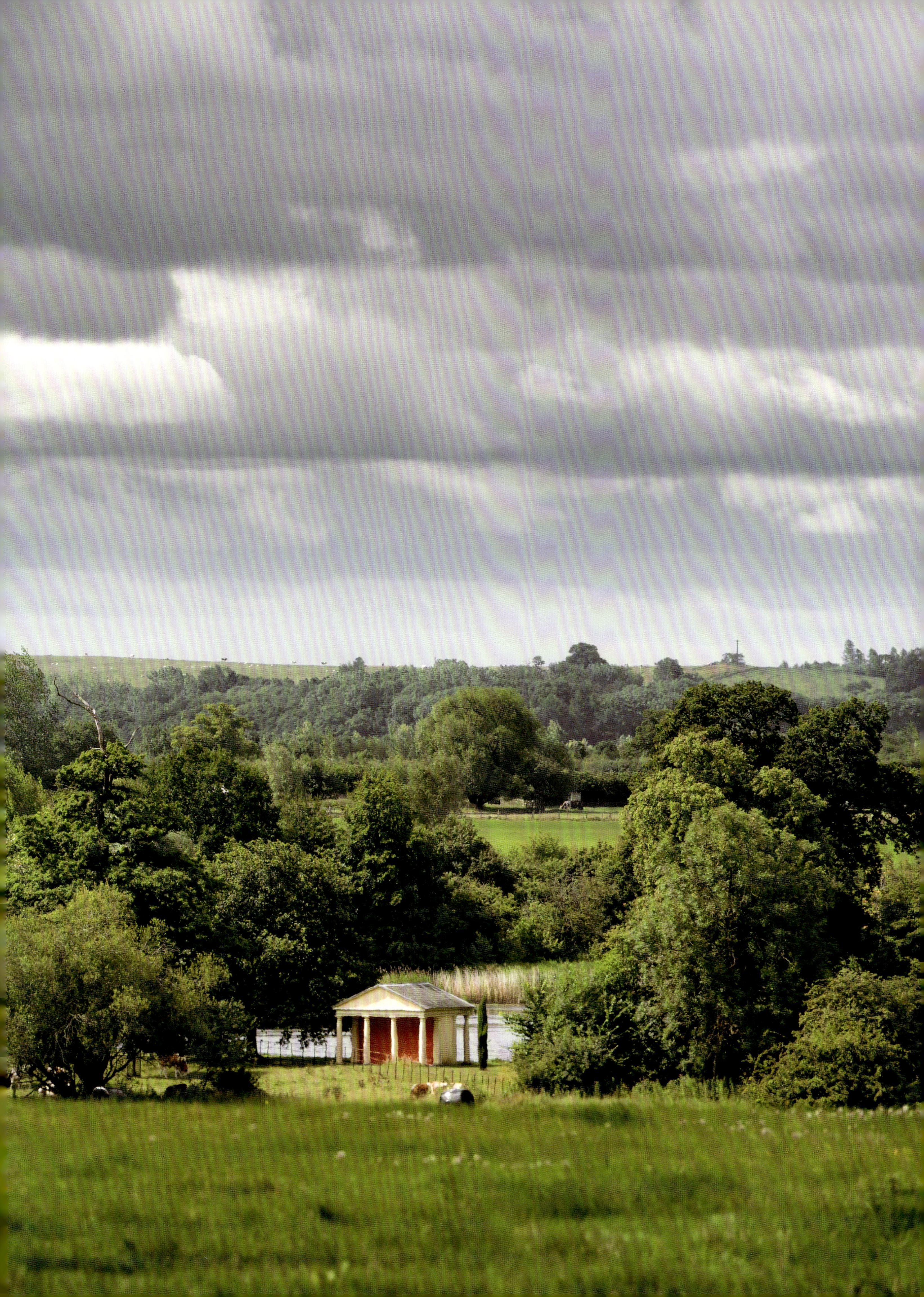

at 36-degree angles around the Turk, leading one to expect a ten-sided building on the site. The Turk is a half-octagon but has accommodated this relationship by spreading its front; while a true octagon would have eight equal sides of 1 unit length, the northwest, or principal, front of the Turkey Building is 1.5 units. The result is a single composed view of the Rotunda, in which the sightlines to the Grotto and the Poplar Urn play the part of side panels. The scene is predominantly, if not entirely, broad-leaved and deciduous, between framing wings of yew and evergreens. Close to the Turk, the view to the Rotunda was framed on one side by this shrubbery and on the other by an appropriately associative Turkey Oak (*Quercus cerris*), some six meters north of the building.

above: In the nineteenth century the horse-chestnuts, planted in Brown's time, had their branches pinned to the ground to encourage them to root and so in time become new trees.
opposite: The Five-Arch Bridge at Wotton may have been copied by Brown from Kent's similar bridge at Stowe.

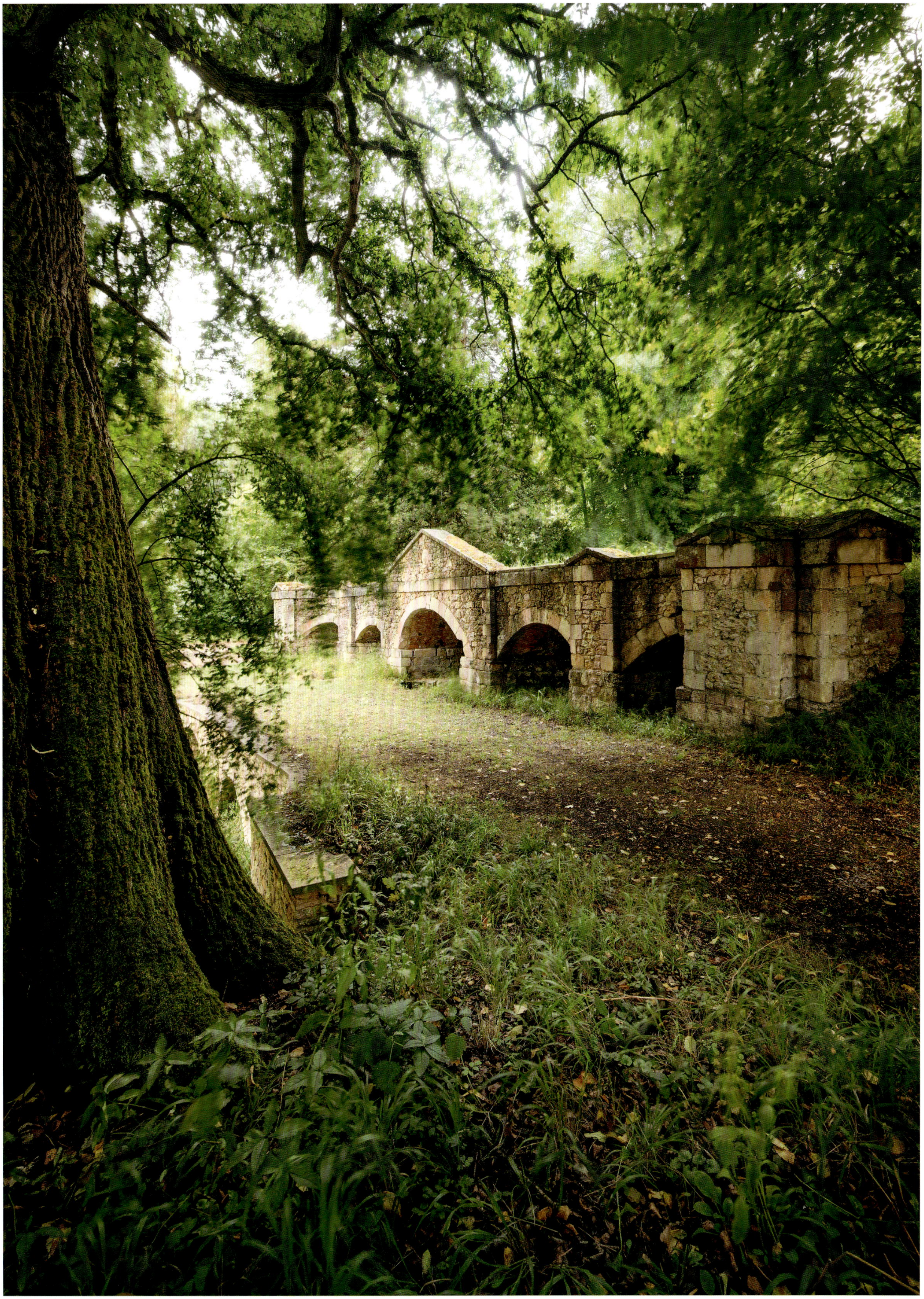

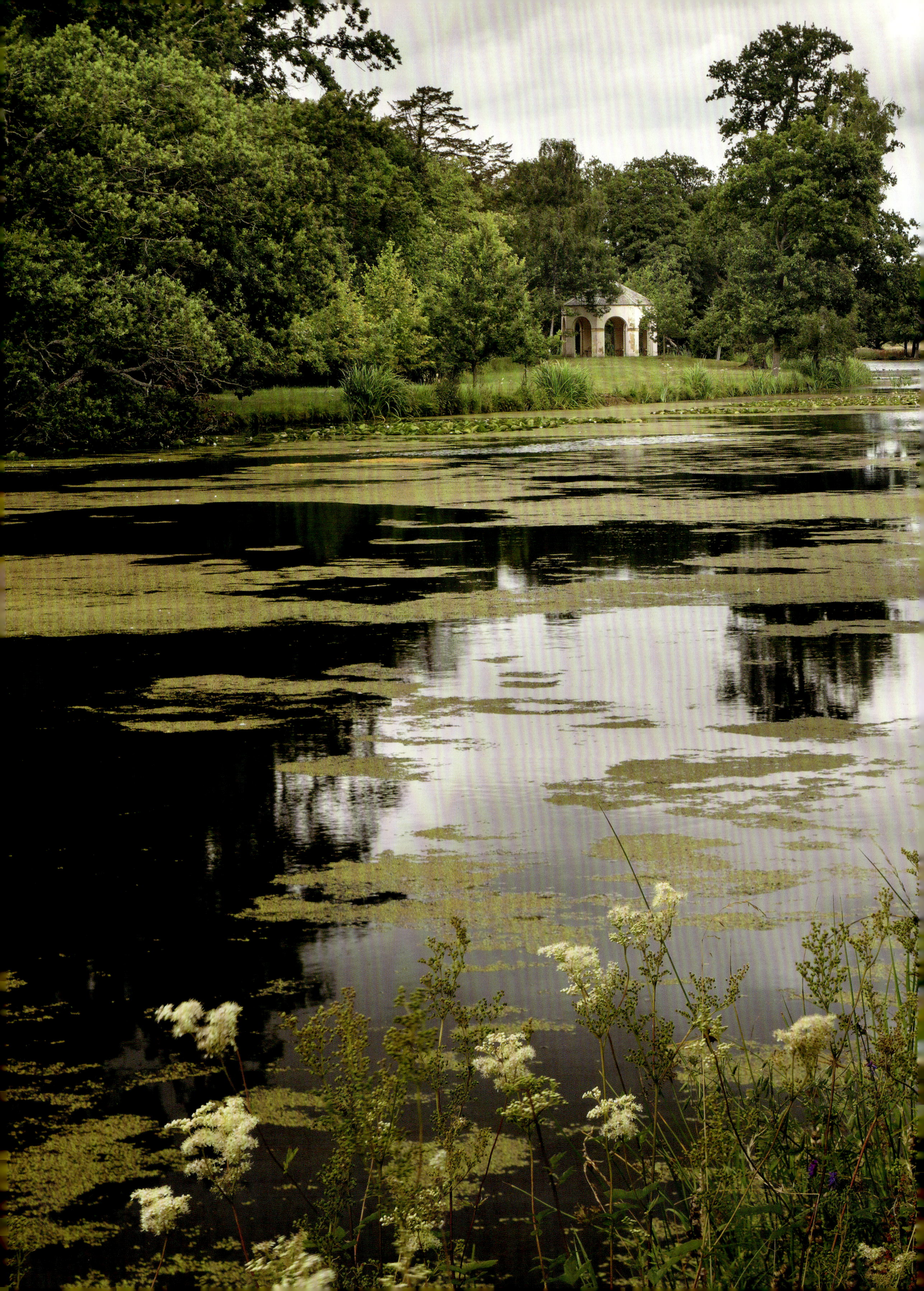

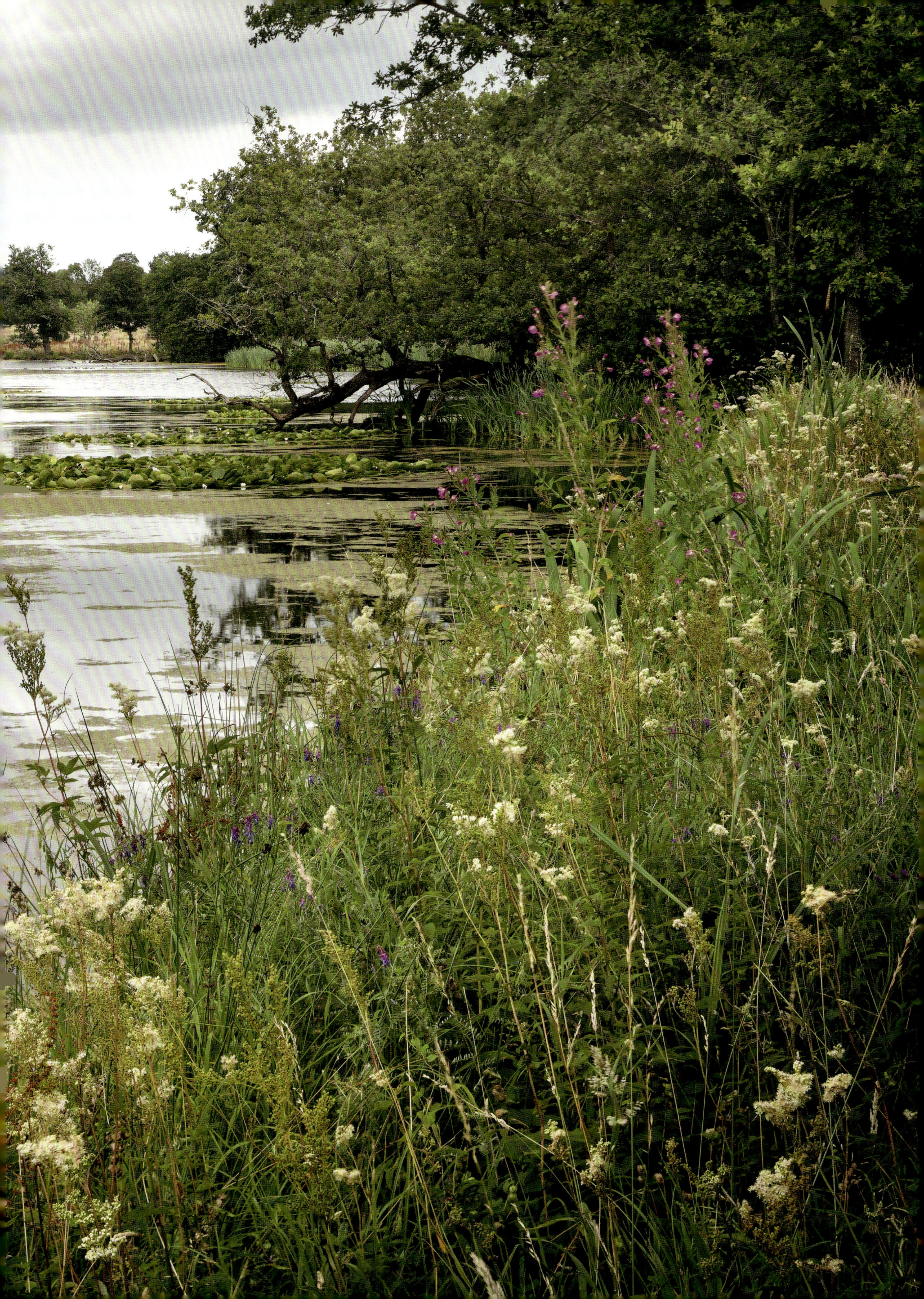

One would expect this framing to be asymmetrical, like a painting by Claude Lorrain (1600–1682), and, indeed, the composition flows down from the Rotunda toward the lake and to the south—the Rotunda appears to be sunk deep into woodland but is lit by the sun shining through the open ground on its south side. However, the overall symmetry of the composition is reinforced by the sightlines to the Grotto and the Poplar Urn. The first may still be traced from yew to yew along the slight scarp between the Turkey Building and the fence. The Grotto will have appeared to float above the trees; Brown often planted a single oak on a rising sightline and then headed it to show off a building above it, like Milton's Eden "embosom'd high in tufted trees." So here, there is an oak beside the lake that was cut to show off the Grotto. The Poplar Urn was a smaller structure than the Grotto, but it is only 150 yards from the Turk. This was graced with a planting of the elegant grey poplar, *Populus × canescens*, from which it takes its name.

However far Brown moved from such early essays in design, we should not forget Wotton. He did succeed in the *ferme ornée* tradition that he inherited, before he began to transform it.

previous pages: The modest Octagon is dwarfed by the immensity of the lake.
above: The sight-lines between the Rotunda and the various structures that surround it are broken up by a series of horse-chestnuts, apparently planted randomly around it.
opposite above: The Turk.
opposite below: There are three set-piece views from the Octagon: one to Wotton House, one to the Grotto, and one to the Turk. These are framed by views to urns set on large earthen mounds.

66 · CAPABILITY BROWN

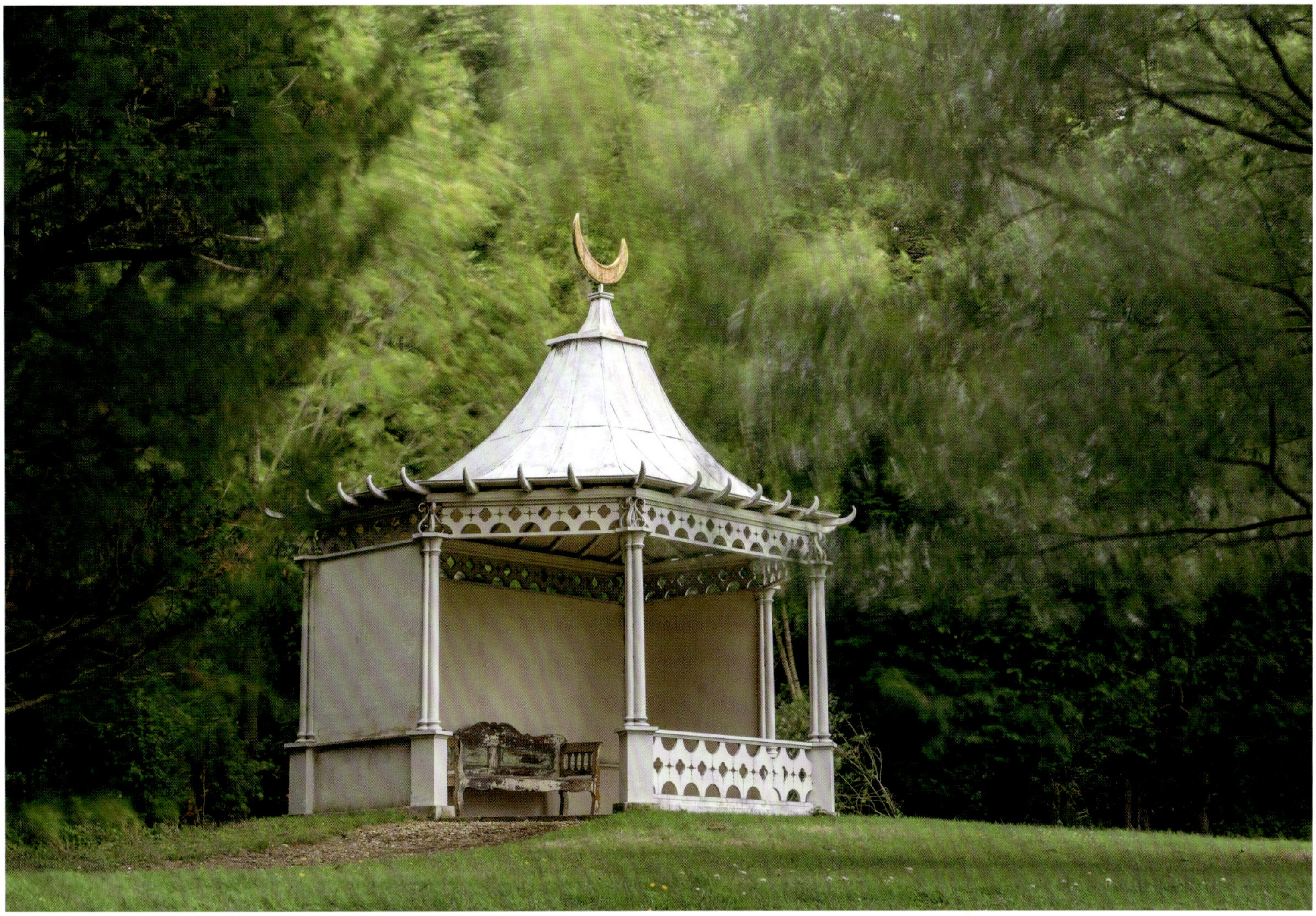

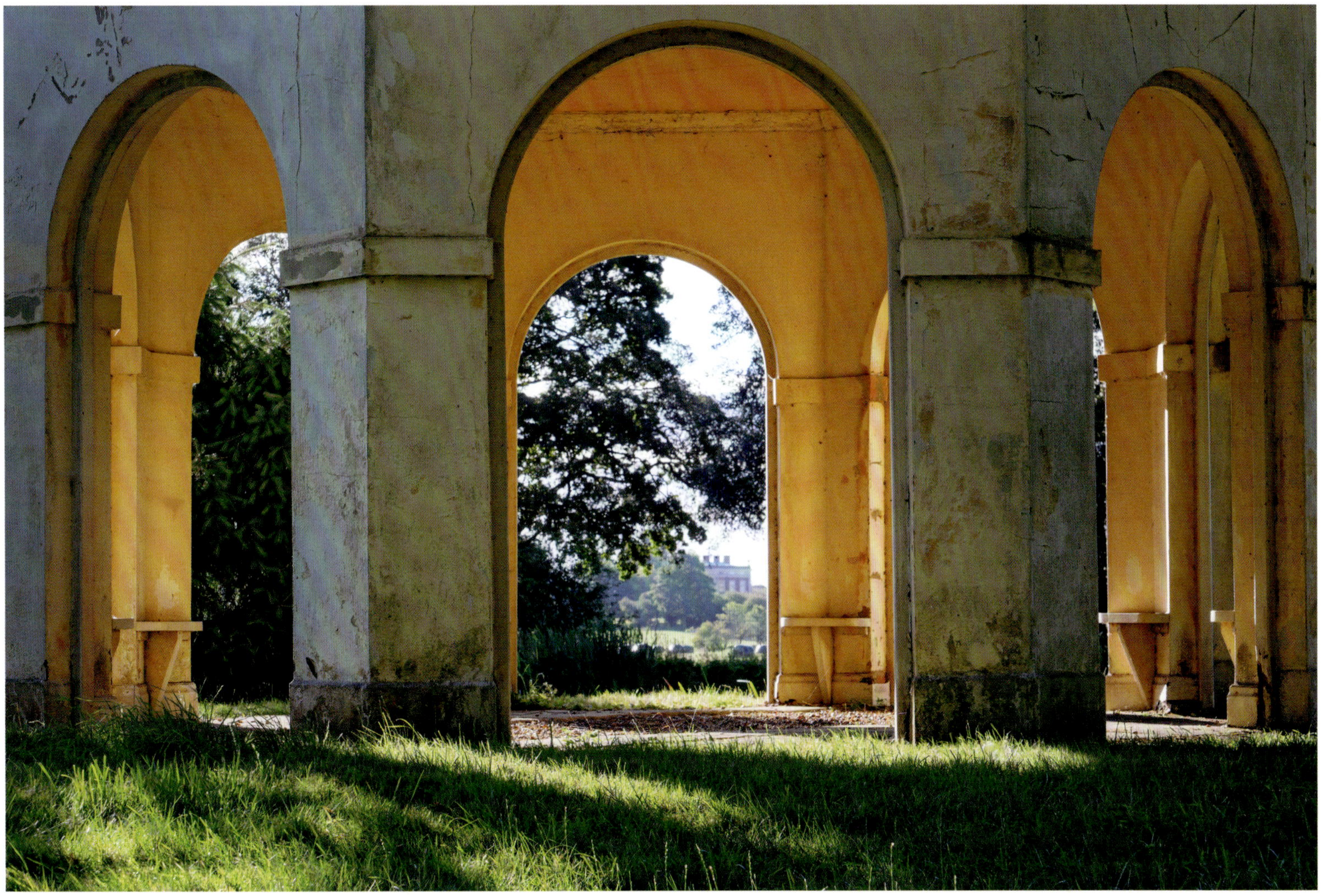

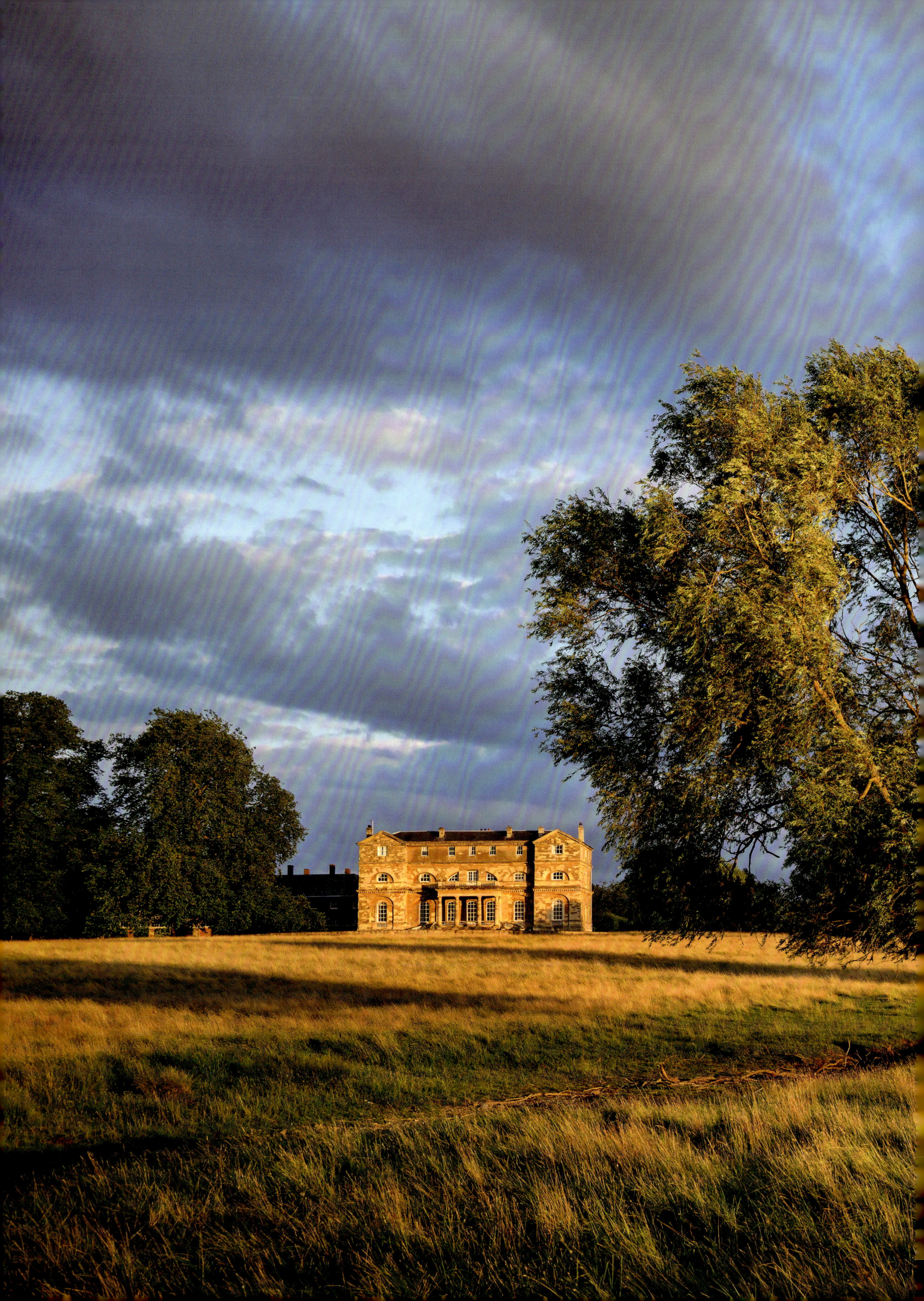

WAKEFIELD LODGE

— NORTHAMPTONSHIRE —
FROM 1750

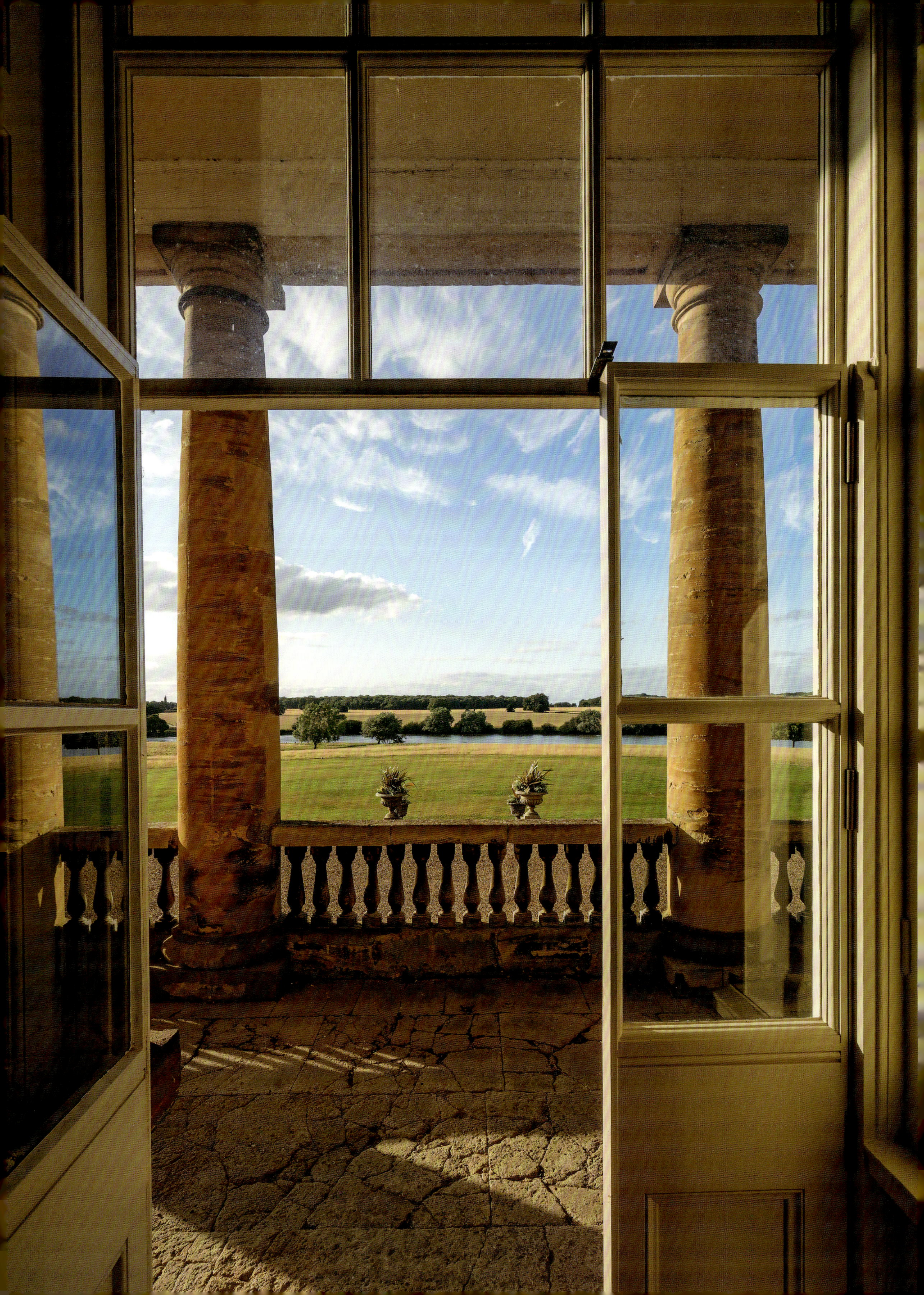

— CHAPTER FOUR —

WAKEFIELD LODGE

WAKEFIELD LODGE IS a strikingly ancient site, only about one kilometer from Watling Street (a Roman road, now the A5), lying within the twelfth-century Royal Forest of Whittlewood, and having at its core a grassy clearing in the forest known as Wakefield Lawn. There had been a lodge on the Lawn since the Plantagenets, but in the 1740s and 1750s Charles FitzRoy, 2nd Duke of Grafton (1683–1757), had this house greatly improved by William Kent (1685–1748). Brown must have visited before this remodeling was complete (he was first paid in 1750), and the Duke would have been a catch for him so early in his career. A politician and courtier, the Duke was also a celebrated foxhunter and Wakefield was his sporting seat. During the 1750s, he was to spend at least forty nights there a year, rather than at Euston, his principal house, and the Grafton Hunt was formed at Wakefield at the beginning of that decade.[1] As at Chatsworth a large new stable block was an essential element of these alterations, and its construction had begun in 1748.[2]

This was Brown's first experience of an estate designed primarily for hunting, and its landscape is best understood as a clearing in a hunting forest. It was not a park because it had no pale—deer might be attracted to the Lawn to feed, but they were always free to roam within the bounds of the forest, and it would have been illegal to confine them. This created the paradoxical situation wherein the parkland could have stock-proof fences, which would allow sheep, cattle, and horses to graze, so long as they were not tall enough to restrict the deer. The same forest law still applied when foxes replaced deer as the quarry of choice.

After hunting, fishing was important, but less so than shooting. Driven shooting had not been developed at that date, and this would have been rough shooting—going out alone or with a few friends, perhaps with horses and a few dogs, perhaps only a spaniel and a setter. However, pheasants were among the birds being shot, and small-scale pheasant rearing would also be required.

Brown then was coming to a place that would need water, a pheasant-rearing area, and plenty of

*previous pages: The parkland had hidden fences to keep stock off grass that was to be kept for hay.
The line of the fence is marked by a visible crease in the ground, which runs diagonally from the bottom left.
opposite: The portico at the lodge is relatively modest in scale. The view was to be had from the balcony, overleaf.*

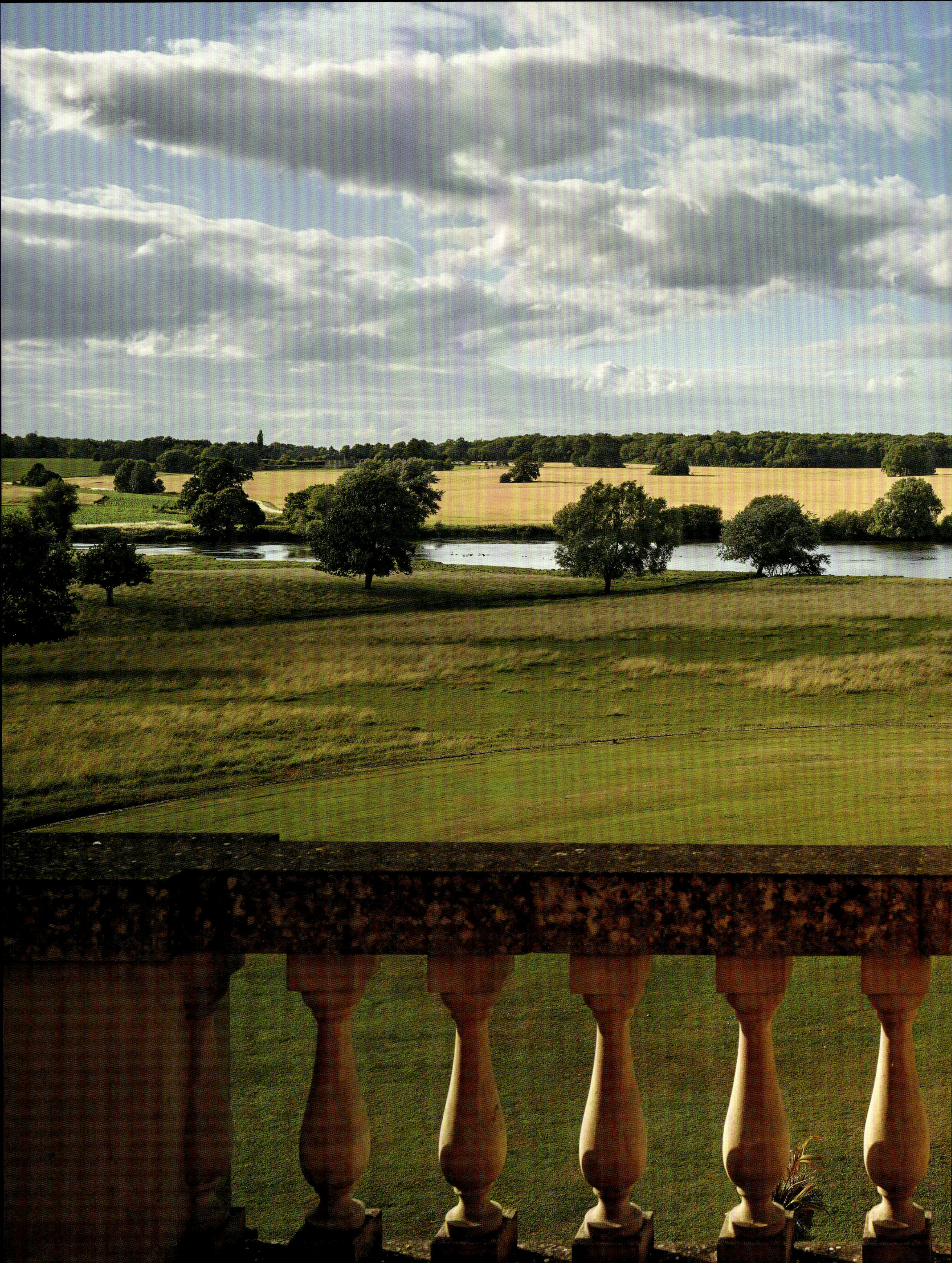

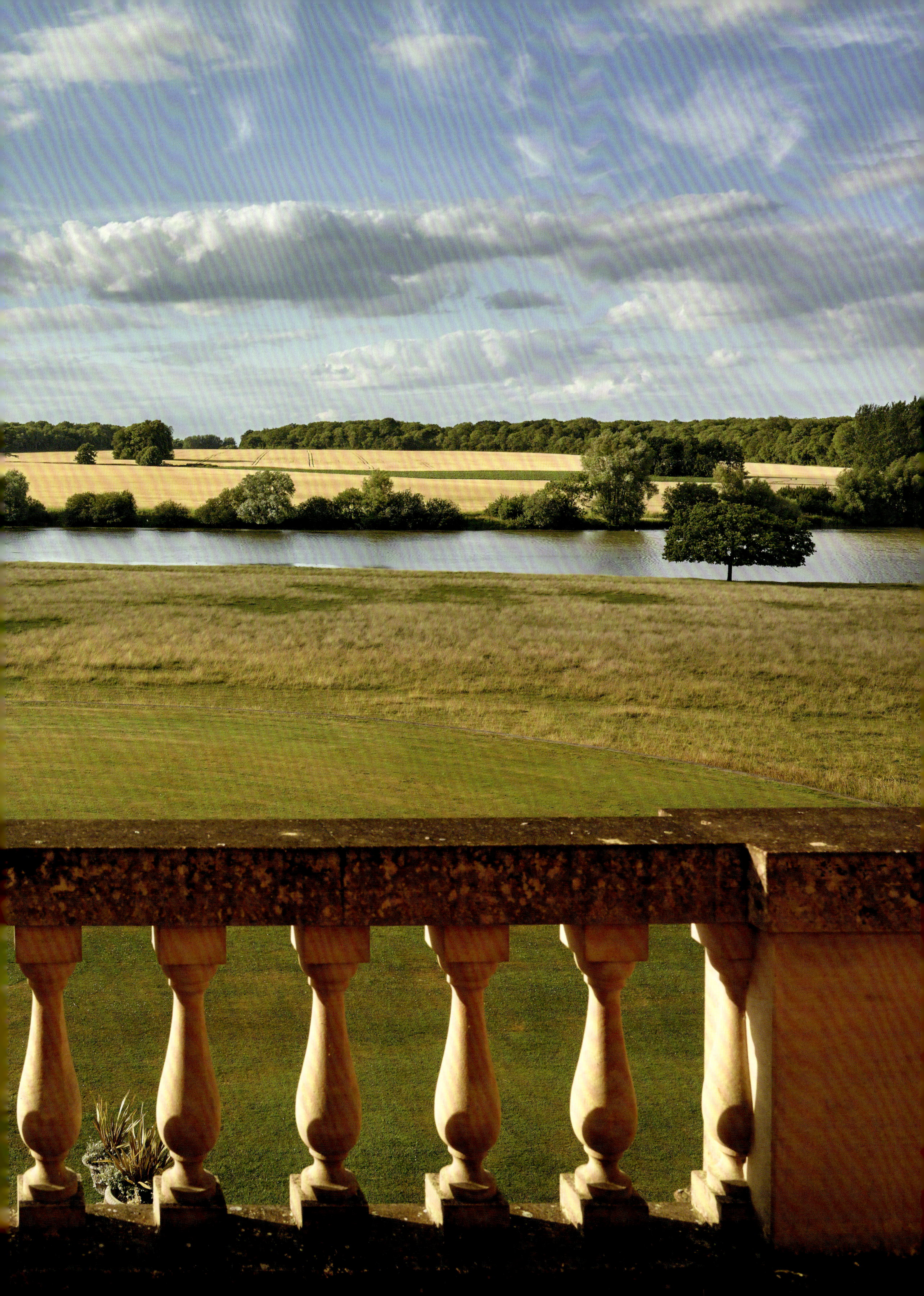

grass above all to cope with the additional numbers of horses needed for regular fox-hunting—at a great hunting estate like Welbeck, the Duke of Portland needed stabling for fifty horses in 1750,[3] by 1770 he had "about 130."[4] Horses were stabled for most of the year and would have required feeding with cut grass throughout that time. In addition they would also have needed paddocks and a training ground or racetrack for exercise.

Grass was thought of as something peculiarly English. So, in comparing English with Italian culture, Horace Walpole wrote, regretfully: "As our poets warm their imaginations with sunny hills, or sigh after grottoes and cooling breezes, our painters draw rocks and precipices and castellated mountains, because Virgil gasped for breath at Naples, and Salvator wandered amidst Alps and Apennines. Our ever-verdant lawns, rich vales, fields of hay-cocks, and hop-grounds, are neglected as homely and familiar objects."[5] But above all grass had a value, it was the transport fuel of the time, as pleasing to an English landowner as the sight of oil wells to a Texan billionaire.

As we shall see in the accounts of Petworth, parkland was to teem with animals and, with its wildflowers and natural character, grass had its part to play in creating a prelapsarian abundance that the farmland beyond had lost. Brown catered for these requirements in a design that was deceptively simple, by working with the medieval character of the Lawn.[6]

above: A cedar of Lebanon was planted on the far side of the lake but directly opposite the house to indicate the point along the approach at which one might stop to take in the view. opposite: The deer herd at the Upper Lake.

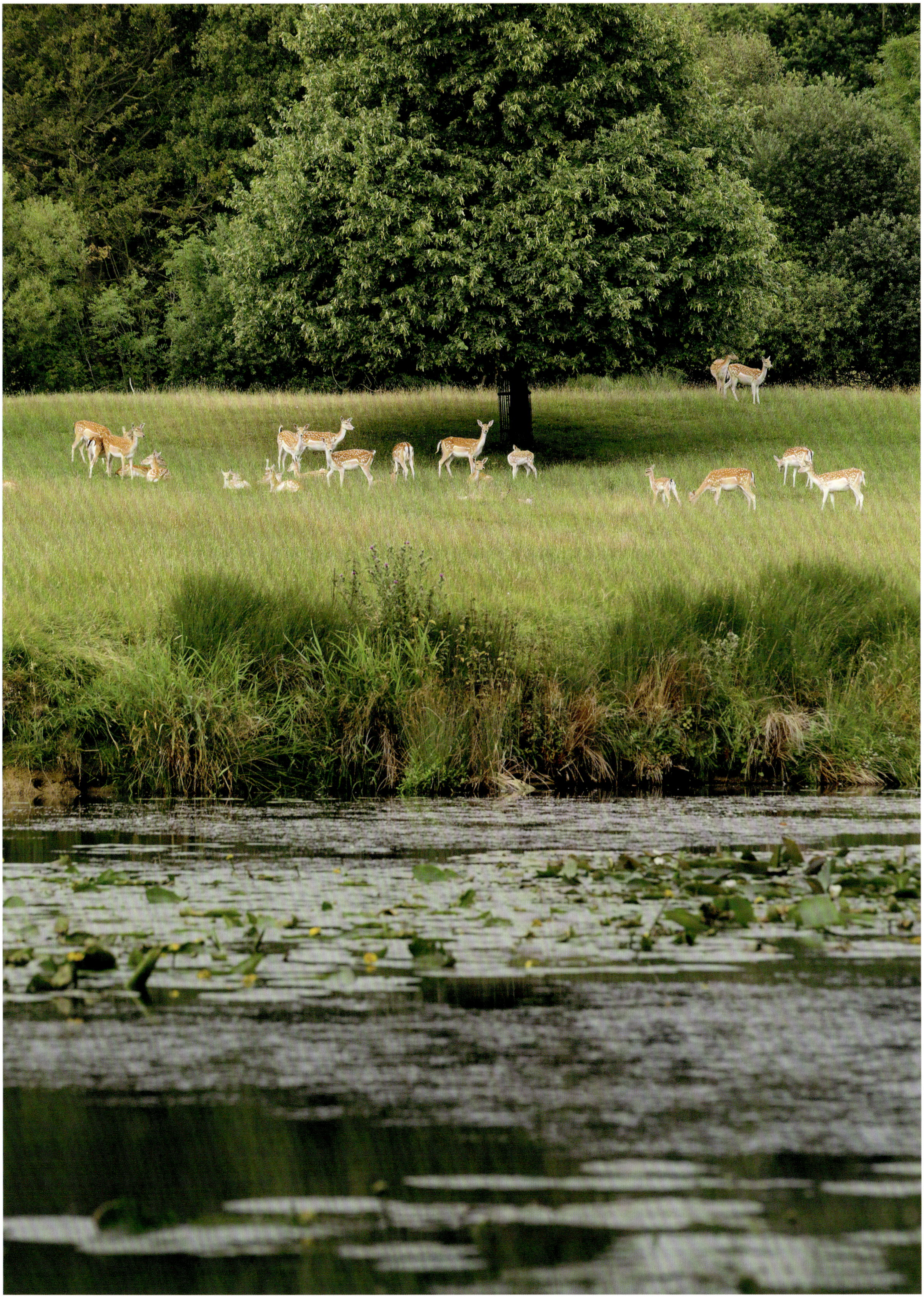

above: The parkland and lake at Wakefield are
surrounded by the forest.

overleaf: The New River. Brown favored weeping willows, and those still growing by the New River are very much in his style.

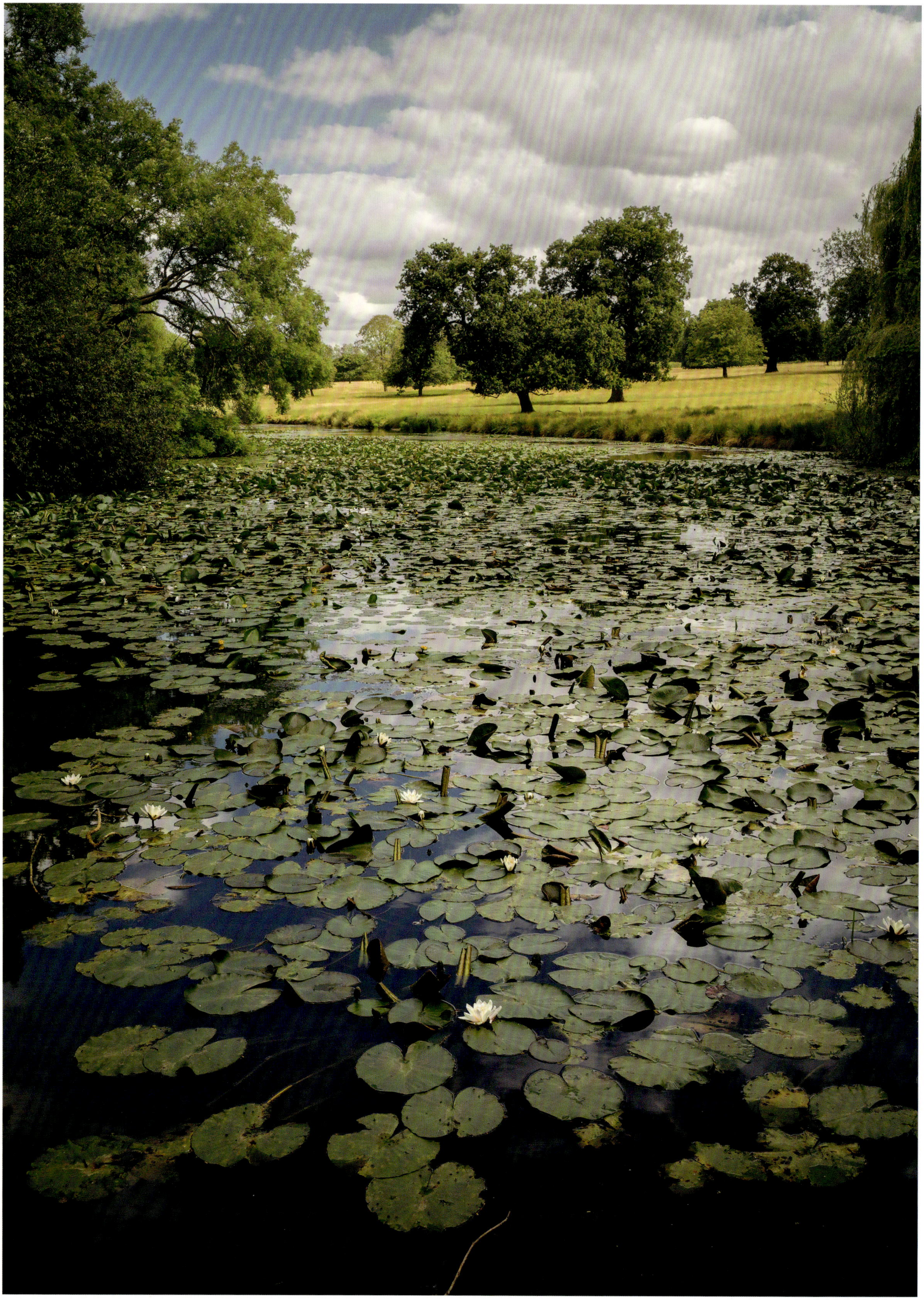

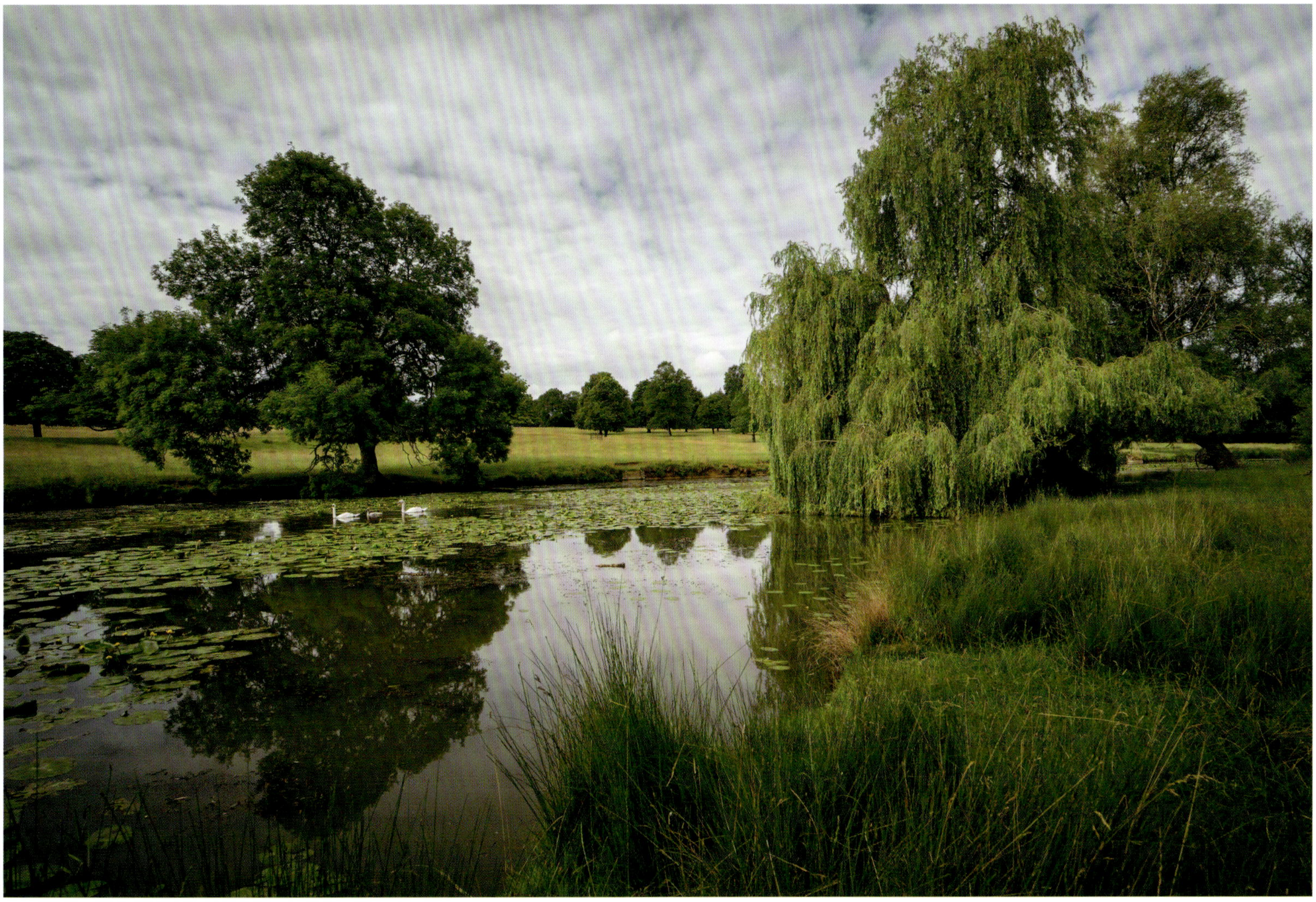

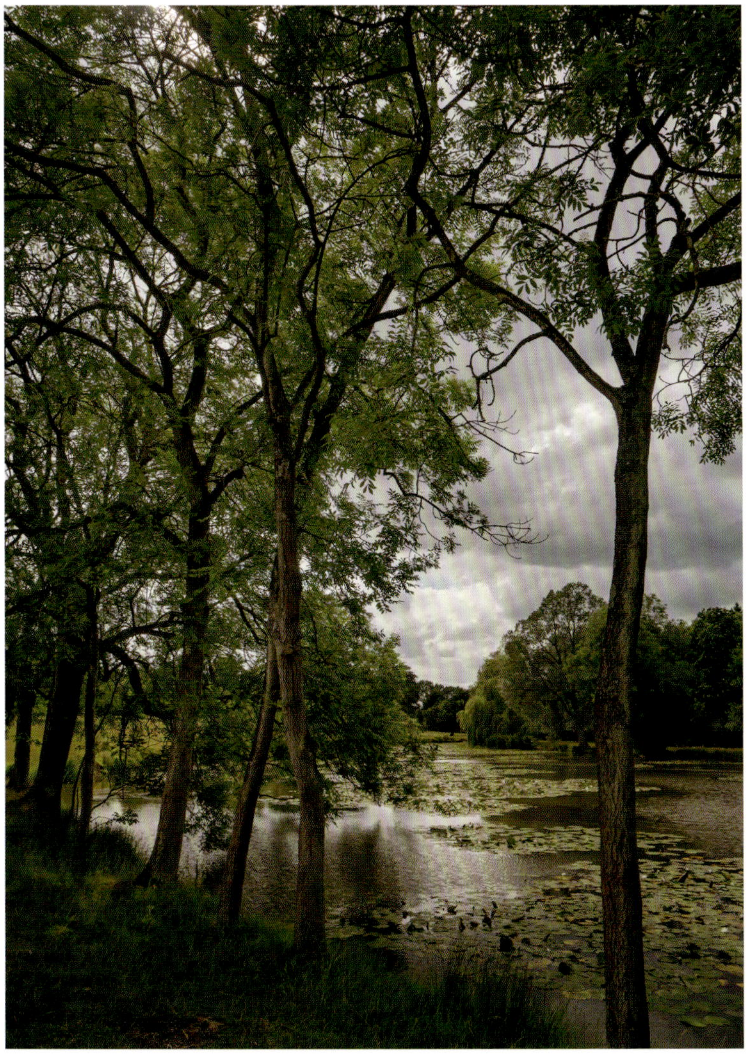

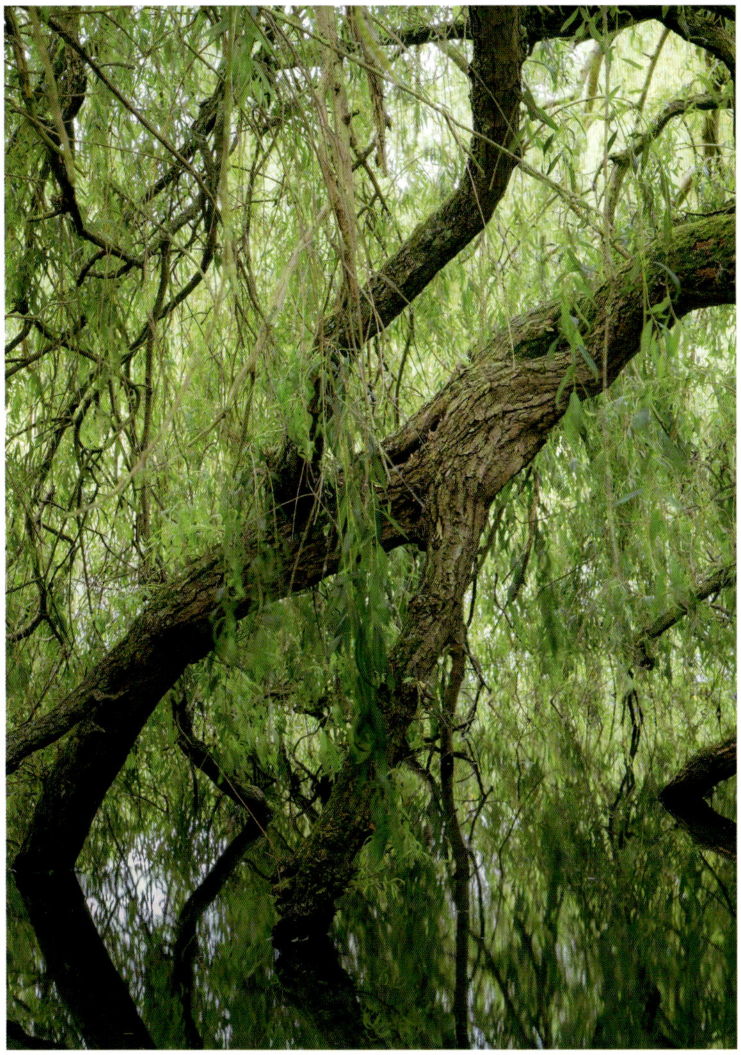

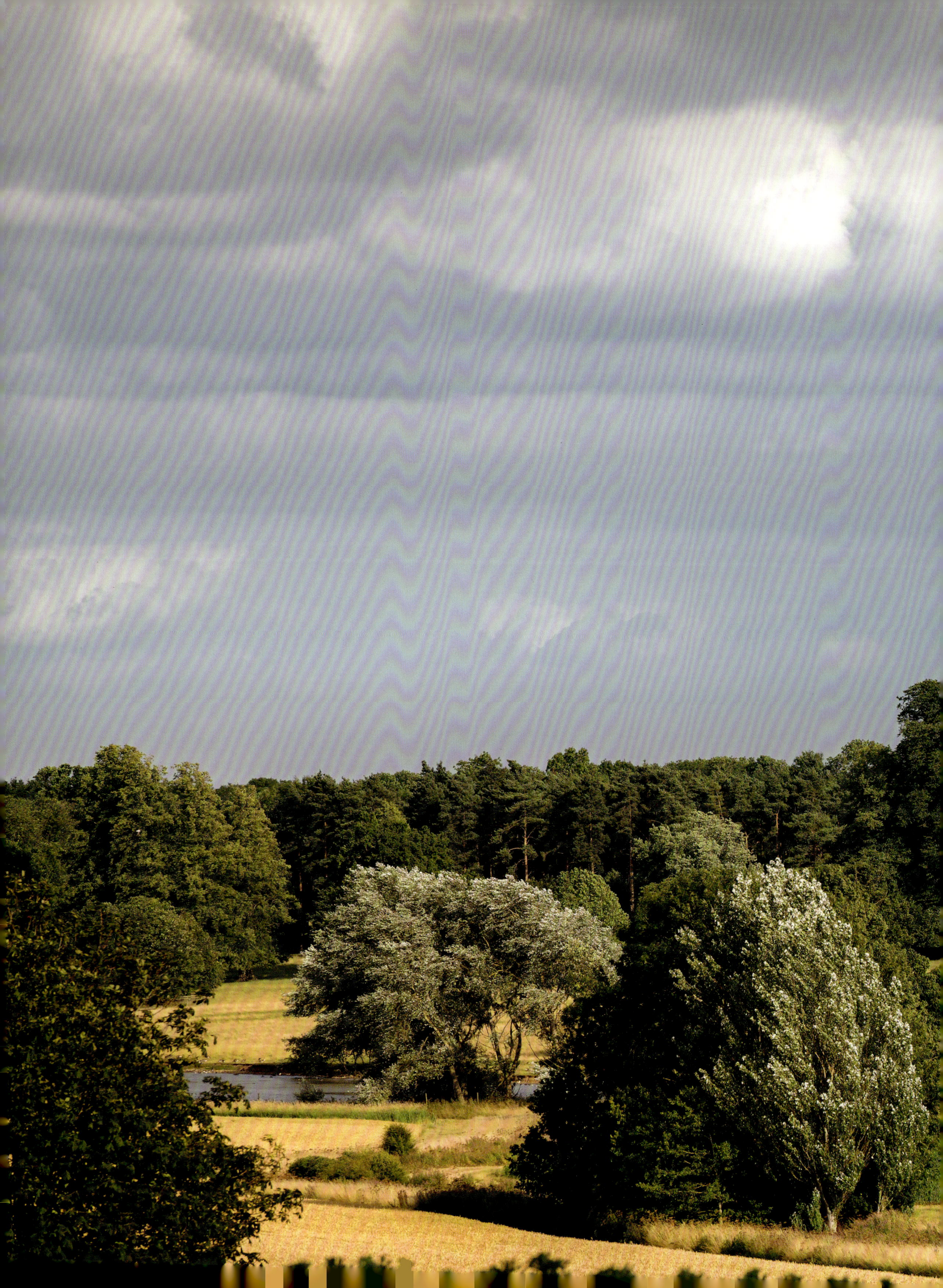

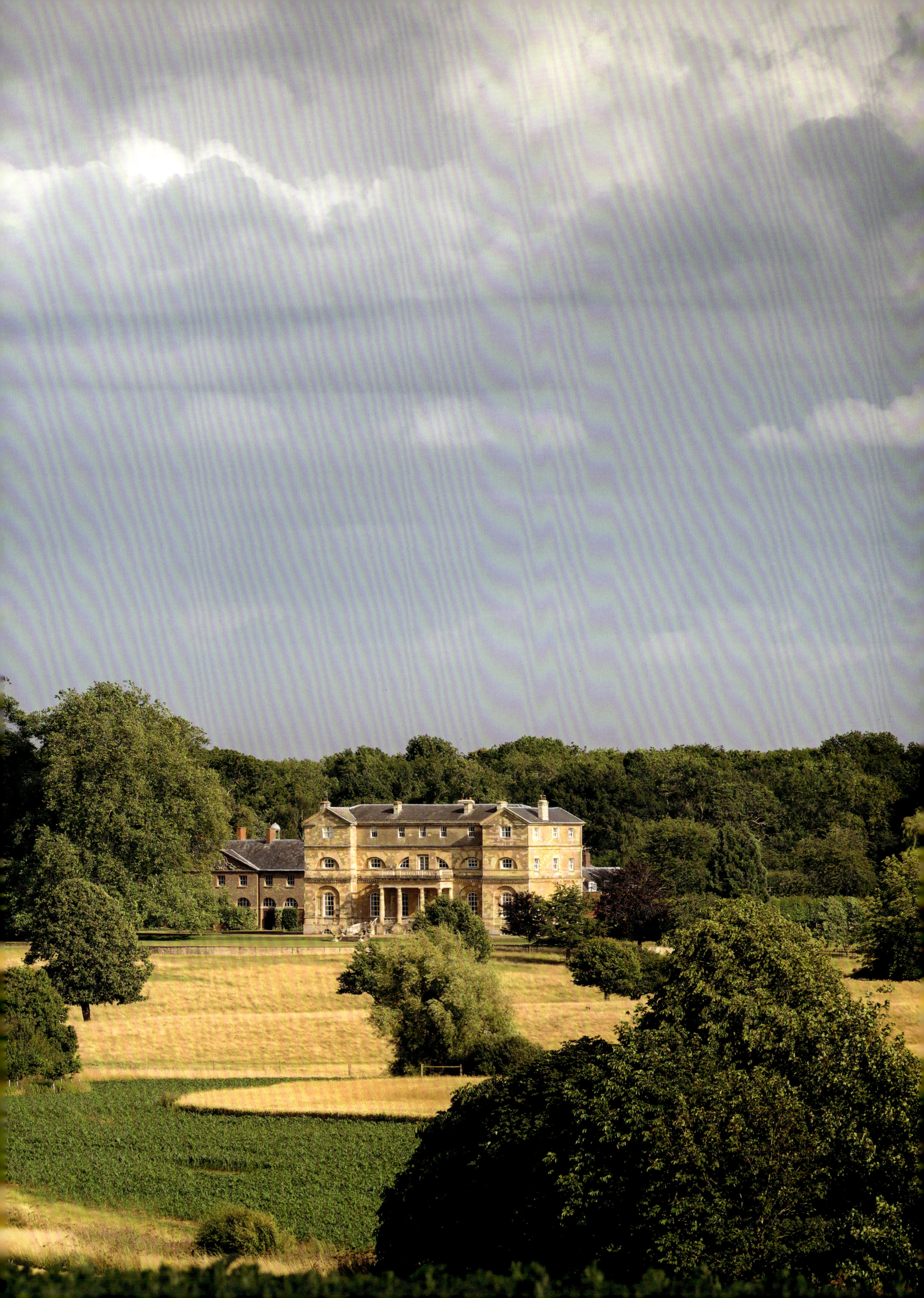

previous pages: Backed by the Pheasantry, Wakefield Lodge stands on the edge of its parkland.

As so often happens, by the time Brown was called in, works were already underway, and just as often, plans may have been going awry. So, Great Pond was already a substantial body of water in 1608, but was in repair in 1745, and grading work around it was carried out in 1747 to tidy it up. This seems to have been unsatisfactory, and in 1750 Brown was brought in and paid nine bills from December of that year to May 1755, totaling £702.10.[7] Except for one, these bills were unambiguously for "making the water at Wakefield." There seems little doubt that Brown extended the existing Great Pond to make the present Upper Lake by building a dam across its eastern end, and then constructed the New River. There is a fall of more than three meters between the two lakes, but Brown designed it to look like a single river in views from the house.

We shall see at Dinefwr that Brown would contribute much more than was asked of him, and it is an open question how far he was involved with other work on the landscape here. Vistas were being cut through the woodland, ha-has were under construction, and the Towcester Approach was built. The land was drained and leveled, enabling the 3rd Duke to establish the Wakefield Lawn Races in 1760, and everywhere trees were being planted, watered, pruned, and fenced. In addition, the place has one feature that is particularly Brownian: despite its being a medieval landscape, in the parkland north of the house there are no ancient pollards (that is, trees regularly cut above the point where the new shoots could be reached by an animal). They remain in some concentration in the paddocks on the south side and on the fringes of the landscape, unsurprisingly in Oaks Field, away to the

right: When Brown created his New Rivers, as he did on a number of landscapes, he had in mind the upper reaches of the Thames.

82 · CAPABILITY BROWN

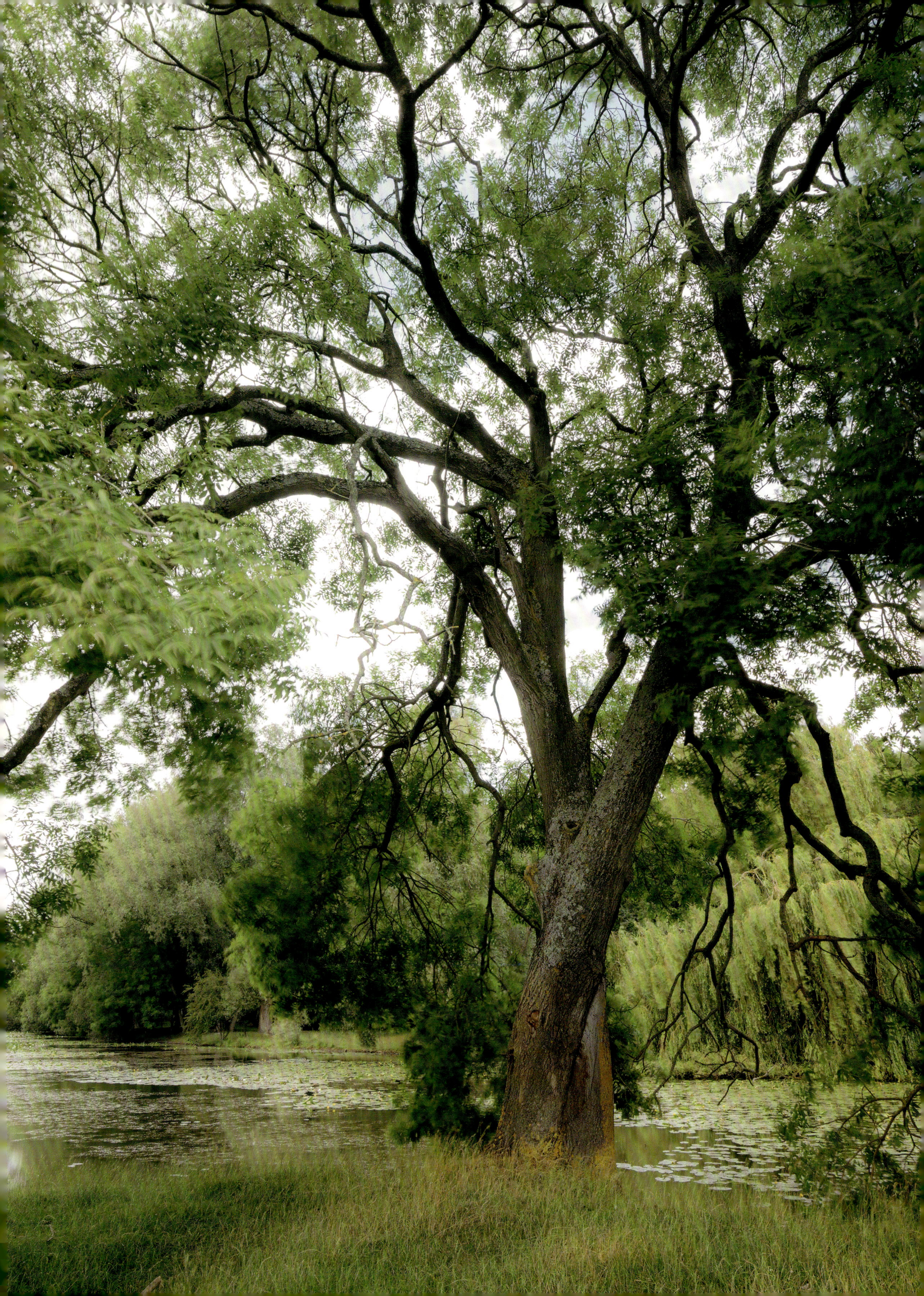

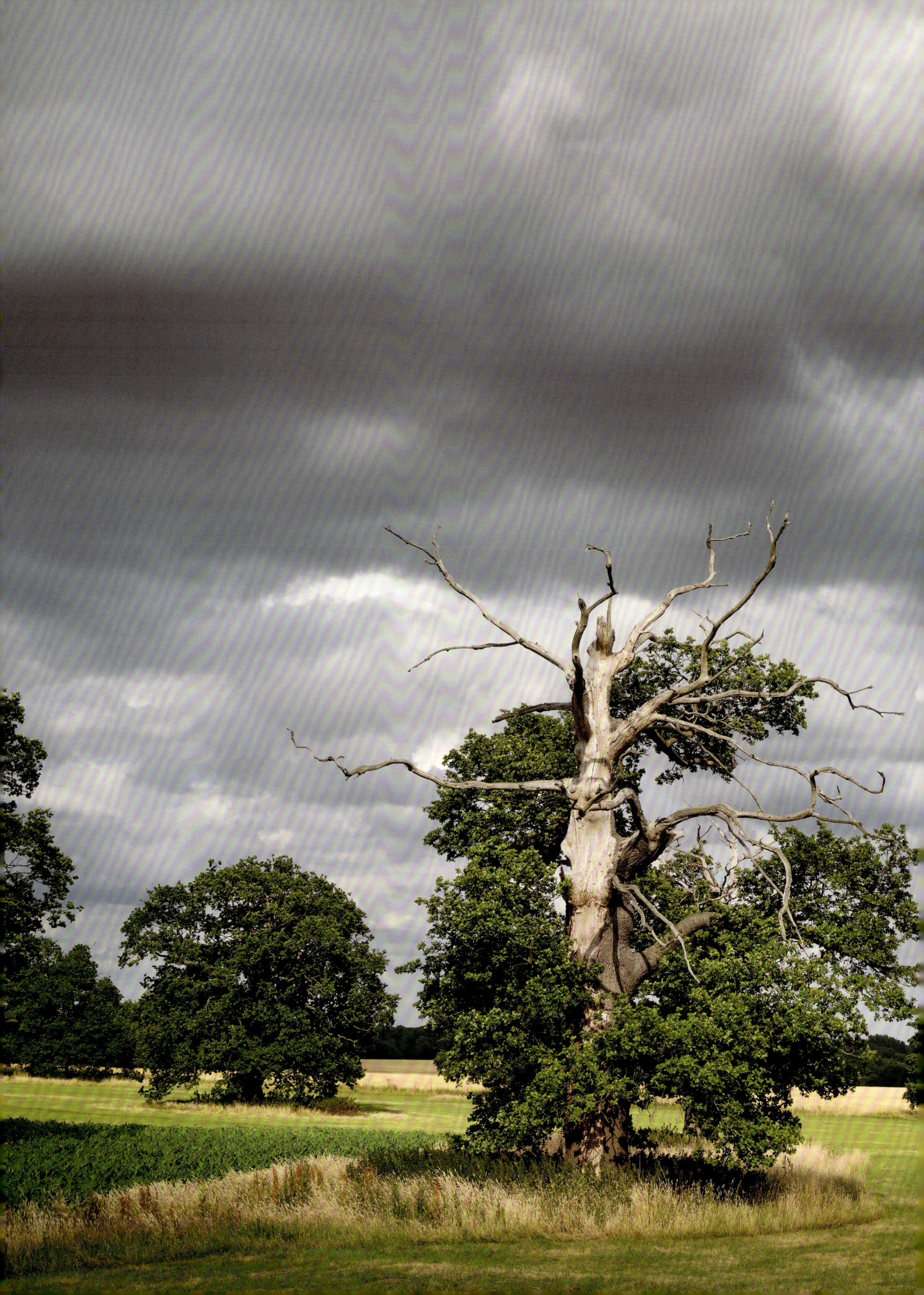

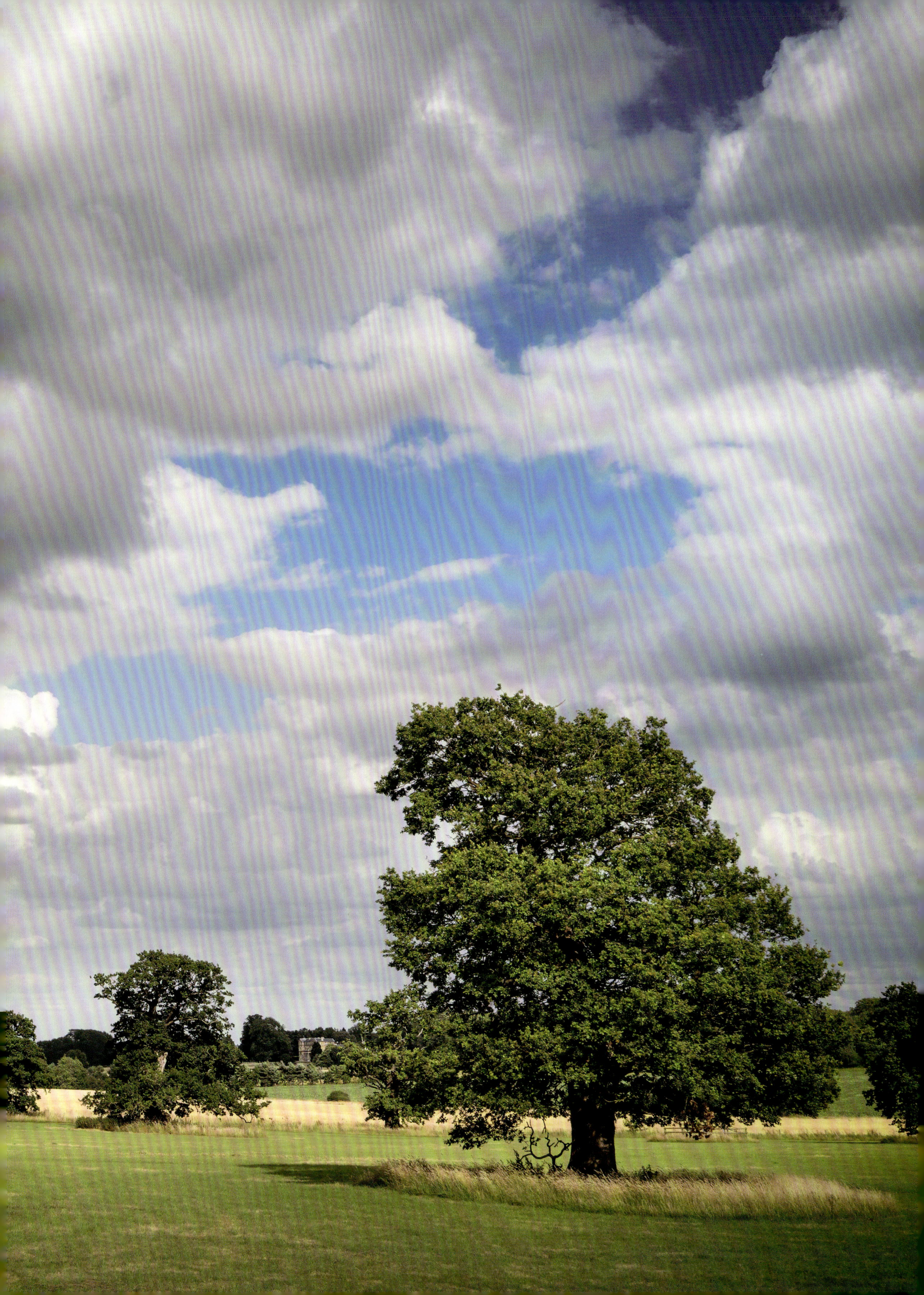

west, and there they retain variety in the landscape, and a reminder of Wakefield's medieval past, but in the heart of the landscape they are gone. They were felled in large numbers throughout England during the eighteenth century, and Brown was of his time in removing them unless they had some sentimental value for the owner, as at Petworth. Several reasons were given for this—the hacking and pruning they had sustained made them so evidently unnatural, they seldom had much value as timber, and often they were diseased. Nowadays, of course, there are no trees we value more highly for their character and, rather than indicating dangerous sickness, the fungi that bloom upon them announce a fruitful biodiversity.

The only obviously ornamental improvement of Brown's day at Wakefield was the Pheasantry, the woodland that runs off from the house to the southwest. This remained essentially a hunting wood, with wide, straight drives cut through it in the 1740s, and serpentine paths (for rough shooting) probably added during 1755–1756.[8]

These straight drives were required for hunting and were described by the agriculturist, Arthur Young:

There is one feature at Wakefield Lodge equal to most in the kingdom; a lawn of delicious verdure, even in this drought, which may spread 500 acres, sloping to a water, of which it is sufficient to say, that it was formed by Brown; scattered groups of trees chequer the scene, and all surrounded, in every direction, by the shade of a forest impervious to the eye; not the poverty of a limit planted to screen and deceive, but the deep recesses, the umbrageous gloom, in which you may wander without boundary, and roam as in the wilds of America, did not numerous ridings cut in strait lines, and very neatly laid to grass, facilitate a passage to every part.[9]

If the idea of the straight drives had been taken directly from France and Versailles, the Lawn itself drew from the traditions of the English forest. Wakefield Lodge is a thoroughly Brownian landscape, which is at the same time deeply embedded in the medieval tradition and in an understanding of the medieval countryside.

previous pages: There will have been hundreds of pollards in the parkland. However, they were only retained at the edges.
opposite: Numerous straight rides ran out from the lodge.

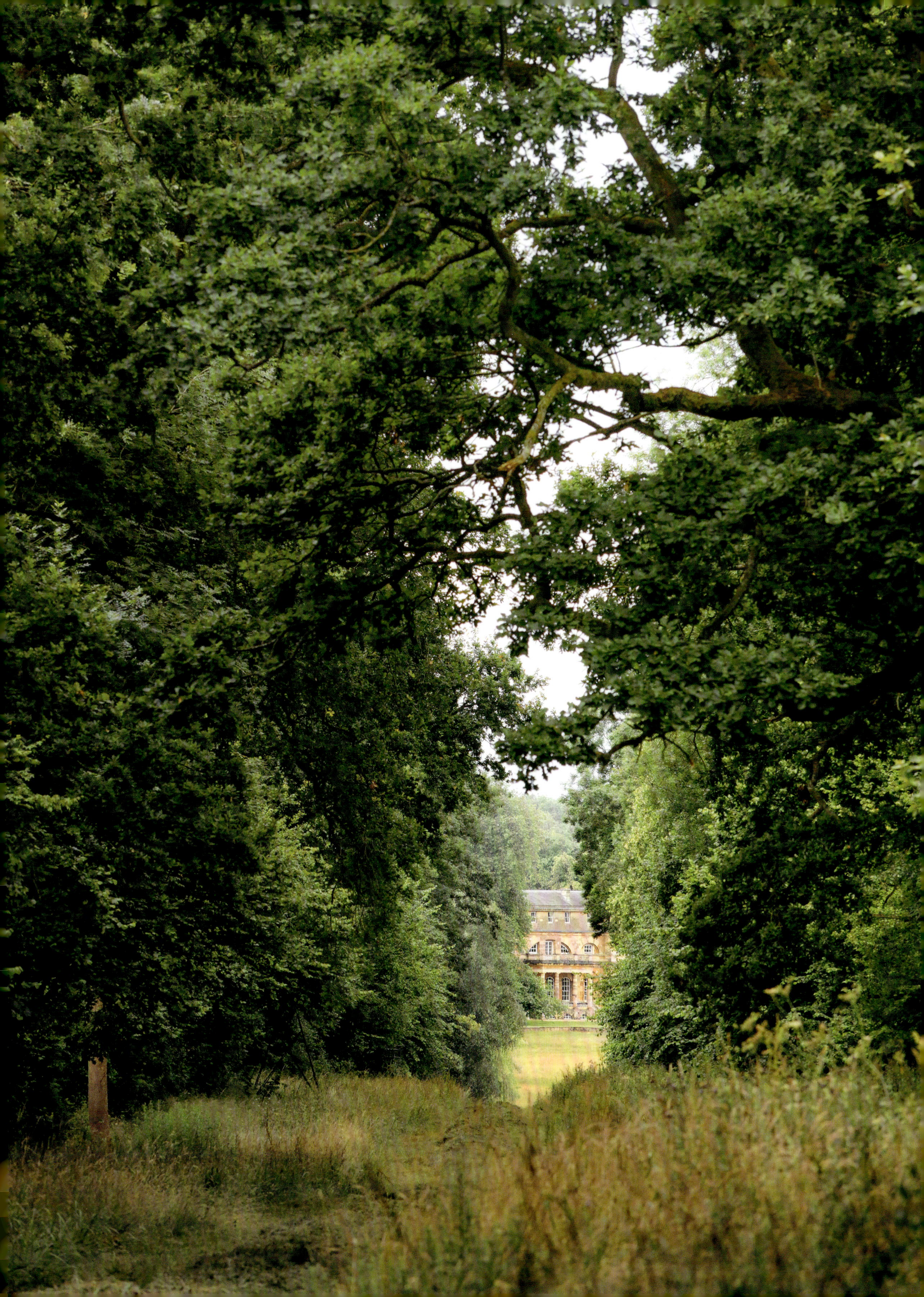

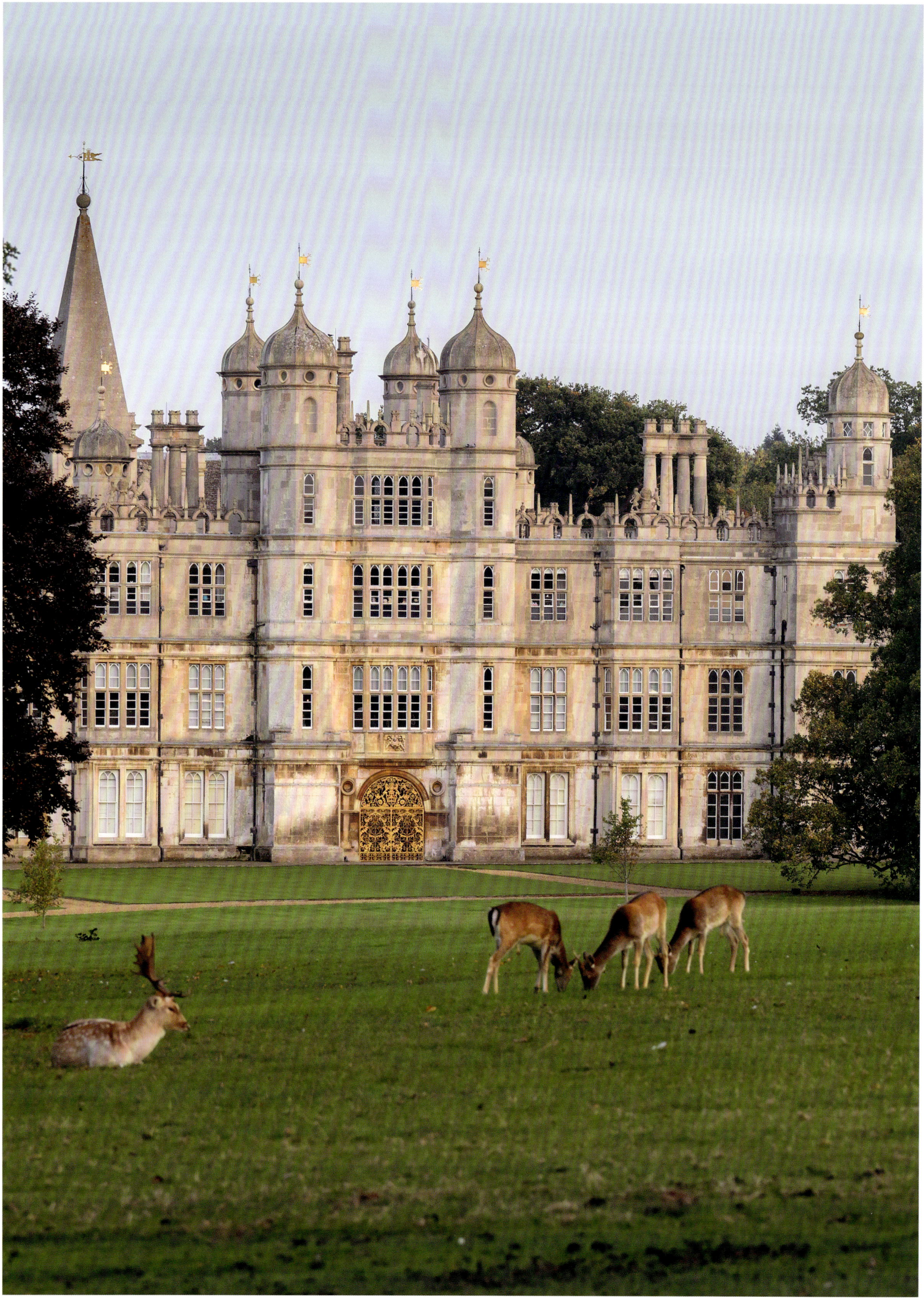

1751–1764
THE MIDDLE PERIOD

THE FOUR ESSENTIALS THAT BROWN TOOK WITH him when he left Stowe were confidence at working on a large scale, an understanding of the *ferme ornée*, an appreciation of medieval landscape (and of forests in particular), and a good experience of construction and architecture. He was immediately to recast this knowledge in a new form.

We have seen that the *ferme ornée* was capable of limitless extension, but limited variation. To deal with this problem, Brown's work in the 1750s tended toward a graduated design, moving from the polished lawns around the house to wild forest scenery, and from polite behavior within view of the windows, to the unlicensed roistering of the hare course and race-track. A typical sequence might run from a garden or pleasure ground around the house, to a deer park, running out from the garden boundary, and then at least one other grass field, which might be a sheep walk, or a hare course, which might double as a race track, and was often apparently indistinct from the deer park, then farmland, traversed by ridings, or a "rough park" or warren, and finally, perhaps, the medieval forest, if there happened to be one nearby.

opposite: Deer graze in Low Park, immediately beyond the polished lawns of the pleasure ground at Burghley House.

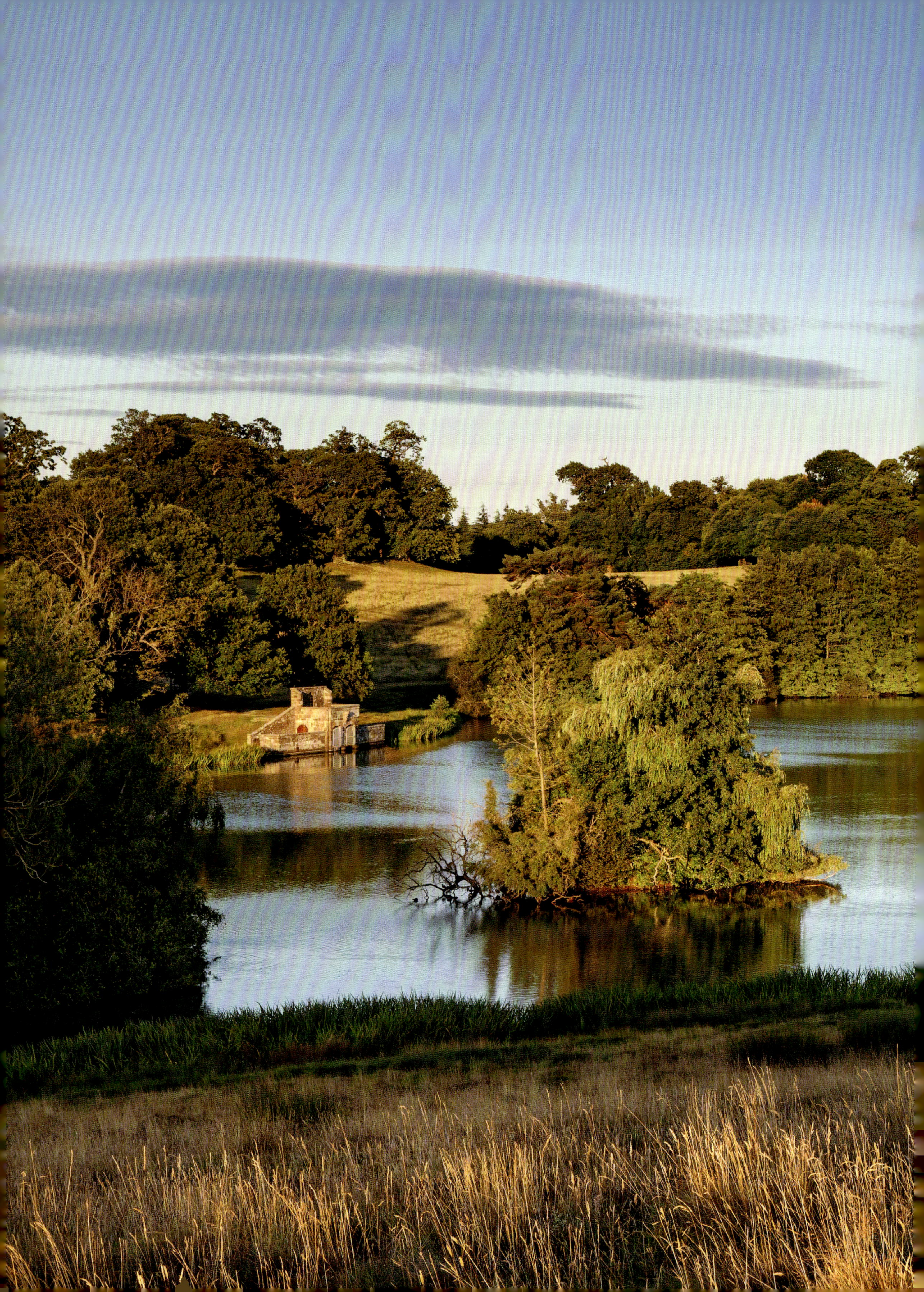

PETWORTH HOUSE
— *WEST SUSSEX* —
1751–1763

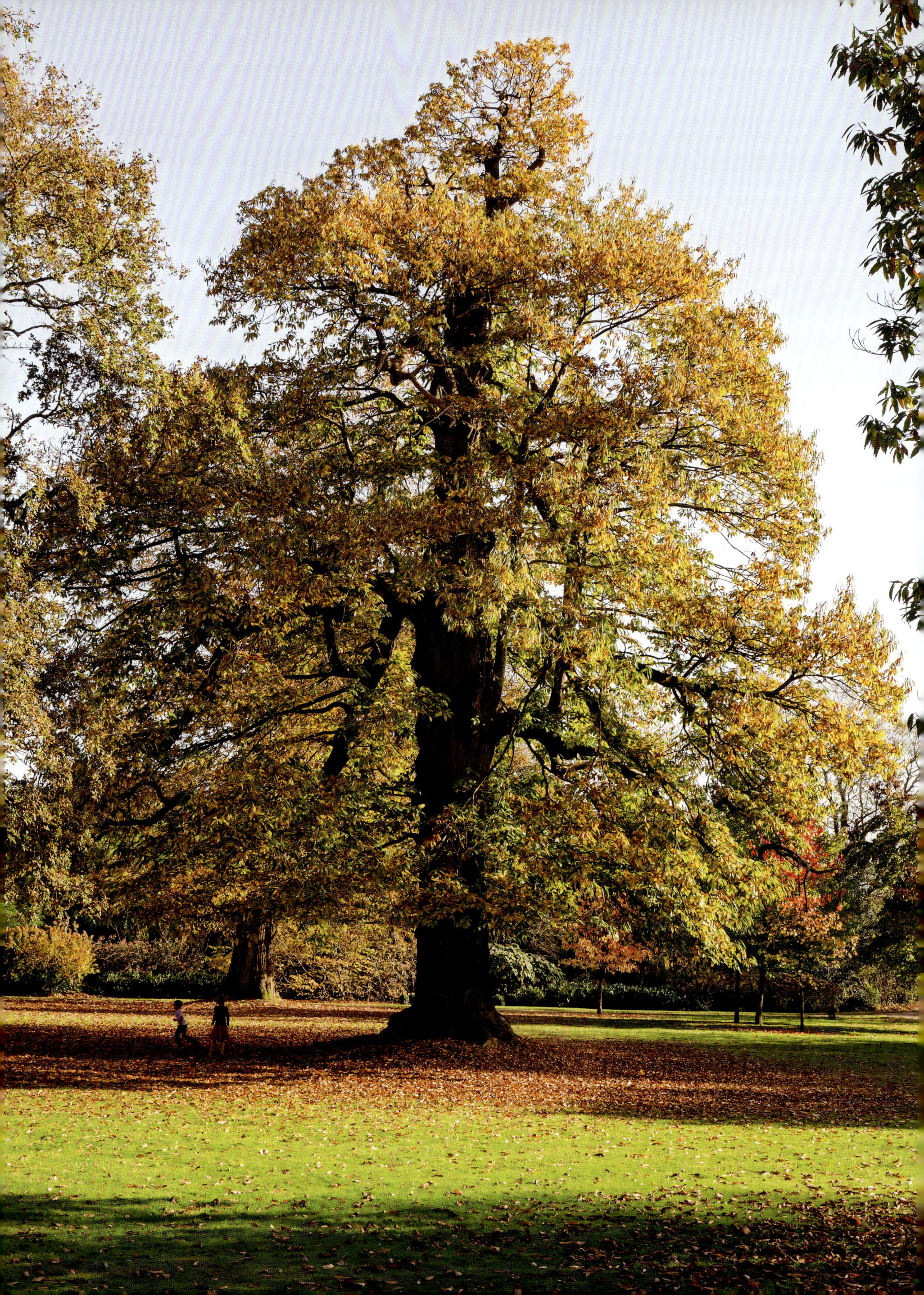

— CHAPTER FIVE —

PETWORTH HOUSE

AFTER THE DEATH of the Proud Duke, the 6th Duke of Somerset, in 1748, and of his son the 7th Duke two years later, the Petworth estate passed to Charles Wyndham, 2nd Earl of Egremont, who employed Brown from 1751 until his early death in 1763. We have detailed records of five separate commissions for Brown as a contractor there, sometimes with a foreman, Peter Blair, and the contract was on a large scale—the payments for which we have records add up to at least £5,600.

The acreage covered was also large—at more than seven miles from one end to the other, Brown's design was at the scale with which he had become familiar at Wallington. However, the different components of the landscape at Wallington are in no particular order, whereas the Petworth model was graduated, moving from the polished to the wild, from the ornamented parkland to farmland. This was the paradigm of the English landscape style as it was idealized by Thomas Whately:

The most perfect composition of a place that can be imagined, consists of a garden opening into a park, with a short walk through the latter to a farm, and ways along its glades to ridings in the country ....[1]

So, as one traveled north from the house, the elaborate pleasure ground gave onto Home Park "quite decorated & smooth," joined by "a fine large coppice of Spring wood [Pheasant Coppice] thro which are cut 3 paralell Ridings" to Stag Park, for red deer, turned into farmland by the 3rd Earl in the 1790s, but planted by Brown and described in 1770 as "quite in the forest stile exhibit[ing] a pleasing Wilderness." Brown's ridings continued, across the London road (A283), through a mixture of commons and unplanned farmland with small, hedged fields and numerous woods and copses. This land would have provided good rough shooting and had a keeper's lodge in the middle for that purpose. Thence the riding looped back to the London road three miles farther north, west of the neighboring park, Shillinglee, where Brown also worked.

These ridings were a component of landscape that is very much associated with Brown. Rather

previous pages: The town of Petworth lies immediately behind Petworth House, but is entirely hidden in every view from the park.
opposite: Brown retained ancient pollards and timber trees, which had sentimental value for the family.

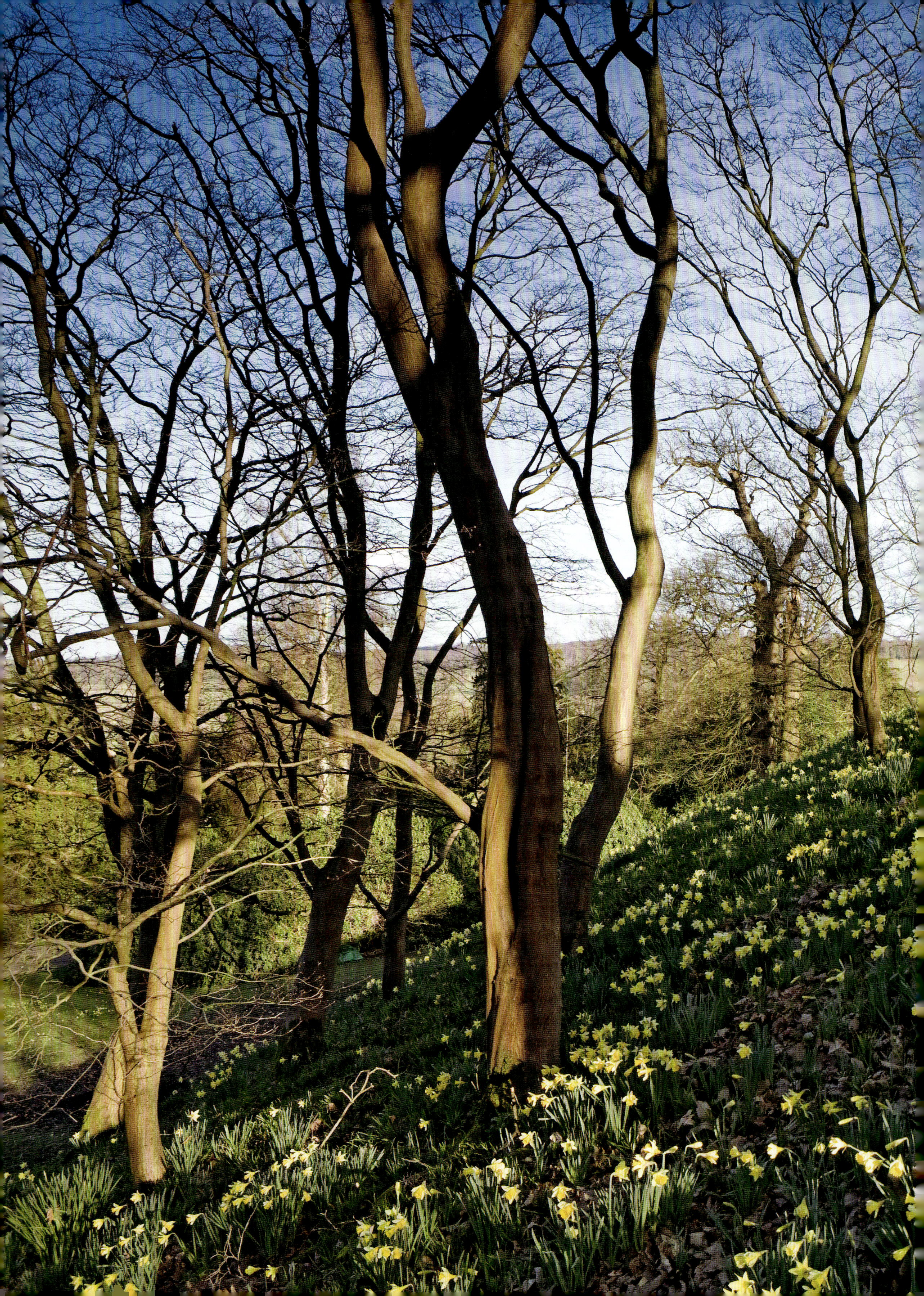

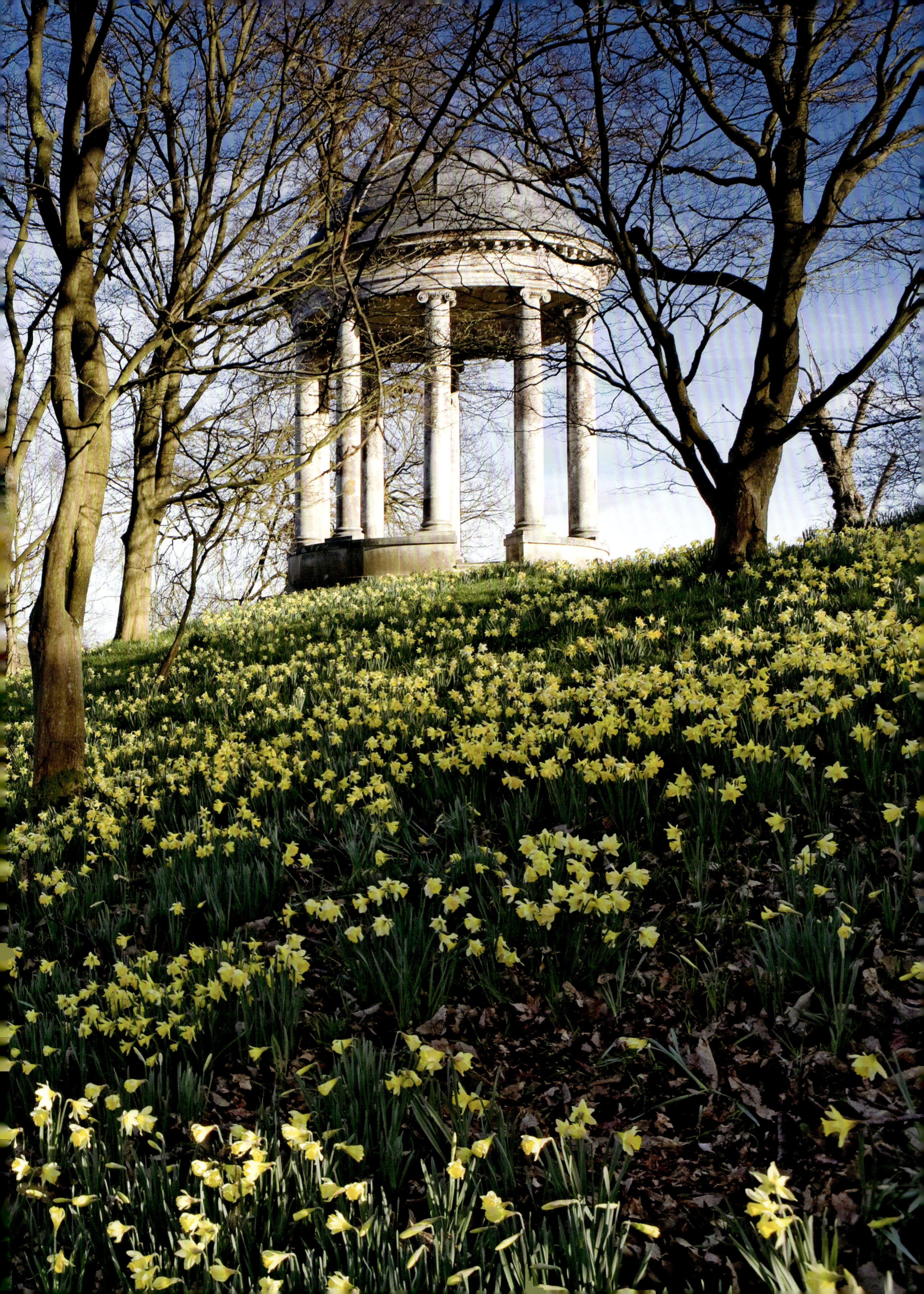

than creating landscape by earthworking and planting, "the use of a riding is to lead from one beauty to another, and be a scene of pleasure all the way." The route was intended to show off the best of the countryside rather than change it; nonetheless, such a road "admits more embellishment and distinction, than an ordinary road through a farm" and thus could "*extend the idea of a seat*, and appropriate a whole country to the mansion."[2]

The length of the Petworth ridings is by no means exceptional, as we shall see at Chatsworth and Milton Abbey, but it may have made sense to provide a private and safe passage in Sussex, which had infamous public roads: the wit, Horace Walpole, was "thrice overturned" in 1749 in its "Alpine mountains."[3] Ten years later, a street in Petworth (presumably the London road that ran down the east side of the deer park) was reported to be "two hundred yards long, full of deep holes, and a precipice on one side of the street, without so much as a rail for twenty yards, though exposed to every drunken traveller or stranger on horseback."[4] It is understandable that in a riding "the pleasantness of the road, not of the spot, is the principal consideration" and hence, "very

previous pages: The Rotunda on the high ground at the far end of the pleasure ground, overlooking the park.
above: The landscape stretches away indefinitely north of Petworth House. Lawns and the wooded pleasure ground south of the lake give way to the deer park, the sprawling clumps of Stag Park, and finally to the wildness of the commons.

moderate views are sufficient to render its progress agreeable."⁵ However, Brown's career coincided with the high tide of turnpiking, a system during which the main roads were greatly improved through tolls exacted from those who used them—and this may explain why ridings lost their currency so rapidly after his death.

Approaches (the links between the public road and the house) were by contrast closely connected to views. Above all, the road's surface should not be seen from the house and secondarily, they should provide, if possible, a triumphant burst—a first dramatic reveal of the great house. So at Petworth Brown moved his approach to the southern edge of Home Park, having seen that from the top of a great smoothed-out quarry in the hill, the Concave, he could get his burst—and there is nothing finer in Brown's entire oeuvre. Here the house appears at a great distance, against a broken horizon, above Brown's lake, the Upper Pond, with trees balanced at its shoulders, in a scene of perfect symmetry, though, in fact, Ash Grove, the hill on the right, is higher, and the land has been cut away and built up onto the left-hand side (Arbour Hill) to match it.

above: Sweet chestnuts had been planted at Petworth since the reign of Charles II. Many were retained by Brown, though at Chestnut Grove they may have been moved, to give the clump a more relaxed appearance.
overleaf: Petworth is regarded by many as the finest park that Brown ever made.

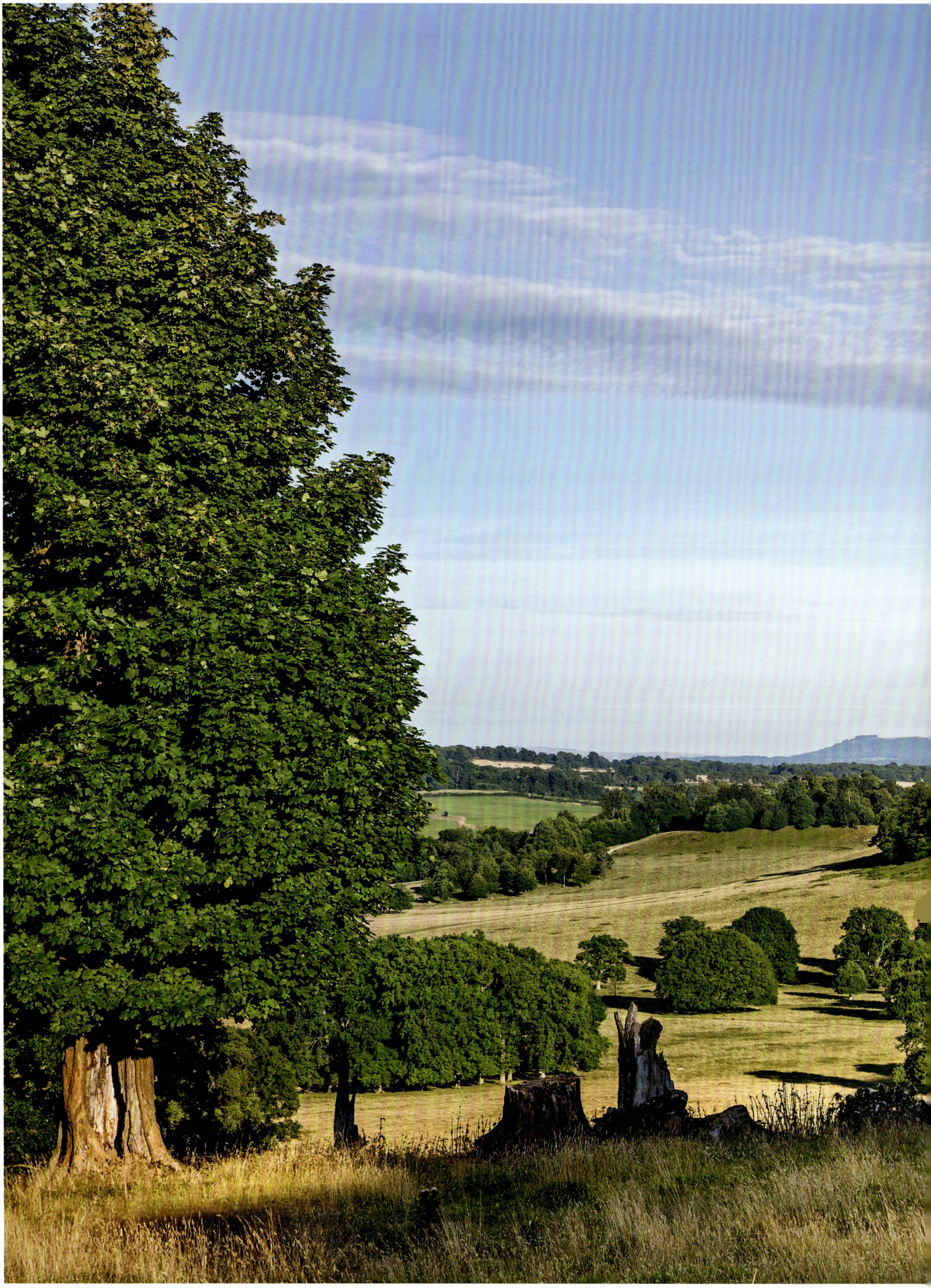

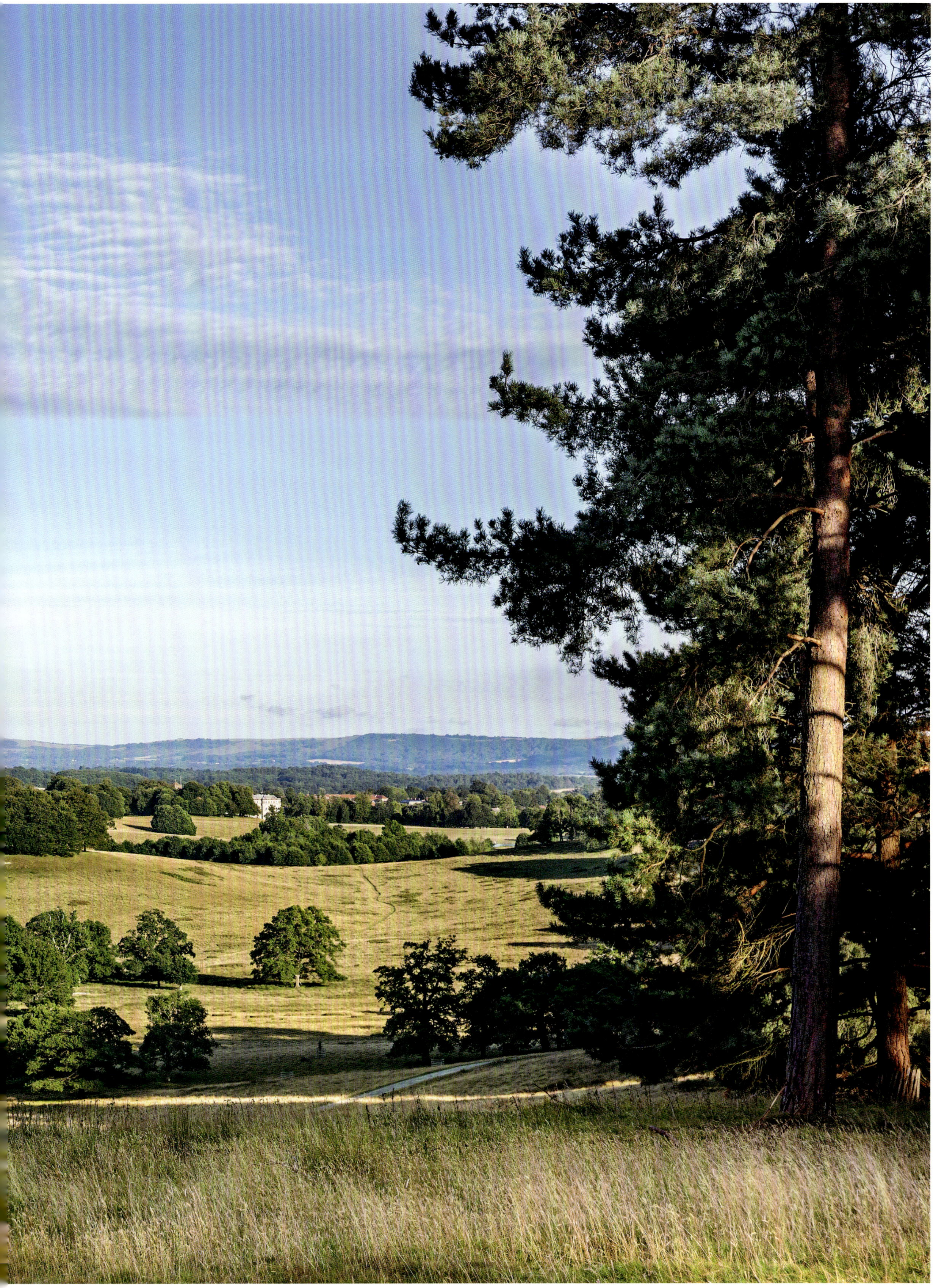

Arbour Hill, like the nearby clump Chestnut Grove, also has a flattened top, perhaps to accommodate tents and picnics in the summer, and both these two clumps have further superb, composed views, the latter to Brown's Lower Pond on the north side of Home Park. Although this parkland was more polished than Stag Park to the north, it still had an undesigned texture, the rolling topography, the groups and clumps of trees creating a space that was not just a frame for views but a space in its own right. It had its ancient trees, the Cecil, Northumberland, and Beelzebub Oaks, retained for sentimental reasons, and the Northumberland Thorn "split in a most uncommon manner" by a vengeful fairy, as an account of 1770 has it: "The Tradition is that a Fairy fell in love with an Earl of Northumberland and they had constantly interviews every day but in time she grew jealous of his wife, but dissembling it she made him a present of a fine girdle but he in going home girt it round this thorn." It had also a mixing of the agricultural and, a sop to the curious, the exotic: "either cultivated, or stocked with the finest breeds of cattle, among which are some Calmuck, and Tartar sheep, distinguished by a member in place of a tail, of enormous size, and exquisite taste. Here is likewise seen the shawl-goat of Thibet."[6]

The gradation at Petworth extended to the planting, so the ridings had all the native trees that one might expect to find in the English countryside, while Stag Park was largely planted with oak (a patriotic choice, but with a suitably uncouth rough habit), and Home Park was dominated by that mix of species commonly found in Brownian parkland: oak, sweet chestnut, horse chestnut, lime, beech, and hawthorn.

Other species commonly found in Brownian parkland might include alder, cedar of Lebanon, and Scots, Corsican, and Austrian pine. While Brown constantly experimented with the way in which he used these species, he rarely planted trees newly introduced from overseas into parkland.

above: The deer herd was established at Petworth long before Brown arrived. By confining much of his new planting to clumps and woodland, he was able to protect his trees from their depredations. opposite: The pleasure ground at Petworth.

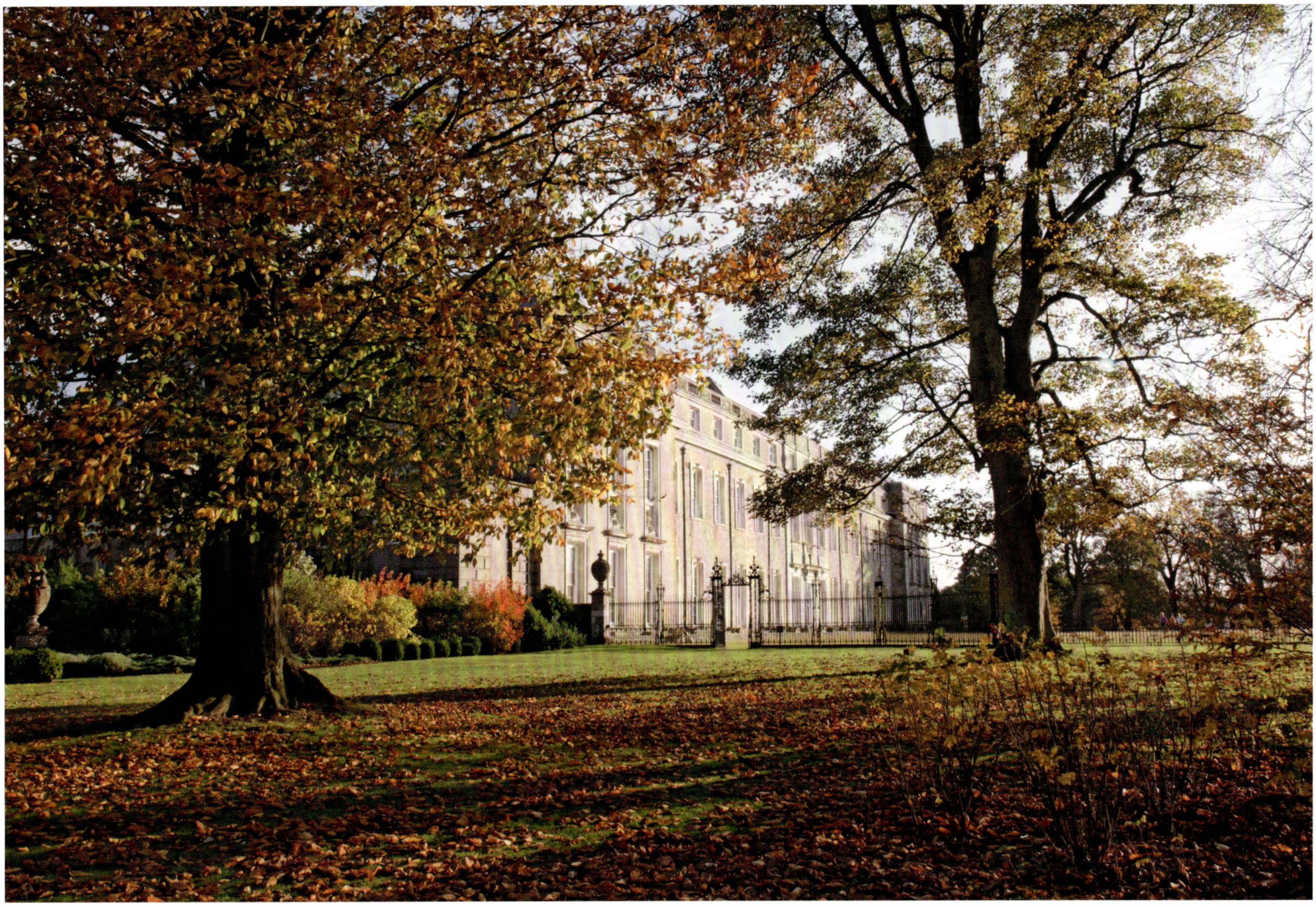
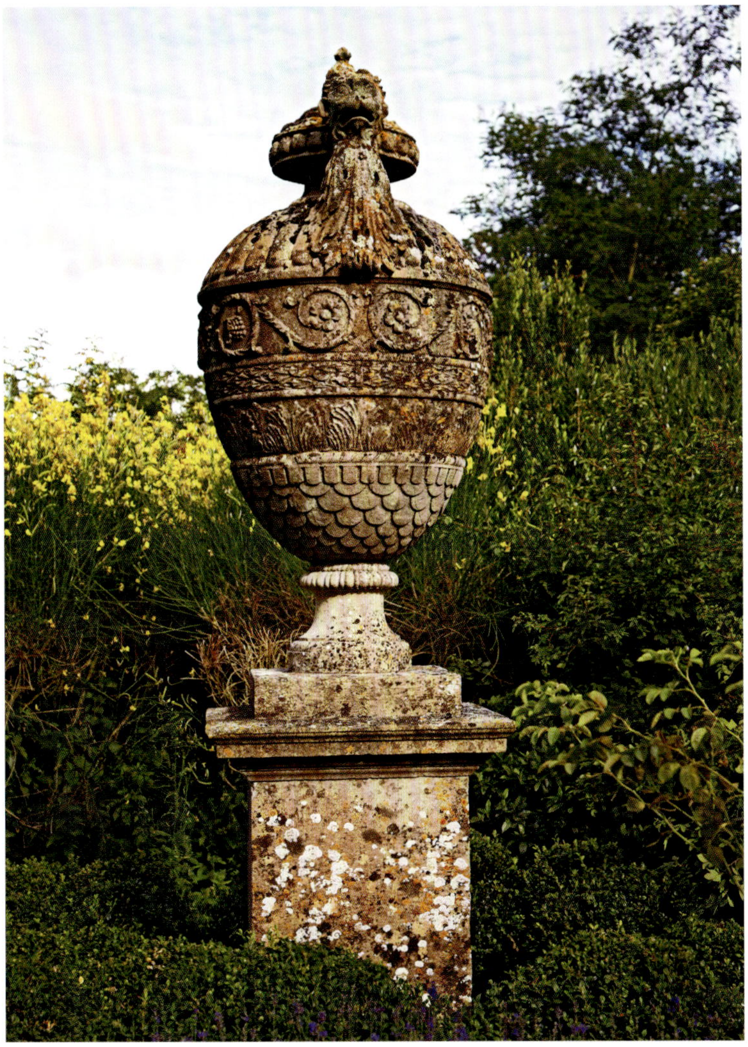
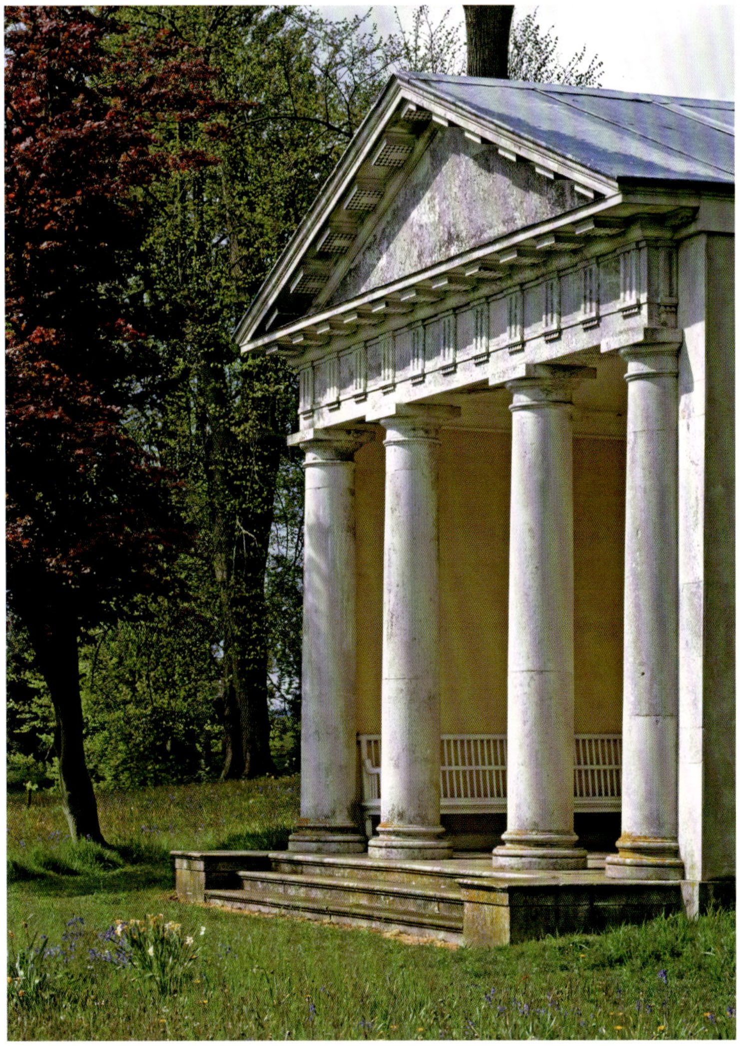

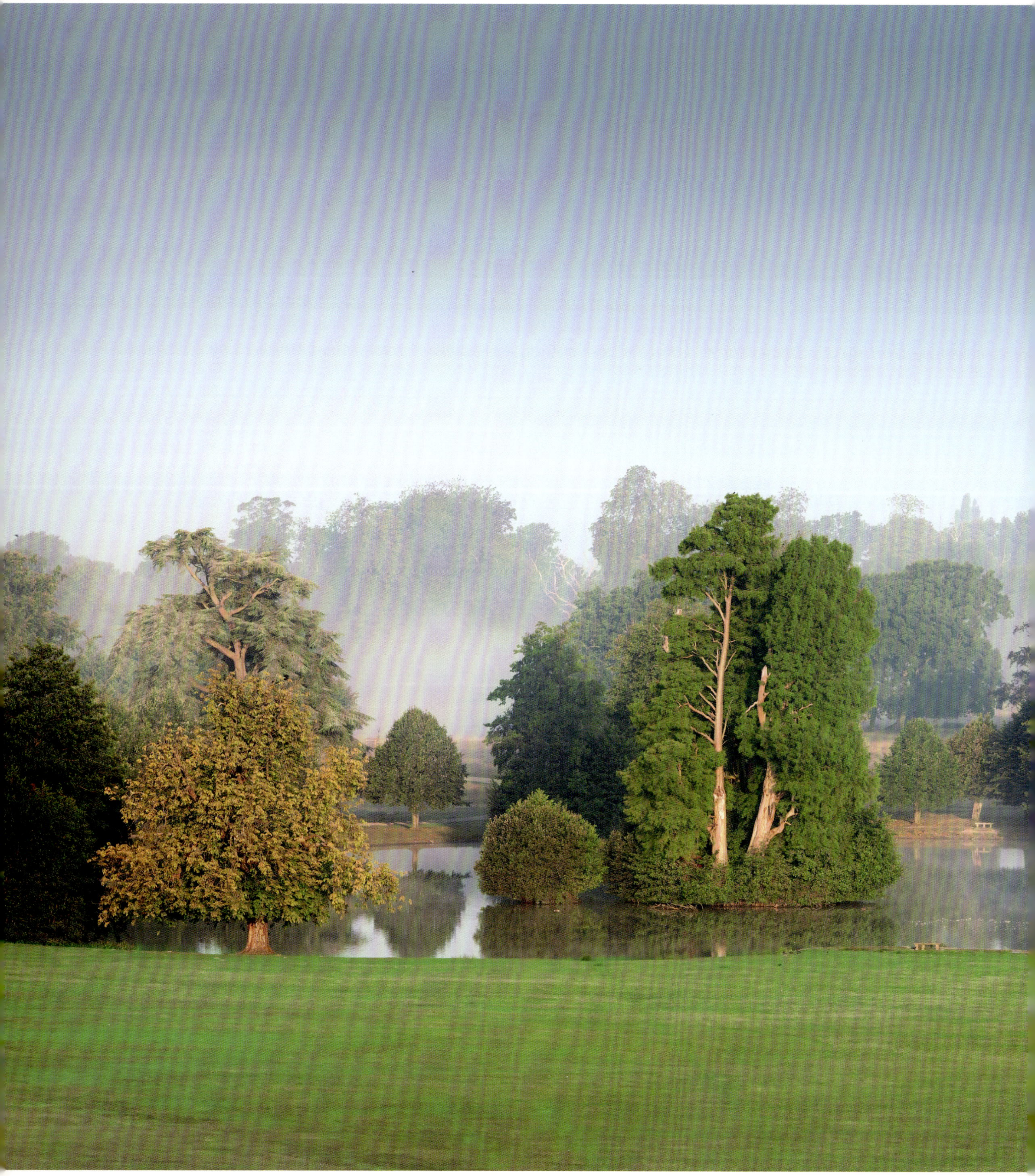

In fact, a good deal of xenophobia was extended to exotics amongst his contemporaries, Horace Walpole complaining to the Rev. William Cole after a hard winter, "Half the cypresses have been bewitched and turned into brooms, and the laurestinus is perished everywhere. I am Goth enough to choose now and then to believe in prognostics, and I hope this destruction imports that though foreigners should take root here, they cannot last in this climate."[7] This was a prejudice that Brown seems to have come to share, as we shall see at Dinefwr.

The pleasure ground at Petworth, however, was known for its exotics. In 1752, Brown proposed that London and Wise's early eighteenth-century parterre be replaced by a new parterre and a greenhouse garden in the form of Pliny's classical hippodrome.[8] The old orangery garden was to be an aloe garden and on the south side of the house there was to be "A Garden for the Bay trees &c." While the gravel path through the Menagerie was to have "Borders Adornd with flowering Shrubs."[9]

Brown may also have made his first essay into more naturalistic "grove" planting here. This style would ideally consist of shrubs grown under forest trees that had been thinned out of an old wood, to create grass walks and glades in imitation of natural forest planting. Hence Walpole's witticism of Petworth: "The portion of the park nearest the house has been allotted to the modern style. It is a garden of oaks two hundred years old."[10]

The graduated Petworth model remains a paradigm for Brown's style in the 1750s, and although the effect is quite different, the same model underlies his design for Burghley.

left: The mist clears at Petworth to show off a Scots Pine (Pinus sylvestris) in its finery.

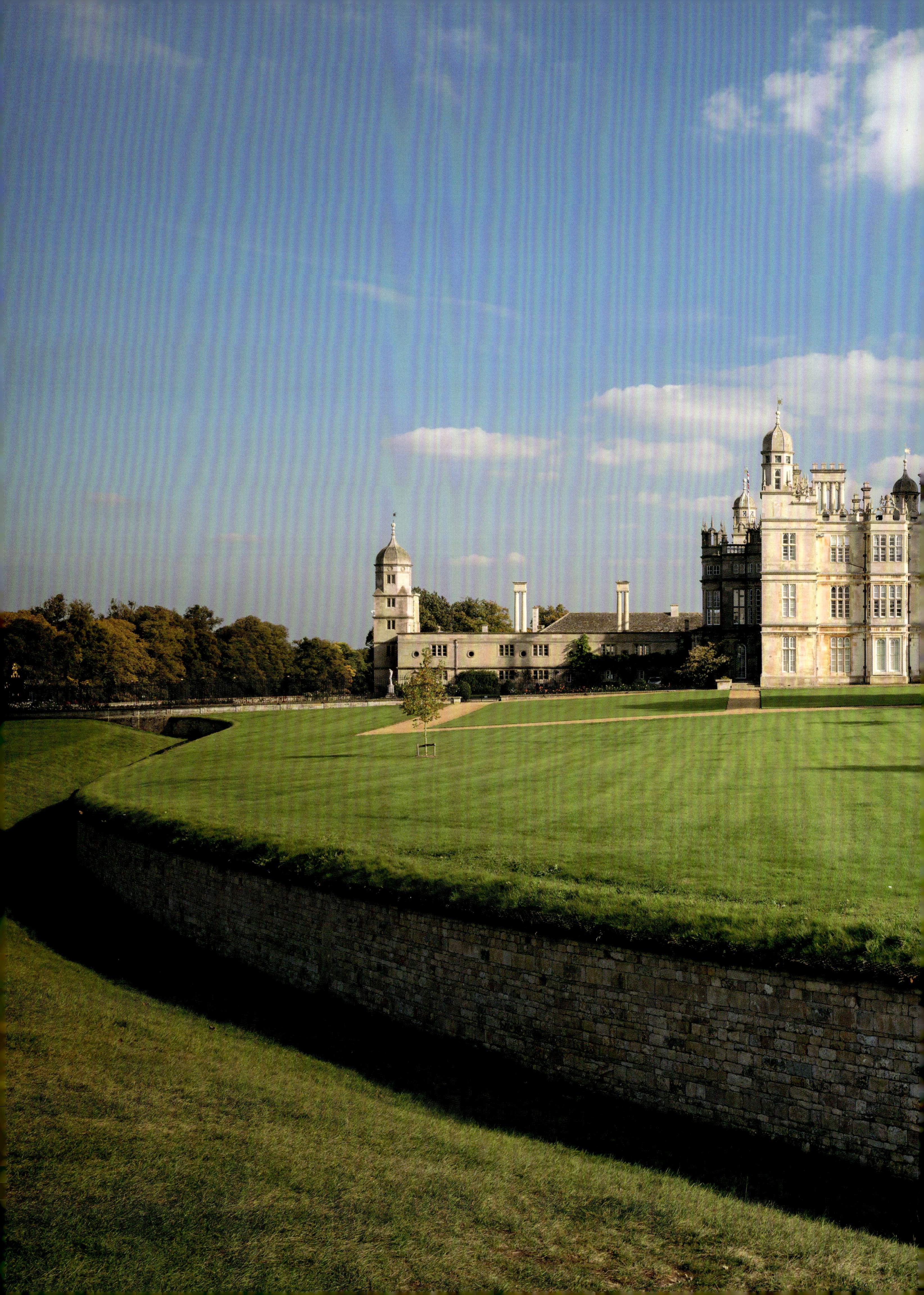

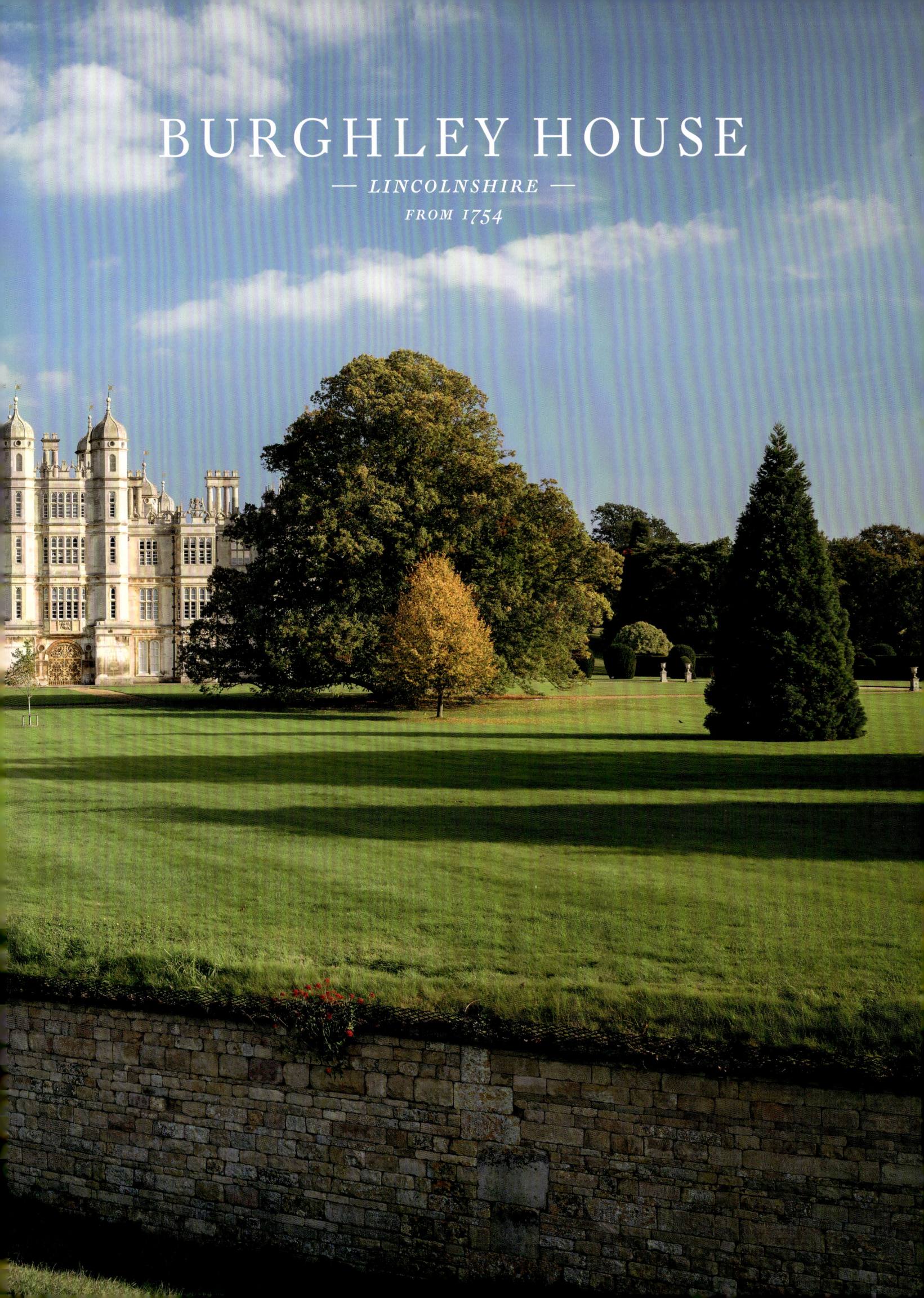

BURGHLEY HOUSE
― LINCOLNSHIRE ―
FROM 1754

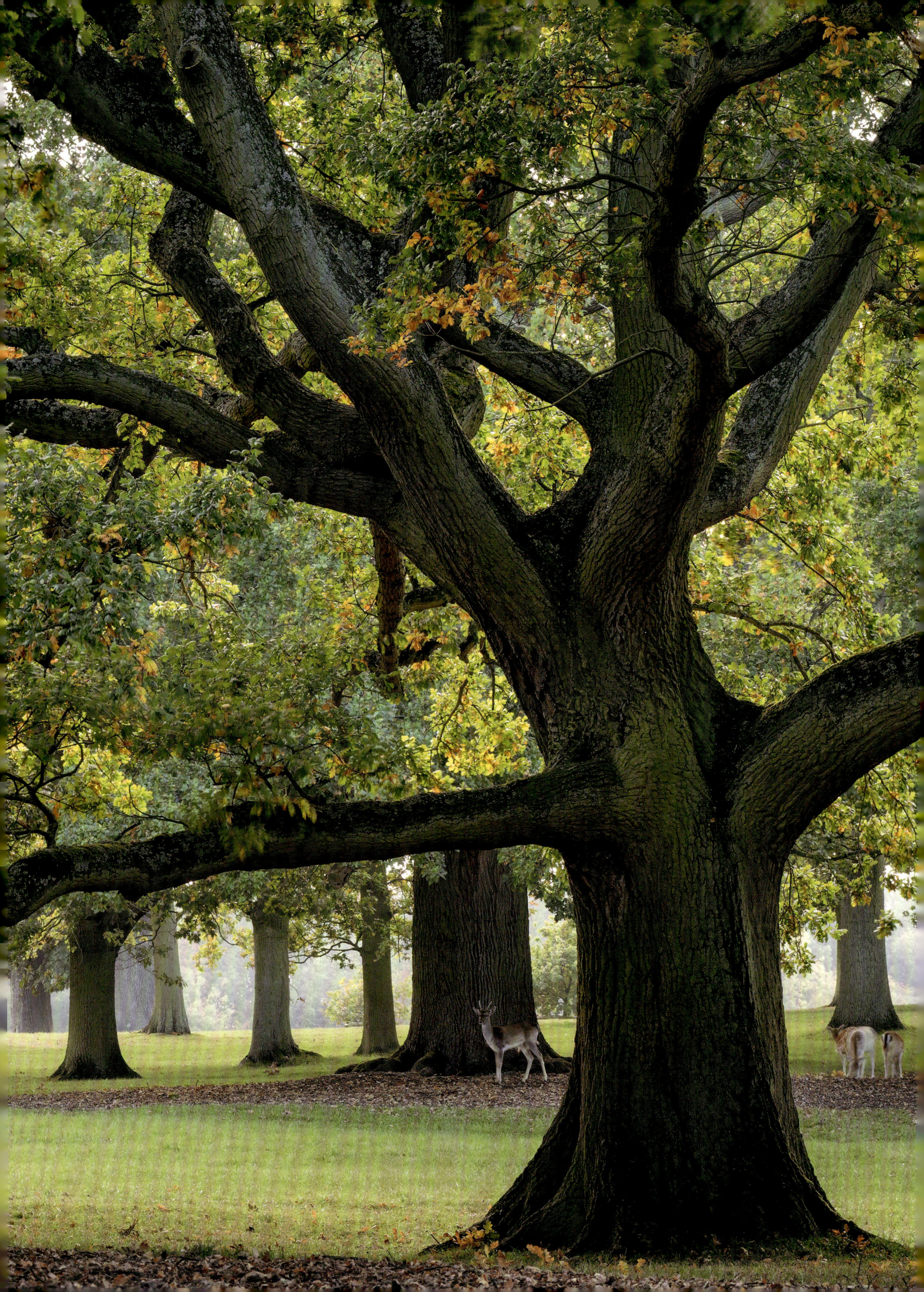

— CHAPTER SIX —

BURGHLEY HOUSE

Brown was paid around £10,000 for his work at Burghley and he was retained there from about 1754 to 1779, with William Ireland as his foreman from 1764 to 1779. Characteristically we do not have his complete accounts, nor do we have any record of what he did, but in his own words, he had "twenty-five years' pleasure in restoring the monument of a great minister of a great Queen."[1] We also have a plan of the place before he arrived and another made after he left, and it is reasonable to suppose that Brown was largely responsible for the changes made between one and the other.

Burghley was the magnificent show house of William Cecil Lord Burghley (1520–1598), favored statesman and Lord High Treasurer to Queen Elizabeth I. The mansion is placed on a knoll on low ground facing square onto a slight valley to the south beyond which the ground rises steadily up about 25 meters. To the north, the land continues to fall toward the open country of Leicestershire and Rutland.

When Brown arrived, the house had the usual accoutrements of sixteenth- and seventeenth-century design; formal parterres close to Great Pond, a roughly square water body, and a mount from which to view it; and a complex network of avenues in Low Park on the north side, and to the south Queen Anne's Avenue, a mile-long double avenue of limes, running away over the horizon.

Brown saved most of the avenues north of the house, just as he was to save the avenues east of the house at Blenheim, grouping some trees and removing others, but conserving its strongly formal air, which was emphasized by the handsome columns of lime trees, all of a dark-leaved clone. His friend, the poet Rev. William Mason, argued his case: "If, therefore, vistas [avenues] are ever to be admitted, or rather to be retained, it is only where they form an approach to some superb mansion, so situated that the principal prospect and ground allotted to picturesque improvement lie entirely on the other side; so much so, that the two different modes of planting can never appear together from any given point of view."[2]

Toward the west, Brown (and one assumes that it was he) had worked out that the Pagoda Room

previous pages: With its spires and turrets, Burghley House is picturesque from any viewpoint.
opposite: The spreading habit of the oaks on Oak Hill might be explained if these were planted large and set out at wide intervals so as to avoid damaging their roots and branches.

and the Prospect Room above it line up exactly with the two church spires in Stamford. By opening a cut through the woods, therefore, he was able to give a peep from these rooms to the town and make it appear to have only a single spire. Brown's portrait hangs in the Pagoda Room today and has him looking down this cut, as though still enjoying the trick.

In order to bring off this view, he appears to have reshaped the high ground west of the house, and to have framed it with the oaks of Oak Hill to the north, and with a second wood, Chabonel Spinney, on the higher ground to the south.

The south front offered him similar difficulties in reconciling the existing landscape with any proposed alterations. The most obvious of these was the pleasure ground, which already had a substantial mount in it, presumably made up of soil excavated from the valley floor to make Great Pond. Brown dramatically increased the size of the Mount (it is at least as high as the staterooms of the house) with the spoil excavated from his own much larger lake, then proposed it as the site for a Menagerie and planted it with widely spaced oaks. Such woods near the house had been recommended by Stephen Switzer at the beginning of the century: "If [a] House is without Coppices and Woods at a reasonable Distance... I would advise the Fencing in and sowing a Wood or Coppice."[3] Burghley's was a grove, such as are also to be found at Petworth, Blenheim, and Chatsworth. This grove had loose shrubberies and grass walks through the

above: Burghley House shows its more relaxed side in the view from the Mount.
opposite: Brown planned to develop a menagerie on the Mount; it looks as though this was set out, but it is now called Oak Circle. In whatever guise, one would expect it to have been studded with seats and commemorative ornaments.

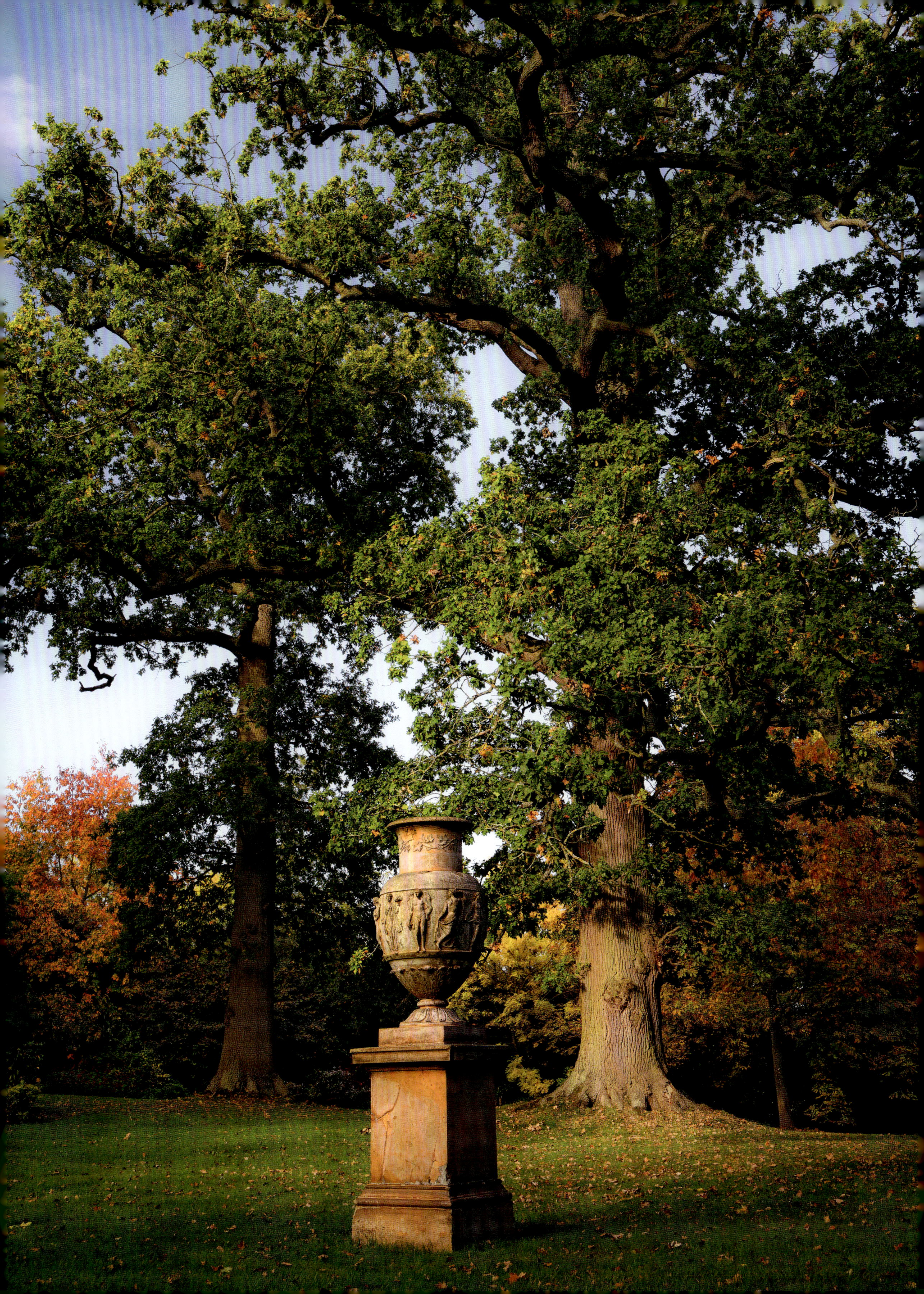

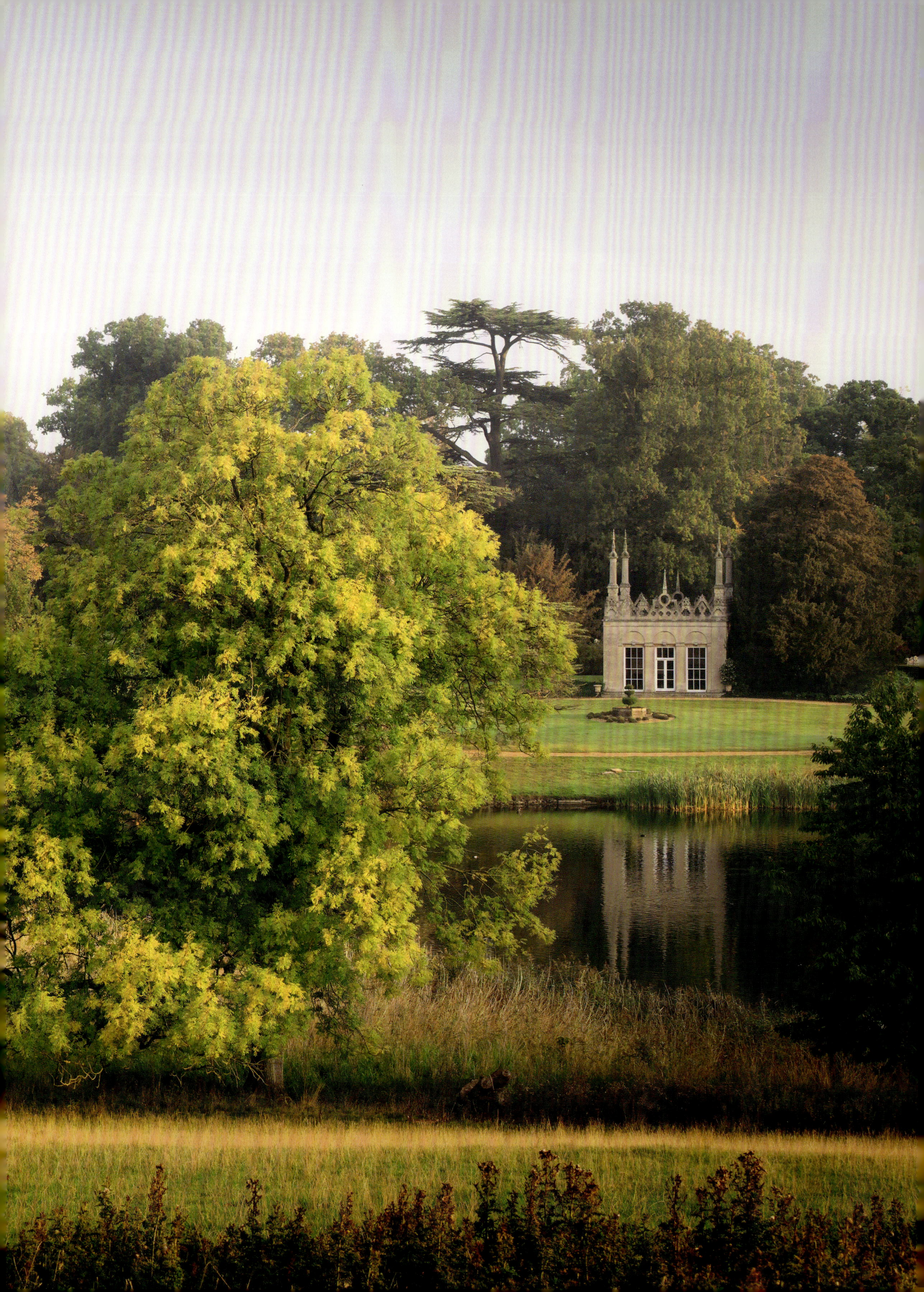

opposite: Brown's Gothic Temple made another eye-catcher in views across the lake from Middle Park. Despite its name it is essentially a neo-classical building with added finials.

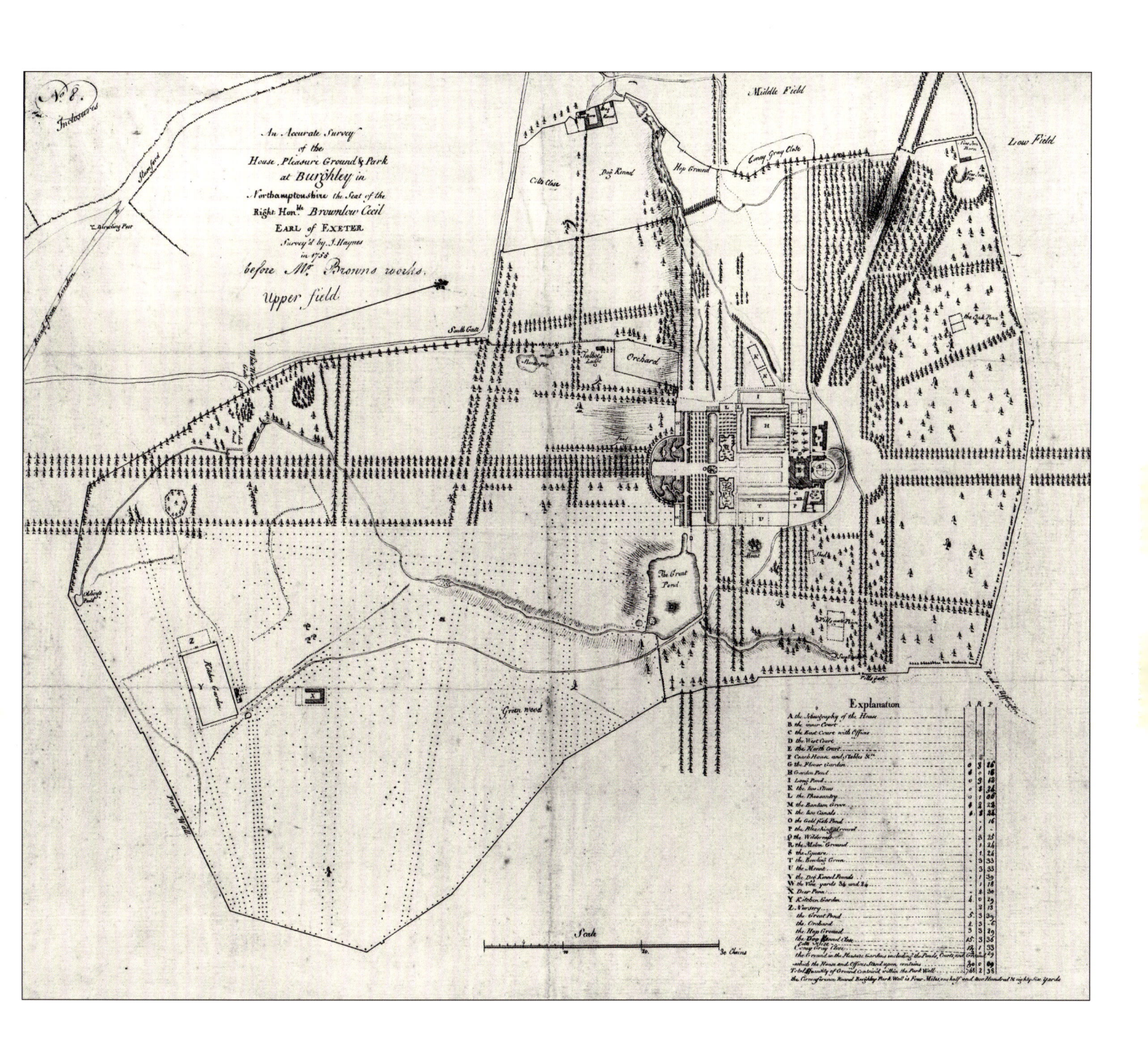

above: "An Accurate survey of the House, Pleasure Ground & Park at Burghley... Survey'd by J. Haynes in 1755." Another hand has added "before Mr Brown's works" by way of explanation.
overleaf: This lime avenue in Low Park has been patched with a single sweet chestnut in the left-hand row, near the lower corner of the photograph. It is as though by using this species out of place, the designer acknowledged both that he had noticed the avenue and that he had elected to retain it.

BURGHLEY HOUSE · 111

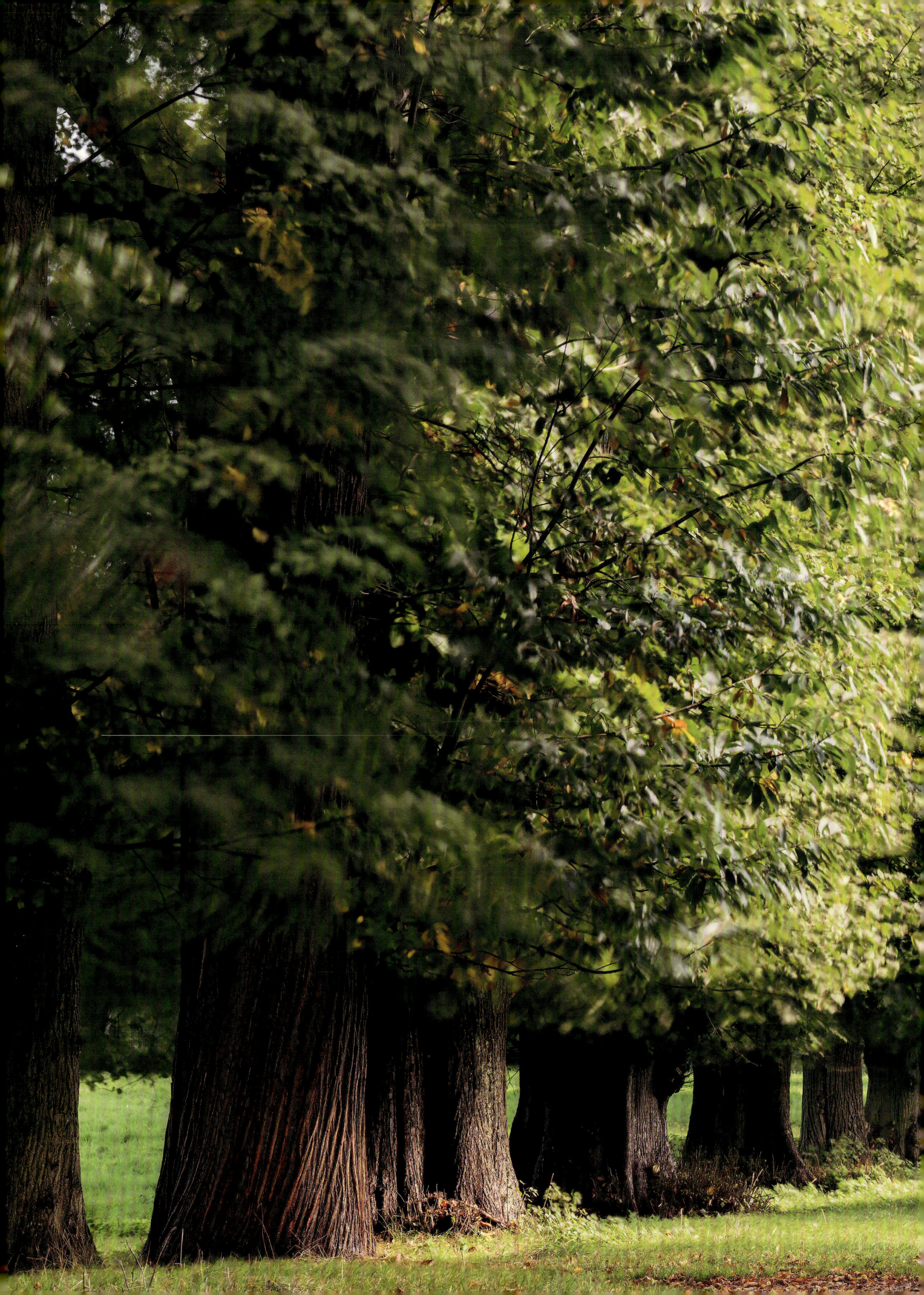

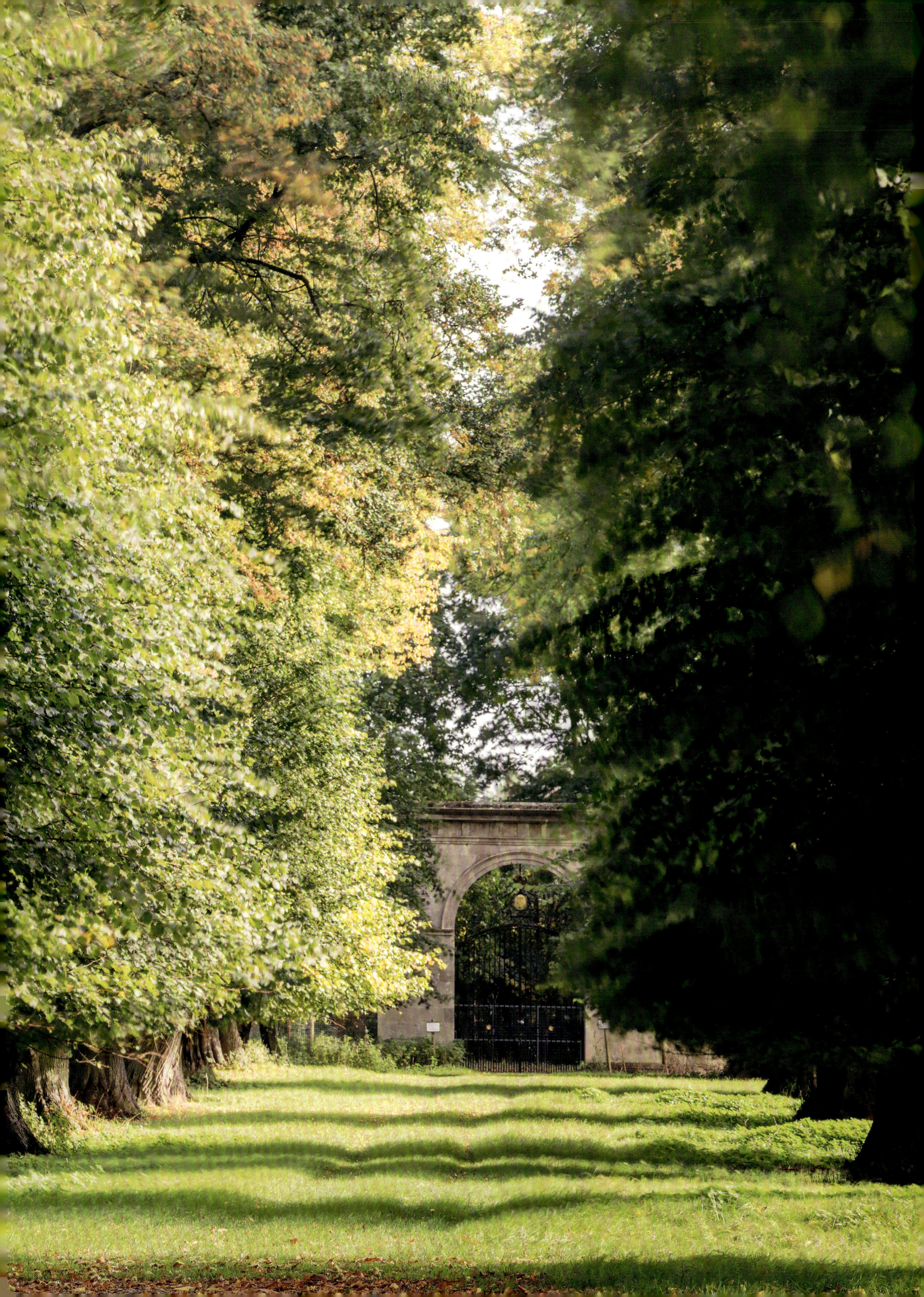

trees to a central circuit walk, and might be regarded as a horticultural version of coppice, which is a distinct but related form of management. Coppice is the ancient woodland practice of cutting trees to the ground every fifteen years so as to harvest the poles for making hurdles and for building wattle and daub walls. It was known to be a valuable habitat for songbirds, and after cutting would have a rich native flora of primroses and bluebells. Shrubbery was a similar management system but with the emphasis on exotic planting, described where it was invented, in the West Midlands, as "little enclosures of coppice or other woodlands—where at the same time flowering shrubs may be Introducd...."[4]

Brown could link this grove to the house with a small formal garden outside his new Orangery, but that left the central problem, that the landscape essentially reads from the staterooms of the house as a flattish panorama. Brown seems to have decided to create out of this level plane the sense of a valley square on to the house. Thus, he extended the existing pond to make "a pretty piece of Water, which when finished will have the appearance of a natural River,"[5] running east-west in the bottom. He also clumped Queen Anne's Avenue, "removed trees of the most enormous bulk, from place to place, to suit the prospect and landscape,"[6] and planted single parkland trees just up from the lake in Middle Park: "a Noble Park, thickly planted with full grown Oaks, that give the place a solemn appearance, the Groves

above: Brown's Gothick architecture was regarded as faithful to Burghley's Tudor fabric, though the two styles are easily distinguished, as with his Orangery here.

being pretty large." This had already been suggested by one of his mentors, Philip Southcote (1698–1758): "The finest spot for planting a wood is on the sloping side of a hill that you look up to from your house, or from any other principal view."[7]

Behind these trees he then wound a drive through Middle Park, opening narrow gaps between them to show off "the Views confined to narrow spots"[8]—views back toward the house and his Gothic Temple and Grotto Boat House (the last now disappeared).

We shall see that at Broadlands he found a more sophisticated solution to what was a perennial problem for him—that the houses he worked on tended to be built square onto a valley, and so they naturally enjoyed short views across the low ground, rather than long reaches up and down the valley. Nonetheless the foreshortening of the horizon at Burghley has brought to the landscape something of the quality of a medieval scroll, unrolling with a variety of incidents (the Dairy, the Kennels, and Lion Bridge), as one looks south from the windows of the great house.

In fact, Middle Park was the area reworked most intensely by Brown, who may have built the enormous sunk wall that retained the deer, and, in the interests of improved agriculture, under-drained the valley between the Maltings and Dog Kennel Brakes, and culverted the watercourse that once ran along the east boundary of the park. He undoubtedly had a reputation as a drainer, so Henry Hoare of Stourhead

above: The best viewpoints from the drive on the south side of the lake are either marked by trees or, in exceptional cases, by earthworks. Here, the ground has been built up to form a level platform, which is now surrounded by thorn bushes.

BURGHLEY HOUSE · 115

above: Each viewpoint on the drive across Middle Park picks a different part of the house and makes a new composition of it, framed by the trees.

congratulated his son-in-law Lord Ailesbury for getting Brown into Tottenham, Wiltshire: "He will remove Damps."[9] His drains will also have fed the new lake. The easy smoothness of these valley floors is to be contrasted with the consciously "tumbled" (that is, disorganized) banks loosely scattered with single trees that he used to conceal the boundaries of Middle Park.

As his final stroke here, he built the Lion Bridge (1773–1777). This had to go up more or less out of sight of the house in order to accommodate the existing avenues, but he angled it so as to frame a fine "peep" view of the house through the arches, and also managed to use it to conceal the termination of the lake (which seems to have been extended farther west after his time).

Once above Middle Park, Great Park was planted in quite a different style, described by the Rev. William Gilpin's nephew, William Sawrey Gilpin, a fierce critic who wrote a generation after Brown's death. Gilpin had praised Low Park, but ignored Middle Park and reserved his scorn for Great Park: "Compare the circular and oval plantations of the outer park with the original planting of that magnificent scenery

… where shall we find any grandeur, beauty, or variety, in the oval and circular clumps and plantations of the outer park, scattered here and there with no reference to each other, or the general character and scenery of the place…?"[10]

To the west of Middle Park were the Kennels (later converted into Maltings) surrounded by Kennels Park with its bigger clumps. Beyond that and Great Park lay the racetrack and Grandstand, on the highest ground, accessed via Carpenter's Lodge Avenue, which Brown is said to have laid out.

The Round House, a thatched Gothick cottage, in Great Park may post-date Brown's involvement but it was a keeper's house, with kenneling for a few sporting dogs such as could be used for setting, retrieving, and, in particular, for hare coursing. This is what Great Park was intended for and it explains Brown's use of clumps here. He was, of course, famous for them, but they came in many shapes and sizes and had many uses—as tree nurseries, as a more effective and very much cheaper planting than single trees, where the land was extensive and was grazed, and as havens for game, such as hares.

The Burghley design thus comes across as another

above and overleaf: The Lion Bridge is reasonably attributed to Brown. However, he was not averse to plagiarizing the designs of others, and the close resemblance has been pointed out between this and the bridge at Compton Verney. The bridge was so angled as to frame views to the house through its arches; the views would only have been seen from boats in the lake.

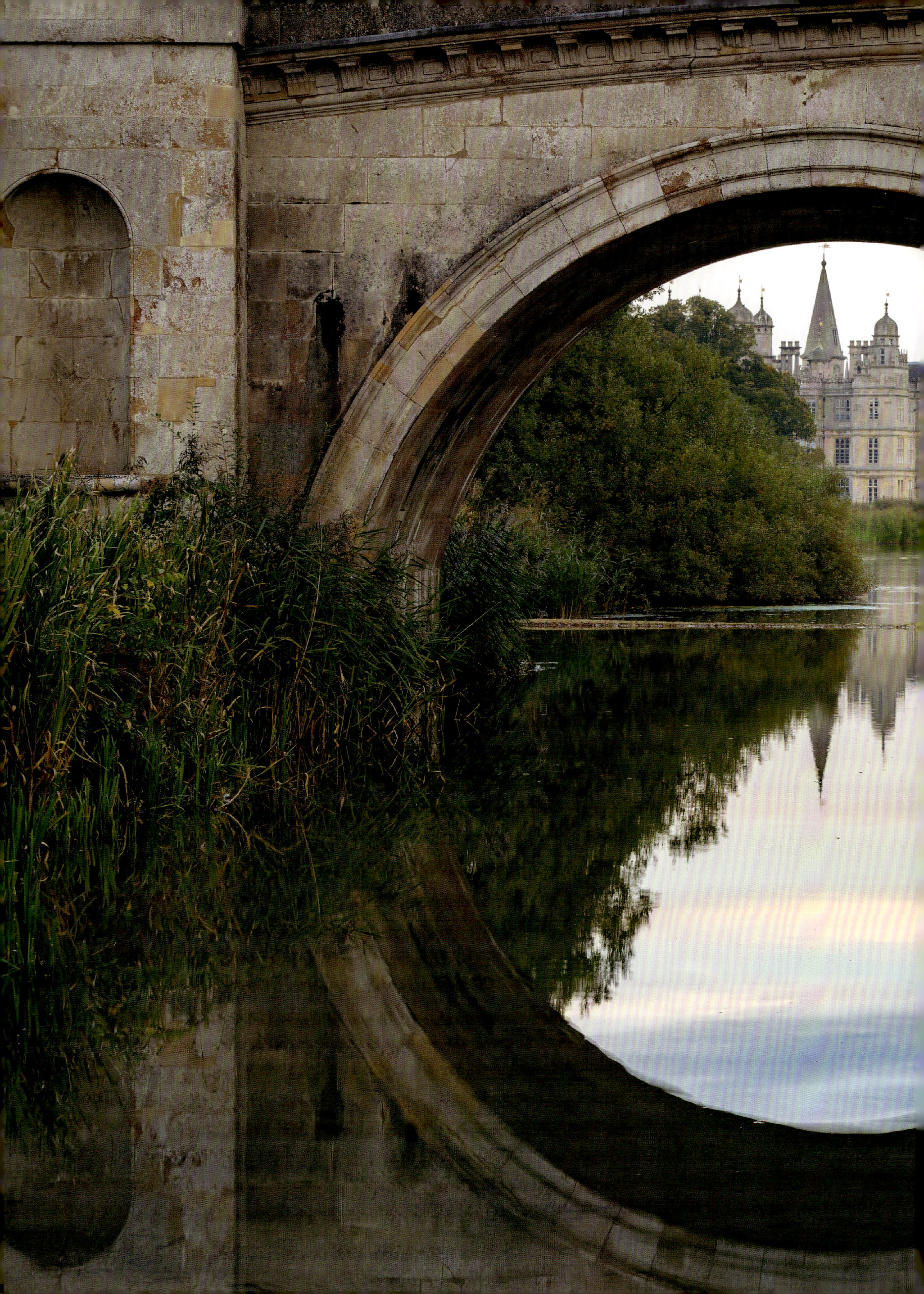

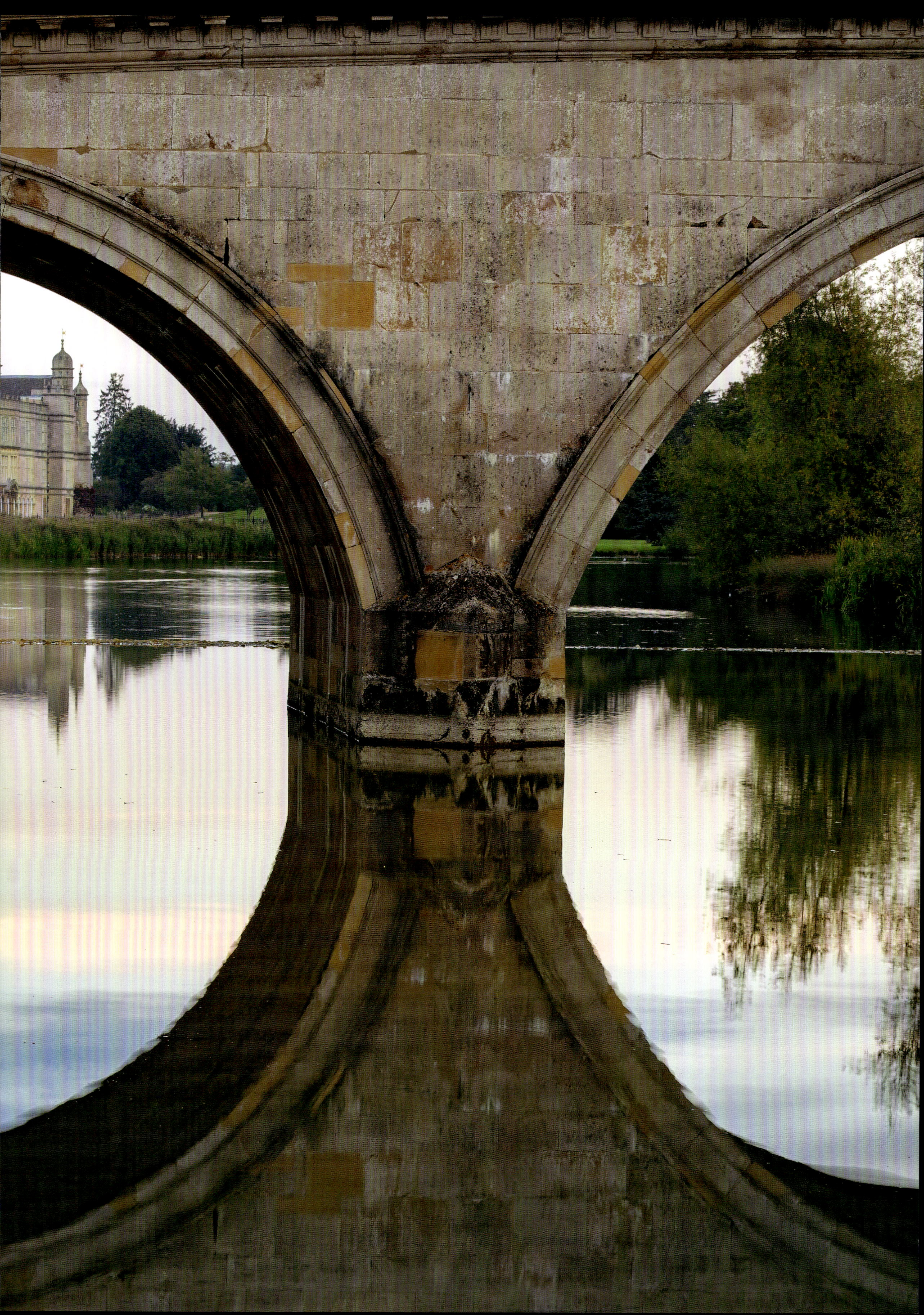

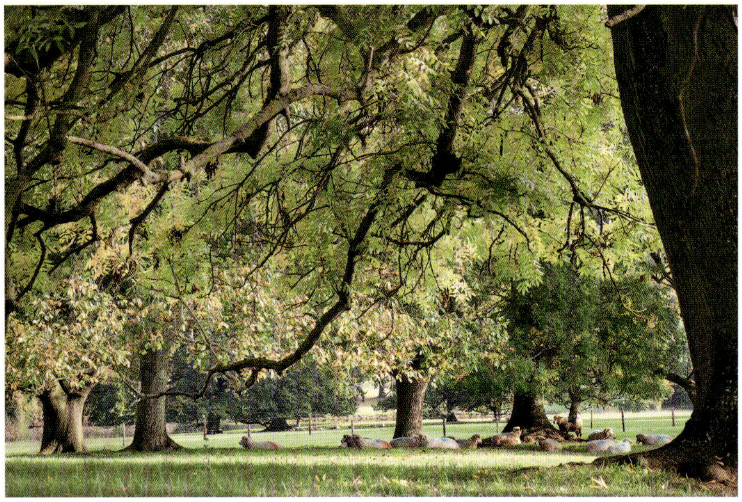
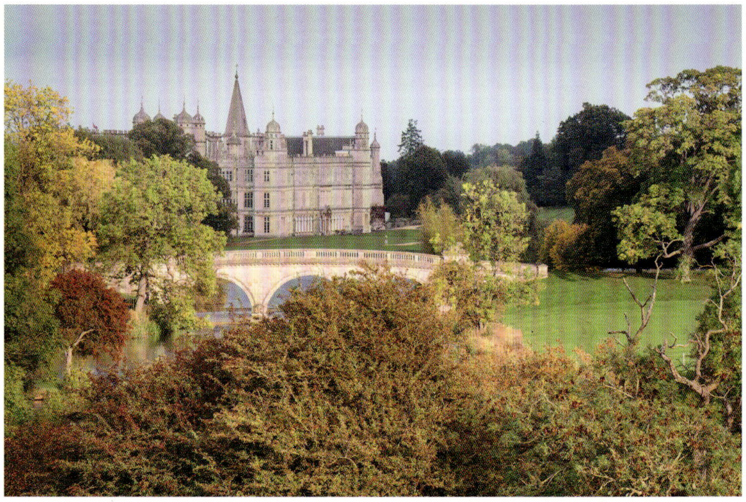
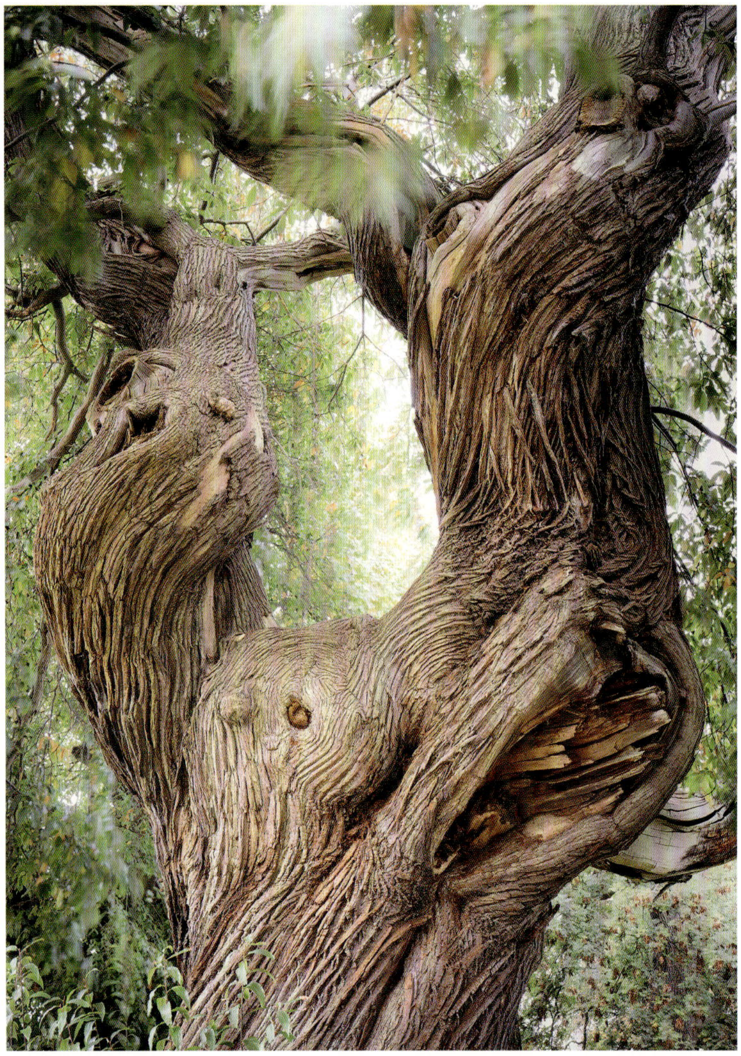
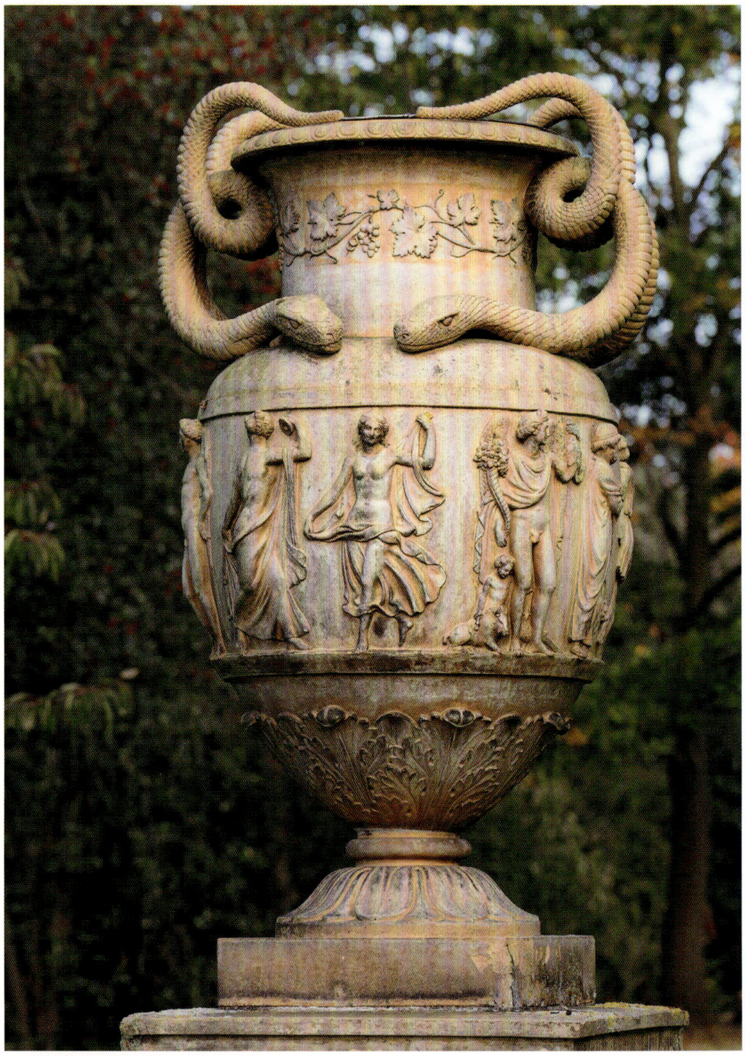
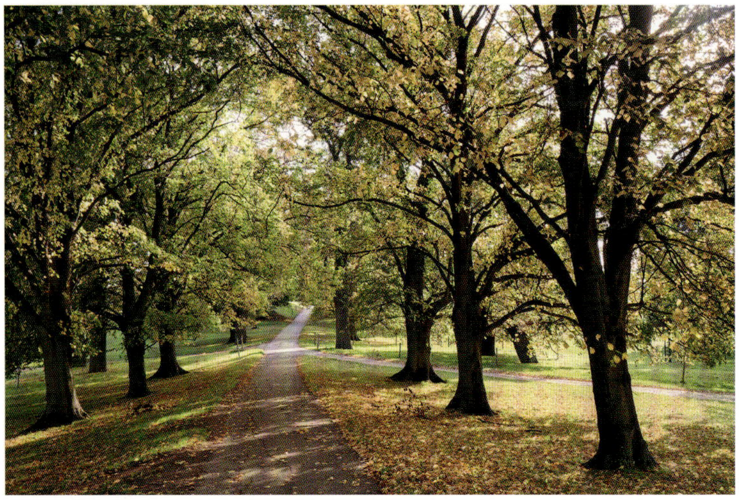
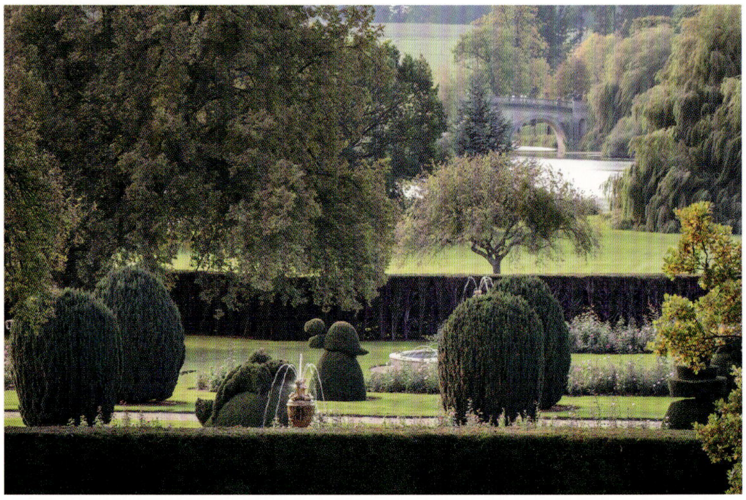

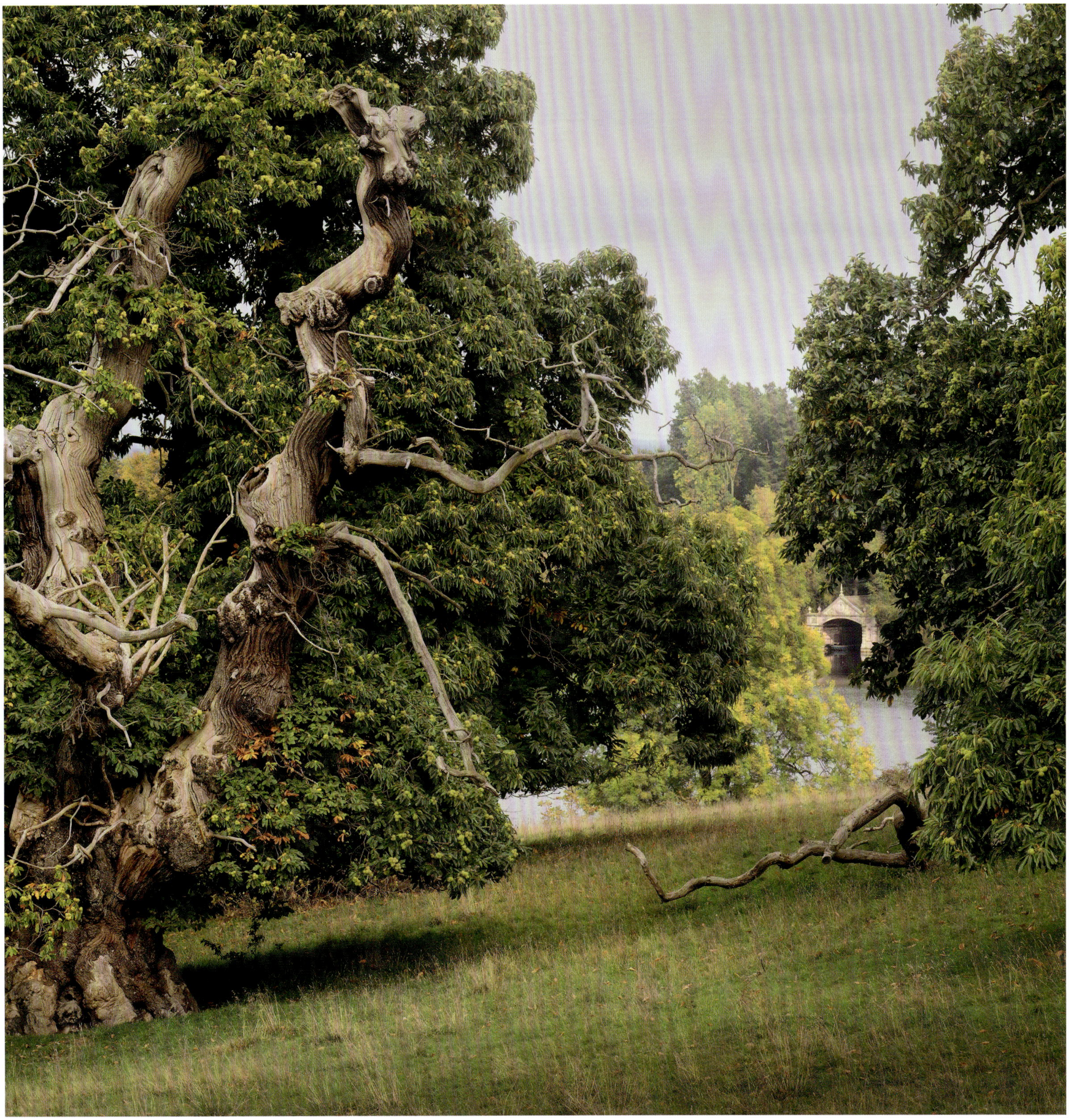

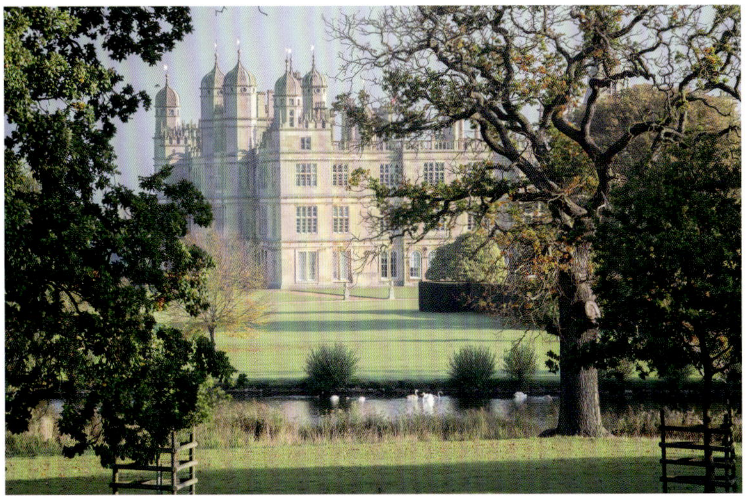

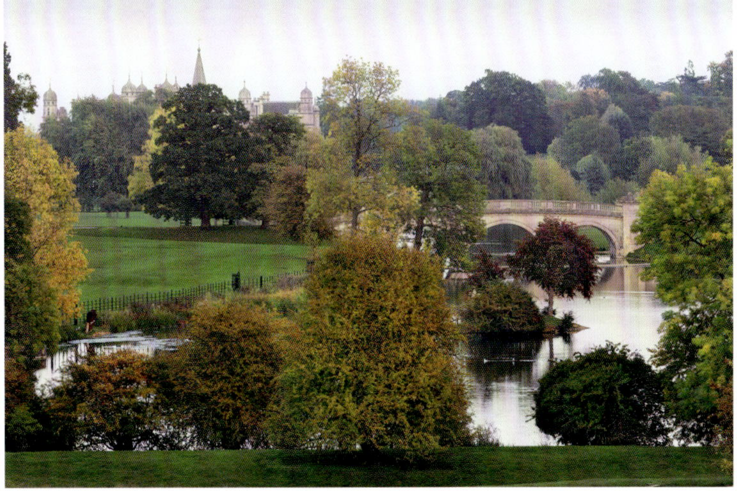

previous pages:
*Details of the parkland at Burghley.
Brown's trees are carefully grouped so as to frame
views without unnecessarily drawing attention to
them; the old sweet chestnuts that Brown retained
from the avenues in Middle Park at Burghley
are amongst the largest in the country.*

excellent model of the gradation that Petworth displays: moving smoothly from the tamed landscape of Low Park, and the polish of the pleasure ground, to Middle Park, the Dairy and kennels, thence to the hare park, and finally to the race course. It is the use of gradation that gives it its overall coherence—there is variety in the landscape, but there is also a kind of logic that prevents any sense of a disruptive contrast. It might be regarded as a development from the Petworth model in retaining the lime avenues around the house; but it remains instinctively right that one should look out from that tamed landscape to the more natural terrain of Middle Park.

With its various compartments, such a landscape might still be as productive as a *ferme ornée*, but Brown was now concerned to conceal all the evidence of fences, rather than use them to bound each of the discrete scenes. The reticulated landscape of the *ferme ornée*, consisting of a number of discrete components, was to be replaced by a graduated one, in which each component would blend into the next, becoming insensibly wilder as one moved away from the house. So the farm idea was retained, and one could see from Lion Bridge all at once, at least seven hundred "black and white Spanish sheep,"[11] and "droves of cattle" (presumably on their way down to the London market),[12] besides the deer. With so much stock to be fed, and the horses in particular, there would still have had to be room within the parkland for hay meadows, as well as pastures for the dairy cattle, and all this was achieved by Brown without the hint of a fence in any of the important views.

Burghley is unique in Brown's oeuvre in that he made explicit his ambition to restore "the monu-

*right: The tradition of keeping unusual breeds at
Burghley has been maintained.*

122 · CAPABILITY BROWN

BURGHLEY HOUSE · 123

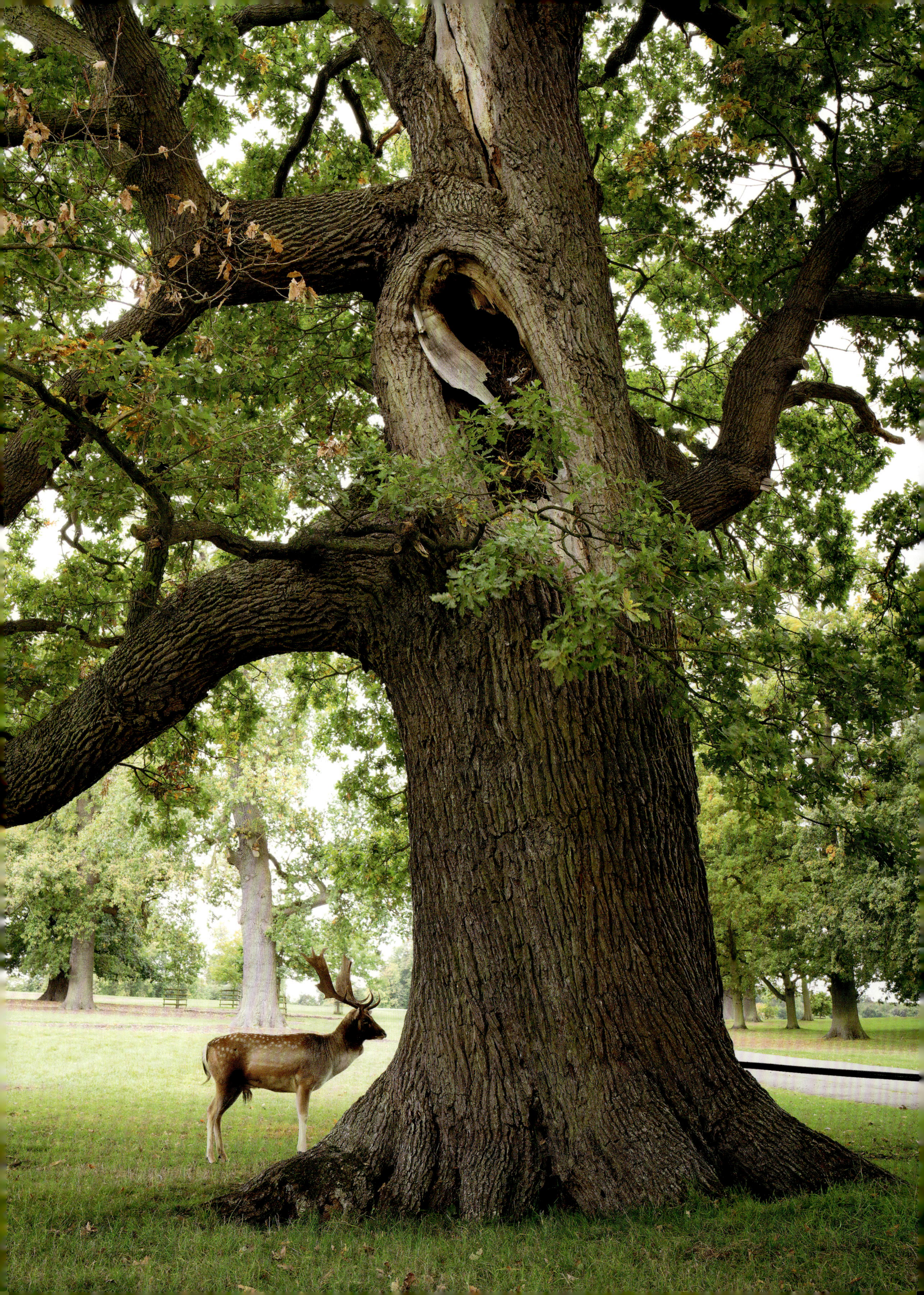

ment of a great minister of a great Queen." The significance of Burghley, for Brown, resided in its antiquity, and in the honor due to Cecil, but it is worth making the point that with one or two exceptions, the landscape he made here is not a restoration of the Tudor garden, but is recognizably in his own style. He was criticized for this by William Gilpin: "How far the fashionable array, in which Mr Brown has dressed the grounds about this venerable building, agree with its formality, and antique appendages, I dare not take upon me to say. A doubt arises, whether the old decoration of avenues, and parterres was not a more suitable stile of ornament. It is, however, a nice question, and would admit many plausible arguments on both sides."[13]

However, rather than attack Brown for failing to make Burghley a restoration project, one might argue that his more natural, unfenced landscapes were themselves attempts to get back to medieval and post-medieval landscapes as they were imagined in eighteenth-century England.

The Earl commissioned numerous paintings of the house and its landscapes, and all of them confirm what Brown's contemporaries also emphasized in print—the coherence of his achievement: "It was the genius of the late LAUNCELOT BROWN which, brooding over the shapeless mass, educed out of a seeming wilderness, all the order and delicious harmony which now prevail."[14] This apparent coherence is particularly marked in his treatment of the house, for which he was also the principal architect during the period of his employment at Burghley. This was the centerpiece of the landscape. It was described as a "Sumptuous Structure," the indulgence of a "Luxuriant fancy." However, while leaving it with this apparent coherence, Brown actually did nothing to simplify or rationalize the structure: "What added much to our Satisfaction in this Place was to see it in such good repair and having undergone so few alterations, such as Sashing some of the Windows, and Modernising a few of the Rooms. In every other respect it still appears nearly the same as it must have done when first finished, to the great Credit of its Noble Possessor."[15]

Finally, one reads the praise given to Brown for his work at Burghley by William Sawey Gilpin's uncle, the Rev. William Gilpin (an acquaintance of Brown's, but not an unquestioning admirer):

It has no advantage of situation; being buried in the dip of a park, which indeed possesses no where much agreeable scenery. The house formerly was approached by descending avenues; which were as displeasing as formality, and awkwardness could make them. Mr Brown was employed to reform them; and if possible to give some air of elegance to the approach. Much he could not do. The situation of the house forbad; and the unaccommodating form of the park. Everything however, that was disgusting he has removed. He has closed the avenues: he has varied the slopes; and has led the approach through a winding valley, in the very path, which nature would have chosen, as the easiest. The magic of these improvements is such, that it has given the house a new site. It appears, as you approach it, to assume even an elevated situation.[16]

opposite: Brown could not have been aware of the principles of ecology as they are understood today. Nonetheless his parks, with their numerous mature oaks and their wounds and hollows, have become highly regarded for their nature conservation value.

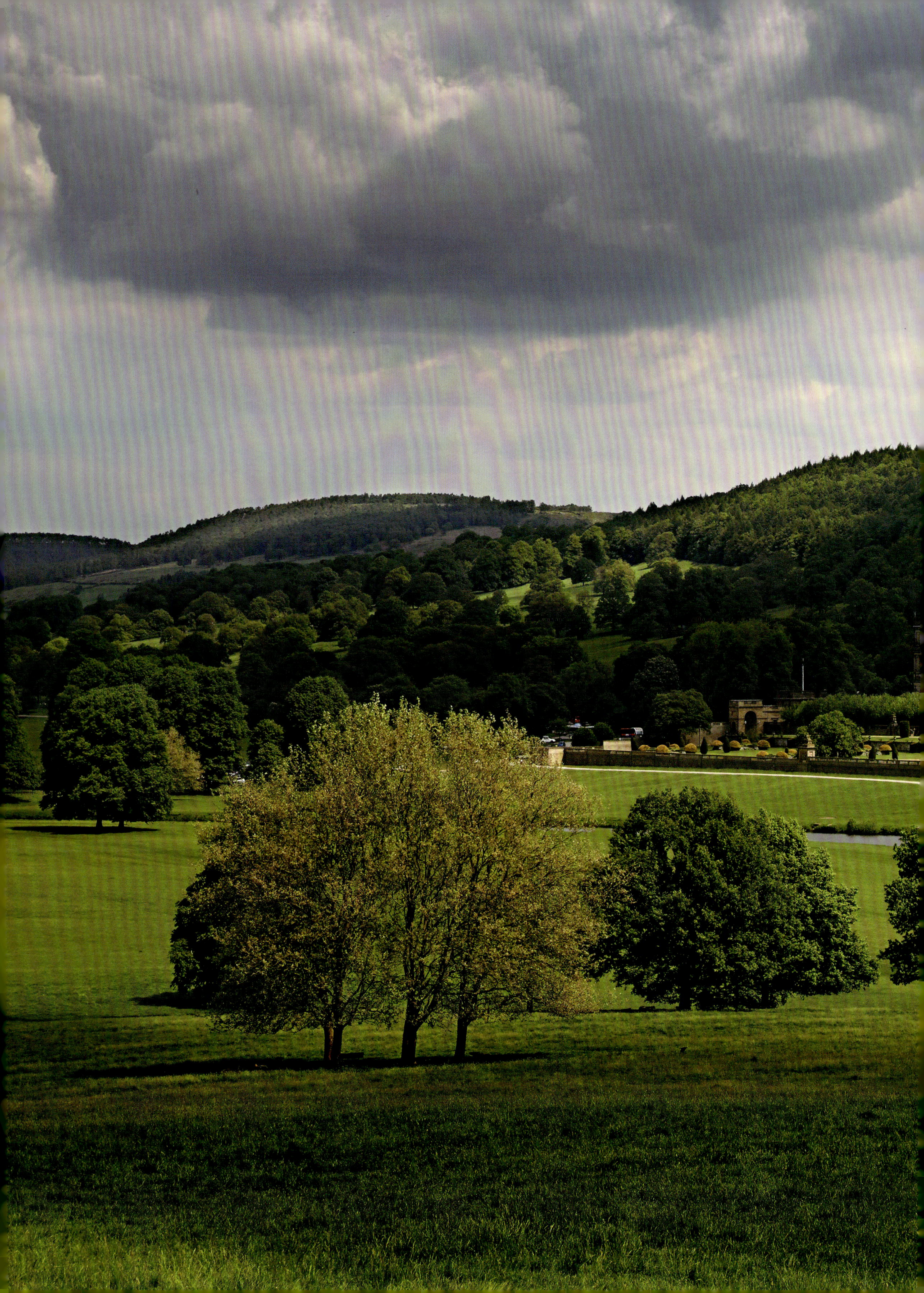

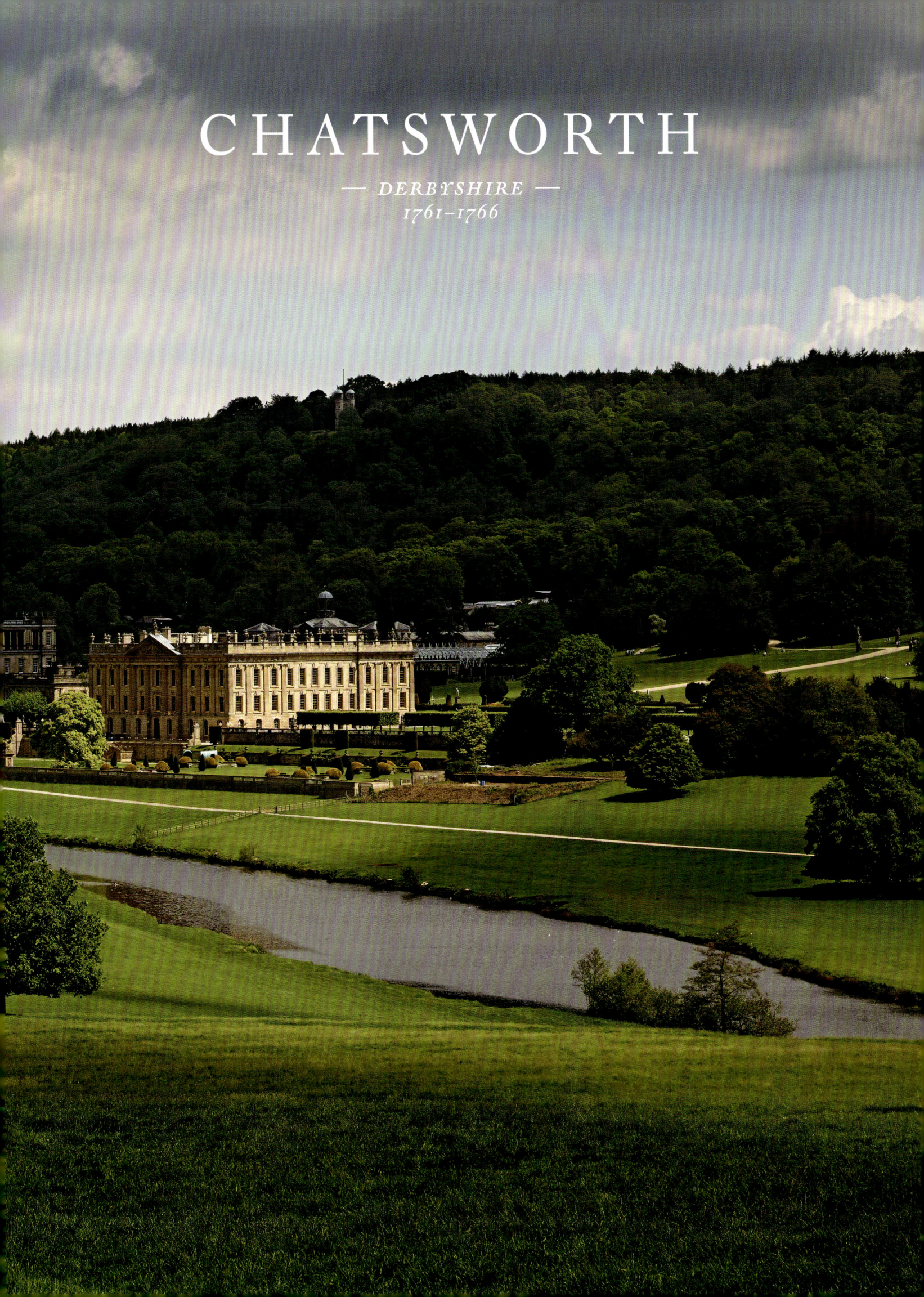

CHATSWORTH

— DERBYSHIRE —
1761–1766

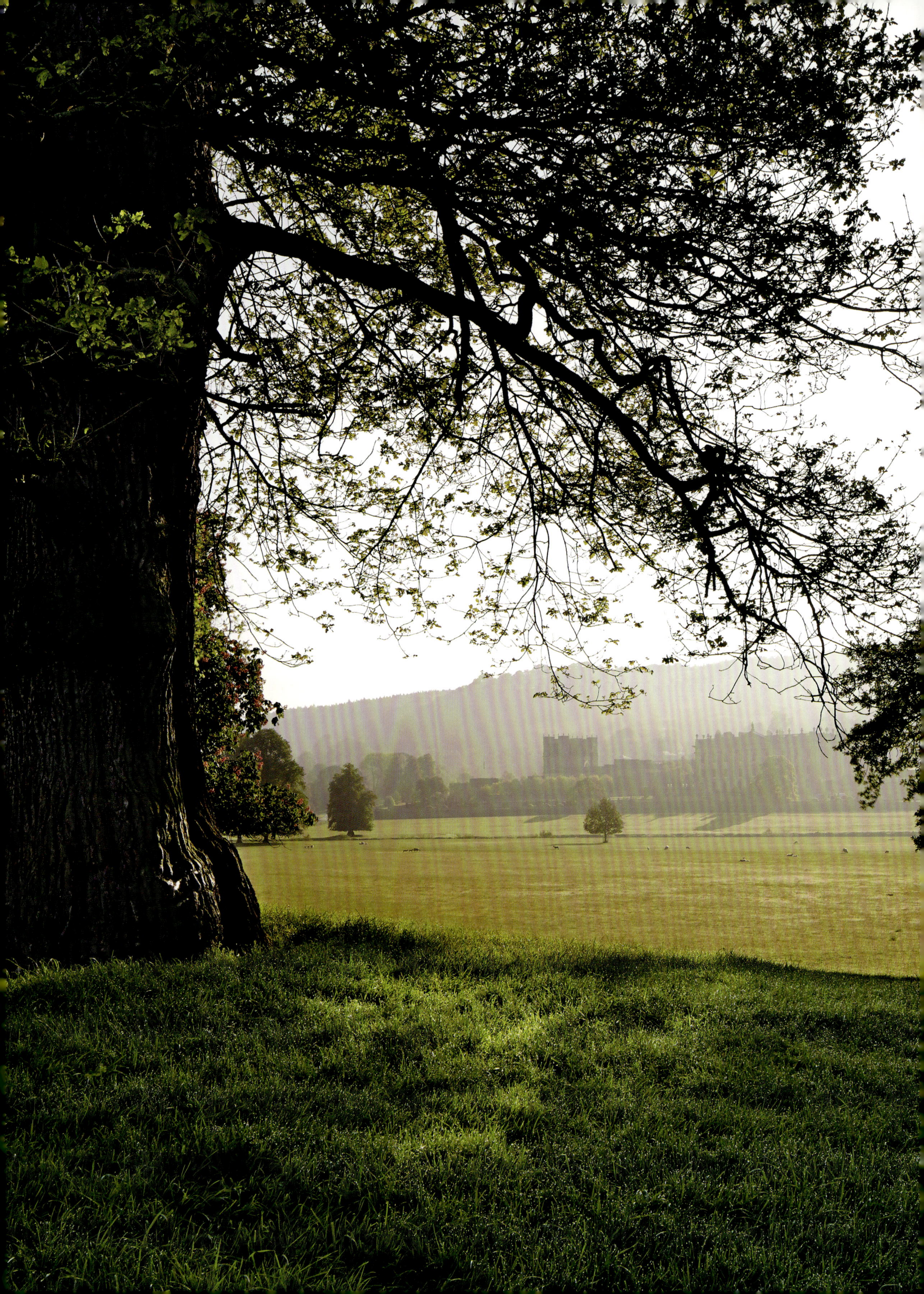

— CHAPTER SEVEN —

CHATSWORTH

No one standing at the west front of the house at Chatsworth and looking out beyond the terrace to the west, across the River Derwent and into the trees—no one could deny that they were in the presence of a masterpiece. But here, as so often, it is not at all clear what makes it a masterpiece.

We do not know exactly what Brown did. We have none of his proposals; he is only mentioned five times in the estate accounts, which list payments of £100 per year from 1761 to 1766. Astonishingly, our best testimonies for his involvement are the casual references of visitors such as Horace Walpole, who noted in 1761 the various works underway "under the direction of Brown."[1] We do know, however, that during the whole of that time he had a foreman, Michael Millican, in place, and Millican was paid a total of £3,010. Millican's accounts and recent research show that a great deal of this money was spent by Brown, as Edward Knight noted in 1760, "sloping off the banks to shew the River Derwent."[2]

However, the most striking change may have been the removal of the old deer park, which had been on the high ground east of the house, and the creation of a new park in full view of the west front, replacing the medieval warren and an array of small fields abutting Edensor village on the west bank of the Derwent. The park wall was begun in 1759, so it seems possible that the idea of creating a new park preceded his arrival, but Brown made the project his own. Overall his treatment of the Derwent Valley was akin to his work in Middle Park at Burghley: the deer park was to unfold like a medieval scroll, presenting an ever-changing scene of clumps rising and sliding over hillocks, with a depth of field continually varied by the planting of single trees and illuminated by occasional buildings, each evoking different scenes, while the great house itself, as at Burghley, remained a constant in all the views from the west. Immediately east of the house, on the steeply rising ground, it seems certain that he made at least one drive, where, visiting in 1768, Horace Walpole mentioned the "oaks and rocks" taken into the pleasure ground.[3] This was grove planting, of the kind that we have seen at Petworth. The drive provided access to Thomas

previous pages: Much of Brown's work at Chatsworth turned on creating an Arcadian view to the west.
opposite: A combination of earthworks and careful planting has concealed the surface of the approach from Edensor, making James Paine's bridge appear to float in the landscape, connecting nothing with nothing.

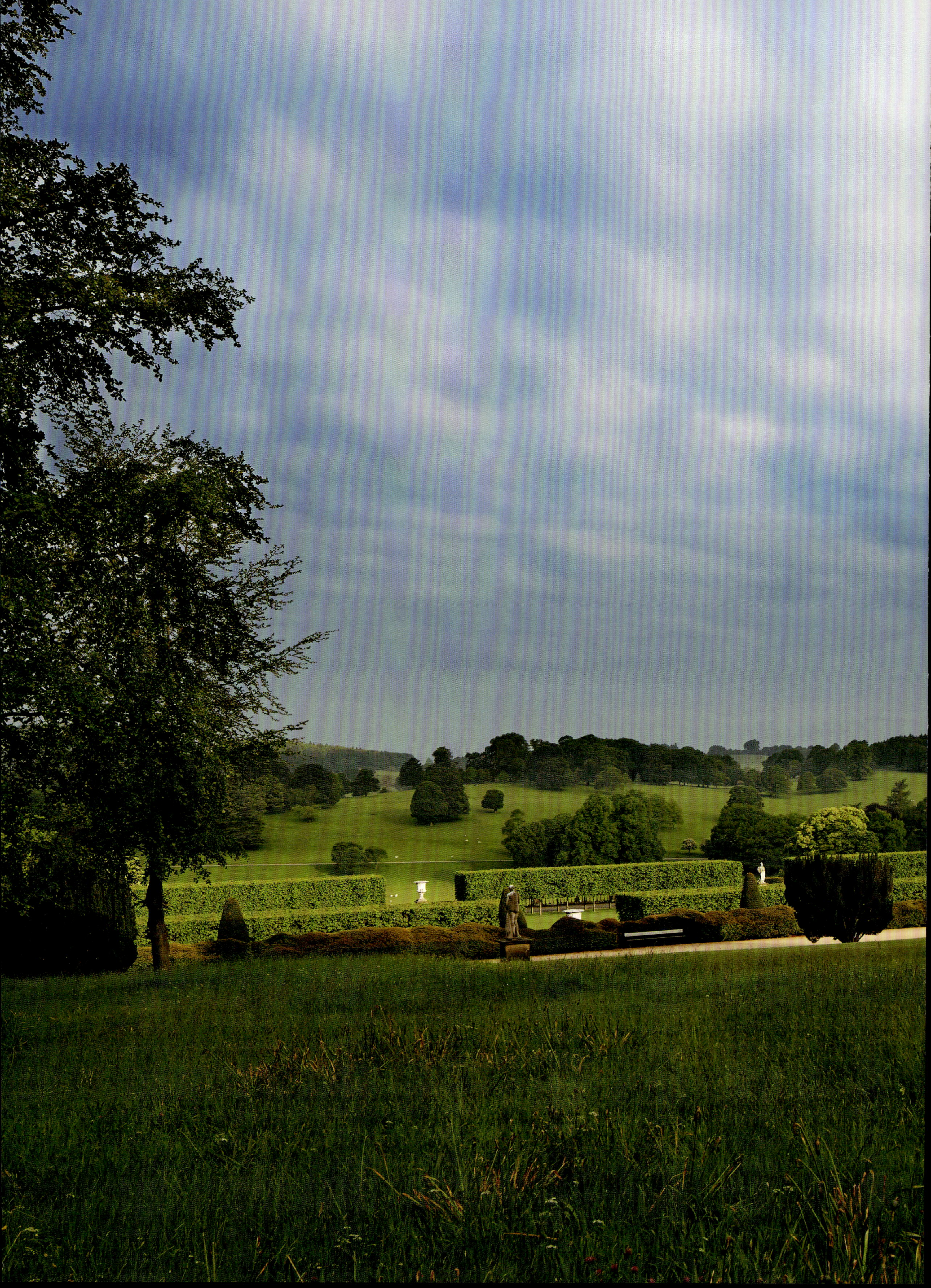

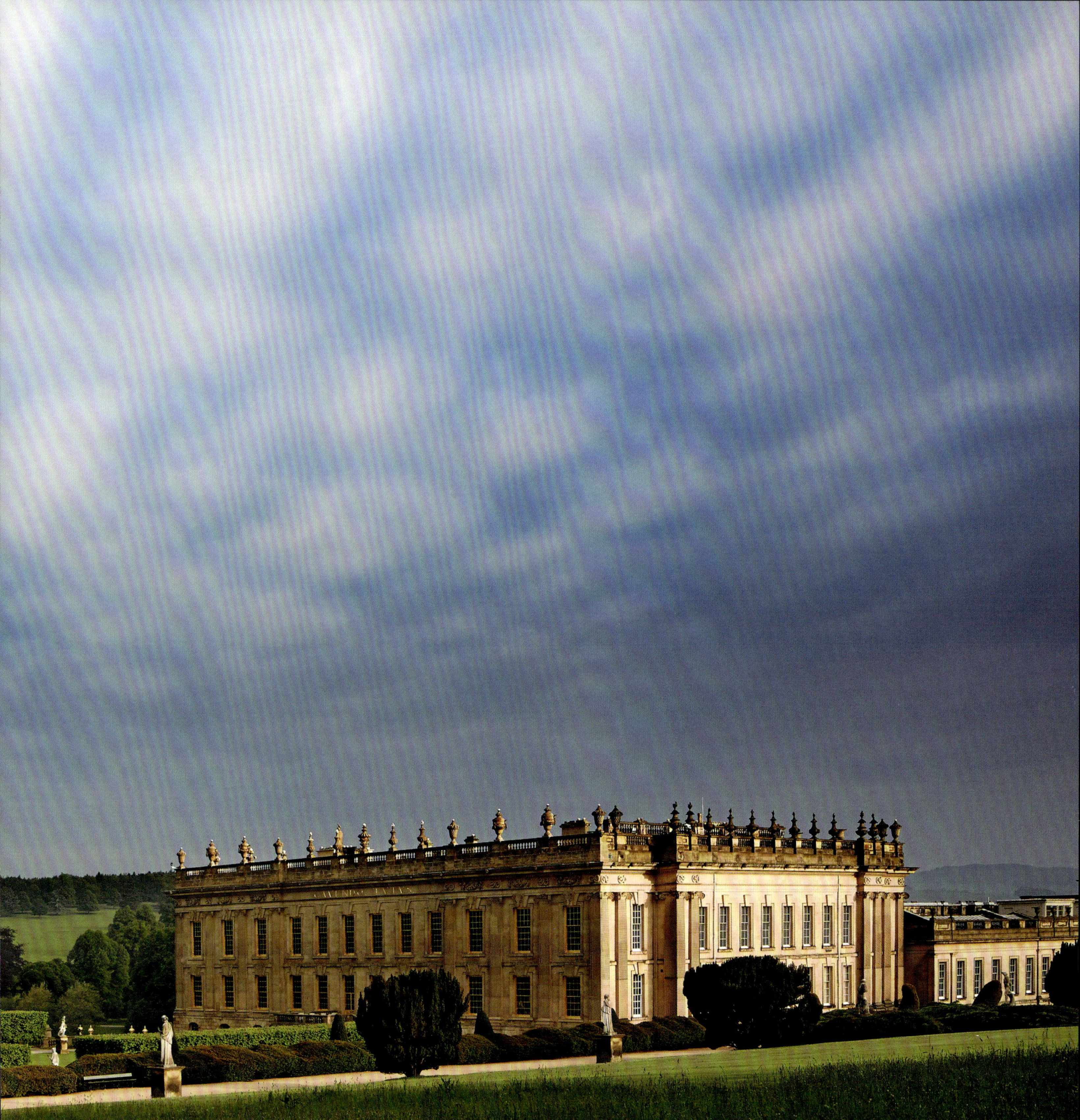

Archer's Cascade House (1703–1712), and offered a still more varied range of views across the dramatic scenery of the deer park to the west.

This opening up of the countryside beyond the parkland was in itself a radical departure. In 1727, George Vertue had noted that "the house looks like a small model... in a bottom & overtopt by Mountains. The Park round it is stony & rocks almost barren,"[4] and even in the seventeenth century it was a "Diamond... set in a vile socket of ignoble jet."[5] In short, for one hundred years before Brown's involvement, the surrounding wilderness had been regarded as disgusting, and at best as a frame to set off the order and beauty of the house and gardens. After Chatsworth, Brown was to begin to turn this idea inside out, making the gardens the frame from which to contemplate the wilder naturalistic countryside beyond. So complete was this reversal that Brown's successor, the landscape gardener Humphry Repton, was to take for granted the role of "shrubs & flowers to enrich the foreground."[6]

One challenge for the new park was to bring the principal approach, which ran in past Edensor, conveniently to the very grand stables on the north

previous pages: Led by Brown, the English landscape style has taught us to find beauty in setting apparent disorder around a very disciplined architecture.
above: The drive followed the contour along the higher ground east of the house.

132 · CAPABILITY BROWN

side of the house, built in about 1764 and designed by James Paine (1717–1789). Since the walled gardens were being moved, presumably by Brown, to their present position some 700 meters north of the house, the road had to run in full view across the face of the landscape in order to avoid passing under the windows of the house en route to the stables—hence Paine's very grand bridge (circa 1764), which was built as far north as it could be without forcing carriages into an obvious detour to use it. Brown so constructed this approach, as he always did, that its surface is concealed for the full length of this traverse.

Repton subsequently made sarcastic comments about this "aversion of *showing a road*"[7]—"Such, alas! is the blindness of system, that, in a place where several roads are brought together (like the streets of Seven Dials), within two hundred yards of the hall door a direction post is placed, as necessary to point out the way to the house."[8] We shall see a different method of concealment at Berrington, but here, and most often in Brown's work, the road surface was concealed by a very slight bank running along its downhill side, between the road and the river.

The "aversion" gave the landscape what Repton

above: Edensor was extended in the nineteenth century, but only the church spire was visible from Chatsworth. overleaf: Several houses in Edensor were taken down in Brown's day, but he left at least one that was fully in view of the house. It was not taken down until 1770—after Brown had finished the commission.

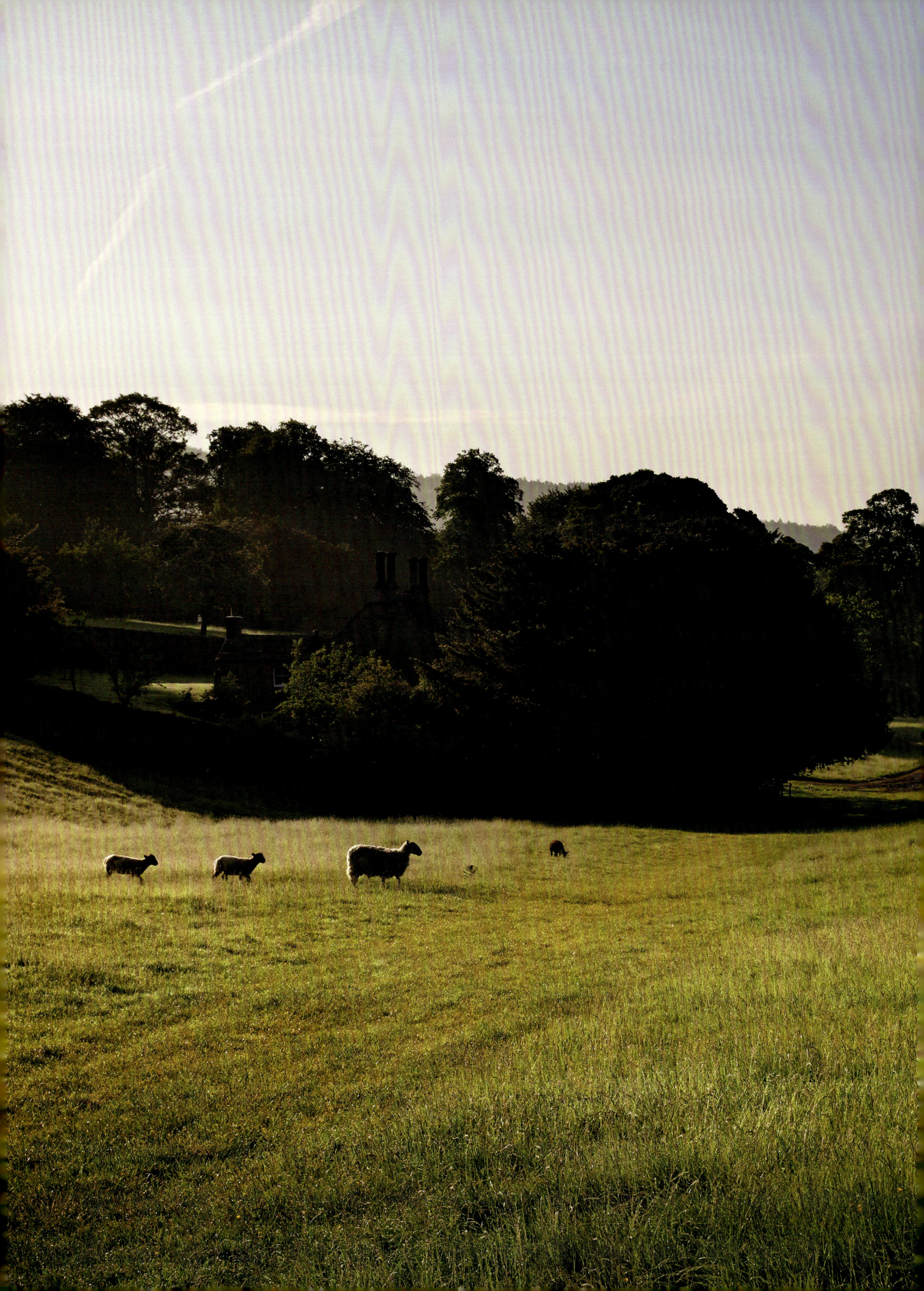

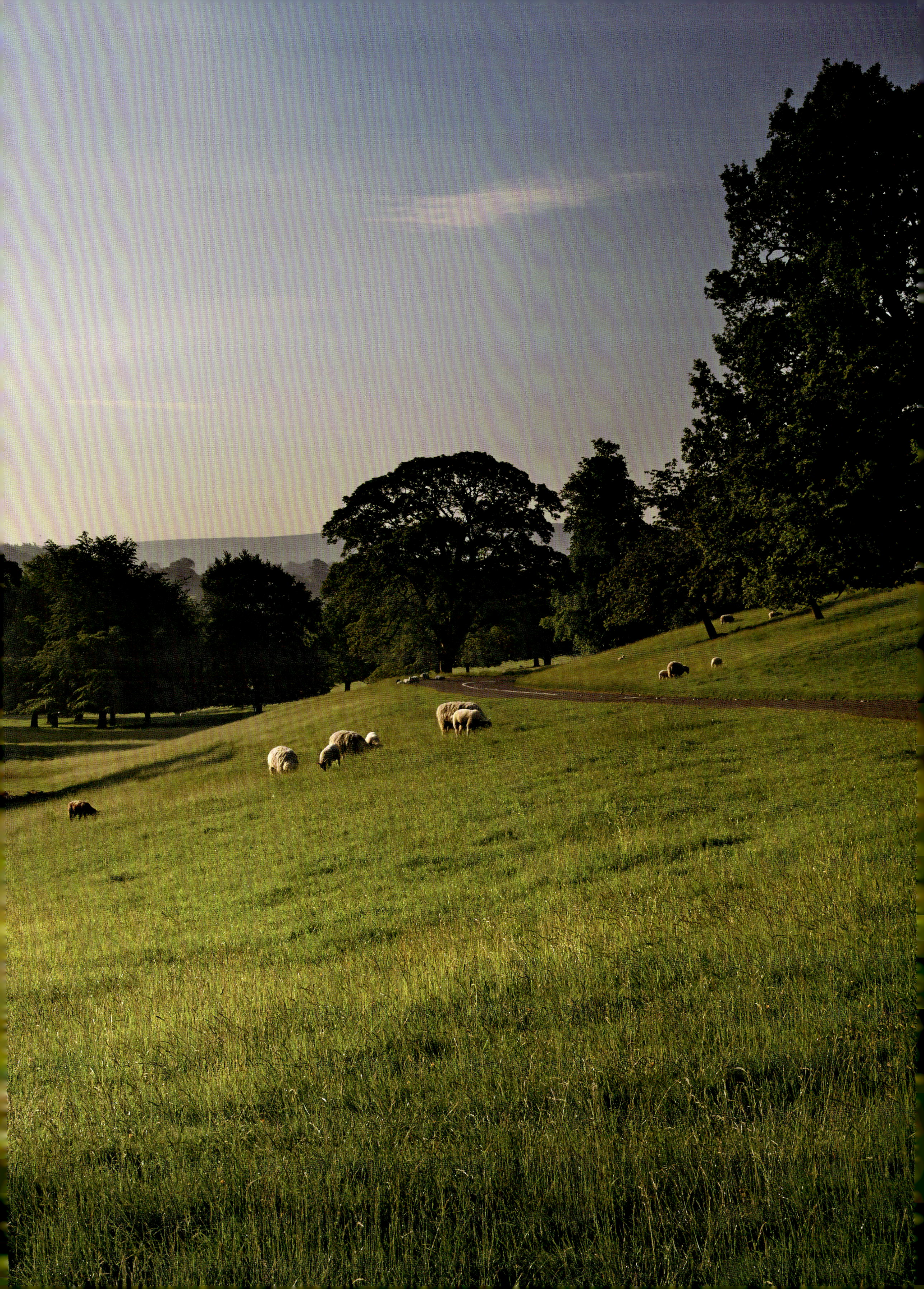

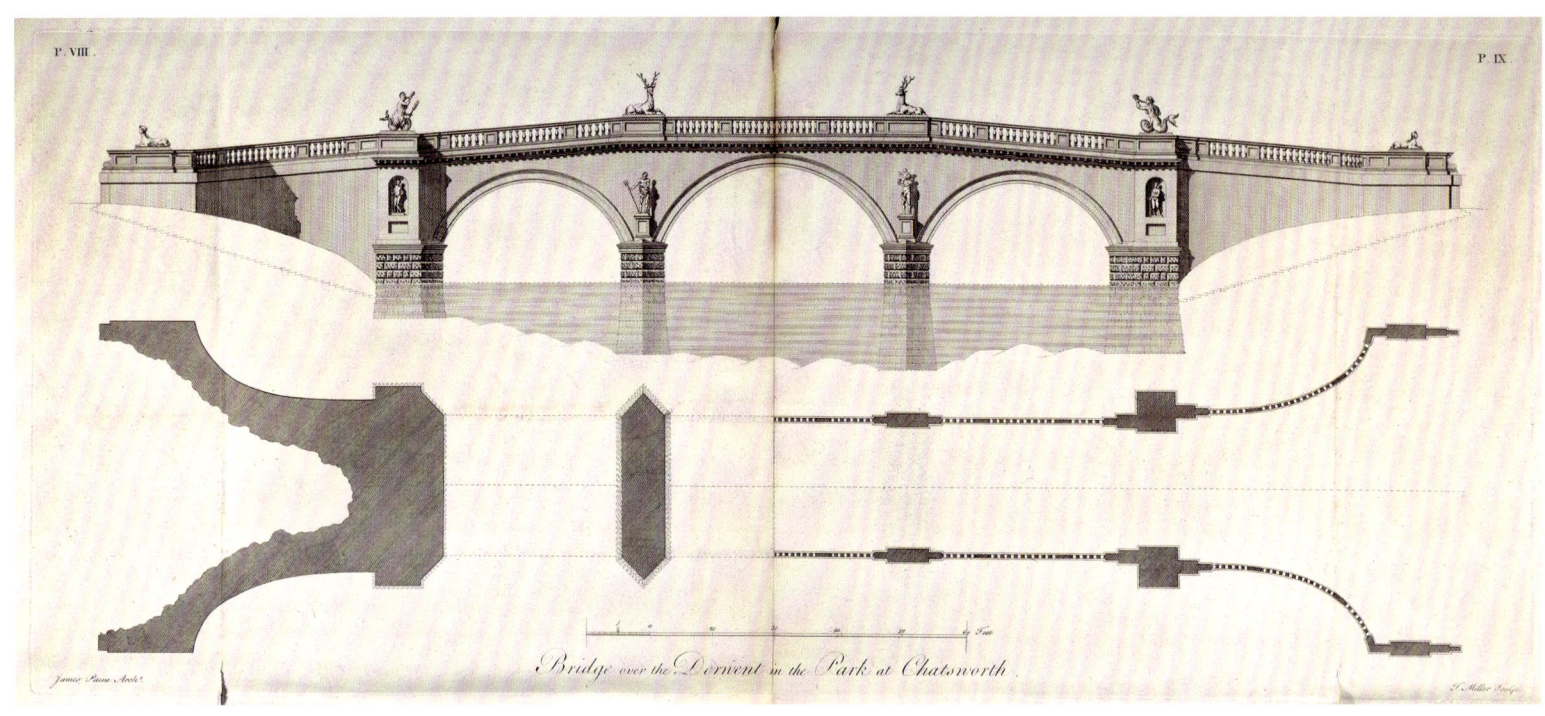

*above and top: James Paine's bridge plays a crucial part in
framing the view west from the house.*

136 · CAPABILITY BROWN

above and top: The stables, designed by James Paine, demonstrate the importance of horses to an estate in the second half of the eighteenth century.

was to call a lack of "connection." A critic might ask why such a fine stone bridge should be stuck in the middle of nowhere, and what the strange stone block of Queen Mary's Bower was doing in the middle of the view (it was said to have been built in the sixteenth century for Mary Queen of Scots). Then there was James Paine's Mill (1761–1762) apparently isolated within the parkland, and the Old Parsonage, left standing when the east end of Edensor was removed from the view (although it was more or less directly in front of the mansion, it was not taken down until 1770). One might ask what place these buildings had in a landscape that had reverted to the wild, and how they were connected with the people and carriages that were daily to be seen passing down the approach. However, the removal of obvious points of connection gives the landscape all the timelessness of a painting by Claude Lorrain, divorced from any diurnal cares. The very suppression of all the links that might connect these components and encourage one to look for a functional relationship between them, bestows upon the scene a dreamlike magical coherence.

It is an extraordinary testimony to Brown's creative ability that this appearance of dissociation (the isolated buildings, the enclosing belt) was mistaken for reality by his successors. Repton explicitly criticized houses where the principal entrance was "like an enchanted castle, without the least appearance of ever having had a horse or carriage at the door," and devoted himself to re-establishing the visible and tangible connections that Brown had done away with: "The waters with very little assistance of Art might be rendered apparently connected... This ruined bridge... shall appear as the natural link of connection betwixt a wood and a dressed sheep walk."[9] Brown's

above: The mill was given an Arcadian setting on the valley floor. There was a fascination for Brown and his clients in what was then a highly engineered and effective machine.

successors unthinkingly accepted the illusion created by Brown that the gentry lived in paintings by Claude Lorrain and felt it was incumbent on them to make their landscapes explicable and everyday, without realizing that by doing so they had broken into the reverie that he had induced.

The picturesque character of this new deer park was contrasted with Calton Pasture, a sheep walk south of the house, created while Brown was at Chatsworth, and highly characteristic of his work. This is a large area of gently rolling grassland, with a sinuous drive on its skirts, four clumps and a pond. Deer parks on the other hand (like Stag Park at Petworth and Goodwood Park in Sussex) were characterized by "rough features... abounding in fern, broom, &c. being, in fact, a forest of large spreading oaks" and were altogether "opposed to the neatness of the sheep-walk."[10] These sheep walks occur frequently in Brown's works (we shall find another at Blenheim), but their role is currently unclear. It seems quite likely that, like High Park at Burghley, they could carry valuable grazing and could also be used for hare coursing, horse racing and training—pursuits that could not be carried out within the rougher ground of the deer park without frightening the deer and risking the horses.

Any view of Calton Pasture from the house is blocked by Lindup Hill, but it would be a mistake to think the view south unimportant. We know that in about 1702 an enormous amount of work had been commissioned there by the 1st Duke of Devonshire (1640–1707): "levelling a hill... by which he hath gained a distant prospect of the blue hills and made on the same level with this house and garden a canal."

above: Calton Pasture is an entirely separate and very extensive parkland. The drives that cross it wind along the valley to a high point at the south end. A great terrace there offers a wide panorama.

CHATSWORTH · 139

In fact, this was described by Sir Godfrey Copley as "the Duke's chief work."[11]

One should make the point that Chatsworth, despite the enormous amount that had been done over the previous centuries, was a muddle when Brown arrived. A good deal of ground given over to a series of seventeenth-century and earlier gardens had been part removed and part simplified in the 1730s by the 3rd Duke. But his son and Brown's client, the 4th Duke, was in a perfect position to transform the place. He inherited the estate in 1755 at the age of thirty. He was a close political friend of the elder Pitt, an acknowledged leader of the Whigs, and had married one of the greatest heiresses of the age, Lady Charlotte Elizabeth Boyle (1731–1754), through whom he inherited very substantial estates. Unfortunately he died at age forty-four in 1764, when his son, the 5th Duke and husband of the famous Georgiana, was only sixteen. The latter finished off the works begun by his father, but then let Chatsworth alone, spending much of his time in London. Visitors were often critical of what seemed a half-completed design, so when John Byng, Viscount Torrington, visited in 1784, he attacked the formal Canal Pond: "The ground remaining unsloped to the vale and river; which the gardener said might be completely done for 2000£."[12] The fact that the gardener himself seemed to have costed the work and approved it, makes it reasonable to suppose that Brown had proposed this project, but work came to an end with the 4th Duke's death (after which Brown brought Michael Millican away to Richmond Park). The magnificent set-piece view to the south that Brown might have intended was eventually captured by the Broad Walk, designed by Jeffry Wyattville in 1820, which now runs to an urn put up to commemorate Lady Blanche Howard, who died in 1840. It is the one long-distance composed view in the landscape, off the moor and down into the quiet villages of Beeley and Rowsley in bright sunlight, between the two sharply defined silhouettes of Beeley Hill Top and Lindup.

So Brown left Chatsworth still with a good deal that was not organized, Queen Mary's Bower, with its fragment of an ancient garden (he had saved a fragment of the Tudor garden at Ampthill as well), the Canal Pond, the Cascade, the remains of the old gardens on the lower slopes east of the house—all are awkwardly stranded, they do not build to anything, they are not parts of a greater whole—and yet the overall coherence still compels admiration. It may be that Brown learned from this, too, and it encouraged him to move away from the intricacy of the design he had worked on at Stowe and Wotton, where the precise placing of structures and planting was so controlled, and toward the wilder ambition of Milton Abbey.

First, however, there was Blenheim.

above right: The parkland at Chatsworth is the backdrop to every view in the gardens. It draws a relaxed and peaceful Elysium out of the wild moors of Derbyshire. Nature is interrupted only by the spire of Edensor church in the distance and by James Paine's bridge.

above: Joseph Paxton's nineteenth-century gardens
may be grandiose and extravagant, but they are carefully settled into
Brown's landscape and do not interrupt it.

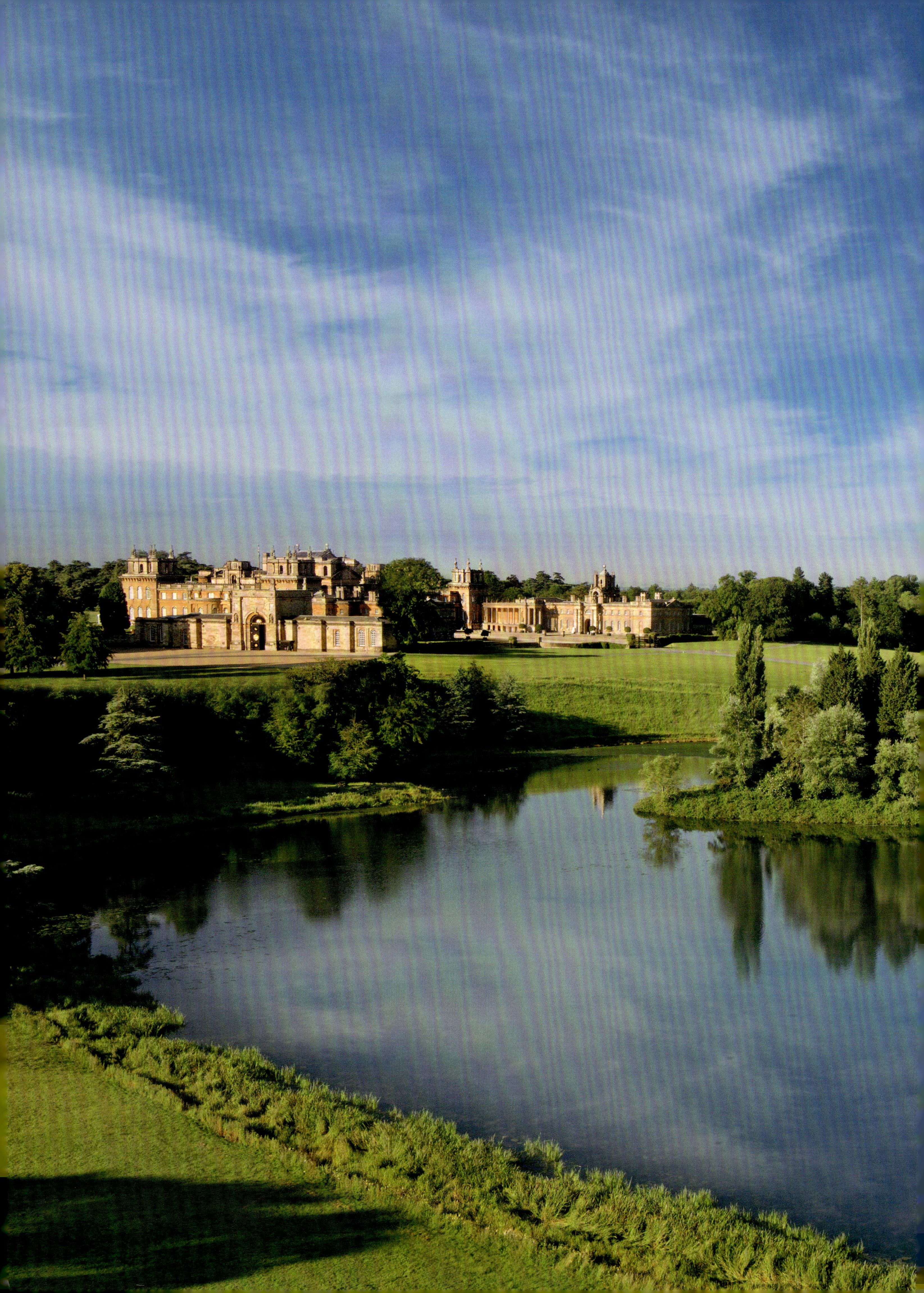

BLENHEIM PALACE
— OXFORDSHIRE —
FROM 1763

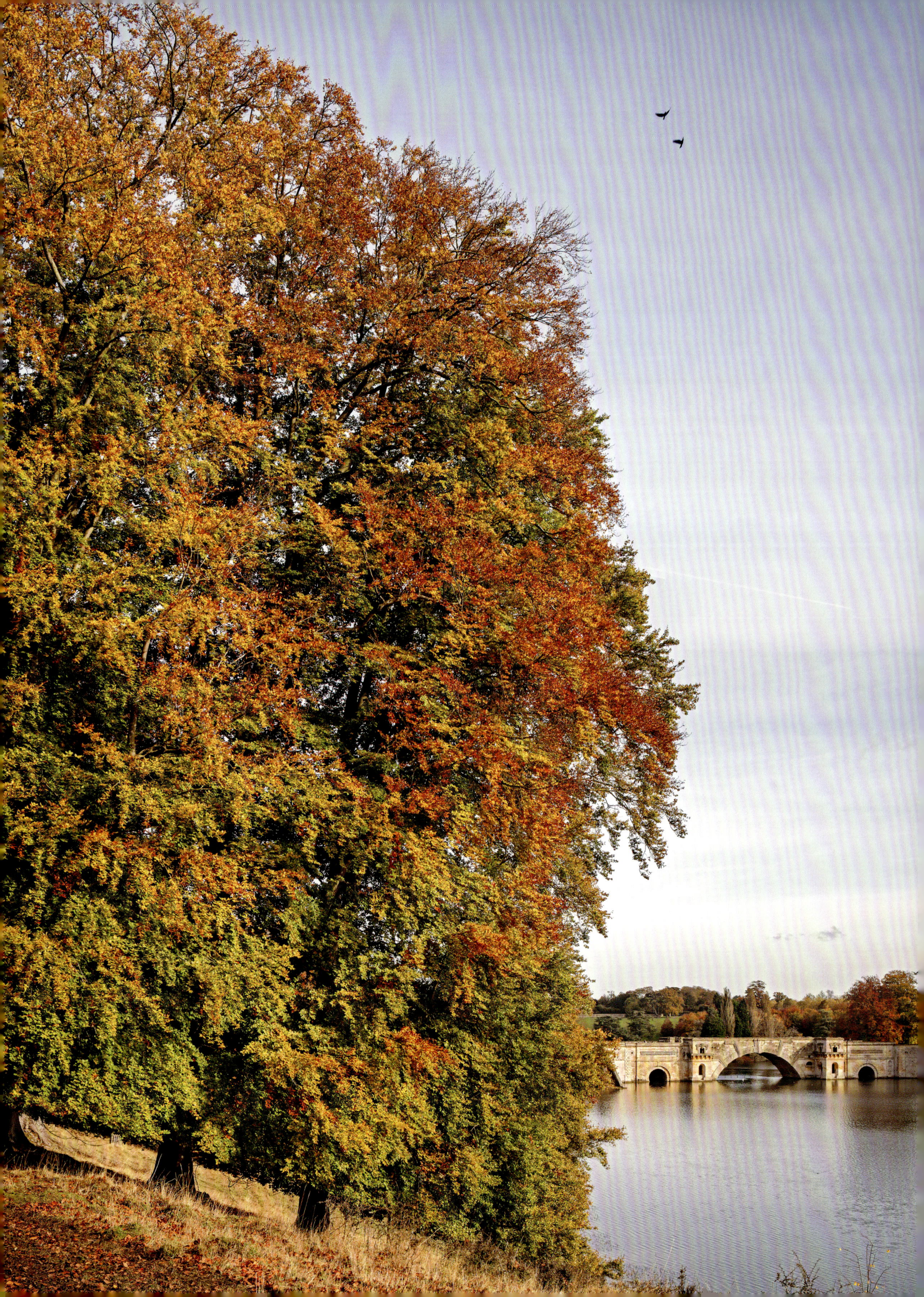

— CHAPTER EIGHT —

BLENHEIM PALACE

In 1828, prince ludwig von Pückler-Muskau found Blenheim upsetting. His admiration for "the grandeur of Brown's genius and conceptions" at Blenheim warranted him his reputation as "the Shakespeare of gardening... who combined lofty poetry with a good deal that was crude, angular and uncouth," but all this was being changed by the 5th Duke, the son of Brown's client, who was "modernizing [Brown's work] in a miserable taste."[1]

Blenheim is a gigantic composition, and like Chatsworth has the blessing of an impeccably researched book devoted solely to the landscape.[2] For Blenheim, too, we have the benefit of a survey of the grounds before Brown began work, Brown's initial proposal, and several drawings of his later refinements of the plan (in general not accepted). We also have accounts that show him to have been paid the staggering sum of £21,537.14s for a project that ran for ten years from 1763. As with Chatsworth, he had a foreman for the work, in this case, Benjamin Read, a "paviour," or water engineer, and "a man of practice and sound direction," as Lord Coventry described him. As with Chatsworth, we know that works were underway when Brown's involvement is first recorded (he had already worked for the 3rd Duke at Langley, and so might conceivably have been involved at Blenheim at an earlier date). As with Berrington, the foreman remained to continue the work after Brown's contract had ended, leaving us uncertain as to whether Brown retained any interest or influence over the progress of the works after that date.

In the eighteenth century, Blenheim was already the greatest show house in the country and Brown was to make its park the equal of the palace, prompting even King George III to exclaim "we have nothing equal to this" when he visited in 1786.[3] The scale of his work and of the lake above all, was such that an unusual system had developed for showing it off, as a German visitor recalled at the beginning of the nineteenth century: "Seated in our travelling carriage... at every remarkable place we looked in the map for confirmation of the information we received from our guide, who rode beside the coach, and calling our attention first to one, and then to another object,

*previous pages: Blenheim and Vanbrugh's bridge, often described as the finest landscape composition in Europe.
opposite: The steep banks of the lake were carefully planted with loose clumps
and single trees so that "the mark of the spade" should not be seen.*

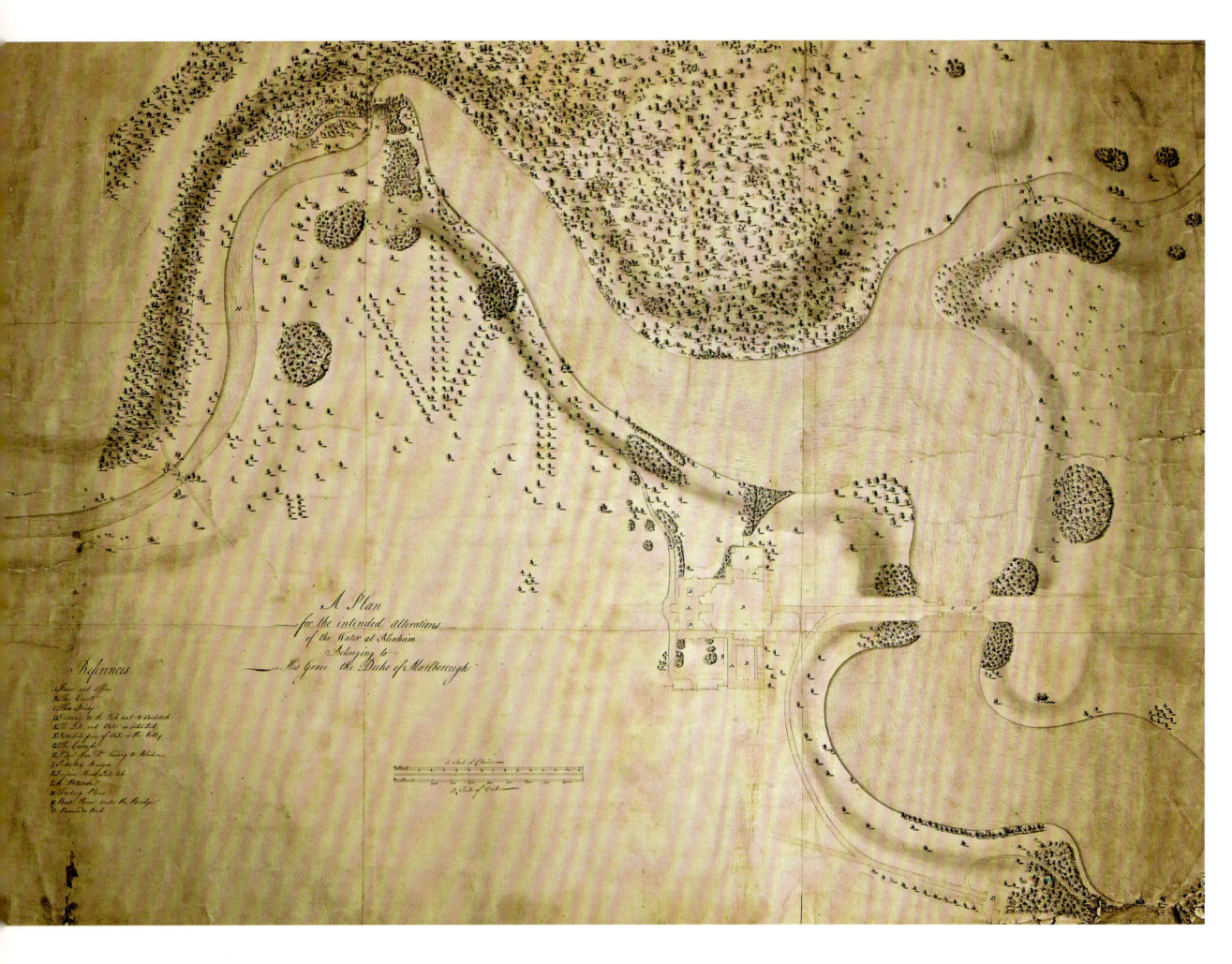

conducted us around the park… We were met by several other coaches, accompanied in a similar manner."[4] John Byng walked there in 1792 and "sneered at the visitors whom I saw driving furiously along, in fancied observation…."[5]

While there were set-piece views designed for stopping at, like those at Petworth, given the sheer weight of numbers in the park, these were always likely to be less important to Brown's design than a pleasing line for the drives taken by visitors, with "a fuller view of the grounds" en route. William Mavor, who had been tutor to the 4th Duke's children, described the route itself more than any specific composition: "This road is almost wholly open. On the Woodstock side, only a few small fresh-planted clumps appear, which assist to conceal the boundary from other points of view, and to break the line of some private houses; a few trees, fancifully disposed, skirt the slope, and others of a larger growth range with the stream on its very edge, and afford some pretty glades into the water between their trunks and boughs; but their heads scarcely rising above the level of the walk, they serve rather to vary than to hide."[6]

Blenheim is a landscape to move through, enjoying innumerable peeps and views as one does so. However, two of Brown's set-pieces will serve to give an indication of his design and his self-confidence. The first, and the most compelling, is the view north from the forecourt of the palace. The eye travels first between the beech clumps that Brown planted at each end of the bridge and down the line of the great triple elm avenue to the Column of Victory (1727–1731). However, Brown's clumps and the column effectively block the view, the eye shies off to the more rewarding landscapes to left and right. To the northwest, these landscapes center on Rosamund's Well and

above: Brown's plan shows perfectly how the formality of the house was to ease into clumps and thence to the wilder woodland on the west side of the lake (at the top of the plan).

146 · CAPABILITY BROWN

the planting around it. This was the garden built for Lady Jane Clifford by King Henry II in the 1170, and an evocative ruin in the eighteenth century—Lady Hertford was one of many who venerated its antiquity and hoped her son would drink from Rosamund's Spring.[7] Beyond the well the land has been cut away for some hundreds of feet into the steep falling slope, which is crossed by a drive, properly ducal in its width and conspicuous expense. The scoop of the earthwork opens a view up through the trees and away toward High Park. The water itself plays little part in this view, but the foreground, on the near side of the lake, is framed to the west by a group of beeches that have spread a little from their line over time.

This northwest view is counterbalanced to the northeast by the long reach of Queen Pool toward Fisheries Cottage, and then, interrupted by the poplars on Queen Elizabeth's Island, the walled town of Woodstock sits on the rising ground above Queen Pool like a Tuscan city. In this view it looks as though it is the town and not the deer park that is walled—in fact, Brown designed a massive Gothick wall for the town, to add to the effect, an idea he might have taken from the architect of the palace, Sir John Vanbrugh, whose fortified wall still survives at Castle Howard (1719–1723).

The straight approach from the victory column and the column itself dominate the composition. By any conventional reading of Brown's "informal" style, one might have concluded that he would have scorned such straight approaches to a house. In fact, however, Brown did retain them, but he treated them in a way that even his contemporaries regarded as absurd.

Samuel Hieronymus Grimm (1733–1794) was a Swiss topographical artist who worked from 1765 for the dean of Lincoln, Sir Richard Kaye, and toured

above: From certain angles the house appears to rise above the lake, like a port glimpsed from the sea.
overleaf: At its north end, the Grand Avenue, while still within the park wall, runs through the farmland of High Park, set with large clumps, very much like Great Park at Burghley.

BLENHEIM PALACE · 147

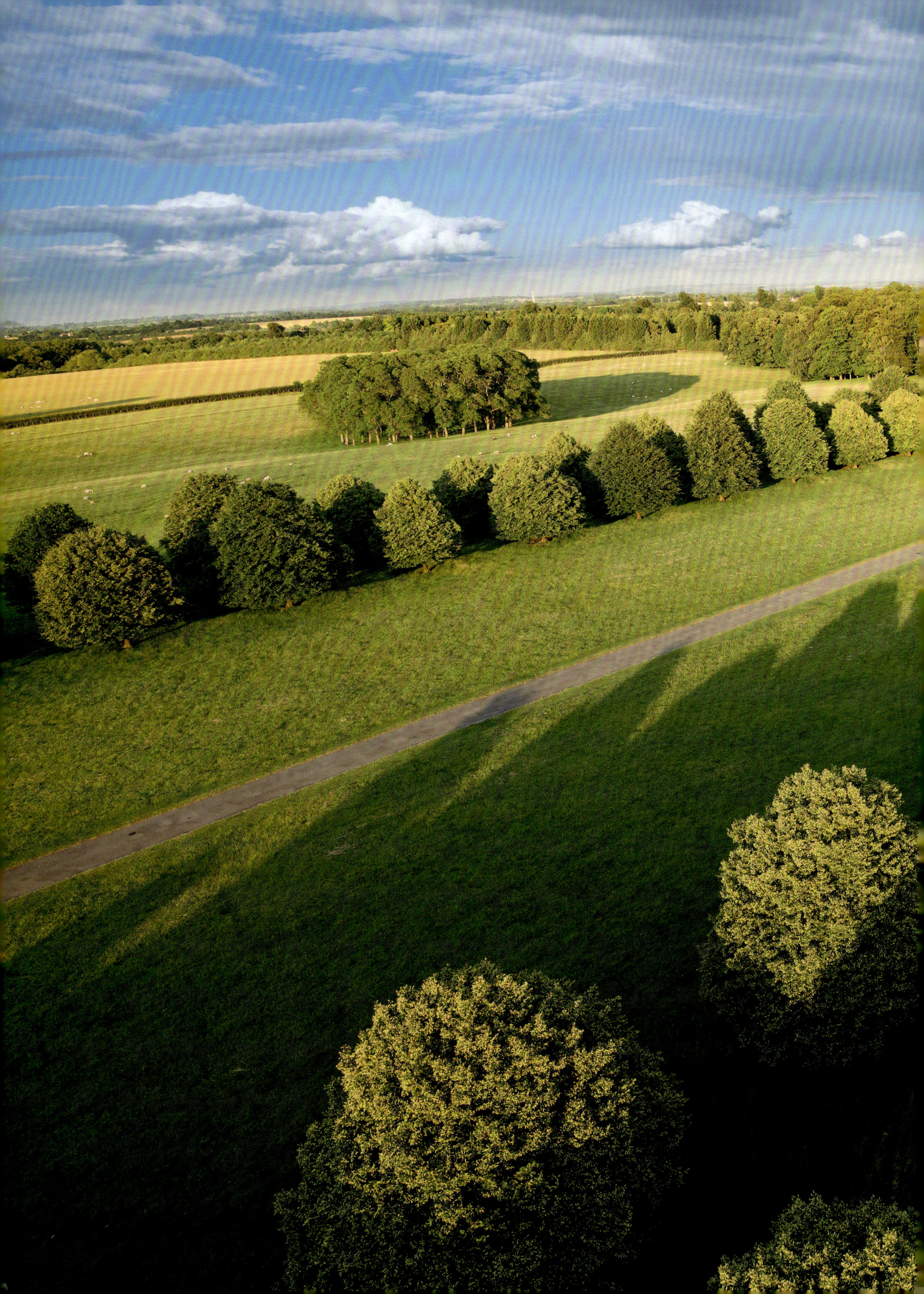

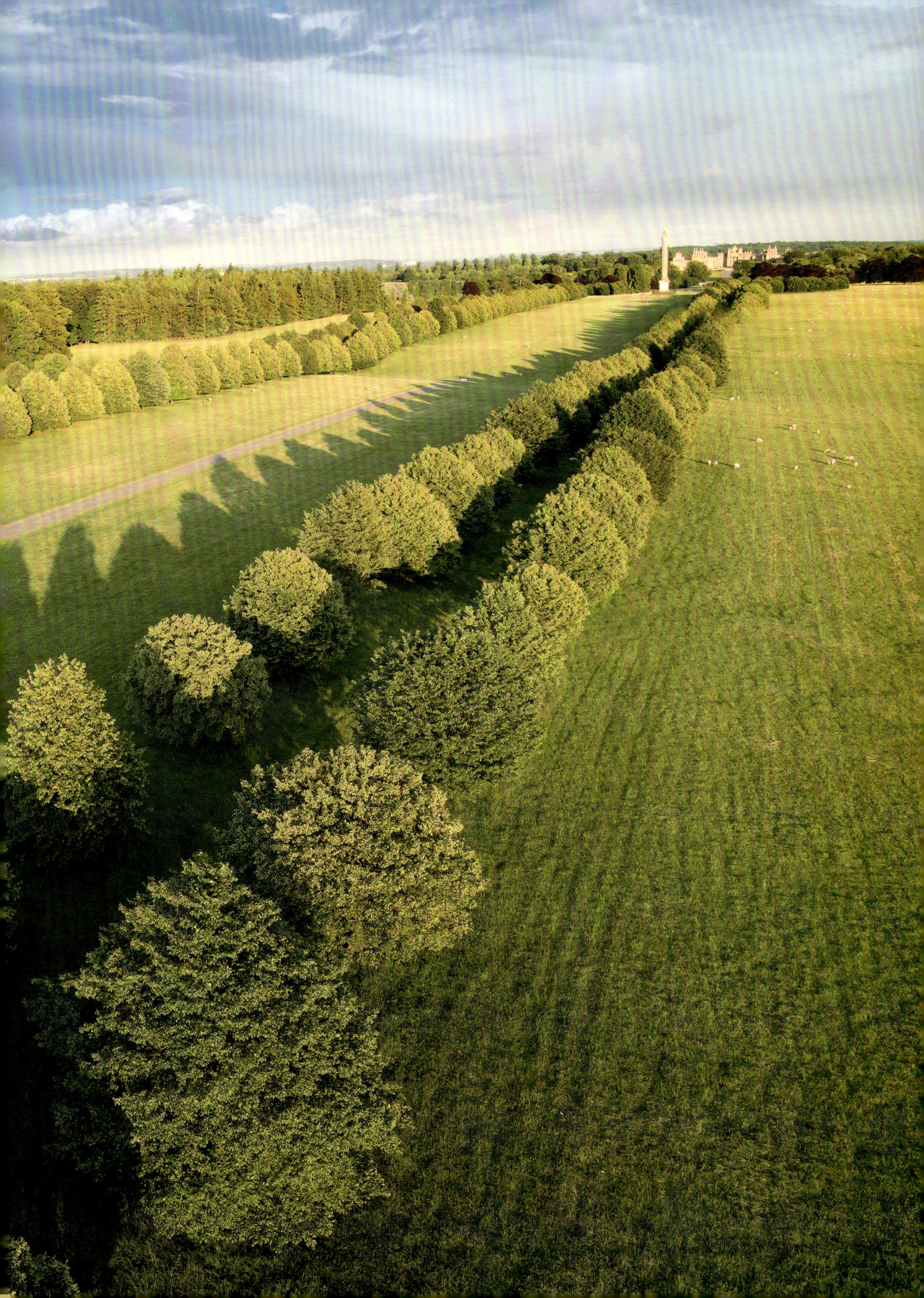

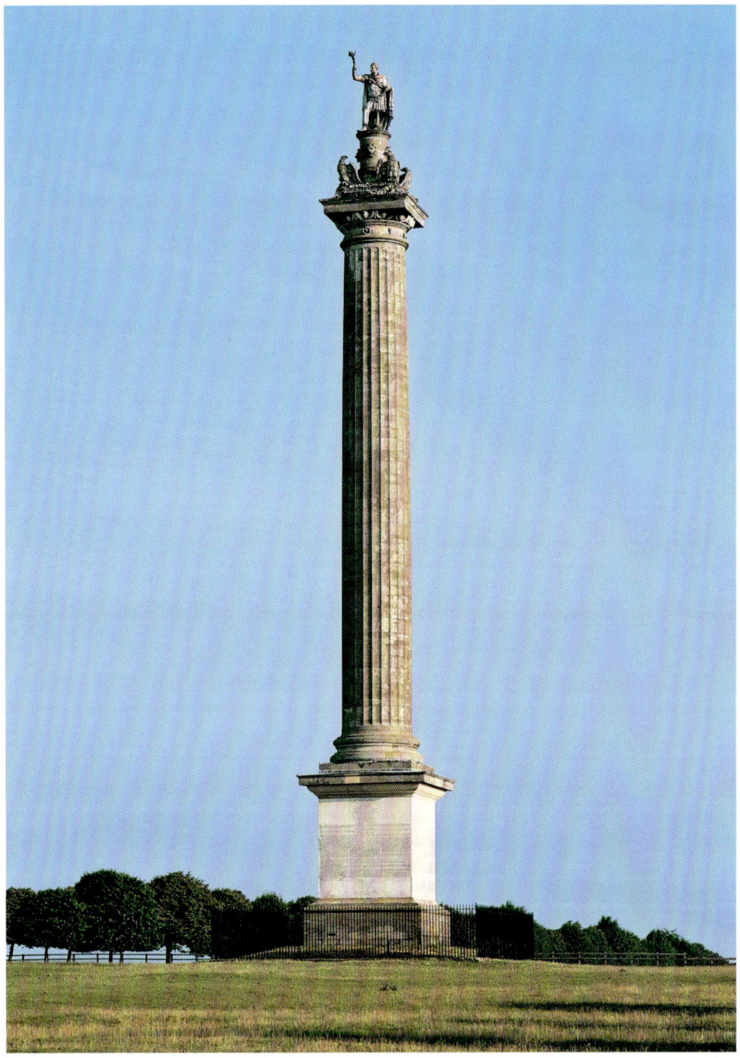
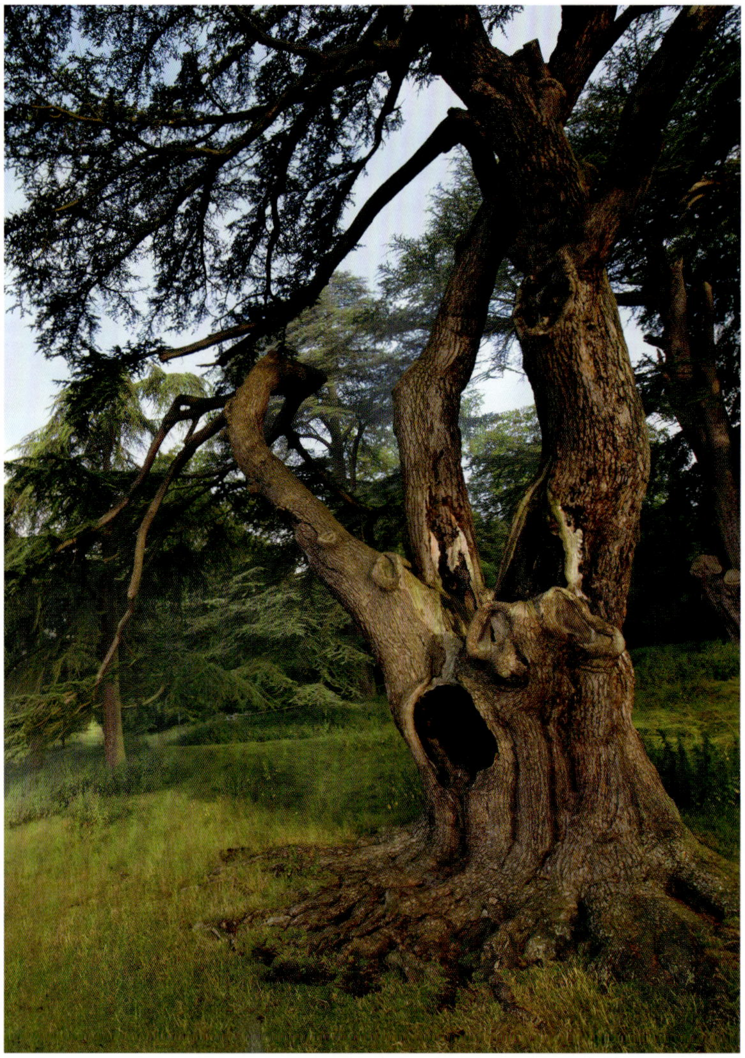
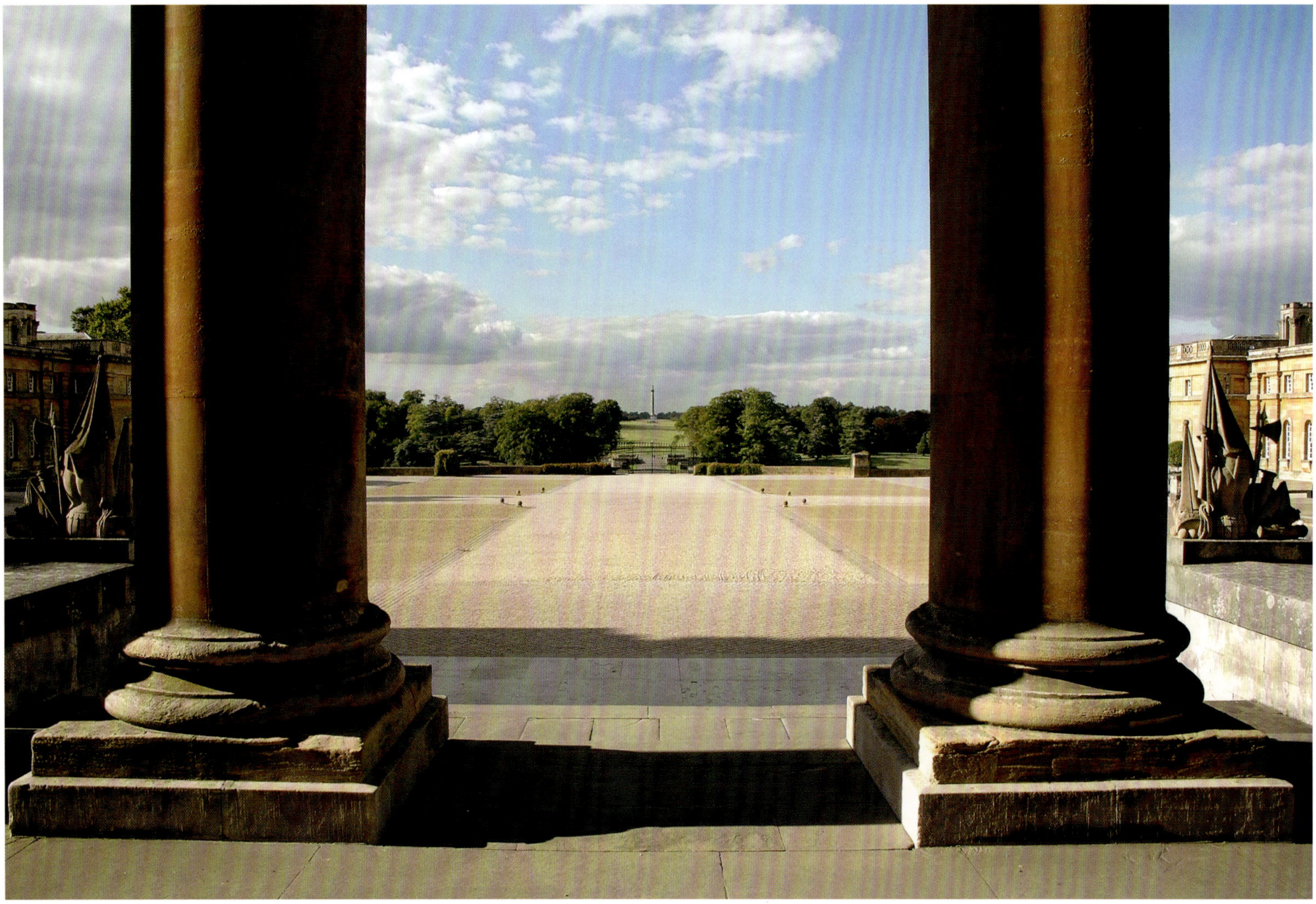

the country for his patron sketching "everything curious"—in the main, church monuments and Brown's landscapes. He got to King's Weston, outside Bristol, in 1788, and sketched a picture from the approach, which ran straight toward the house.[8] Just at the very point at which its roofs and chimneys swayed into sight from the windows of the carriage, at the very moment before one might have topped the hill to see the house in all its glory, with the breadth of the Bristol Channel shining beside it, that "reach of the Severn Sea" that Elizabeth Montagu enjoyed from her dressing room "of near 40 miles in length & many in breadth, the ships lying before my window,"[9]—at that very moment, Grimm shows that the road swung away to the right, into the trees, and the house was lost to sight.

Grimm must have chosen that spot to draw attention to something that he regarded as an absurdity. He would not have been the only person to regard it that way, but something similar happened at Castle Ashby, and at Holkham, where the effect was described: "Rising with the hill you approach the Obelisk... [then] the road branches off to the left leaving a fine expanse of lawn on the south front of the House, which is here seen to the greatest advantage."[10] And it happened at Blenheim.

opposite: At Blenheim, Brown sought to match the magnificence of Versailles.
top: The view from Rosamund's Well.
above: Brown proposed to emphasize the medieval past of Woodstock by building a wall around the town.

BLENHEIM PALACE · 151

The principal approach that Vanbrugh brought through the Ditchley Gate and down the full length of the avenue to Blenheim Palace had lost its primary purpose with the construction of the Woodstock Gate (1723). A graveled road across his bridge will still have been necessary to provide access for heavy goods between the palace and the park, but now Brown turned it off to the east down a dry valley that carries it on toward the lake—just at the very moment where the palace might have come fully into view. The alteration at Blenheim was described by Mavor: "Through this vista formerly lay the road conducting to the grand [Ditchley] approach; a straight reach of more than two miles, without much diversity in the objects, and with too great formality to please. It now takes a happier direction along the edge of the lake to QUEEN POOL, then enters a low bottom with noble steeps in distinct masses, the sides of which are adorned with pendent groves and clumps of different growths."[11]

One might ask why Brown created these detours, and the simple answer is that he was less concerned with views into the house, than with views out from it; and as we have seen at Chatsworth, he was primarily anxious to conceal the surfaces of roads.

The view north from the palace was divided down the middle by the line of the road running to the bridge and the column that continues it into the sky, and this gives an air of formality and balance to an essentially unsorted variety of objects, bringing together the same disparate elements that one finds at Chatsworth—Rosamund's Well playing the part of Queen Mary's Bower and the Fisheries Cottage (which was mapped in 1719 and is likely to be much older in origin) playing that of the Old Parsonage at Chatsworth. It is as though Brown wanted to reflect their long history in his design of these two places.

As with Wakefield Lodge, Brown retained pollards in the skirts of the park, particularly in High Park and on the east side of the palace, but as for the ancient trees that he inherited in this principal view, he "destroyed in Blenheim park, and many other places, great numbers of the finest studies for art that nature ever produced," because, in the opinion of Richard Payne Knight, an unrelenting critic, Brown required "that every thing which indicated decay should be removed."[12]

The second viewpoint takes in the more placid composition of the New River and its bridge, designed by Sir William Chambers (1772–1773). Brown began work on this in about 1768, and his friends laid great store by this achievement. It was acclaimed by William Gilpin: "The banks of ye Wye could scarce have exhibited a more romantic view,"[13] and Brown himself cried it up as "the master-piece of his genius." He is recorded as saying that "the Thames would never forgive him, what he had done at Blenheim."[14] It is as if he were making of the River Glyme a scaled-down imitation of those beautiful lowland reaches around Henley where the Thames circles around the foot of the Chiltern hills, and where (at Fawley Court) he had been working in 1766.

The water was to be brought out of the Great Lake by means of a rocky cascade. Brown would construct cascades in several different ways, but these rocky ones are well represented by Blenheim, and here the Shepherd's Cot built "of the trunks of trees fancifully

above: Brown turned the Ditchley drive off the Grand Avenue and ran it down a dry valley towards the lake, so bringing it past the site of the medieval palace.

arranged," announced the end of one kind of landscape, the deer park, and the beginning of another, the sheep walk.

The New River ran along the west side of the Sheep Walk, "half a mile in length, and through its whole extent abounding with rural imagery. Frequently covered with a flock of more than a thousand sheep, all of the most beautiful and valuable, and some of the most curious kinds." As one might expect, the sheep walk also supported many hares, and John Byng amused himself with "watching them at feed."[15] Beyond them, and below the junction of the Glyme and Evenlode rivers, there were water-meadows that he found he had to wade across. As the Rev. William Mavor put it—"at Blenheim the *ferme ornée* is combined with the magnificent park... In one quarter, the eye is delighted with the sight of waving corn, in another with green paddocks that invite the scythe: here a building dedicated to agricultural purposes, or raised for the accommodation of the necessary offices, just peeps through the deep shade of surrounding trees; there the team rattles down the slope abrupt. On one side appears a herd of deer, on another a flock of sheep, and sometimes animals native and foreign gaze in social peace...."[16]

At Blenheim, however, any humility that might once have attached to the idea of the *ferme ornée* has been stripped away. The place is a stiffer picture of magnificence and pride. The farm has become unlike itself.

*top: The New River and the bridge designed by Sir William Chambers present a less dramatic, Arcadian vision.
above: Brown's cascade was a high point of the landscape. It has been rebuilt
several times since his time but still retains its rough character.*

BLENHEIM PALACE · 153

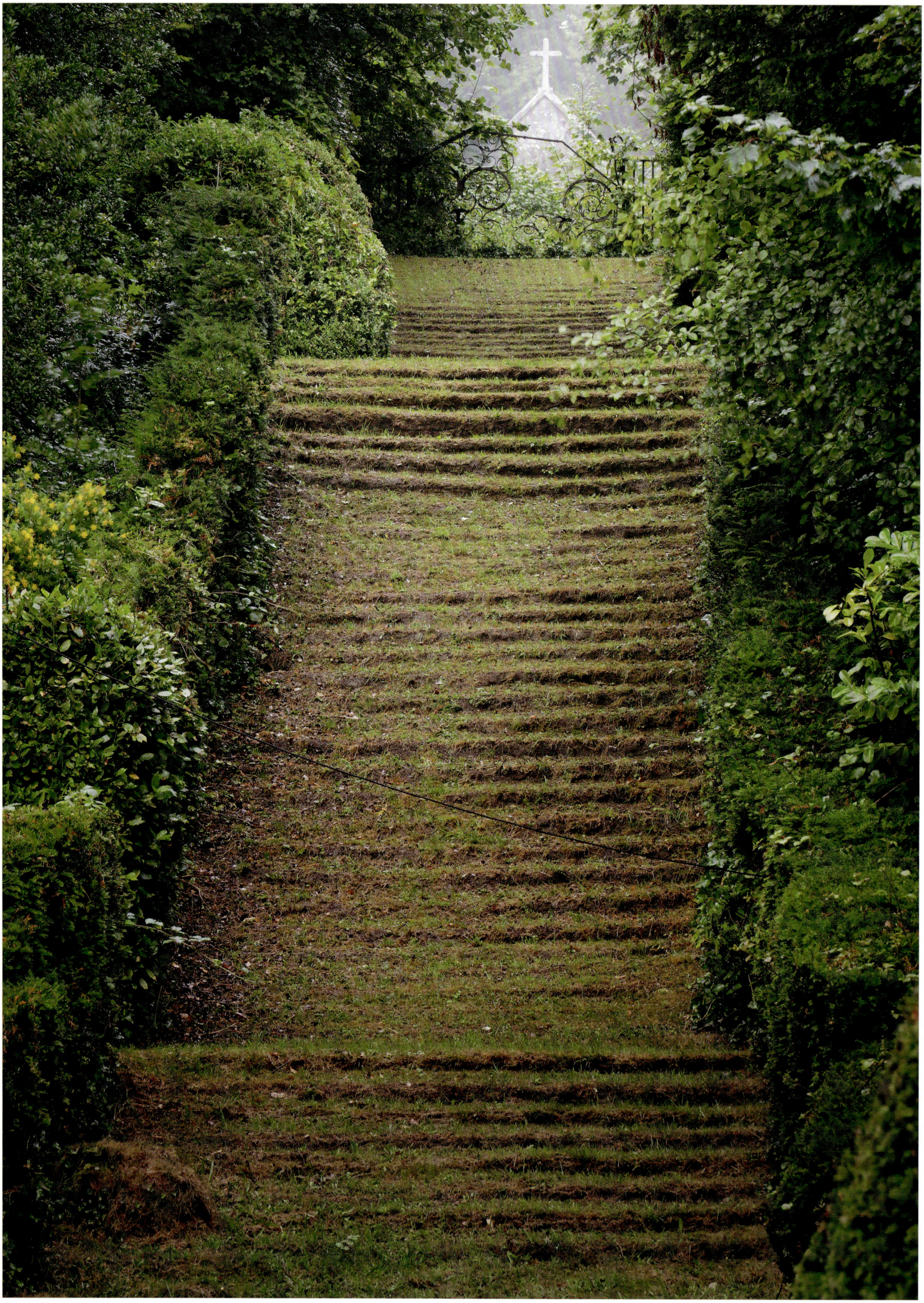

1764–1775
THE PRIME YEARS

In 1764, Brown was made chief gardener at Hampton Court Palace, Richmond, and St. James with an eventual salary of £2,000 per year. He moved then from Hammersmith to Wilderness House within the grounds of the palace. He had been seeking a position with the crown since at least 1758, and it would seem that this regal acknowledgement of his talent released him from the limitations of carefully graduated design that he had developed at Petworth. Extensive though the canvas there was, the graduation was too constraining, too much of an imposition on the spirit of the place. Now his designs were constantly to break his own rules, so that at their best one does not know exactly what kind of landscape one is looking at.

opposite: The Great Stair at Milton runs from the ancient St. Catherine's chapel down to the Abbey church, which dominates the entire landscape. Brown was known for his love of puns, and whether or not he built it himself, the Great Stair—or Stare, for the prospect from the top—ranks with his best.

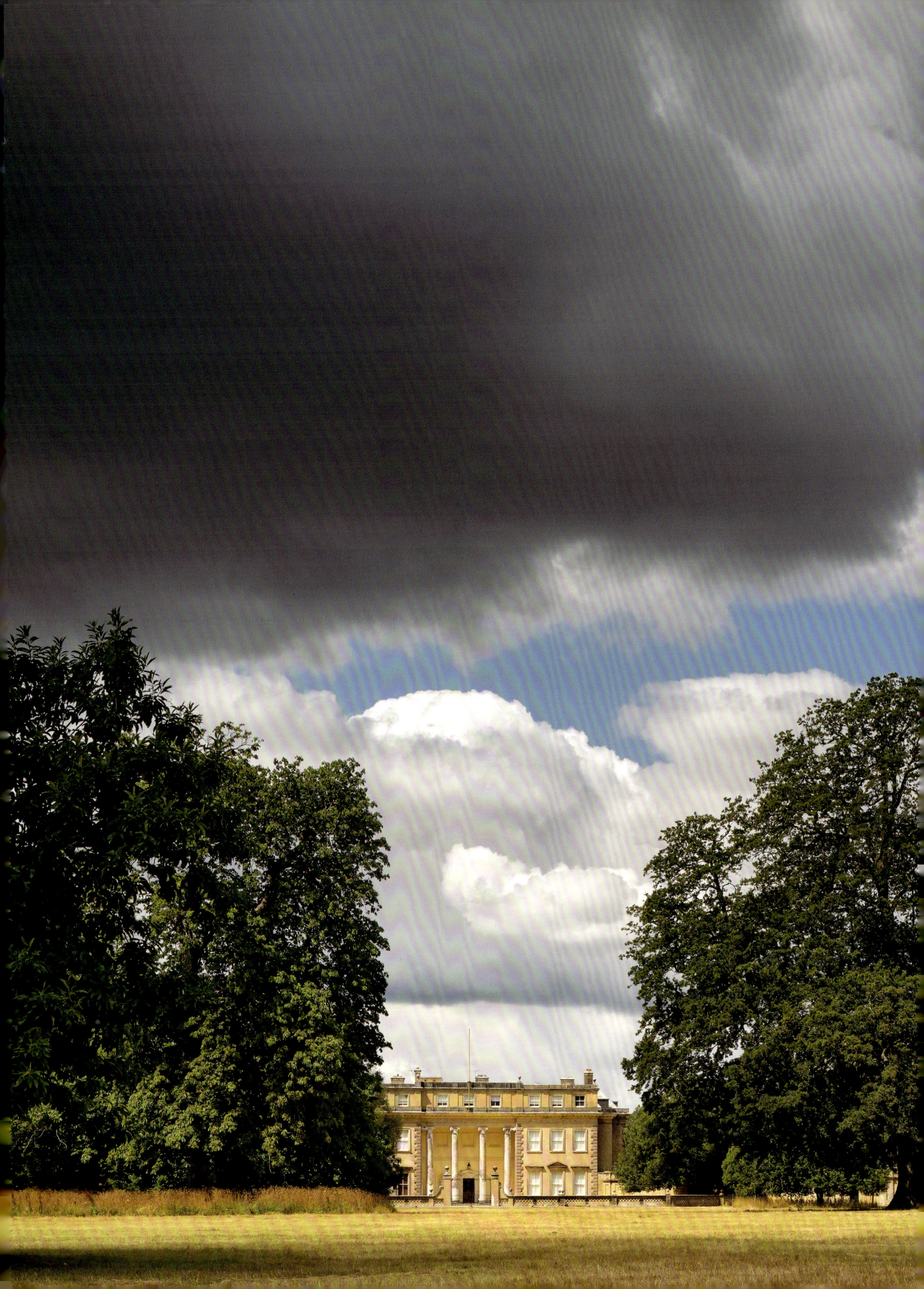

BROADLANDS

— HAMPSHIRE —
FROM 1763

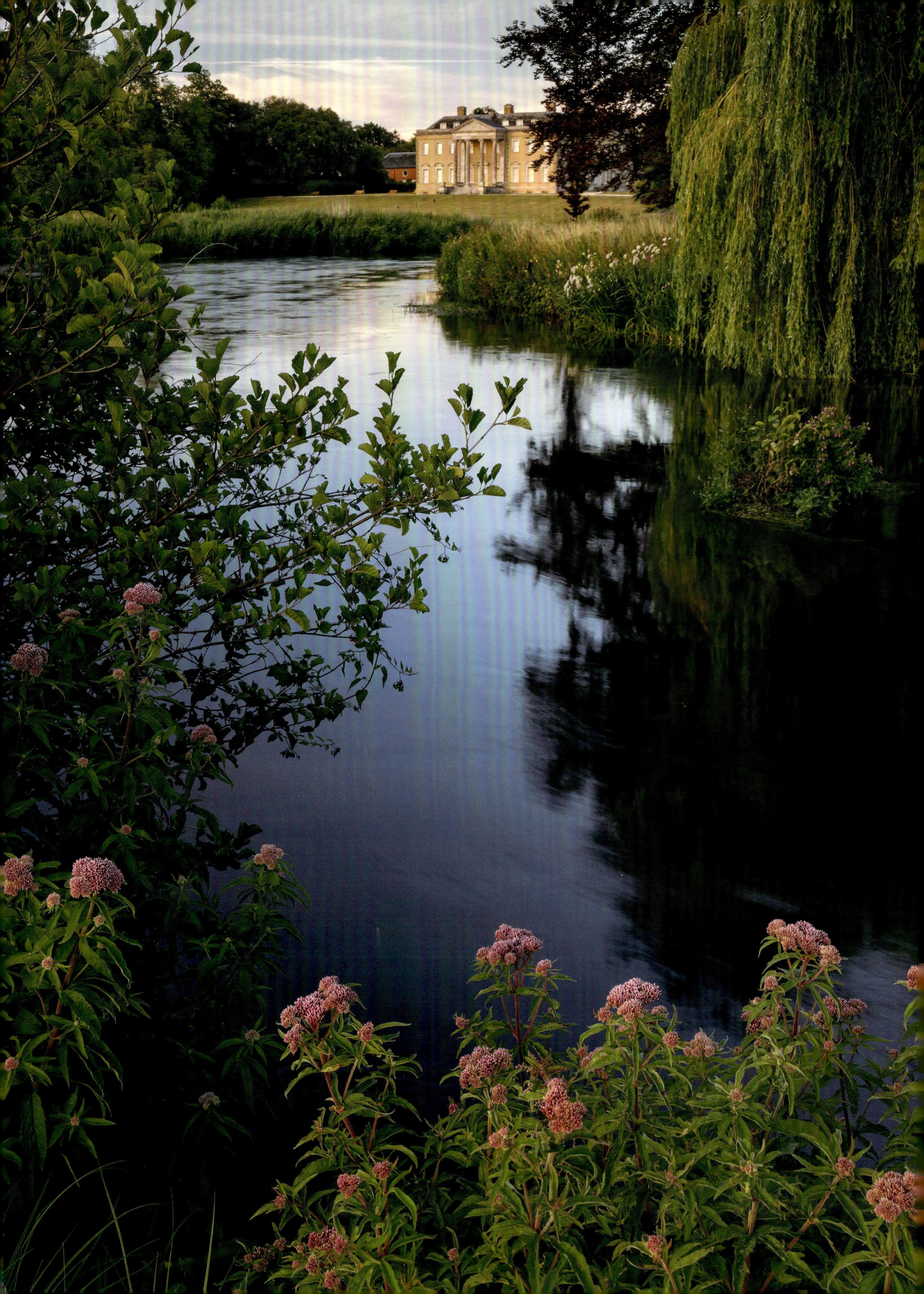

— CHAPTER NINE —

BROADLANDS

Brown worked at Broadlands over a long period (1763–1779), with John Payne as foreman from 1764 to 1772, and he was paid £21,150. The site was an unpromising one. On the east side of the house the land was flat and unprepossessing, with Lee Lane, a public road, running 100 meters from the front door, and the low range of Toot Hill some 2 kilometers beyond that. West of the house there was a strip of pleasure ground up to 100 meters wide running down to the River Test, which had been altered at some time between 1747 and 1767, perhaps by William Kent, to show off two long reaches of water in views from the house. A third strip on the west bank of the river, around 170 meters at its widest, was owned by the estate and was probably retained by Brown as a flood meadow. The meadows beyond that, on the level valley floor, were common fields and outside the estate's control. These, too, were bounded by a public road, but west of that, at last, the land rose in swells and deeps toward the New Forest.

In taking on this challenge, Brown showed little interest in the creation of parkland, though that might be regarded as the sine qua non of English landscape. Instead he used other means to weld these disparate elements into a single coherent, majestic, and apparently symmetrical composition, suspended from the west front of the house. He left the strip between the house and the river more or less alone, but added a rather half-hearted looking sequence of shrubbery clumps to the west side of the river, planted along the carrier, a secondary watercourse which he may have designed to control the estate's water-meadow. These clumps may have helped to break up the panoramic view from the house, and will have gone some way toward concealing the common meadows. Flanking the whole composition was a view to Middle Bridge (rebuilt in 1788) in the northwest, which carried the Salisbury Road, and to an unknown structure shown on an estate plan of 1785, southwest of the house—perhaps an urn on a plinth. At the heart of it, as one looks directly out of the house to the west, there was low ground and a half-mile beyond that, a lane running out of the hill and raised up on a terrace to animate the scene with its passing traffic. Hanging

previous pages: Broadlands House from the east. Lee Lane has since been closed to extend the parkland on the east side of the house, which nonetheless remains undistinguished.
opposite: Broadlands House from the south-west.

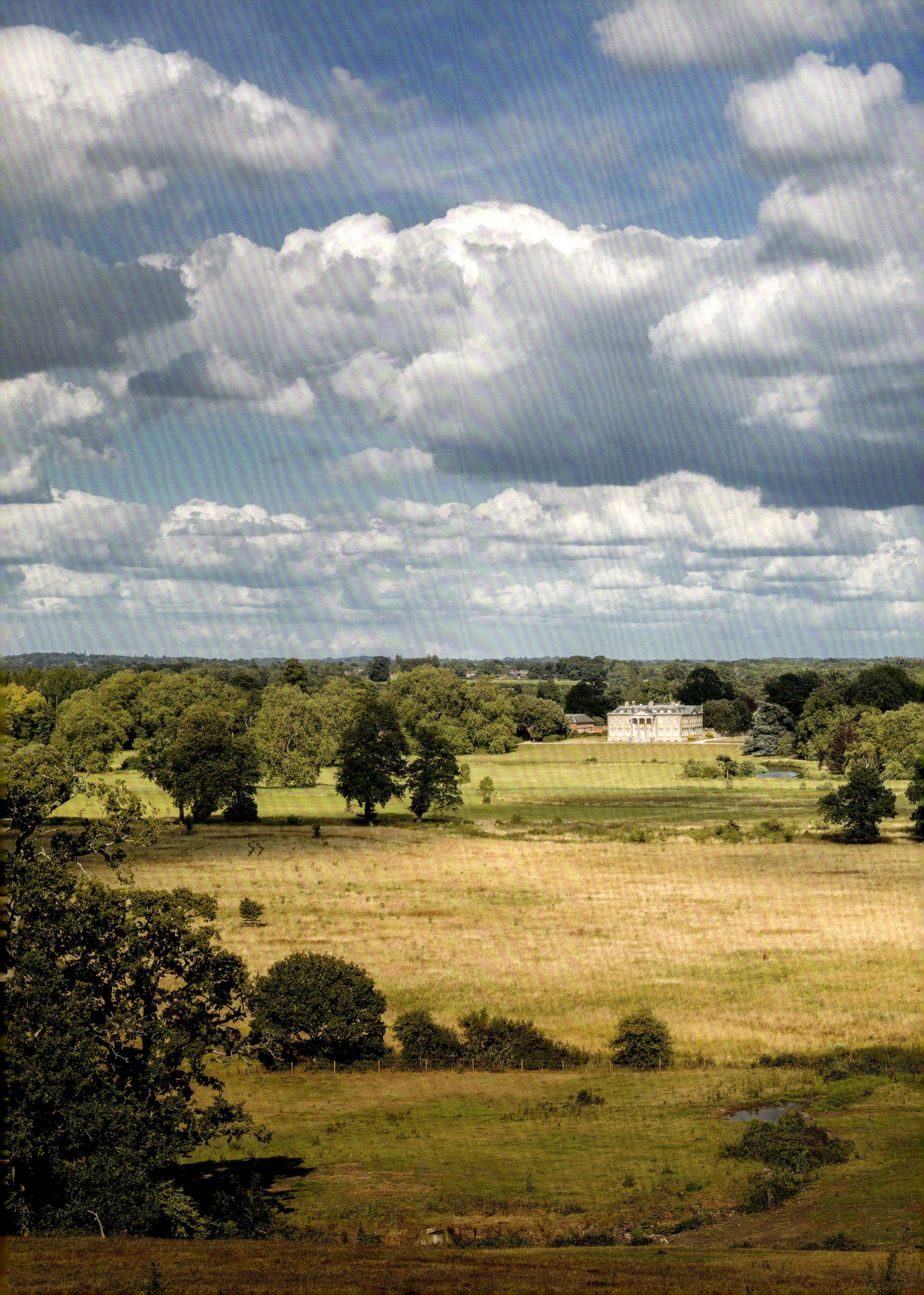

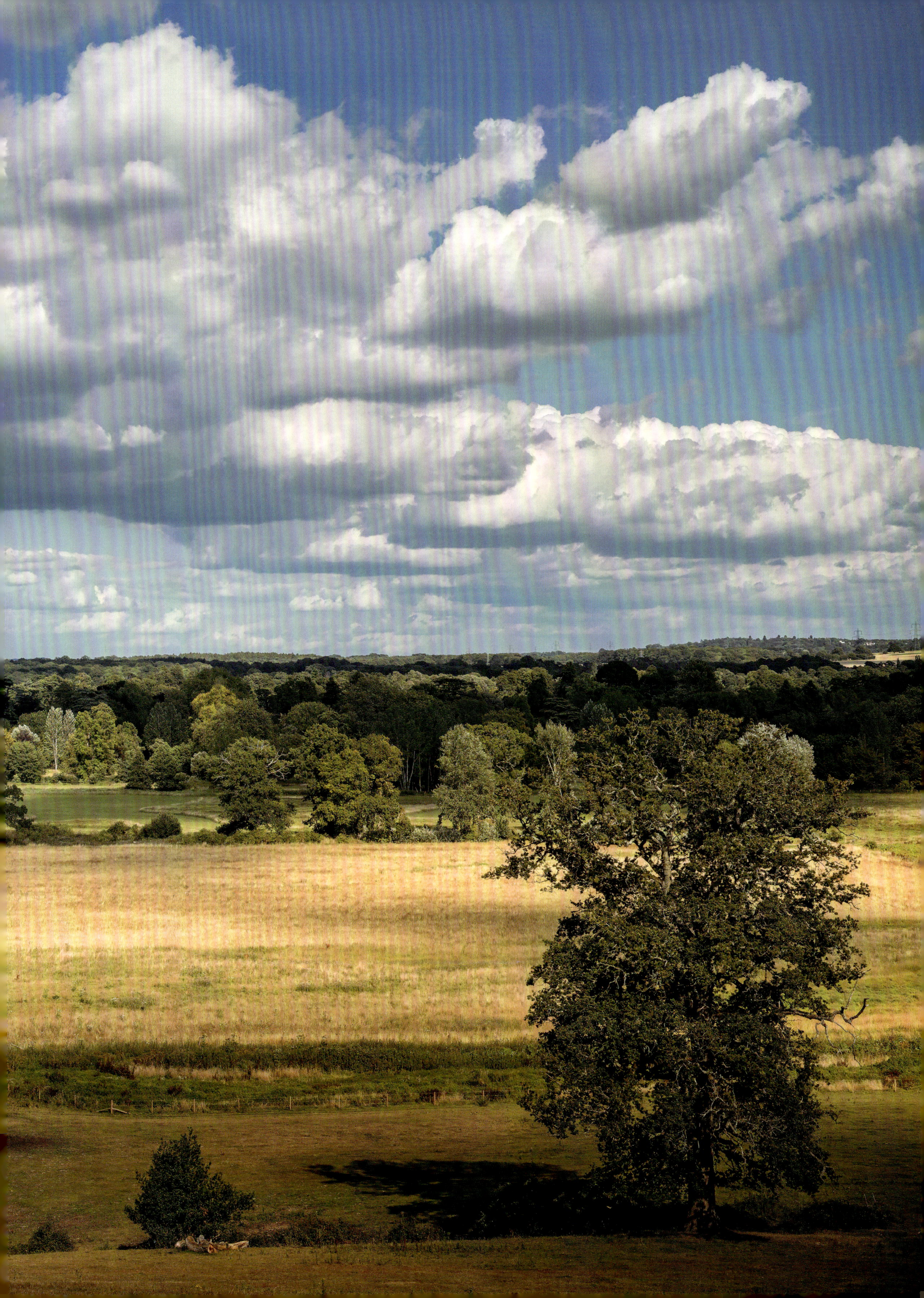

previous pages: The great stretch of level ground west of the river was given over to water-meadows. Brown's landscape simply continued in the foothills of the New Forest, on the far side of the meadows.

over this road, just on its south side, was the ancient Pauncefoot Manor. This had been acquired by the first Viscount Palmerston (1736–1757) in 1750, and Brown had retained it, as he did the Old Parsonage at Chatsworth and Fisheries Cottage at Blenheim. Framing this centerpiece, the horizon is broken by the apparently symmetrical hills, Pauncefoot and Spursholt. In practice these are not equidistant from the house, nor were they the same height. The northern hill, Spursholt, is further away, but its summit has been built up with a substantial platform. Pauncefoot Manor survives, though derogated to a farmhouse, but the lane is now a main road from Salisbury and so has been planted out. In the middle ground, the common meadows were in practice overlooked by the design.

Brown frequently incorporated flood-meadows into his designs. Like these at Broadlands they were generally "wet meadows," defined by the agricultural writer Thomas Hale as "within the reach of natural or artificial Over-flowings." They would have boundary banks and small open drains, "cuts" or "grips" but little else to control the water.[1] They were not complex, yet they gave pleasure: "When the [water-meadow] is at "work"... the entire surface (supposing the operation to be perfect) is covered with one continued sheet of living water; pushing evenly over every part, some inch or more deep. If the grass be very short, the water is seen; and has a beautiful as well as a profitable effect: if not, it steals unseen among the herbage; or

right: Brown addressed the neo-classical west front of the house with an apparently symmetrical composition, made up by these two hills on the horizon and the river in the foreground. The relationship between architecture and its unpromising setting is complete.

162 · CAPABILITY BROWN

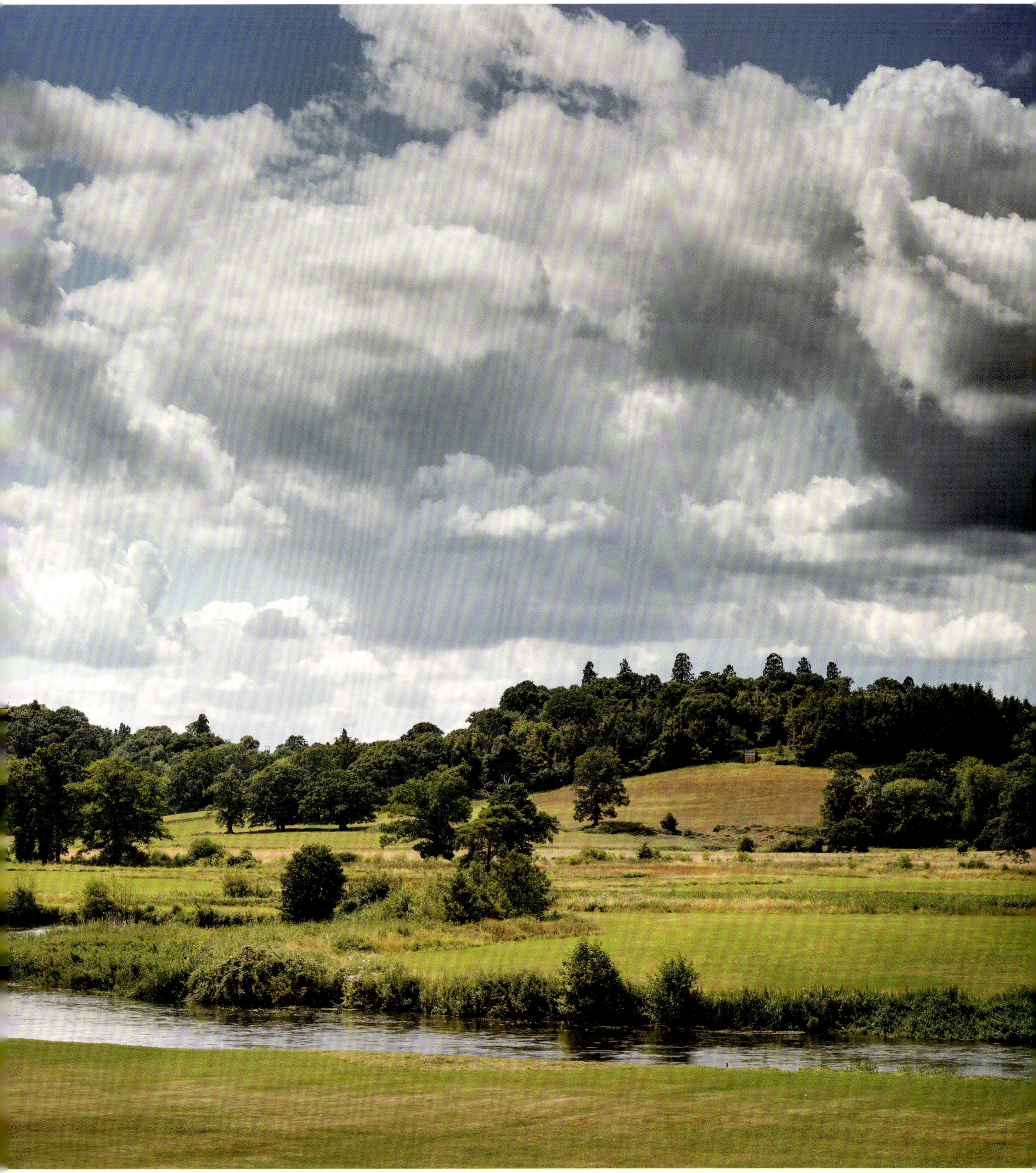

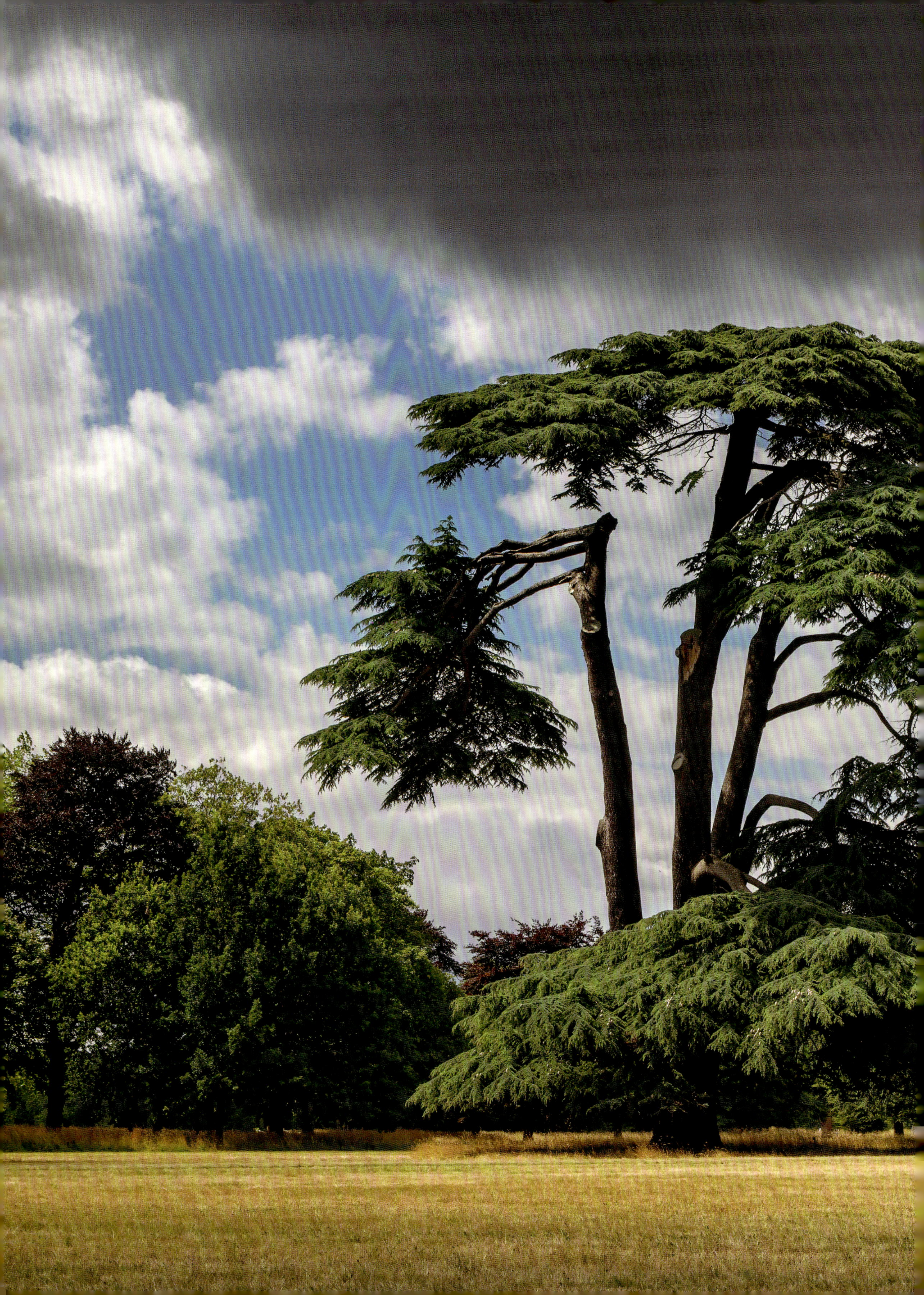

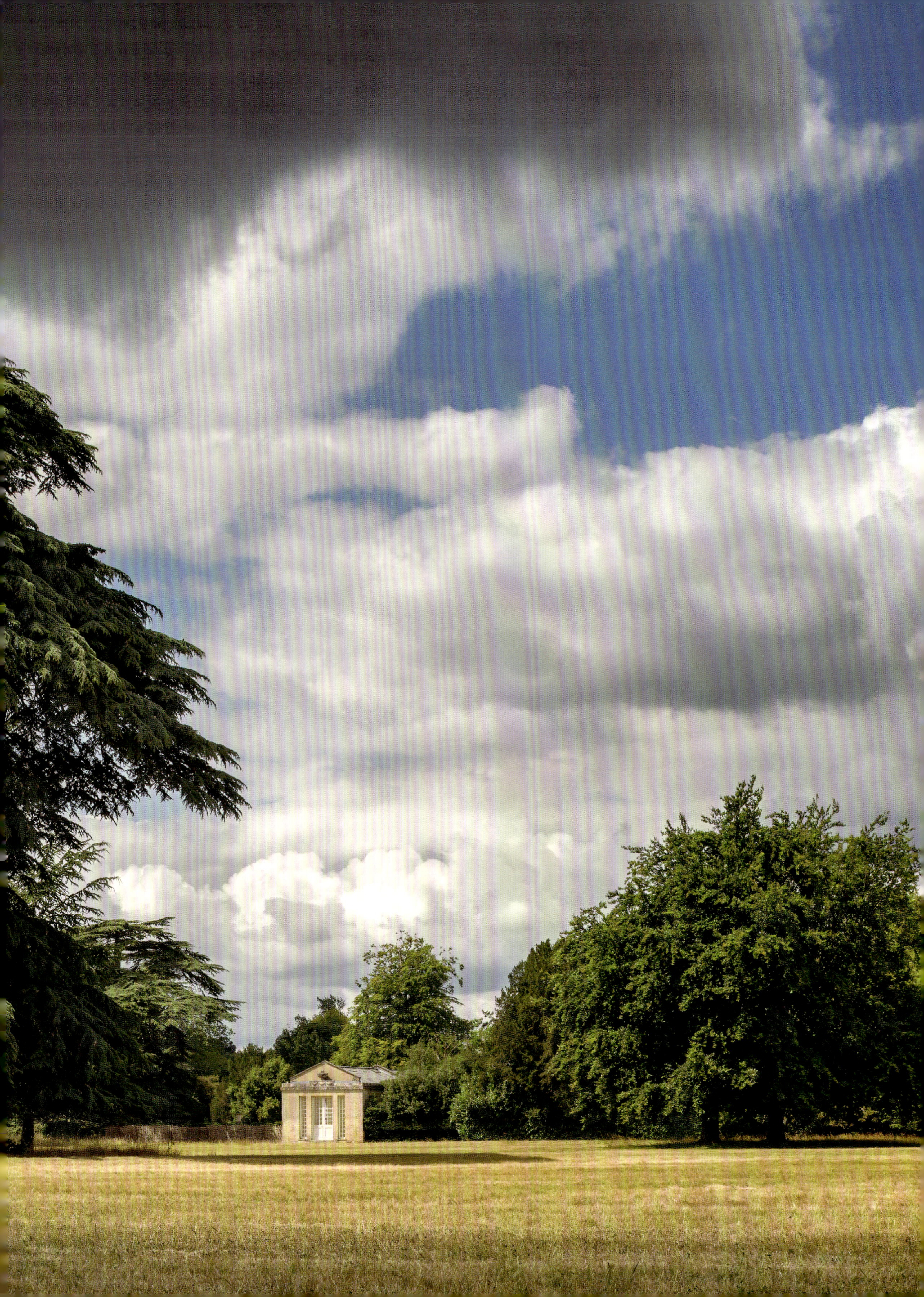

shows itself partially: it being impossible, in practice, to render the sheet, throughout, a uniform depth or thickness."[2] As Uvedale Price, one of Brown's fiercest critics at the end of the eighteenth century, commented, "Sometimes... it happens, that the bottoms of meadows and pastures subject to floods, are in parts bounded by natural banks against which the water lies, where it takes a very natural and varied form, and might easily from many points, and those not distant, be mistaken for part of a river."[3]

The water-meadows might temporarily have widened the river, and so added to its attraction, but Brown may have had no choice about them. The problem over which he is likely to have been more exercized was one he had already faced at Chatsworth and Burghley: a house that faced directly across the valley toward a hillside. Here, however, instead of thickening the trees to conceal the far slope and so emphasizing the course of the valley, he allowed them to climb the hill in patches, so that they appeared to appropriate an indefinite range of country and invite the more distant views toward the New Forest. He found the same solution elsewhere. At Fisherwick, Staffordshire, for example, where he was to begin work in 1768: "The embellishments have been effected by breaking the greensward of the rising ground, behind the house, with planting: the boldest and most beautiful part of it being judiciously preserved in lawn—scattered with groups and single trees. The further extremity is a continued grove;

previous pages: The Orangery at Broadlands was a double-fronted building. Brown would use orangeries to herald the approach of the house—as at Heveningham and Weston. above: Brownian drives rising up to the New Forest can be traced across the hill.

and the point toward the house is also planted; to hide the kitchen garden, and to give to this confined site, all the feature and expression it was capable of receiving ..."[4]

The River Test is still regarded as the finest chalk stream and trout fishing river in southern England, and the first viscount described it as "the main object of pleasure" at Broadlands.[5] Given his experience with water and drainage, it is not surprising that Brown made the river the central element of his design. Lady Palmerston referred in her correspondence to boat trips and haymaking, as well as to the popularity of the place after Brown had finished with it: "I am sure if you were a follower of the fashion you would hasten to England to see Broadlands for every day produces one and [as] many [as] three parties to view our beautiful domain."[6]

The New Forest was second only to the river as an attraction, and the intention behind the Brownian design was to provide a series of drives up into the higher ground of the forest. These drives ran up, via Pauncefoot Manor, to the platform on Spursholt Hill. This was the climactic point of the design, providing an unexpected and open prospect view to the shipping on Southampton Water ten miles away, and hanging over the whole town of Romsey and its abbey. Such long-distant prospects were regarded as vulgar by eighteenth century *cognoscenti*, such as the poet Thomas Gray: "I find all points that are much elevated, spoil the beauty of the valley, and make its

*above: Pauncefoot Manor, defiantly ancient in its character
and vernacular in its architecture, is dwarfed by Romsey Abbey beyond in the view from Spursholt Hill.
overleaf: Broadlands' west lawn is built in two planes, to control views from the house to the River Test.*

BROADLANDS · 167

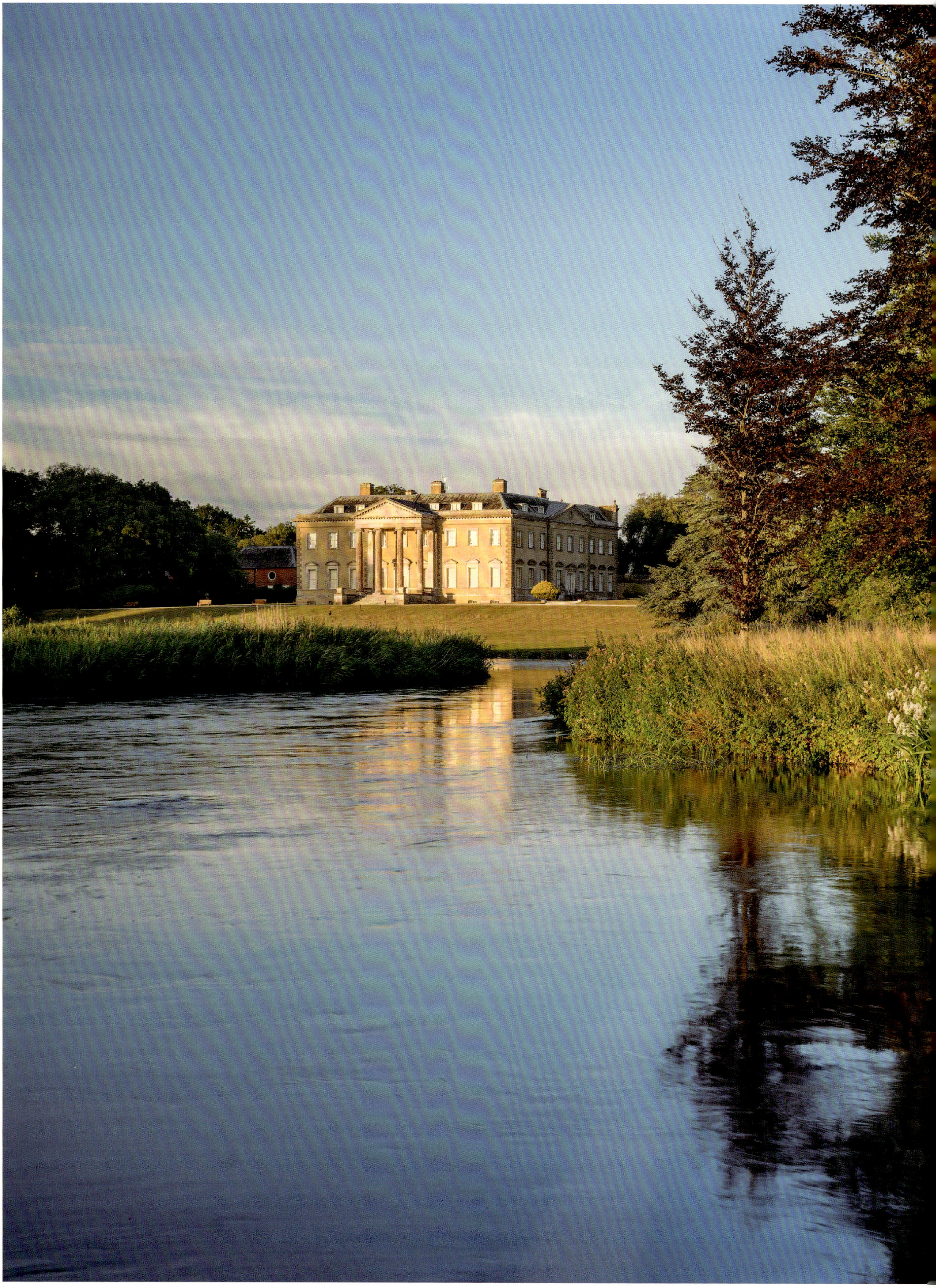

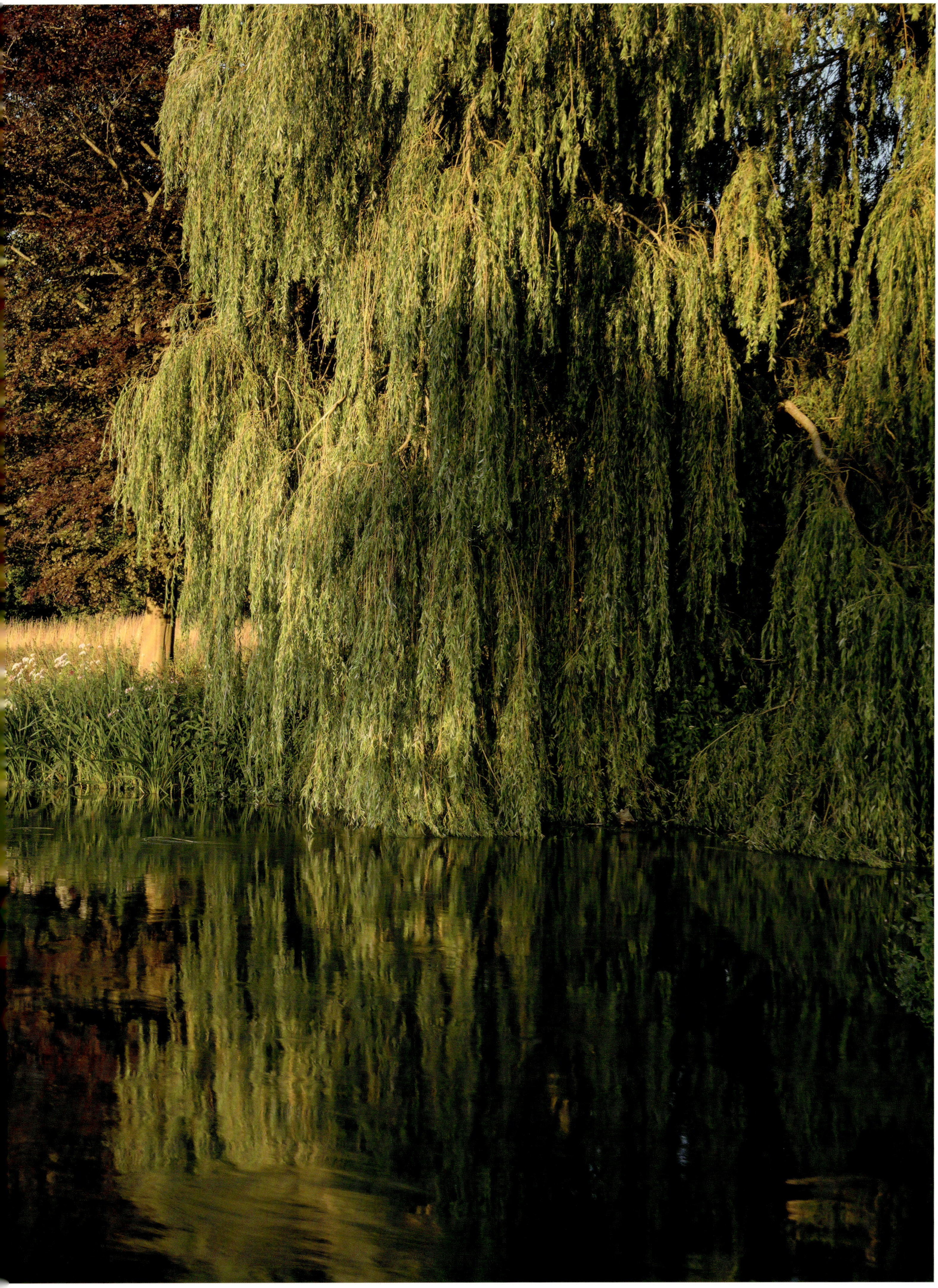

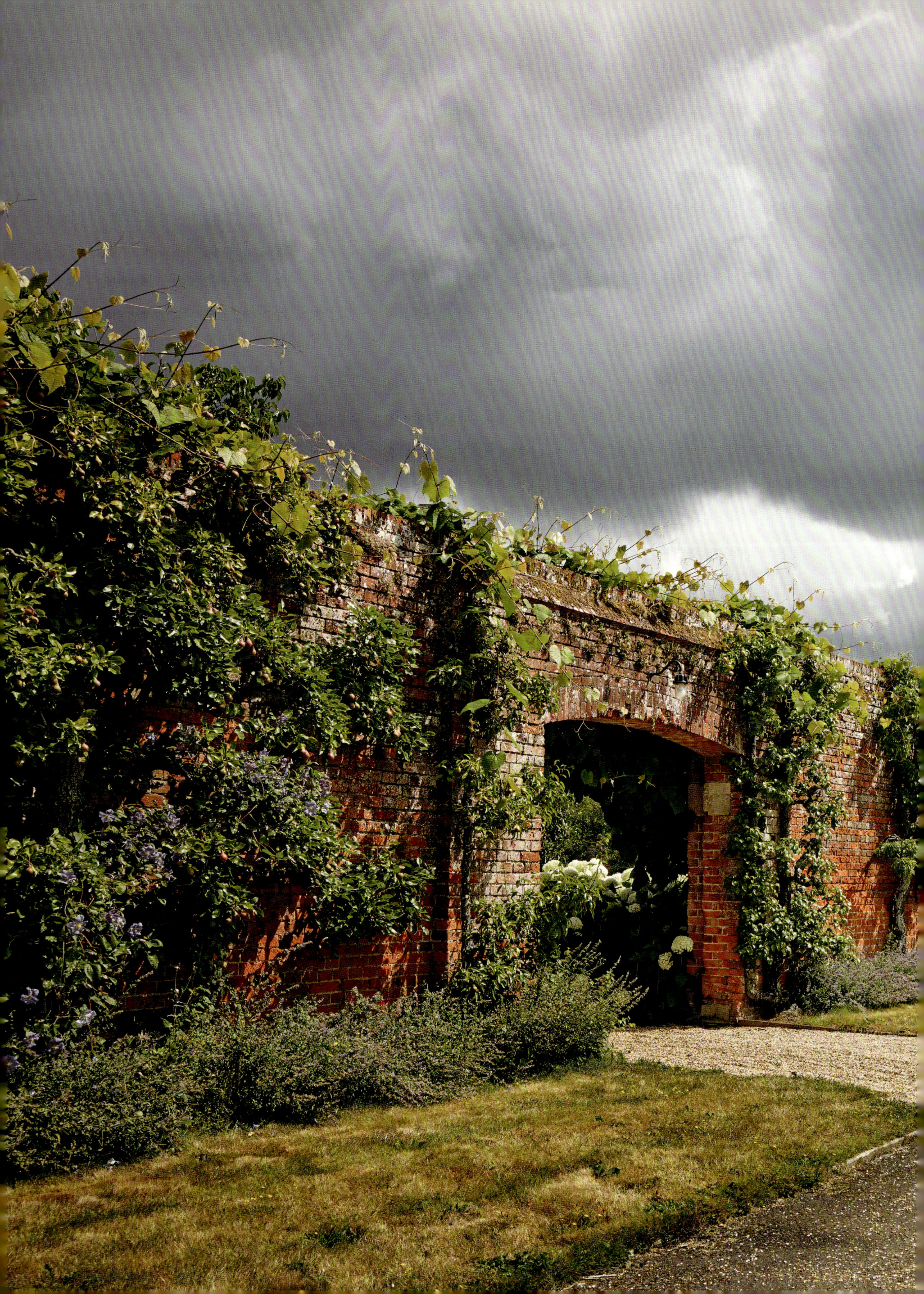

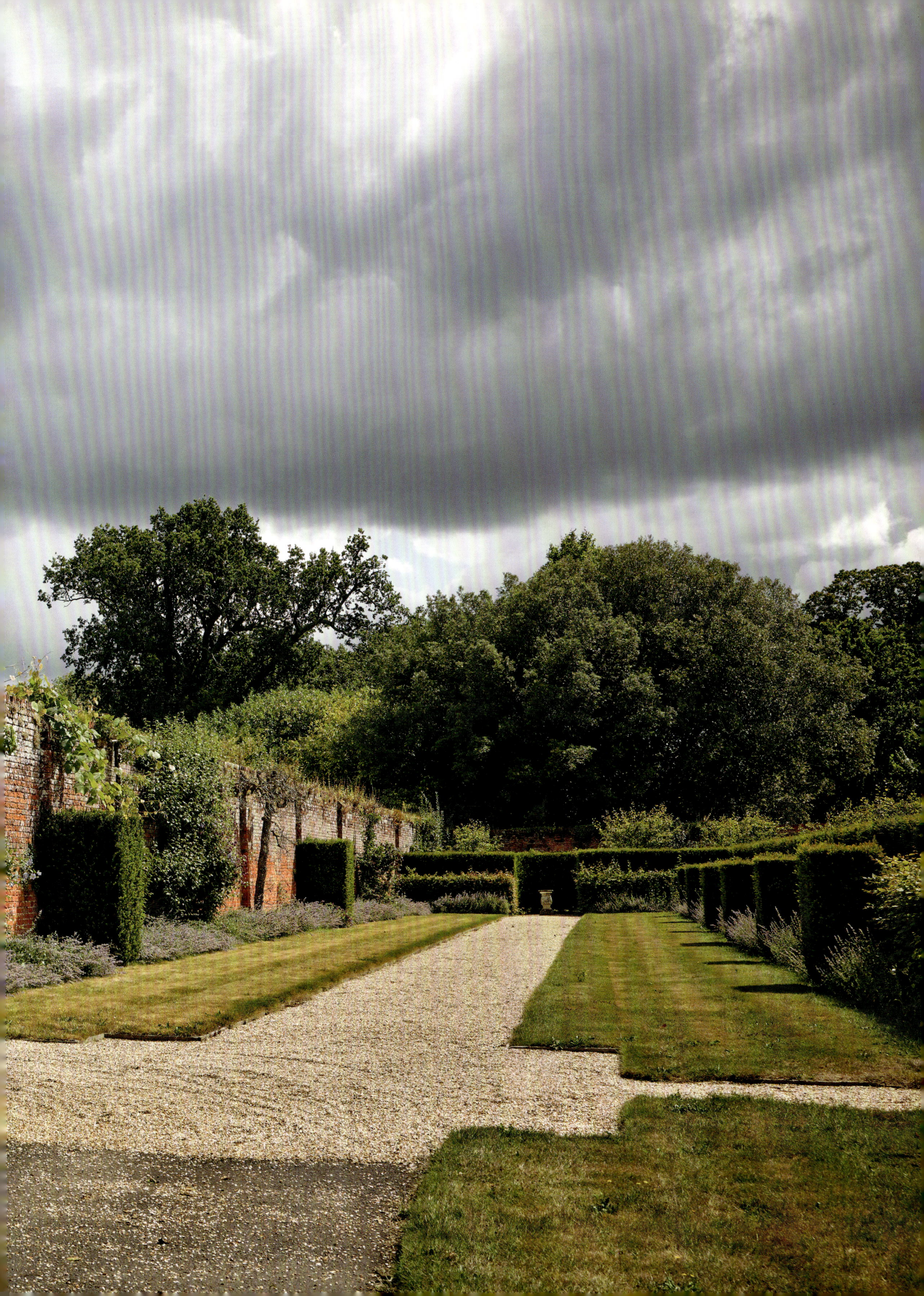

Turnpike Road to Winchester.
Mill-bridge Street
Bell Street
Ben. Hooper.
Benj. Hooper.
Jno Fleming Esq.
Corporation.
Corporation.
River Test.
EASTGROVE
Samuel Wood Esq.
Jno Fleming Esq.
Jno. Figes.
Sir C. Mill.
COMMON WALLDRON
Benj. Figes.
Fredk. Breton Esq.
Fredk. Breton Esq.
Fredk. Breton Esq.
Fredk. Breton Esq.
THE ANDOVER CANAL
Lock.
Sir C. Mill.
Wilt. Fletcher Esq.
Jno Fleming Esq.
Ashfield Green.
Jno White.
Will. Fletcher Esq.
Lee Charity.

parts, which are not large, look poor and diminutive."[7] However, Uvedale Price came to revise his early hostility to the "prospect hunter," confessing that "If I do despise prospects, I am constantly acting against my inclination... In my own place I have three distinct prospects—bird's eye views seen from high hills—of which I am not a little proud, and to which I carry all my guests of every description."[8] Brown would have agreed with Price; he was never hostile to prospects or to anything that could add variety to a landscape.

Although the view west may be regarded as Brown's greatest success at Broadlands, his commission was centered on a rebuilding of the house, which he subcontracted to his son-in-law Henry Holland. This was only one of a number of architectural interventions. Brown may have rebuilt the west front of the Orangery, converted the Dairy, and also doubled the size of the walled garden. His summary of the work he had done between March 1766 and early 1779, in a letter to the second viscount in 1779, emphasized the built elements: "kitchen garden, stores, dairy yard, greenhouse, repairs at Spursholt Farm or the greater part of it, some small matter done to the building in the wood, all nurserymen's bills, the whole house inside and out, the additional offices and the repairs to the old offices."

Walled gardens are pleasant places to be. It is not only the protection that they afford in bad weather, and the wonderful warmth they hold in on good days at the start and end of the gardening year,[9] there is an aesthetic pleasure, too, in a well-ordered onion bed,[10] and besides vegetables, it was often here that the cut flowers for the house were grown. Wherever possible, therefore, the walled garden was made the destination and high point of the circuit walk, uniting "the utmost simplicity with the greatest neatness,"[11] and as Humphry Repton said: "The Kitchen garden... is always interesting in the spring by its blossoms and early vegetation, and in autumn by its fruits."[12] After all, the Duchess of Devonshire was ready to wear a kitchen garden on her head when "very early in spring, when those vegetables were small, and extremely dear, she came in a head-dress ornamented with real carrots and turnips."[13]

Brown had a reputation for moving these gardens away from the house,[14] but this is unfounded, as the garden at Broadlands shows. It is true, however, that it was screened with planting and tucked out of sight off the corner of the house, so as not to obstruct the views. The place is a fine example of making something great out of not very much. One would like to know whether the Palmerstons had given Brown a free hand, for it seems possible that at this stage in his career he was trusted to make his own decisions.

previous pages: The south end of the walled garden is only a short walk from the house.
opposite: The Broadlands estate in 1787. The water-meadows are on the left side of this detail from the plan. Brown has turned the avenue on the east side of the house into an alternating set of clumps.

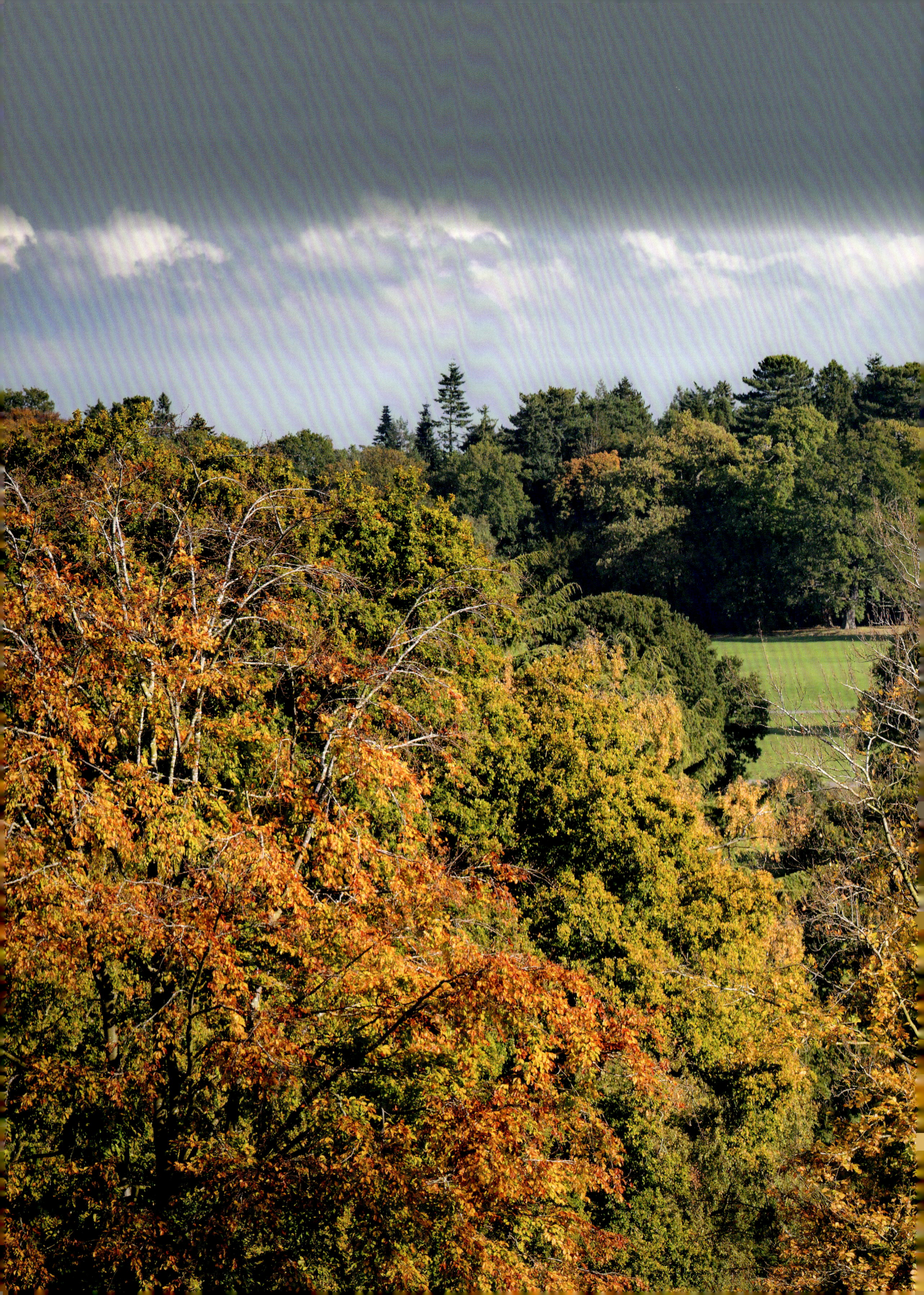

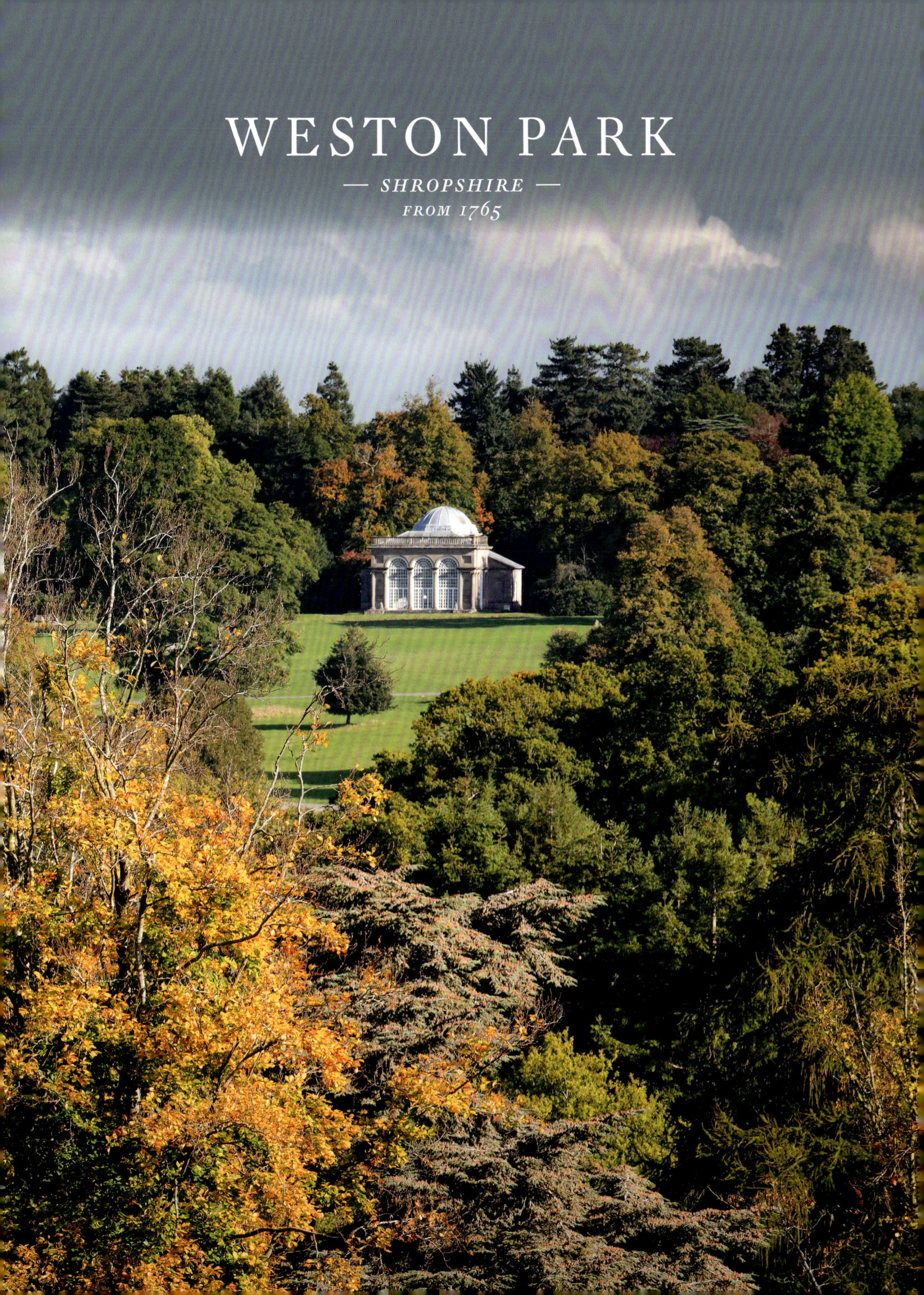

WESTON PARK

— SHROPSHIRE —
FROM 1765

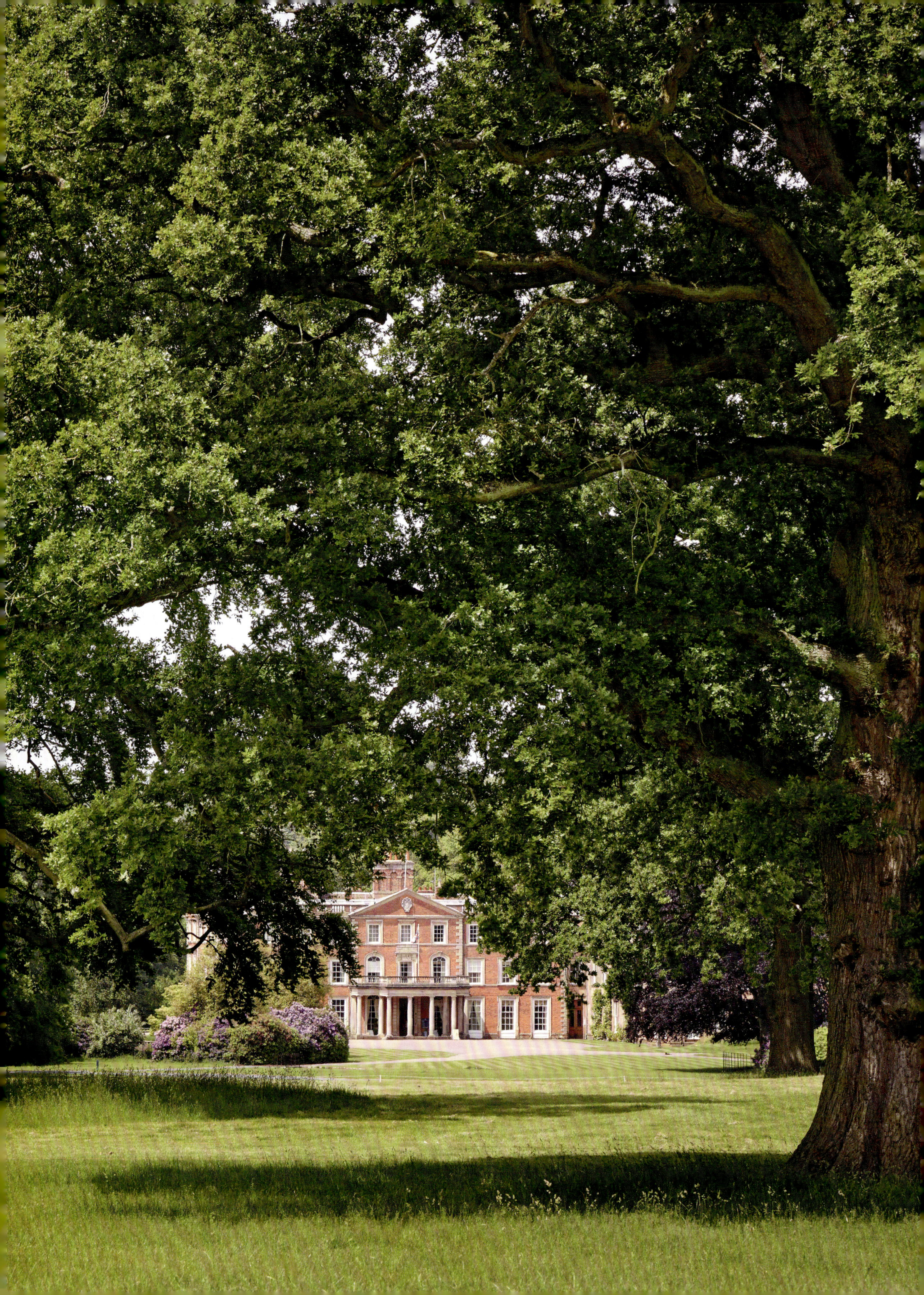

— CHAPTER TEN —

WESTON PARK

Weston was another challenging site. Brown's client, Sir Henry Bridgeman (1725–1800), inherited the estate in 1763 and had taken Brown on within two years, but after 1768, when Brown's second contract was completed, he turned to Joseph Doody, a local man, to continue the work. So, Brown did not have much time to lay the foundations of his design, nor did he have a great deal of space: any expansion of the landscape to the north being prevented by Watling Street, the old Roman road which runs from east to west within 250 meters of the hall.

To the south the hall looked out over gently falling ground with two ancient parks, one for red and one for fallow, licensed in 1346, running out to the southeast. The view was terminated by the distant ridge of Tong Knoll, outside the estate, though Brown was also working at the time with the owner, George Durant I, at Tong Park immediately beyond. To the west an extension of the parkland to Mill Lane was possible, and this is indicated on the plan of proposals that Brown drew up for his first contract. Until at least 1775, Old Park, to the southeast, remained separate, but Weston Park, off the south front of the hall was created in the 1760s, presumably with advice from Brown, and eventually amounting to 1,000 acres.

Brown's intervention at Weston was short-lived, but that is not necessarily a bad thing for a designer. The two contract documents that he signed survive, as well as his plan for the first of them, so we have an unusually good idea of his response to the landscape, which was, as with Broadlands, largely to leave the parkland on the open valley floor, but this time to throw the emphasis on the pleasure ground (perhaps because Sir Henry did not own Tong Knoll). This was no simple pleasure ground, but a lengthy promenade of some 1,300 meters along the north side of the landscape. It took in some new incidents (at one end the primitive grotto, Pendrill's Cave, said to have been the home of a mendicant priest of that name, and at the other, the neoclassical scenes around the domed Temple of Diana). It also reworked others from the existing garden: a Bowling Green, the Fountain Pool, and the East Avenue, for example, which survives as a row of sweet chestnuts near the Temple.

previous pages: The Temple of Diana (also known as the Orangery) stands in the position for which Brown proposed a menagerie.
opposite: Weston Park, built in 1671.

Even this documentation does not give us anything like a complete picture of what was done. We might choose to believe that Brown did discuss the development of the whole landscape with Sir Henry, and his pleasure ground would not make sense if the extension of the park to the west had not been agreed on. We may not, therefore, need to strive too hard to distinguish Brown from Doody, or what Brown actually did from what is merely Brownian.

However, we can see what a successful treatment of the topography Brown provided. It is one that he might have adopted with great success in the similar circumstances of Broadlands. By establishing this lengthy woodland garden on each side of the hall, he provided the house with a backdrop, screened out Watling Street, and enabled the park itself to be seen from numerous different points, as though from a gallery. This might be regarded as the reverse of the treatment that he provided for Burghley, where the house remains the main point of focus and the valley side south of the lake, opposite the house, is heavily planted. Here, by planting on the same side as the hall, he enabled the detail of the design of the park to weigh less heavily in the landscape: trees were to come and go, views to come and go in the foreground, as one made one's way from Pendrill's Cave to the Temple of Diana, and he used trees, shrubs, and carefully molded earthworks to create that effect. Thus the two pleasure grounds may be regarded as opposites. Pendrill's Cave offers a walk west of the house from light into dark; the open lawns giving onto the park and ornamented perhaps with studs of annual flowers end in a dark subterranean cave that faces away from the park and into a stone wall. This setting can only make sense if one climbs the slope to the top of this wall—then the cave makes the foreground to a dim view south, shrouded still and crowded with ancient yew trees. One can find a similar trick at Ansley, Warwickshire, which is also attributed to Brown, but it is a rarity in garden design.

On the other hand the walk east, to the Temple of Diana, begins with a dark tunnel and continues as a close walk, thickly planted with shrubs and with no views out, ending at the back door of the Temple, through which one passes to the Orangery, where by

above: With their tall clean trunks and the light shade they cast, it seems likely that when Brown saved this row of sweet chestnuts from the East Avenue he expected to embed them into a grove. opposite: Pendrill's Cave faces north, away from the parkland.

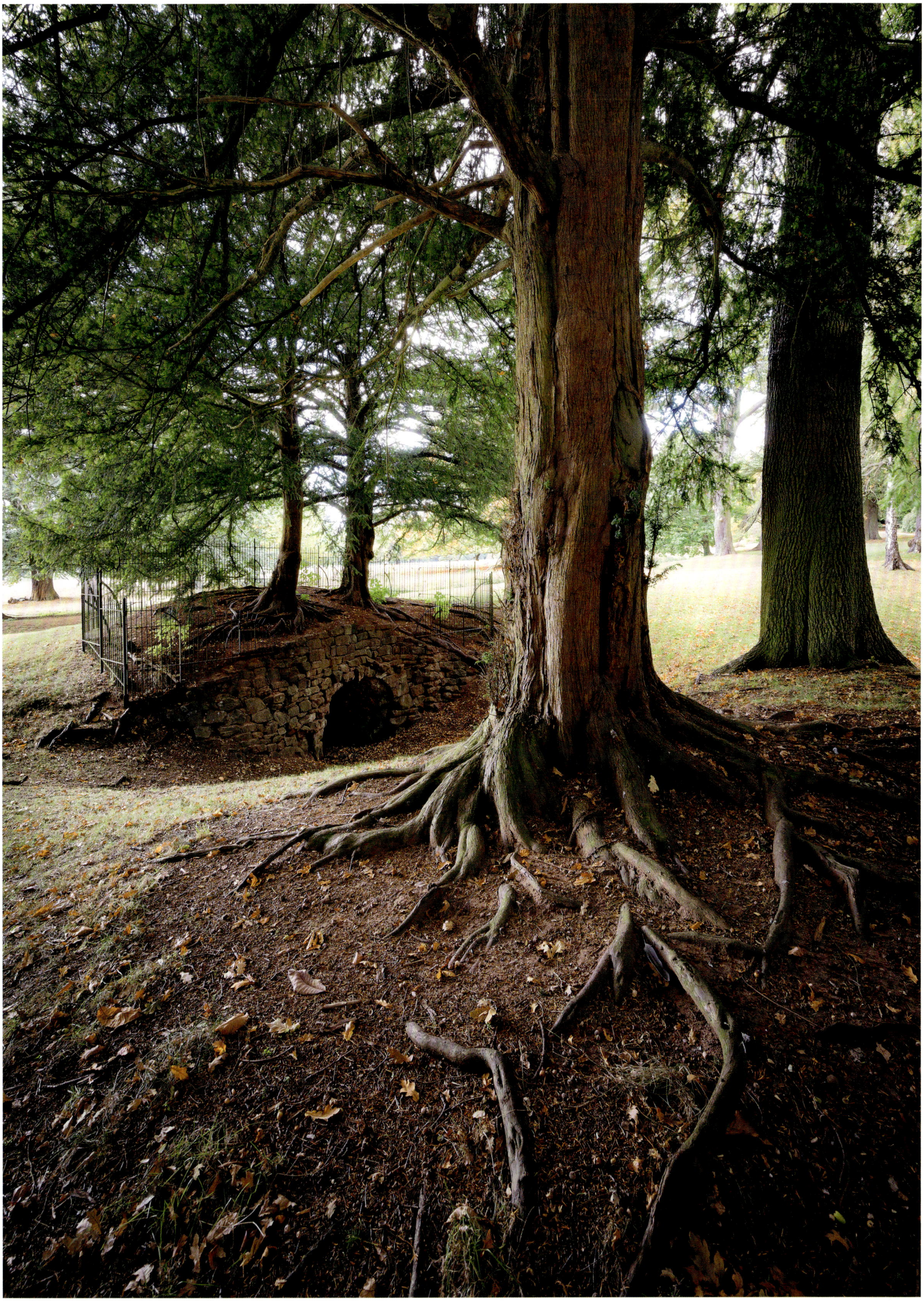

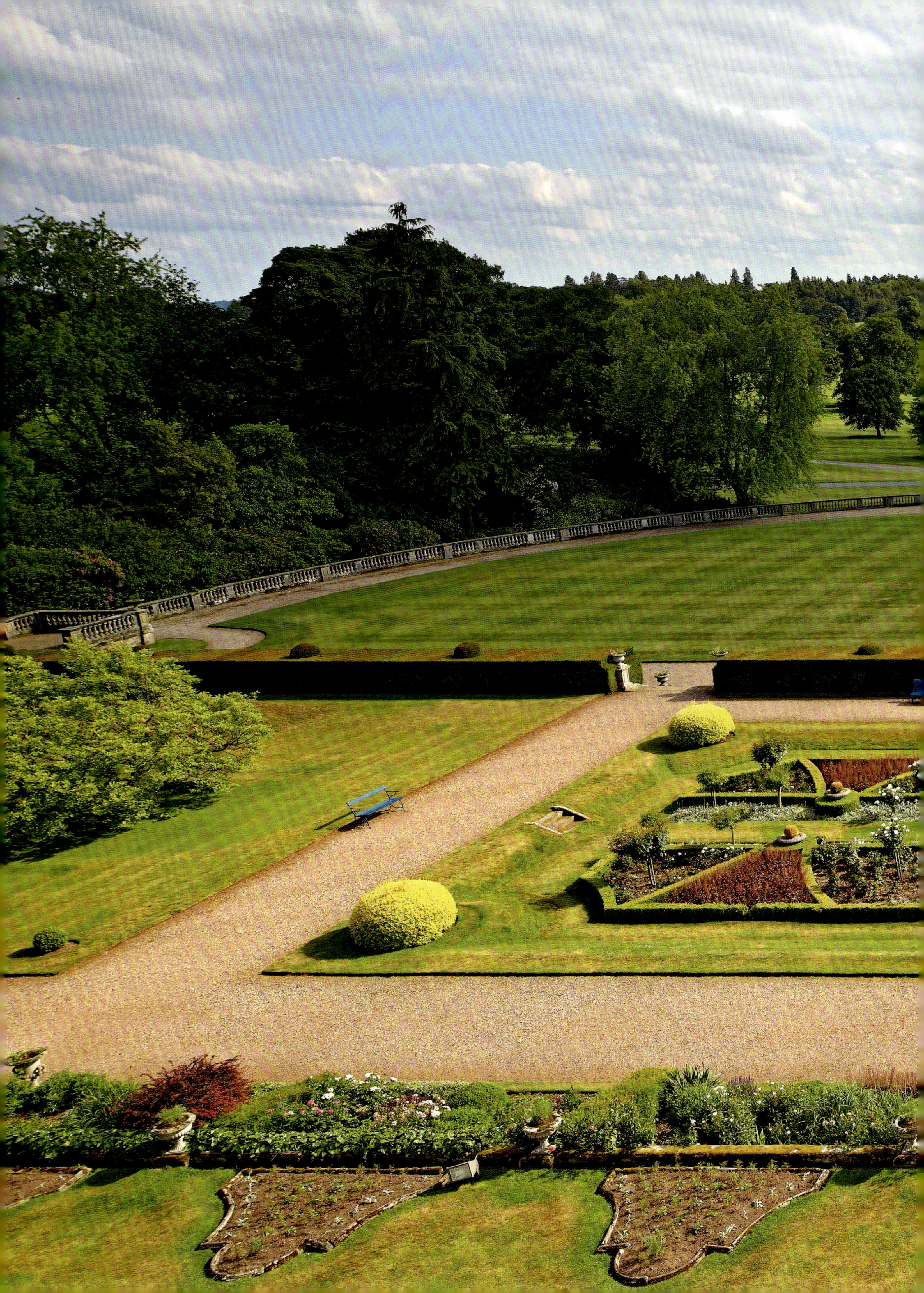

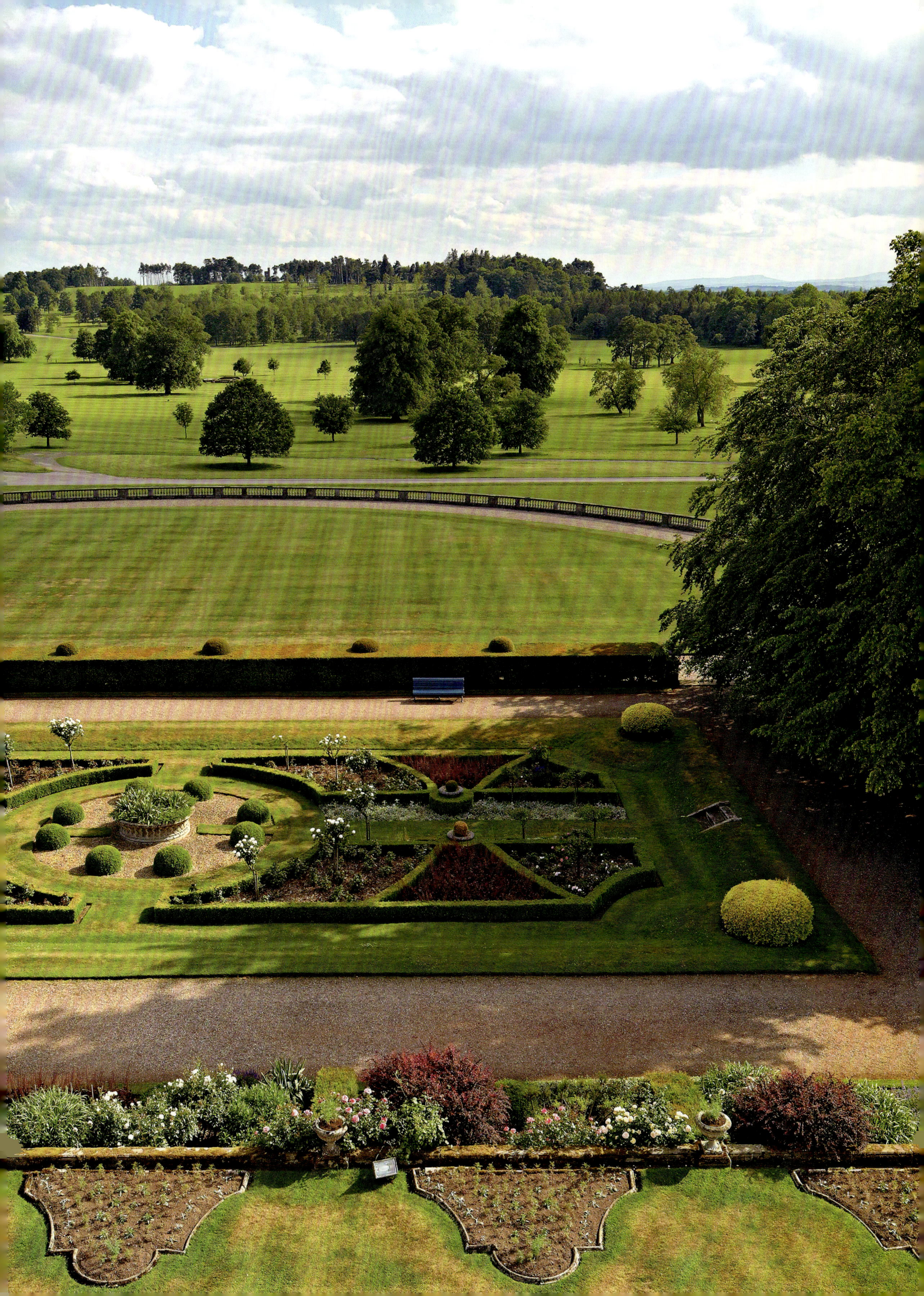

182 · CAPABILITY BROWN

previous pages: The house at Weston looks directly out at the ridge of Tong Knoll.

contrast the light is blinding and the views over the park are wide and open.

The most elaborate element of the whole garden lay at the back of the multi-purpose Temple of Diana (1770), described by its architect, James Paine:

> *The ovalar room... faces south, and was originally intended for a green-house, and consequently to be inclosed with glass; the circular room in the centre of the north front... is used as a tea room; the octagon room... is used for musick; and the opposite room... is the habitation of the dairy woman. Underneath these rooms, are apartments arched with stone, and used as dairies and for other purposes appertaining thereto. Over the dairy woman's room is contrived within the roof, a sleeping room and over the circular room is an exceeding good bed chamber.*

So far as Brown was concerned in 1768, however, it was a menagerie. He designed one like it for Coombe Abbey, and the domed octagon that both buildings have is reminiscent of the Grande Menagerie at Versailles.

Stowe, Wotton, Petworth, Burghley, Blenheim, and Milton Abbey all had menageries, and Brown often accommodated them in his designs. They combined gardening with zoo-keeping (though the animals were very often birds); they were always enclosed and often closed to visitors. They would always include a pool, a place to sit, and exotic planting. We have already seen Brown's recommendation for flowering shrubs at Petworth, and the agriculturist and land agent William Marshall exclaimed of the aviary at Enville: "exotic birds are apt accompaniments to exotic plants; and a shrubery, rather than a seques-

left: Brown was known for his tunnels. This one allowed the walk to pass to the Temple of Diana uninterrupted by traffic on the road which ran above.

WESTON PARK · 183

above: The Orangery, or "ovalar room,"
as it was described by its architect, James Paine.
opposite: The Circular Room.

overleaf: The pool was extended after Brown's death and Paine's Bridge was built to bring the approach across it; the seat was added in 1938. These embellishments were not anticipated in the only Brown plan that survives at Weston.

186 · CAPABILITY BROWN

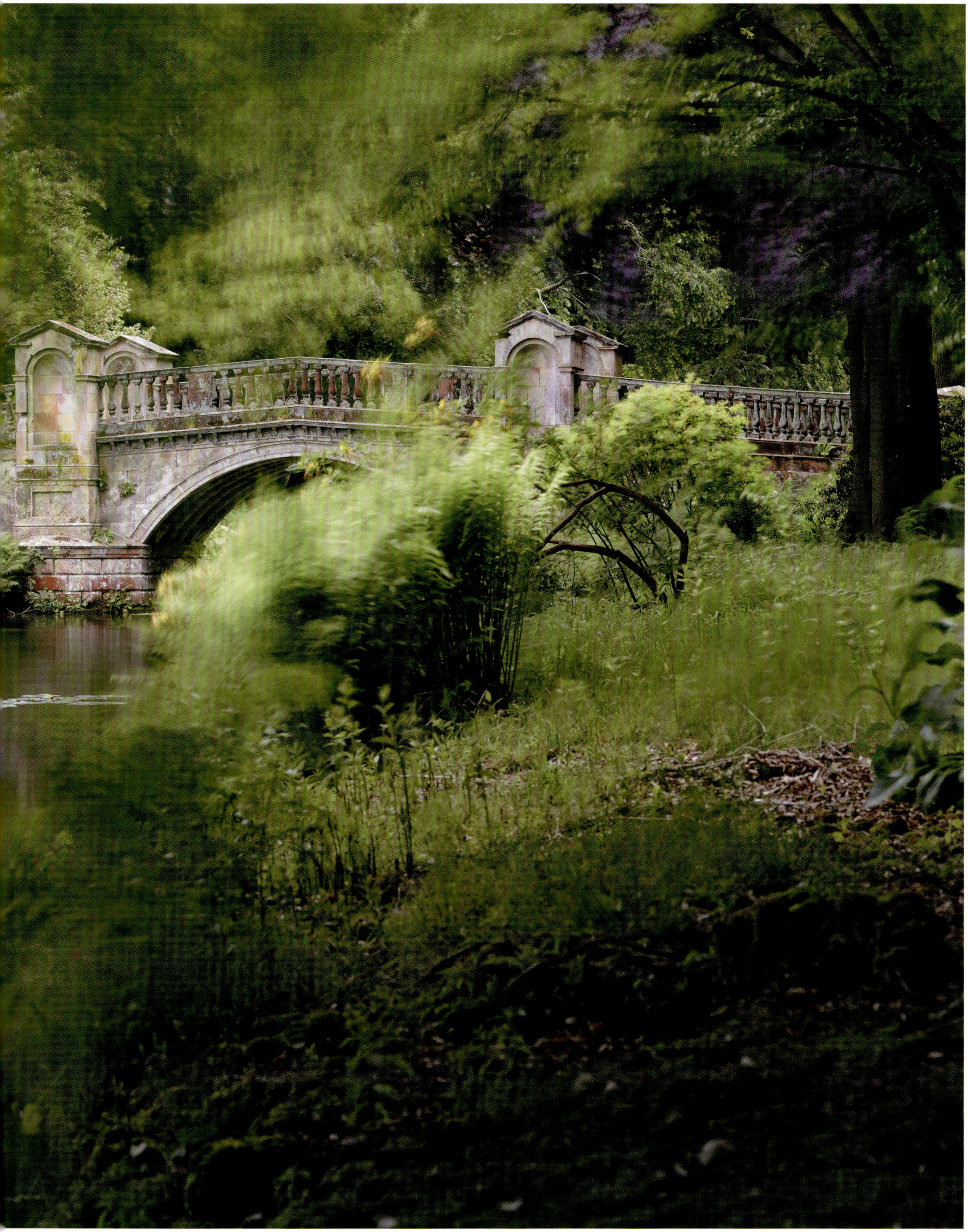

tered dell, seems to be the most natural situation for an aviary."[1]

The artist William Hayes recorded the birds of Sir Henry and Lady Bridgeman's aviary in a series of paintings (1762–1763), and, in fact, in Brown's day pleasure grounds, no less than parks, were expected to be full of animals. The accounts for Wycombe Abbey's volary record constant purchases of songbirds (blackbirds, larks, goldfinches, linnets, greenfinches, bullfinches, "green" and "brown" birds (1752–1755); then a period (1757–1759) in which additional exotic birds (Canada Goose, "sea Gul," golden pheasants, "whisling ducks," "King Bird," and a turkey) were purchased. The idea was to enchant the Baron d'Haussez in the nineteenth century, even when shooting and hunting had really begun to have an influence on landscape design: "Sometimes, at the whistle of a keeper, hundreds of guinea-hens, of gold or silver pheasants, of peacocks, of pigeons of the rarest species, come to mingle the brilliant tints of their colours with those of the flowers which embellish these favourite retreats, and impart to them a life and motion, the charms of which it would be difficult to define."[2]

Indeed, English gardens were known abroad for their birdsong.[3] Lord Temple had his "nightingale Bench" in the Elysian Fields at Stowe, sitting on it long enough after sunset to give himself "a slight feverish Cold."[4] The poet William Shenstone talked to his friend Richard Jago of "planting hollies, pyracanthas, and other berry-bearing greens, to attract those Blackbirds,"[5] and there was a fashion for planting "a more than common quantity of [Bird cherries], that they may have these feathered songsters in greater plenty." Strange to say, hares would also be encouraged: "how peculiarly delightful the sequestered lawn, while the hare is present!"[6] and, noted by the antiquary John Loveday, "hare in abundance abt ye woody Garden" at Ingestre by 1732.[7] Even in the nineteenth century they remained an enlivening incident on the

above: The ha-ha rises up and performs as a terrace where it crosses in front of the temple.

188 · CAPABILITY BROWN

lawn outside the library at Stourhead: "You see every morning a hundred pheasants, intermixed with hares, playing their gambols with a confidence and familiarity that is delightful... there is no satiety, and you fancy yourself in a better world."[8] We should always expect animals in pleasure grounds, and consequently these had to be organized so as to make it easy to protect the plants from them—apparently at Weston the enclosures fanned out around the north side of the Temple, though here the picture is confused because although there is a bill for the replacement of posts and nets in 1771 (presumably for the enclosures), the menagerie had been converted to a Dairy by the end of the century, when the pool was extended to the east and decorated with Paine's Bridge (designed by James Paine and completed in 1793) and with the Swiss Cottage (first recorded in 1806).

One should not overlook other work by Brown either. He may also have designed the village street, and this is the moment to consider the view from the hall to Tong Knoll. Even though Sir Henry did not own the knoll at the time, its west face, directly in front of the hall, had been quarried and was made good at a much steeper gradient. The dramatic effect of such steep falls of ground was also recognized in the view from the west front at Milton Abbey House, and that from the saloon at Wardour, and this is by no means the only quarry to be worked directly in front of the house—the Concave at Petworth and the gravel pits at Berrington are two further examples.

It is pleasing to think that the quarries from which the stone was taken for Brown's ha-has, buildings, and roads were themselves to become features in the landscape (the current Knoll Tower which now dominates Tong Knoll was not built until 1883, though it replaced an earlier building put up by George Durant I of Tong to commemorate his successful divorce; this was blown up by his outraged sons on the night of his death in 1780).

above: The walled gardens and yards occupy the space between the back of the house and Watling Street. The circuit of the pleasure ground took them in on the return from Pendrill's Cave.

WESTON PARK · 189

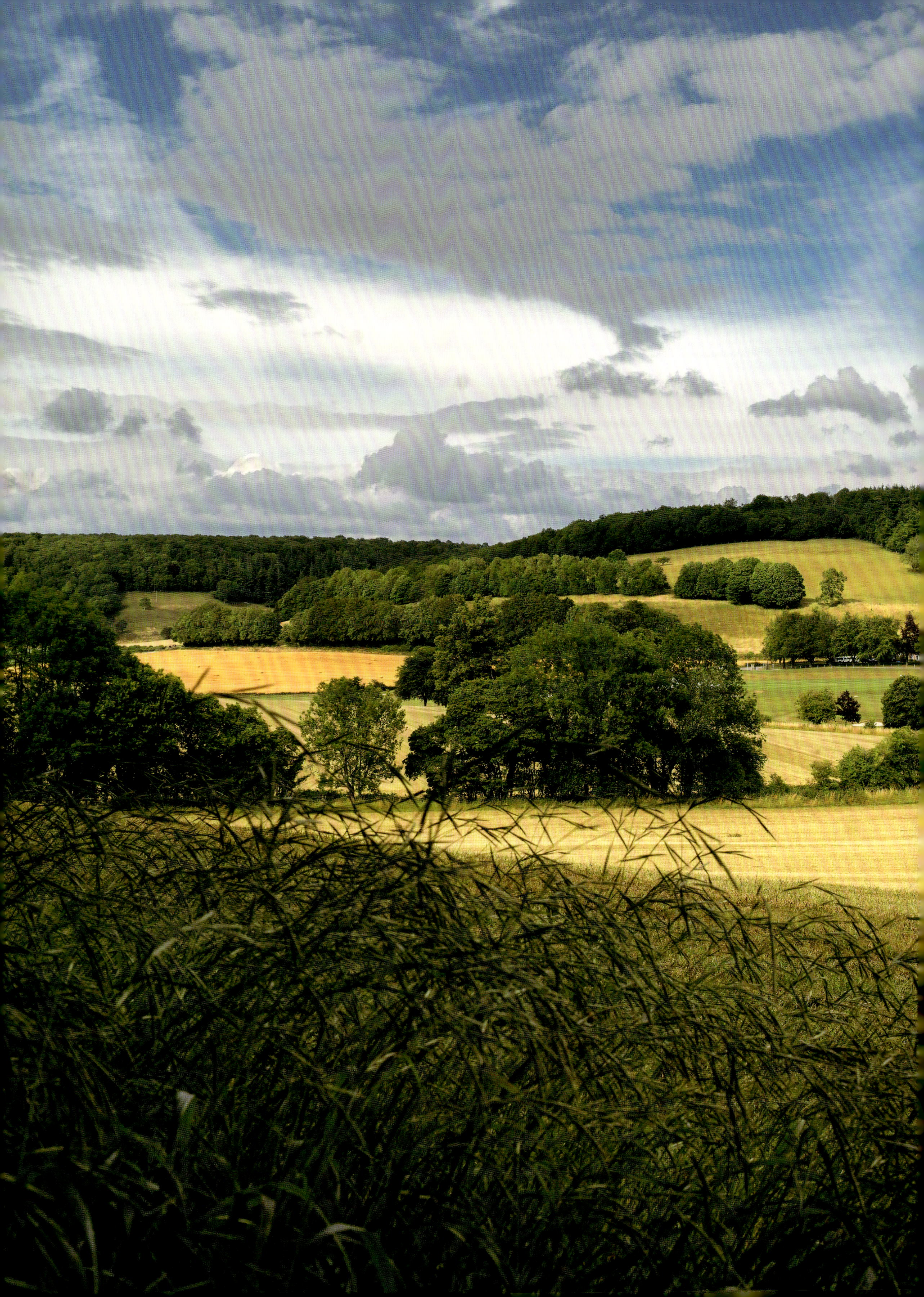

MILTON ABBEY
— DORSET —
FROM 1763

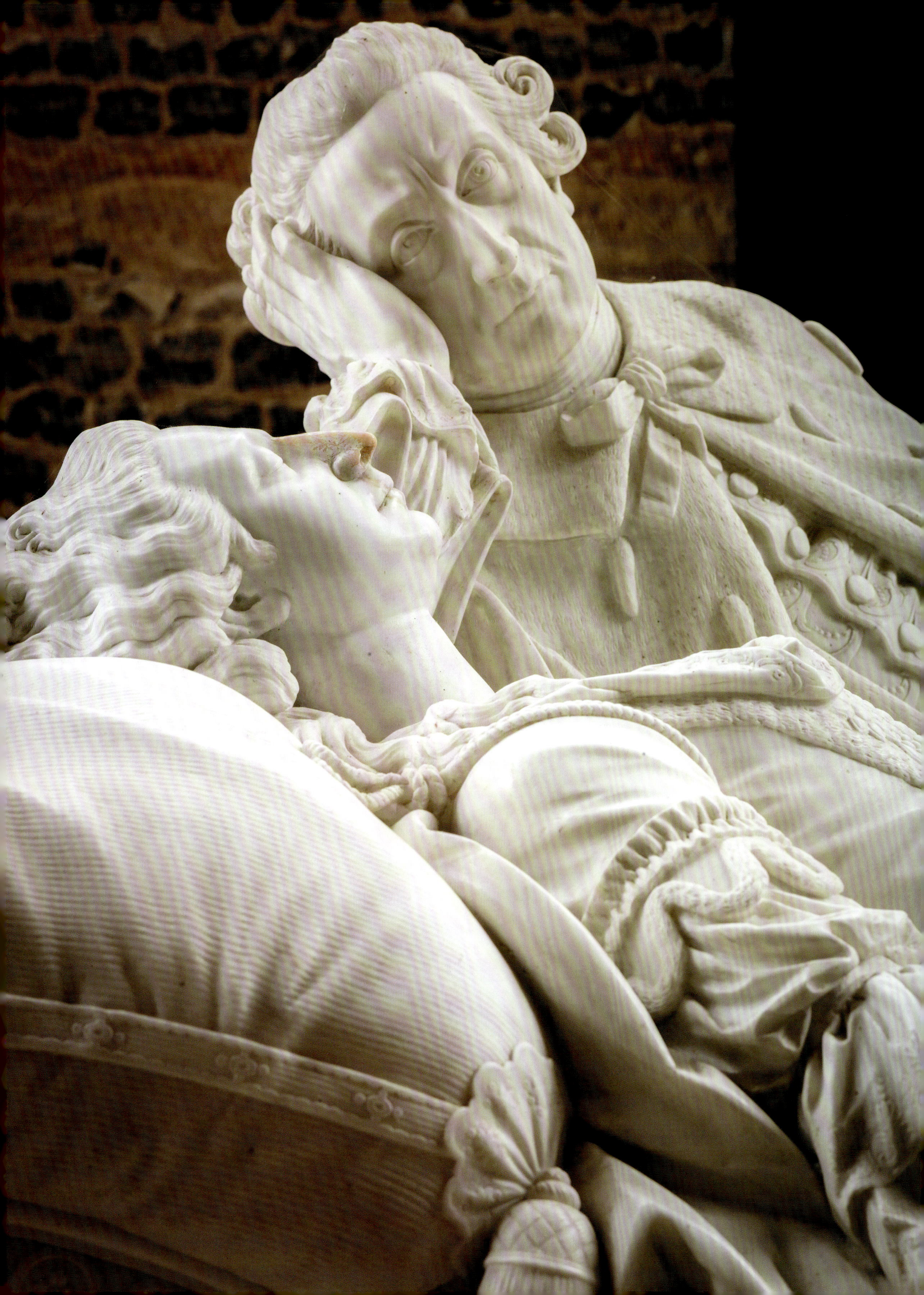

— CHAPTER ELEVEN —

MILTON ABBEY

To judge from his own account book Brown was paid about £4,000 for a series of four contracts at Milton Abbey, running from 1763 until December 1782, and his work there can be divided into two substantial campaigns. First, in the 1760s, the late medieval Milton Park was planted as woodland, and the Blandford Approach was put in, with the whole of the Delcombe Valley landscape, which winds up north of the abbey to Bulbarrow Hill.

His client, Joseph Damer (1718–1798), having acquired the estate in 1752, immediately began to rebuild the house. Ten years later he was elevated to the English peerage as Lord Milton, and was ready to plunge his limitless resources into the creation of his demesne. His ambition may have released something in Brown, whose confidence had already been boosted by Blenheim and his royal commission. "He writes Launcelot Brown, Esquire, *en titre d'office*; please to consider, he shares the private hours of the King, dines familiarly with his neighbour of Sion, and sits down at all the tables of the House of Lords and c." In short, as William Pitt the Elder advised Lady Stanhope: "The character of my friend's dignity must not be omitted."[1] Thus, the great principal approach to the abbey was on the same scale as the long approaches at Petworth and Chatsworth, running for six miles, "chiefly through [Damer's] vast woods" (i.e., Milton Park Wood), from Blandford Forum; and when he visited in 1771, the agriculturist Arthur Young noted that "all the home grounds are to be walled in, which will be a circuit of 16 miles half of which are done; and the tops of the hills all planted with a great variety of trees, to the amount of 500 acres." When one thinks that Blenheim's wall is only just over eight miles long, the scale of the undertaking becomes clear.

Arthur Young was equally overwhelmed by this stupendous reach of grass and woods up Delcombe:

... a remarkable winding valley, three miles long, surrounded on every side by hills, whose variety is very great. It is all lawn; and, as the surface has many fine swells, and other gentle inequalities, the effect is everywhere beautiful. The hills, on the [west] side are thickly covered with wood,

previous pages: Milton Abbey from the Ruins.
opposite: The memorial, designed by Robert Adam, commemorates Lady Caroline Damer, who died in 1775.

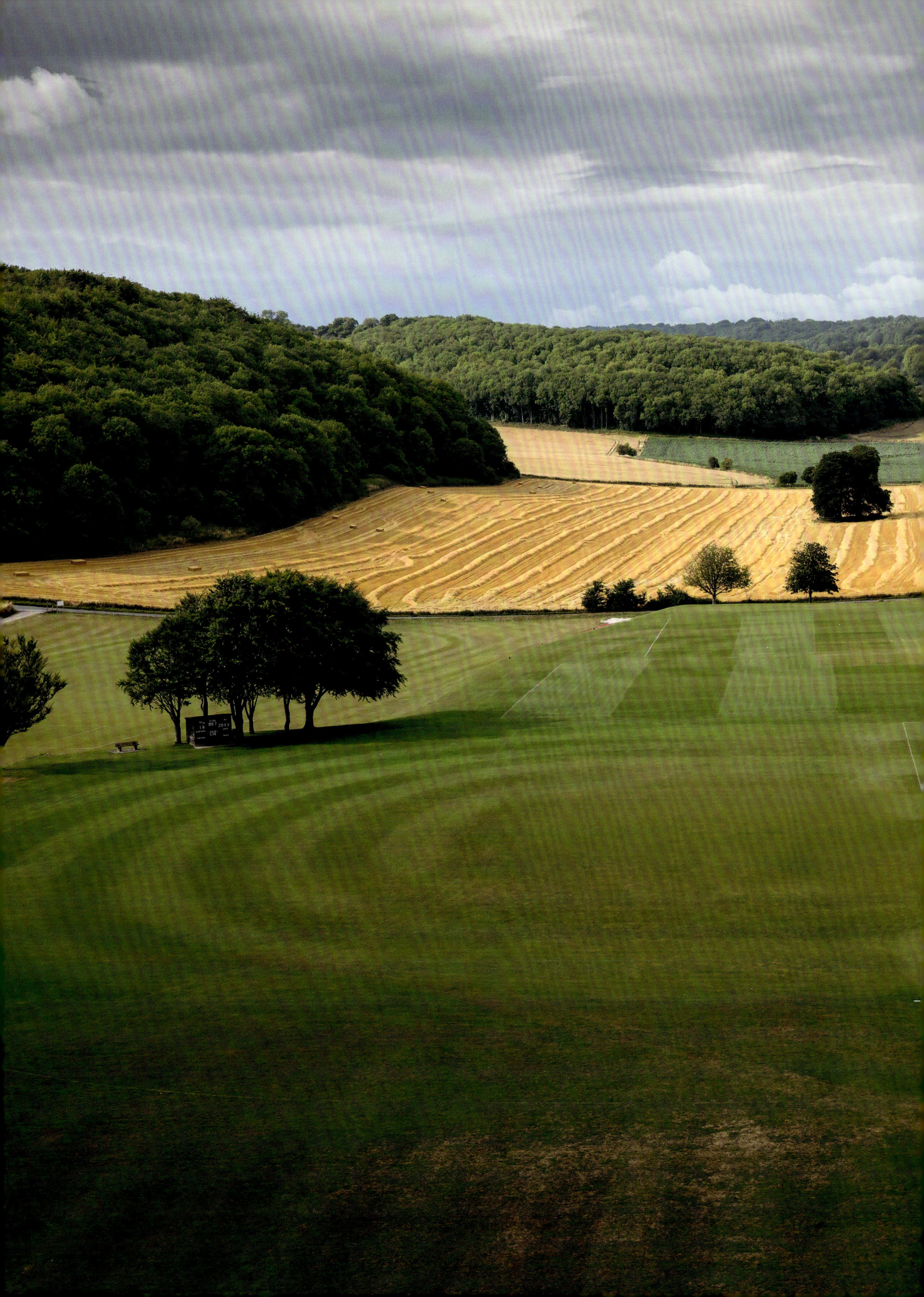

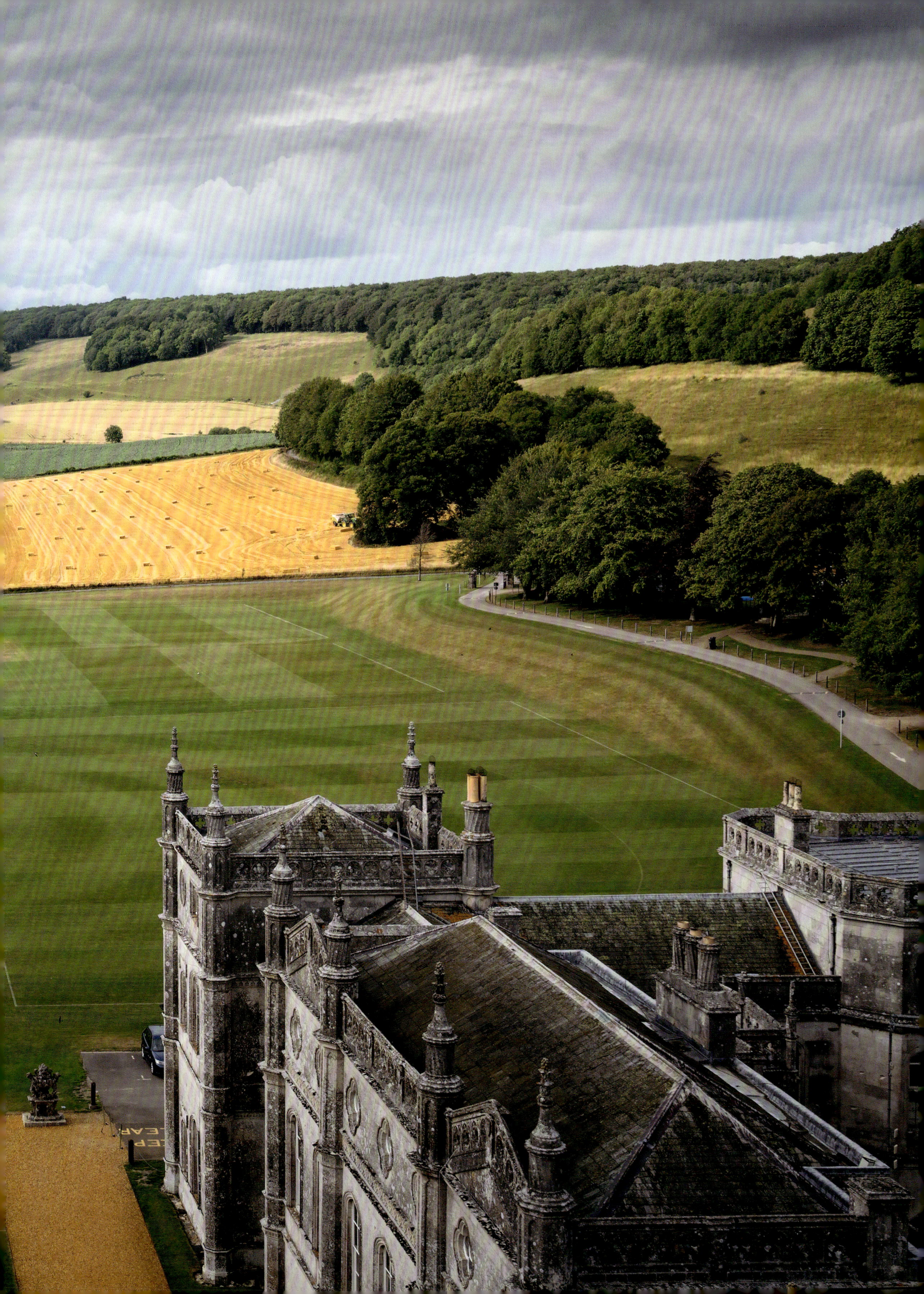

from the edging of the vale itself, quite spreading over the tops of the hills: these continued sweeps of hanging woods are very noble. In some places they form bold projections, that break forward in a great stile: in others, they withdraw, and open fine bosoms of wood, which are as picturesque as can easily be imagined. ... On the [east] side the vale, the hills are partly bare; but are clumped with new plantations, and scattered with single trees and thorns, contrasting the continued woods on the opposite hills in the boldest manner.

The passage is worth quoting, because of the steps that Brown took to show off this strikingly sculptural composition from every angle, by creating small, leveled areas at good points beside his drives so that carriages could stop and take in the view. Again, Young is our guide:

The riding that surrounds the amphitheatre rises the hill on this side, and, skirting the edge of it in the way to the house, looks down on the vale, and has a full command of the vast range of wood[s], which hang on the other sides of the other hills. One of the views is uncommonly fine: it is a projection of the opposite hill; the sloping bend fringed with a filleting of wood, and the crown of the hill a lawn scattered with single trees gently hanging to the eye: a landscape truly pleasing.... In other places, you look down steep winding hollows, in which romantic clumps of wood seem swallowed up by the impending hills.... On rising

previous pages: Milton Abbey sits at the conjunction of Eleanor Combe and Delcombe with the Hilton water, which runs up to the abbey from the west, and then turns away to the south.
above: The house and church at Milton Abbey, from Delcombe Valley.

the hill, if you turn the other way, toward the head of vale of Blackmoor: the vale [i.e. north], you look down from without the wall commanding all the waves of the lawn at bottom, which form a most pleasing scenery, and look full into a vast amphitheatre of wood, which terminates the vale: the view nobly romantic.... From the top of the hill, full northwards, is a very great prospect over the innumerable inclosures are spread forth to the eye; the whole bounded by distant hills.

Young was right to describe this drive with its huge views over the country as a "riding," and his description shows that it was performing just as Thomas Whately had proposed that ridings should. It had a variety of scenery, a prospect at its climactic north end, and the "object of an airing"—the Ruins, put up at some time between 1770 and 1790. In Thomas Whately's terms, "a small spot, which may be kept by the labour of one man, enclosed from the fields, and converted into a shrubbery, or any other scene of a garden, will sometimes be a pleasing end to a short excursion from home; nothing so effectually extends the idea of a seat to a distance; and not being constantly visited it will always retain the charms of novelty and variety."[2]

The campaigns of the 1760s enclosed Delcombe with scrolls and swags of woodland, carefully addressed to the contours "here the woods sweep wildly round, pursuing the course of the valleys." This obeisance to the genius loci may have been

right: William Jennings's plan of 1806 shows Brown's completed scheme. The woods to the north around Delcombe were planted in the 1760s, those that run along the Hilton valley in the 1770s and 1780s. overleaf: The Delcombe Valley was designed by Brown as farmland with a 1,000-acre grass field on its floor.

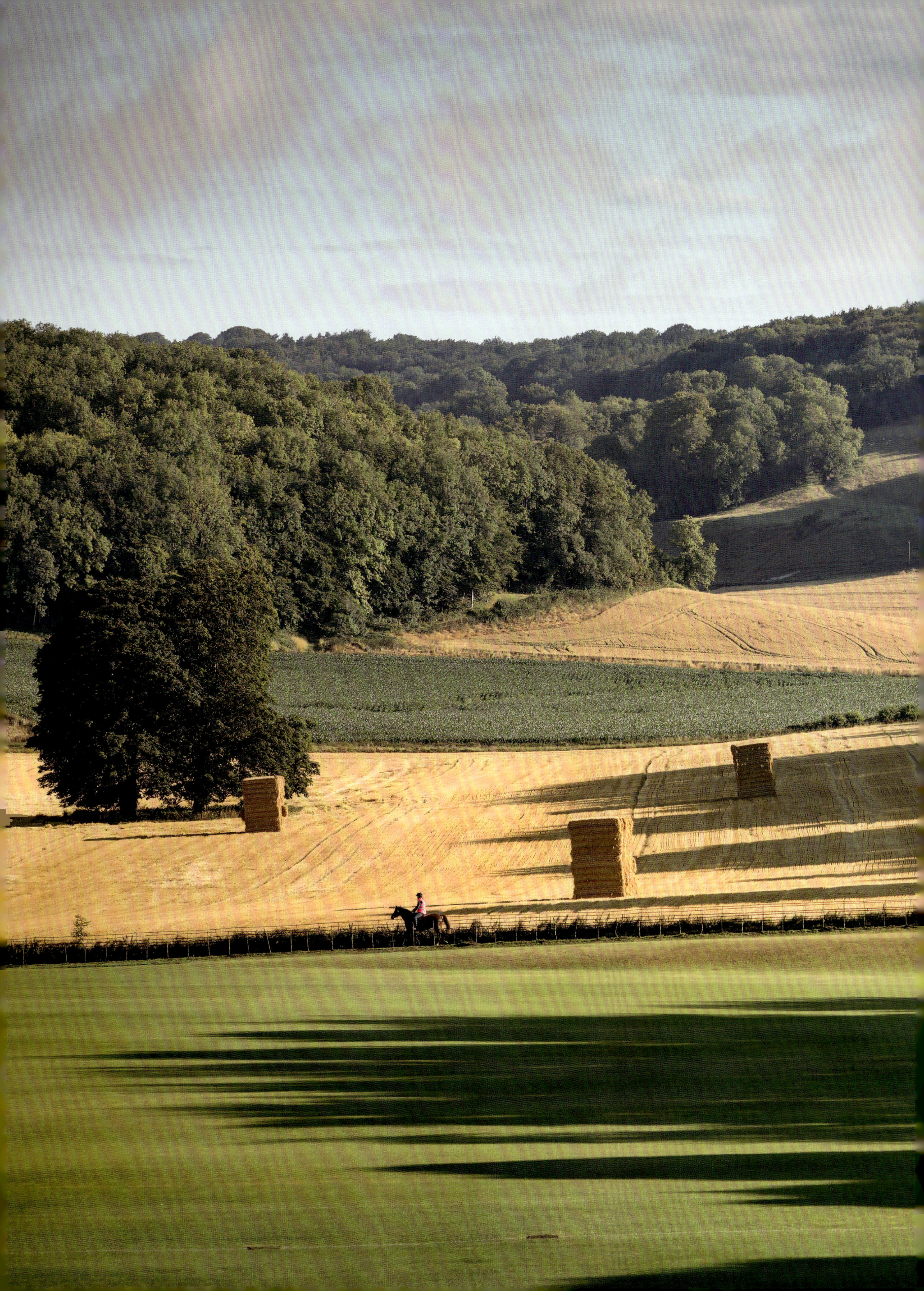

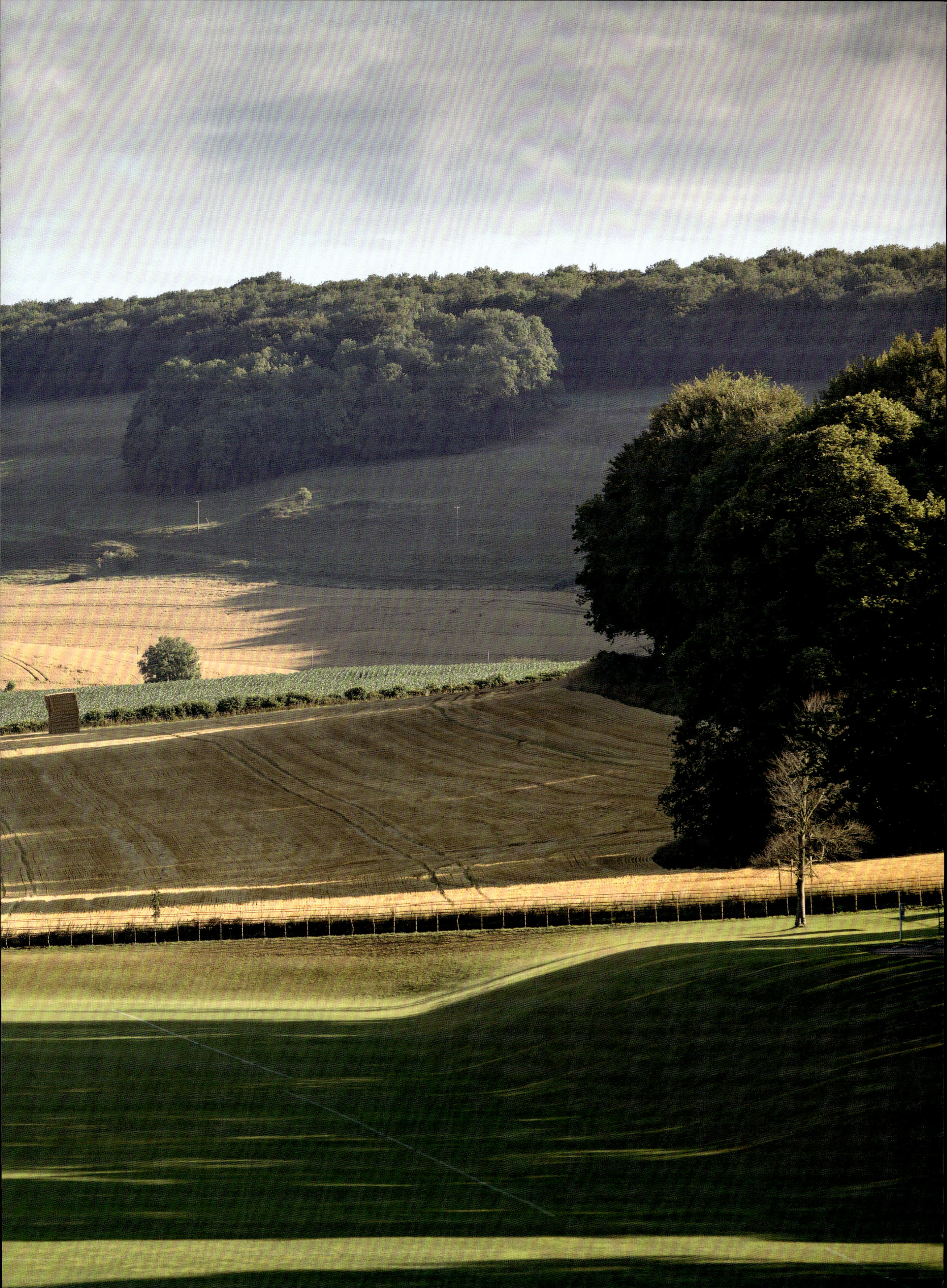

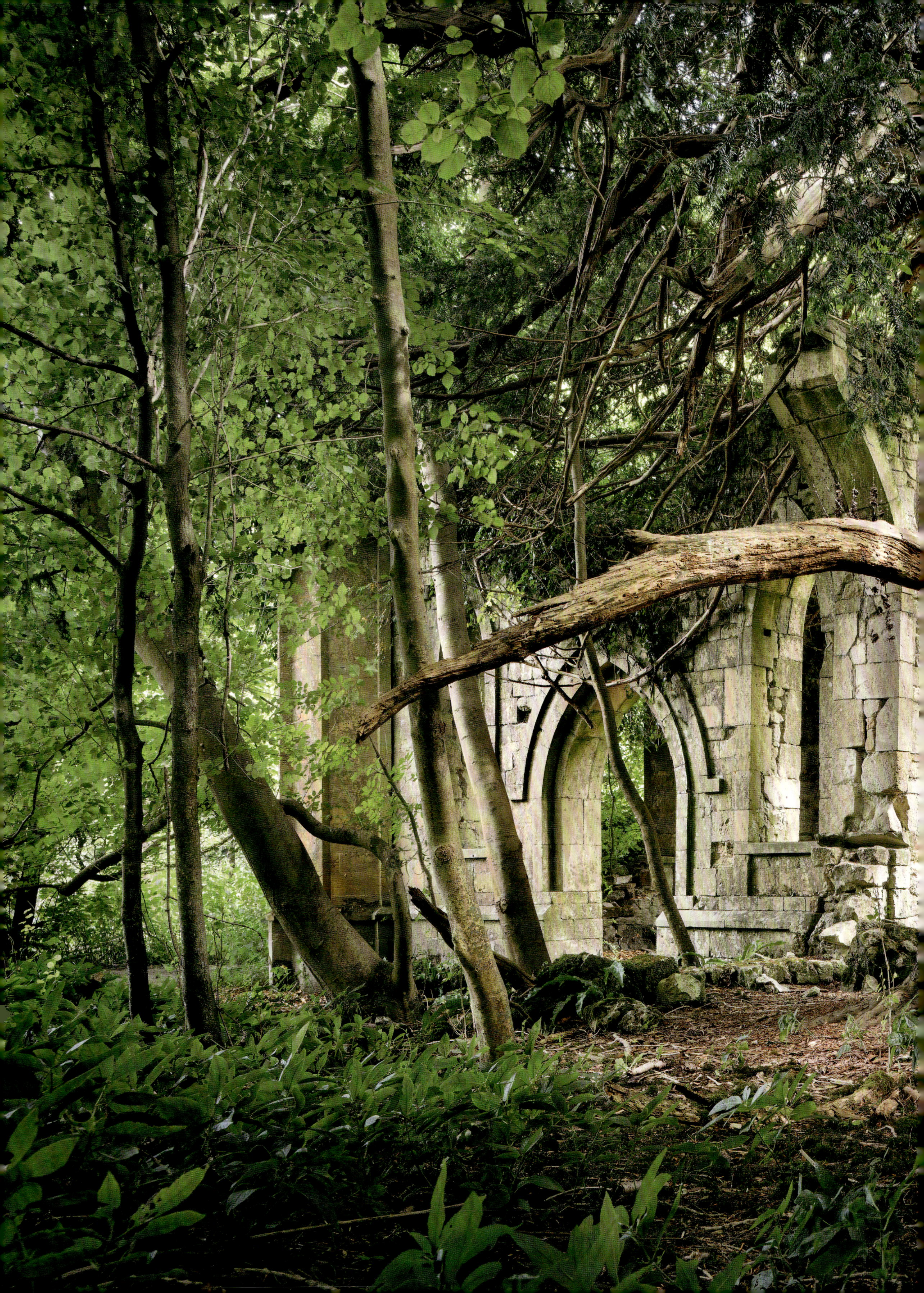

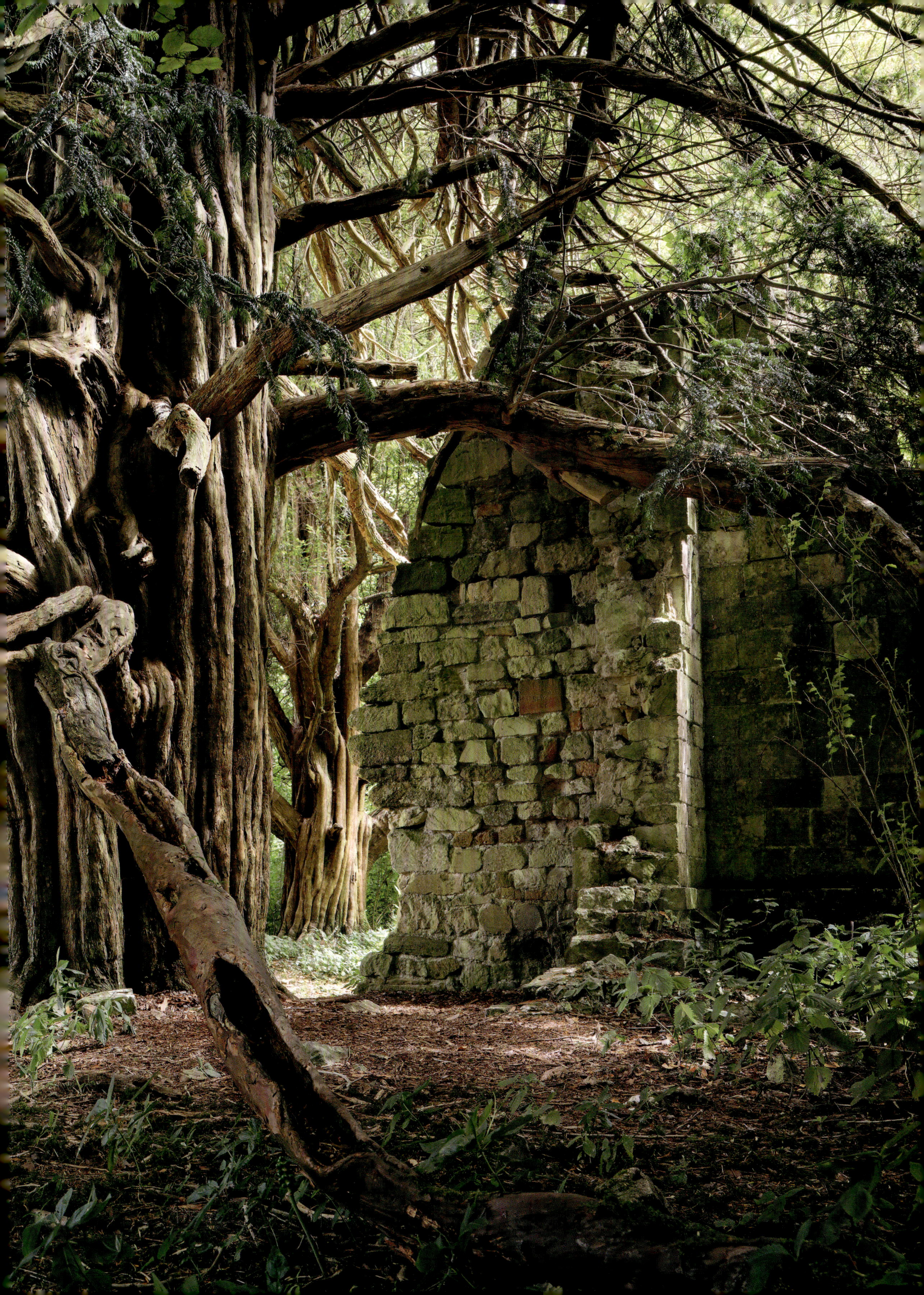

radical, but still more radical were his campaigns of the 1770s, which were to suggest that nothing should be excluded, whether village or arable fields.

Milton thus introduces us to the freedom of Brown's late landscapes. However, the work of the 1770s is better known for the destruction of the old town of Middleton, which disturbed Lord Milton's peace. A new village, Milton Abbas, was to be its replacement. This was designed by Brown and the architect, Sir William Chambers, and built by Brown alone after 1774, when Chambers abandoned the project, describing his client, Lord Milton, with some justice as "this unmannerly, imperious Lord."

The new village was squeezed into a wooded valley out of sight of the house. It was to be made up of thirty-six houses built with vernacular materials— thatch and cob. These are identical in design and were evenly distributed along a serpentine street about 450 meters long, with the church (built in the 1780s after Brown had died) and the alms house opposite each other at the turning point.

To accommodate this design, the valley (Luccombe Bottom) had to be widened at its lower west end, and this required a substantial piece of the chalk hill to be crudely cut away above the Brew-House. Ornamentation seems to have been limited to a series of single horse chestnuts planted between each house. These have been felled, but they were the tree of choice for Brown's ornamentation of villages, and in their prime would have softened what seems today a regimented layout.

Brown designed and built a great many buildings, but his architectural style was never distinguished. He offered a tidied up vernacular, as here, an austere neo-classical, and a Strawberry Hill Gothick. His architecture seems to have been dominated by the sense that there needed to be a building of a certain size in a certain space, the details of the design of the building were of less interest to him. He had no scruples about copying designs—the Lion Bridge at Burghley is a copy of Robert Adam's bridge at Compton Verney (1760s); the ceiling design that was rejected at Burton Constable was put up in 1763 at Corsham. William Mason, who knew Brown well, gave a plausible account of Brown's attitude: "Brown, I know, was ridiculed for turning architect, but I

previous pages: The Ruins screened the entrance to the pleasure ground in St. Therace's Vale.
above: Brown retained Green Lane Cottage from the old town. It sits still inside the pleasure ground.
opposite: Milton Abbas from the west side of the lake. The houses were designed by Sir William Chambers.

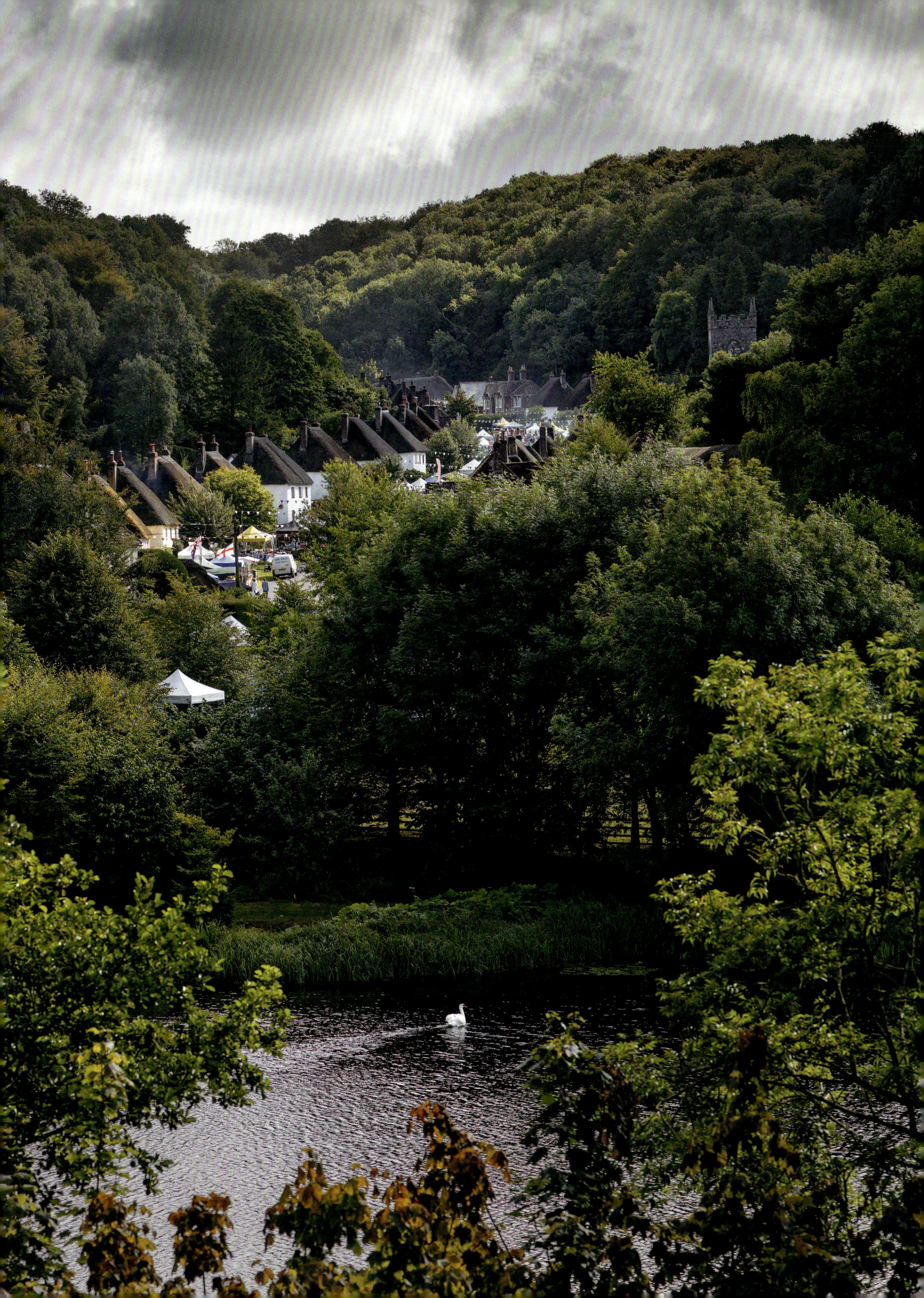

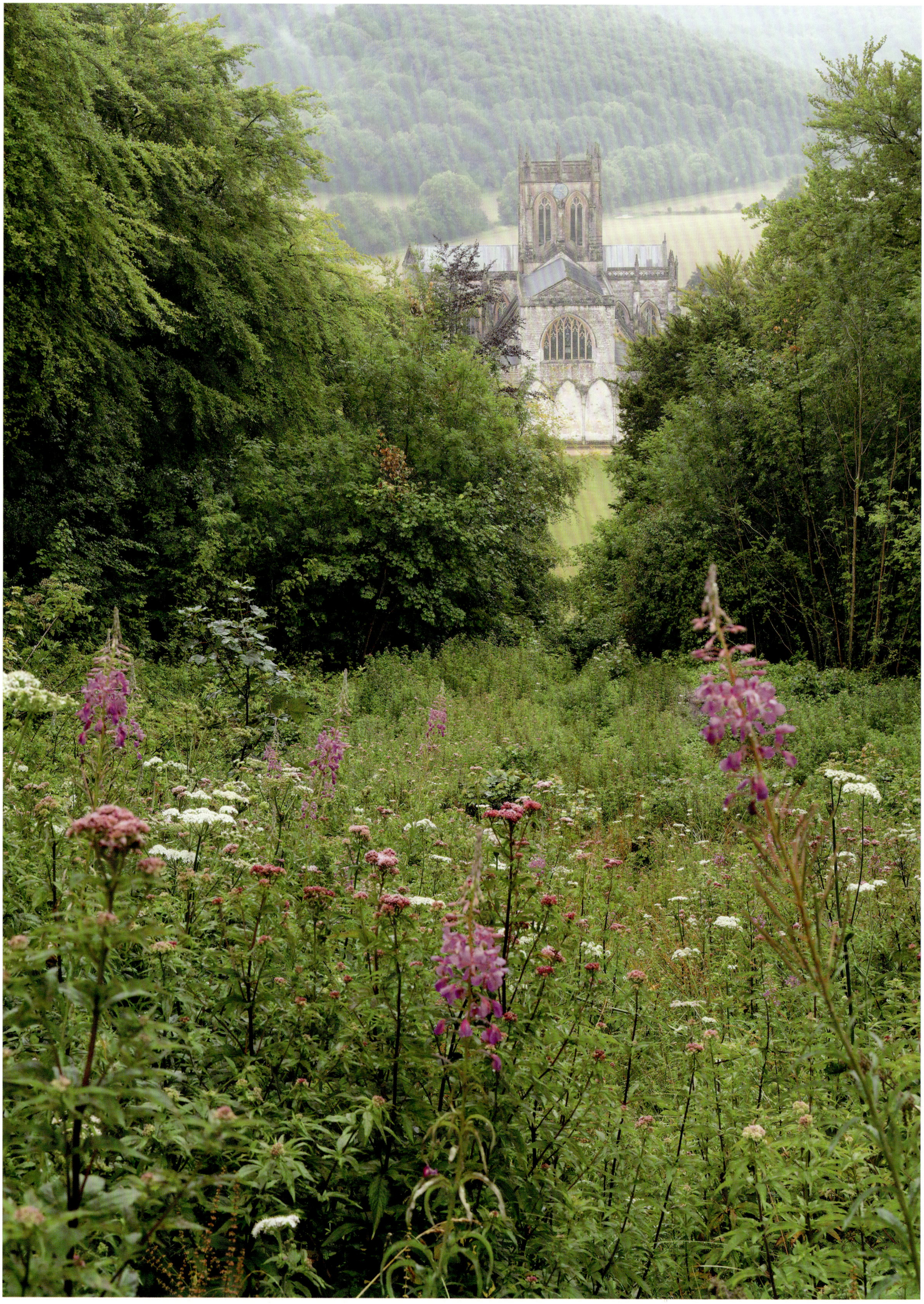

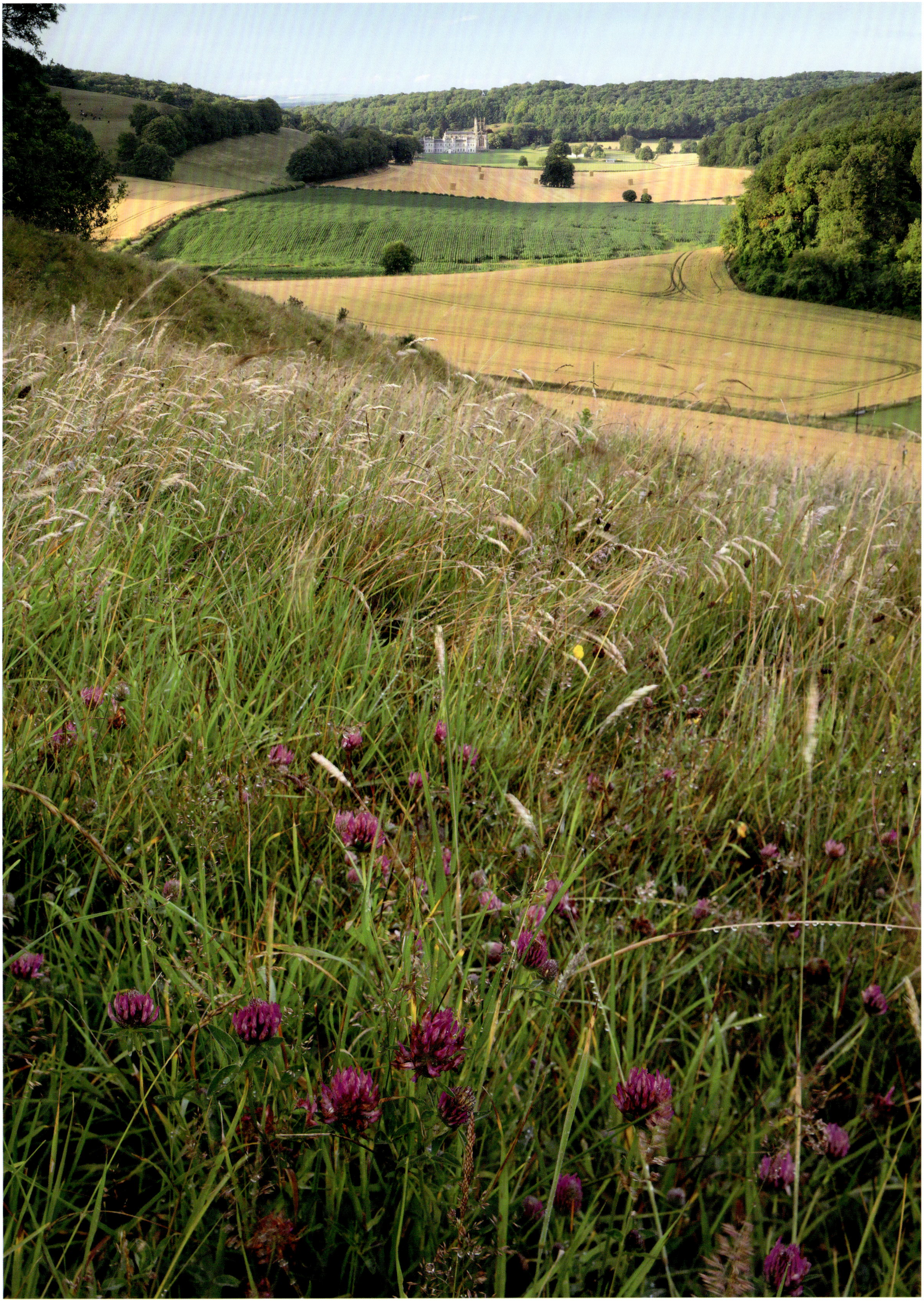

previous pages: The Abbey church, Milton Abbey, is almost on axis with the late-twelfth-century St. Catherine's Chapel that stands above it. Given Lord Damer's hatred of the school in the eighteenth century, it is ironic that the abbey should be a school today. Yet nothing can take away from the deeply peaceful and remote character that Brown has given it.

always thought he did it from a kind of necessity, having found the great difficulty which must frequently have occurred to him in forming a picturesque whole, where the previous building had been ill-placed, or of improper dimensions."[3]

Milton Abbas has with reason been described as the first model village in England, and it was perceptively described by the novelist Fanny Burney in 1791:

After an early dinner, we set off for Milton Abbey, the seat of Lord Milton. We arrived, through very bad roads, to a village, built by his Lordship, very regularly, of white plaister, cut stone fashion, though every House was square, & meant to resemble a Gentleman's abode. A very miserable mistake in his good Lordship, of an intended fine effect; for the sight of the common people, & of the Poor, labouring or strolling in and about these dwellings, made them appear rather to be reduced from better days, than flourish in a primitive or natural state.[4]

Fanny Burney could see that Milton Abbas was providing for a servant class, however, she did not register the scale of the enterprise. In this later stage of his career Brown had become the expressive placemaker par excellence. He would devote himself to the genius loci at each landscape. What made Milton Abbey radical was the "ancient church" at its center, "unwelcome... when it breaks into the design of a park or a garden."[5] Brown retained this as the most important and conspicuous building on the place, but far from furnishing it with a wild "medieval" park, apparently untouched by any improvement, Brown surrounded it with the "common fields" for which Sir William Chambers was to criticise him—in short, Milton was "a very large farm" and Lord Milton was "one of the most considerable farmers in this country."[6]

It may seem paradoxical to claim that Brown was reaching back to the Middle Ages to create this setting, when at the same time he was creating the progressive improved farms of the agricultural revolution. The point we miss is that if the landscape were to be expressive of this monastic character, then the land had to be as perfectly managed as it would have been in the hands of its monks. Sir William Chambers designed the beautiful neo-classical Higher Lodges at the principal entry to the parkland, but they do not fit into the design, and there are no neo-classical temples, no Malayan Huts, no obelisks. Instead two chapels were built at the periphery of the landscape (at Delcombe Manor and the Ruins). These are very rare in a Brown landscape, but they do directly express the spiritual reach of the church—and this quality of Brown's work at Milton was immediately recognized: "from the hill above these rustic habitations, the church tower beyond and the wood hanging from the brows of the neighbouring heights form a singularly romantic scene.—it must be confessed too that the removal of the town has rendered the effect of the valley more highly monastic than ever, and restored it to that seclusion and solitude which recommended it to its original tenants."[7]

If Milton was to be reinvested with the spirituality of the Benedictine idea, then the lay people who supported it had to be moved out of sight, beyond the reredos, as it were, to Milton Abbas and to vernacular houses whose style of construction would have been a commonplace in the Middle Ages even

opposite: Nature is steadily reasserting itself in the surrounding woodland.

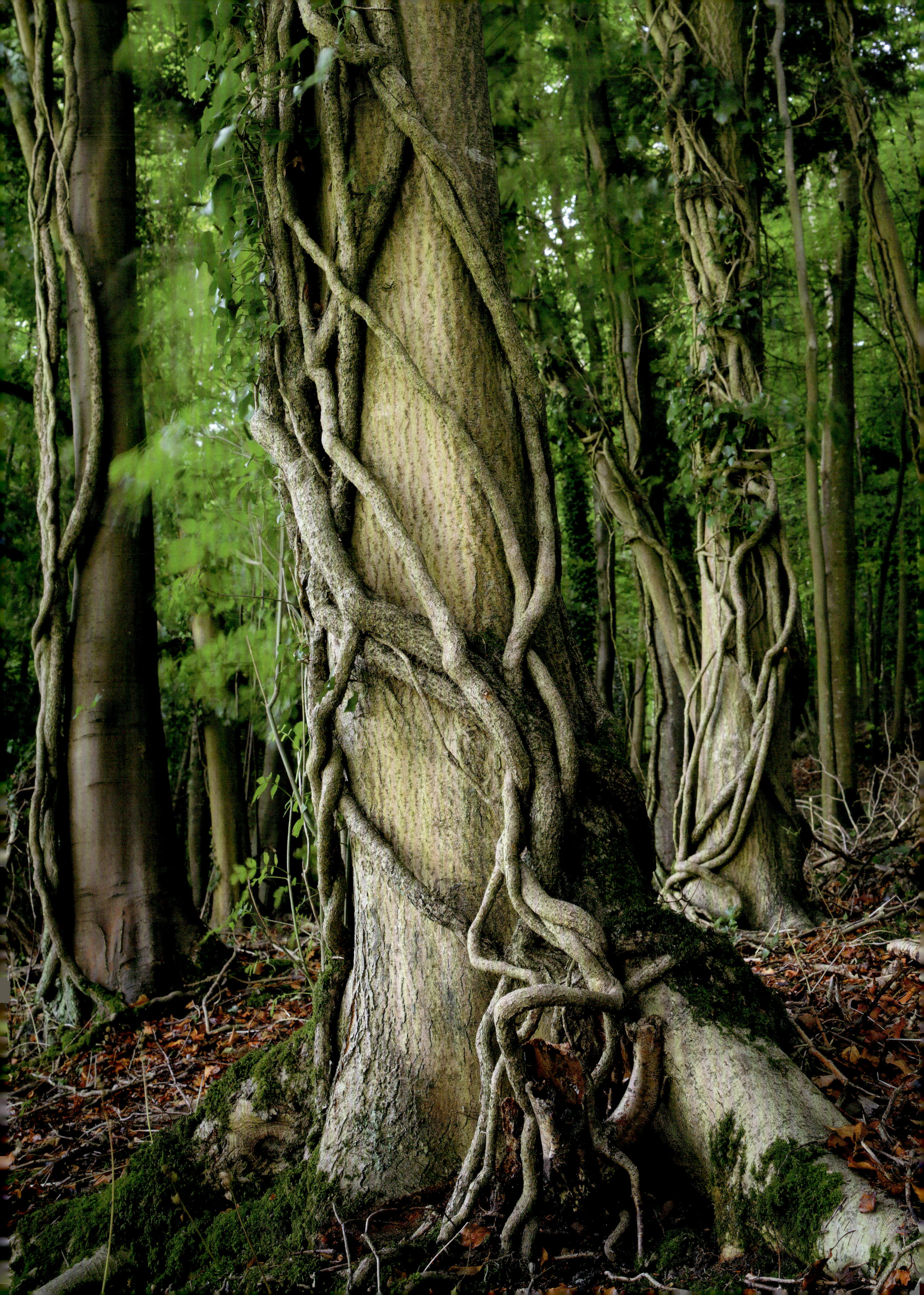

if they were internally commodious and up-to-date.

Remarkable as Milton Abbas may be, Brown's treatment of the neighboring village of Hilton has claims to be still more radical. This is the first ordinary village to be embraced by planting within the landscape and made a central event in the composition, rather than excluded, as had been the custom. Woolsthorpe at Belvoir Castle is another example from the same period in Brown's career. The implications of the design are considerable. It led the way to the painter John Constable's appreciation of the ordinary Suffolk villages around his house, and it illustrates the final stage in Brown's development, in which nothing in England is barred from inclusion in a designed landscape. Today the view seems natural and unremarkable. We cannot believe that it took any skill or profound perception to bring it off because we are the unthinking inheritors of his tradition. Yet the imagination must travel some distance to arrive at this appreciation of Hilton. At Stowe, where Brown had learned his trade in the 1740s, he could look out each morning from his house in the Boycott Pavilion and see that "the Garden is extended beyond its Limits, and takes in every thing entertaining that is to be met with in the range of half a County. Villages, Works of Husbandry, Groups of Cattle... even to the *nicest* taste these rural scenes are highly delightful."[8] However, the village that Brown would have seen at Stowe was a sham, put up at the New Inn in the second decade of the eighteenth century. These "rural Scenes" had been

above: Brown's woods curl round the back of Hilton and embrace the church and the muddle of cob, brick, and flint houses around it.

carefully engineered by Lord Cobham. The view to Hilton shows that Brown had realized that England itself could be regarded as beautiful even at its most unadorned and raw.

With all its indeterminate size, and the village included in the ambit of the surrounding woods, there is no place here for the orderly gradation of scenery that was the goal at Petworth. The basic questions go unanswered: Is there a deer park, for example, and does there need to be? In fact, there was, but it was out of sight of the house and on the periphery of the landscape.[9] Can we distinguish at Milton the park from the sheep walk, the drive from the riding, and the hunting wood from the belt? Does it have a boundary? It should not surprise us to find that the project to build a wall around Milton's demesne was abandoned.

Ecologists today press for the need to take in more extensive ranges of landscape in a kind of threading through and interweaving of landscape and nature. This is what Brown was able to design at Milton. His home grounds were a farm, with 1,360 acres grazed by about 1,400 sheep "not so much with a view to profit as the beauty of his lawns." Here the belt is supplanted by spooling, coiled ribbons of woodland, and the landscape sprawls lavishly over the ground, without any apparent regard to boundaries or land use, public roads, or property. What might have been park has become a farm, but a farm like no other before it.

above: The view south across the lake runs out into open country and the surrounding woods and clumps set off the natural form of the land.

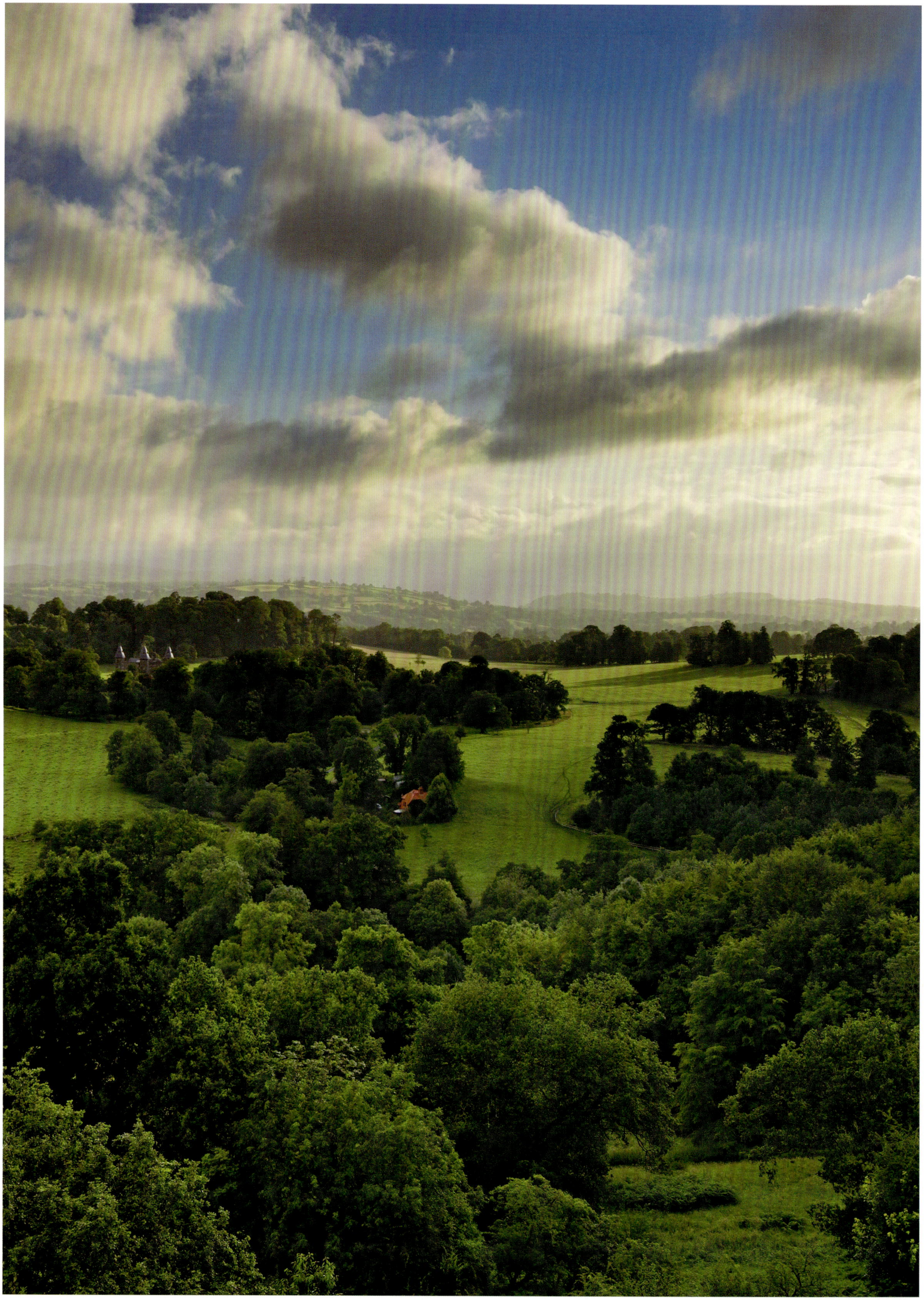

1772–1783
THE LATE WORK

IN 1770, TWO POTENT ADVOCATES OF BROWN AND the English style went into print: Thomas Whately with *Observations on Modern Gardening*, and Horace Walpole with *On Modern Gardening*. Two years later came William Mason's poem "The English Garden," and Brown's elevation to immortality was secured by Sir William Chambers' savage attack on him in *A Dissertation on Oriental Gardening*. Brown was rarely mentioned by name in this literature, but no one can have been in any doubt about the fight that Chambers had started.

At the same time, however, Brown was suffering increasingly from asthma, and his business model had begun to fail him. After 1772, despite the scale of his enterprise, he seemed to need to send out invoices for drawings (at King's Weston, Wilton, and Longford Castle, for example) that he had initially provided without charge, perhaps in the hope of securing the contracts for the execution of the work. Nonetheless his invention did not fail him, and some of his greatest works were still to come, with a new freedom of ideas and ever-increasing diversity in their expression.

opposite: In the view from Dinefwr Castle, the country seems to have been transformed into an enormous grassed valley that winds through the landscape and encircles Newton House.

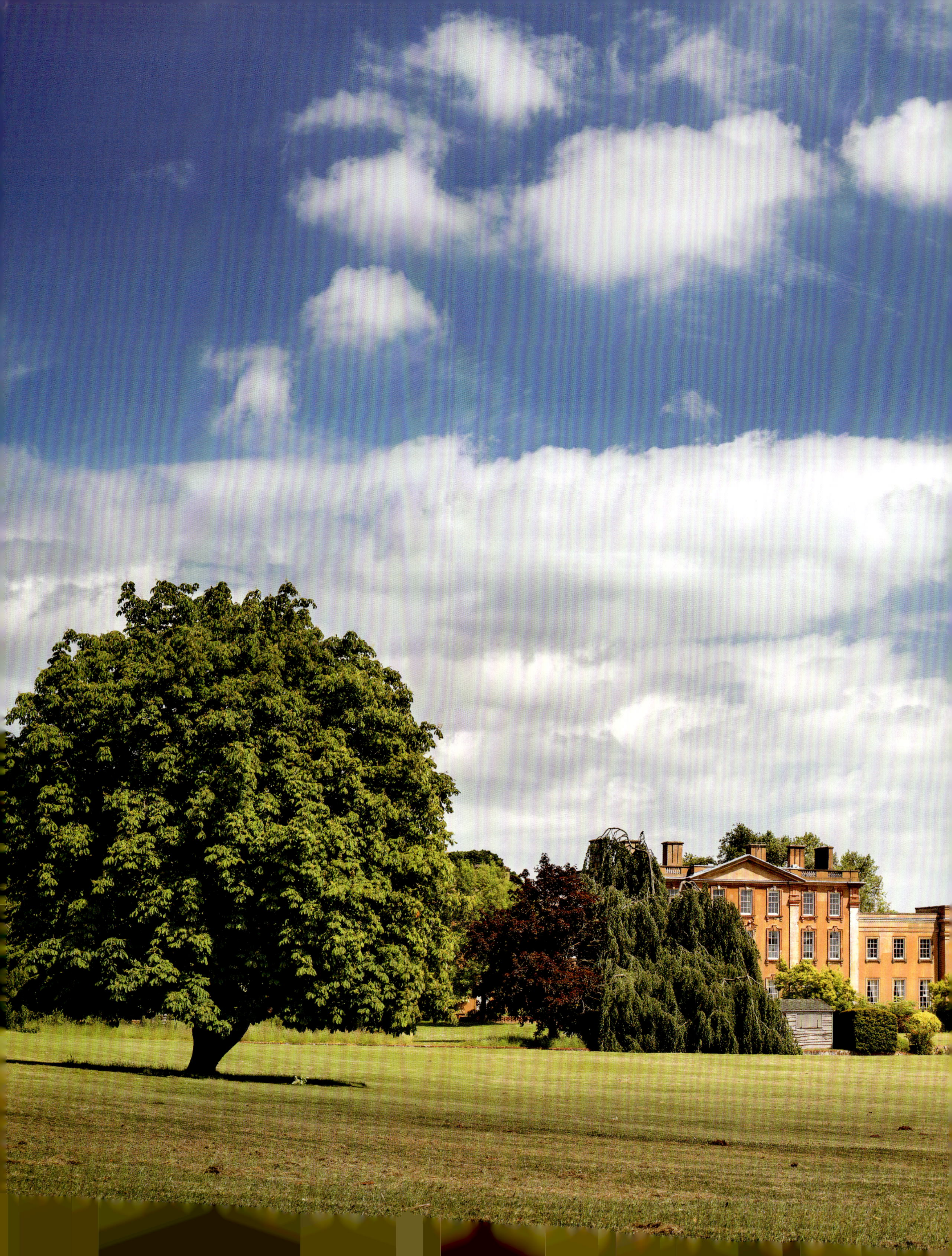

HIMLEY HALL
— STAFFORDSHIRE —
FROM 1774

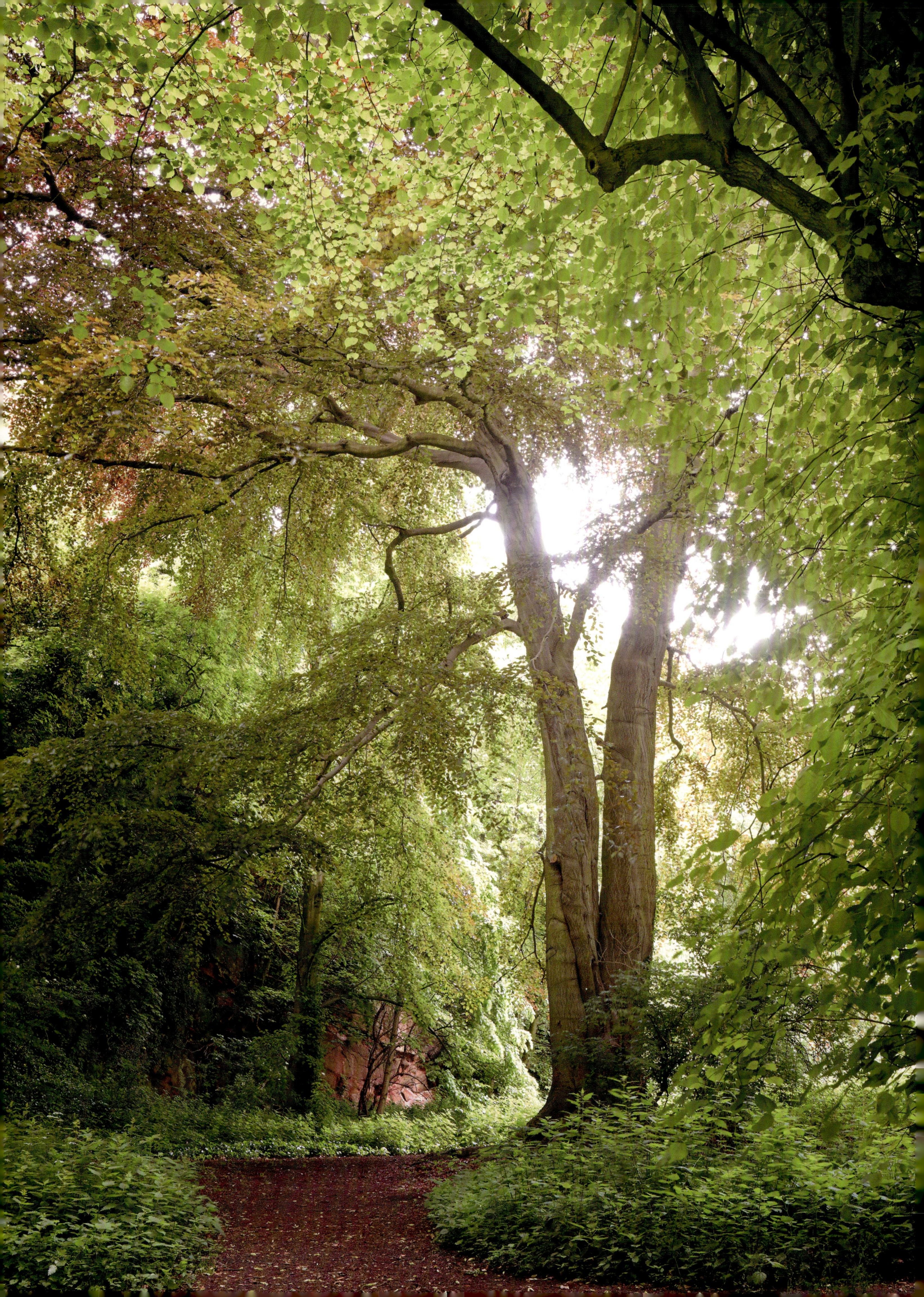

— CHAPTER TWELVE —

HIMLEY HALL

Himley is a late Brown, but it superbly represents his mature work and shows what separated him from his contemporaries. It is a master class in bringing coherence to an essentially incoherent series of spaces. It is a model of balance, and we can compare his design with that of other proposals made before he arrived.

John Ward, the 1st Viscount Ward, had inherited Himley from his cousin in 1740 and built a new house next to the old moated manor. He ordered a survey of the estate in 1752, so he may have been considering work, but in 1765 he commissioned Nathaniel Richmond to redesign the landscape. Richmond had worked for Brown from 1754 to 1760; he had learned much from him and his cartography has Brown's house style, but the design itself has none of Brown's fluency. Richmond found a raw new house with a hamlet of cottages running away to the southwest served by roads, including the well-used Himley to Dudley road. Near the house the old moats were still in place, fed from springs in the ancient Baggeridge Woods to the northeast. Sheltering it to the north was a great plug of red sandstone, The Hill, another geological eruption of the kind that made great the landscape at Hawkstone, Shropshire, a vast somewhat alien object, like a monstrous whale. Beyond that to the north lay the Old Park, established in the thirteenth century, but broken up into fields and returned to agriculture by Richmond's day. Richmond's response to this was to reconfigure the moats into a long river-like series of ponds that would make their way past the house on its way west out of Baggeridge Wood; and to open up views to The Hill, stripping the undergrowth from the rock so that the exposed cliffs would tower over the house and the winding walk around it, so as to provide some views out over Old Park.

The Hill's topography and formation, after all, is not polished, tamed, or classical, but vivid and appealing. Though adjacent to the house, it is country that a painter of the sublime, a Salvator Rosa, would have taken to. Any designer, one would have thought, would have done the same as Richmond, planting pines on the tops, so as to emphasize the drama of the juxtaposition of smooth turf and cliff.

previous pages: Himley Hall was re-fronted from 1824 by the architect William Atkinson, but it is essentially the same eighteenth-century neo-classical building that Brown knew.
opposite: The Hill rises unexpectedly and makes an irresistible setting for the pleasure ground.

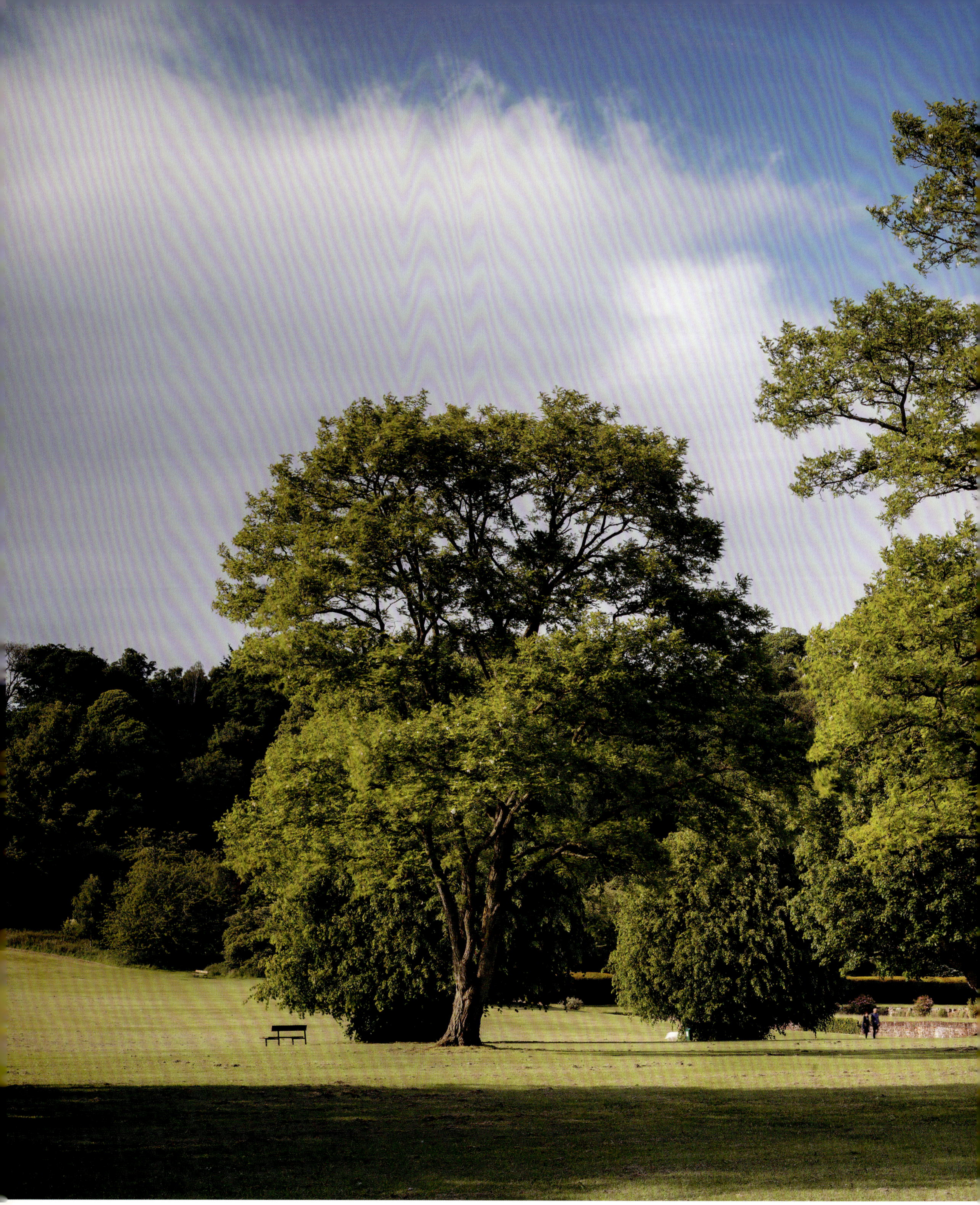

above: Himley Hall with the Hill behind it. The planting of the sandstone plug of the Hill used a mixture of species. Brown was sometimes criticized for this, but Repton regarded it as having a "cheerful" effect, which might be appropriate in a pleasure ground.

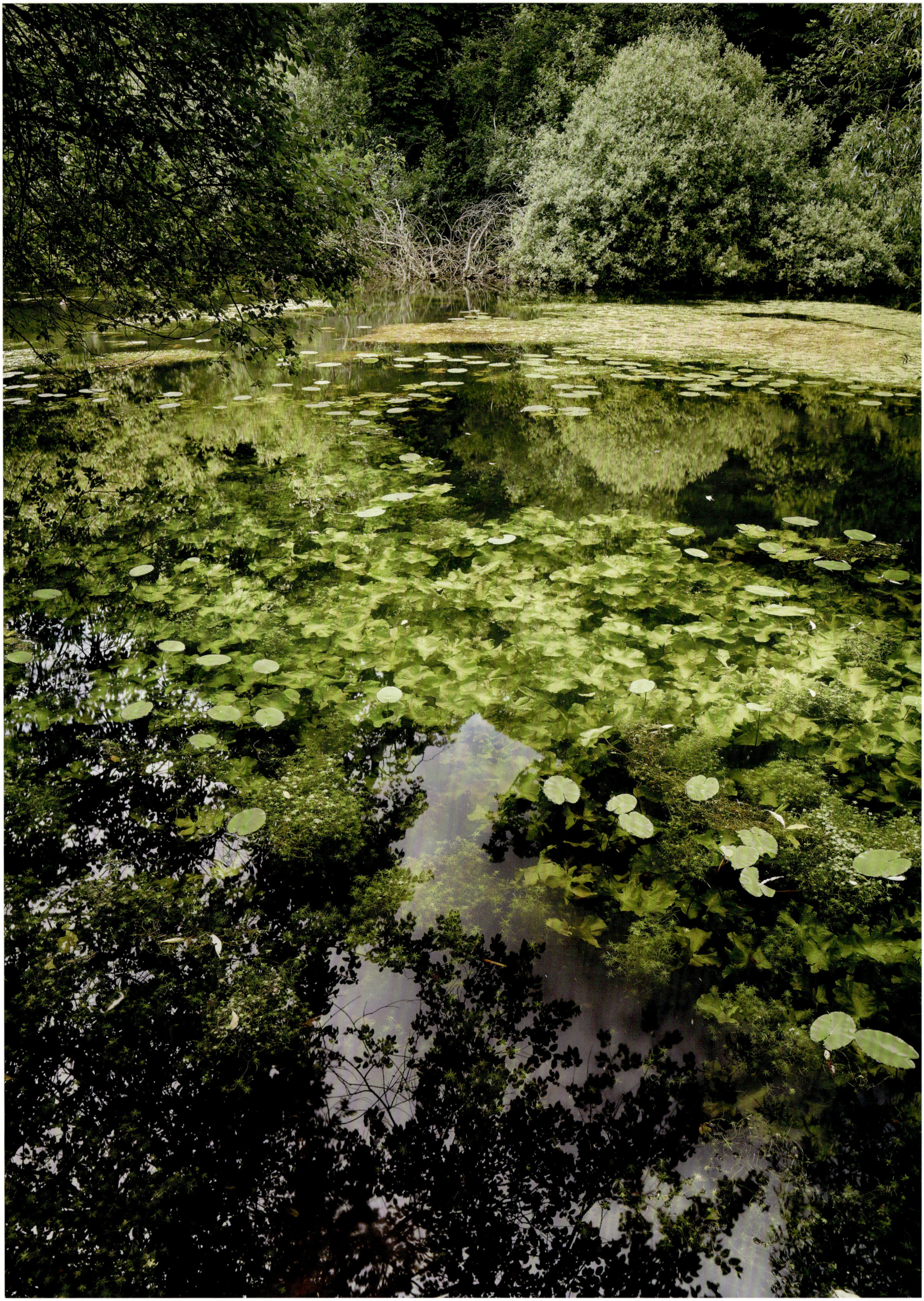

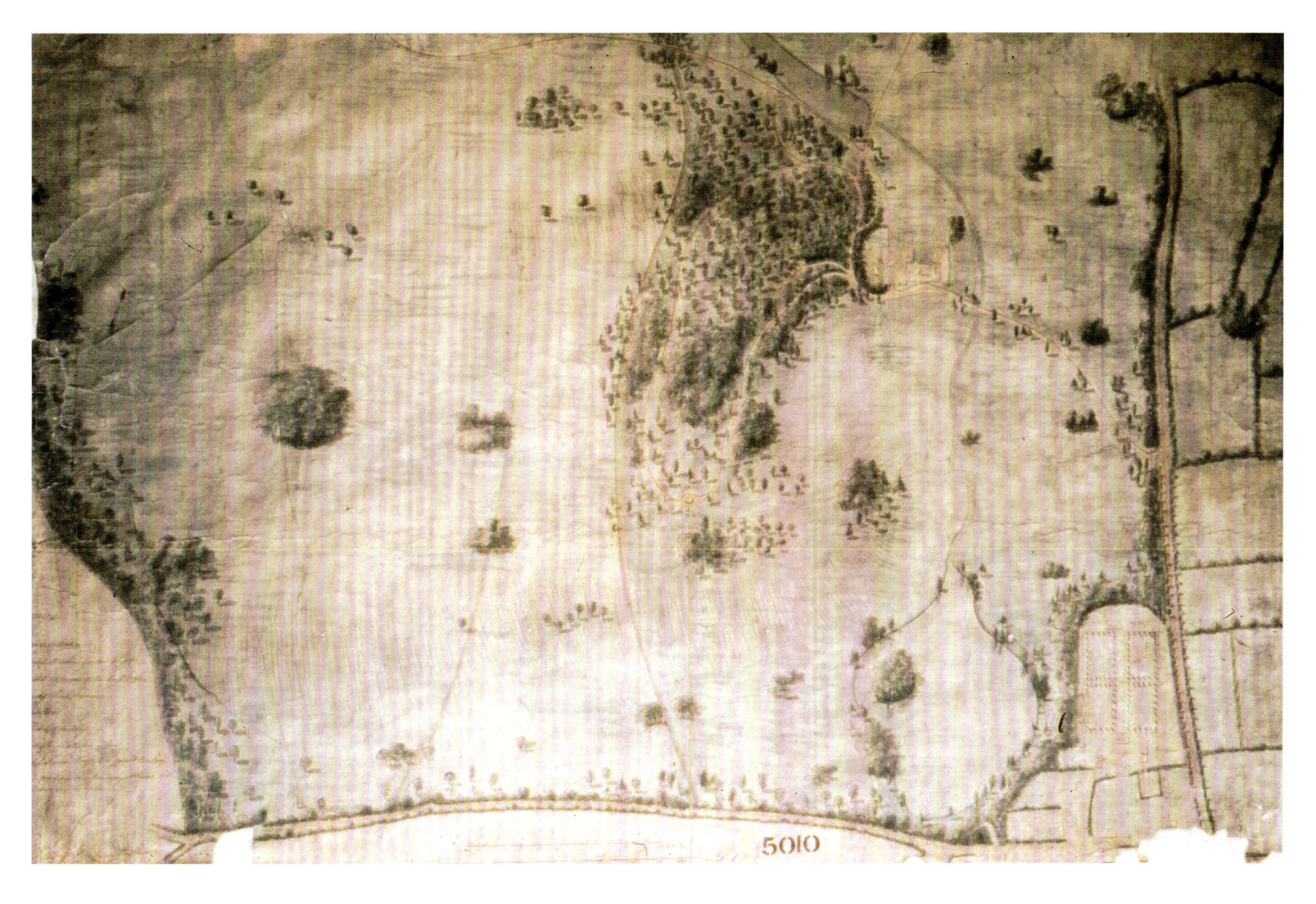

Even Brown's friend and supporter, William Mason, proposed Richmond's solution in his poem "The English Garden":

Yet fair Variety, with all her powers,
Assists the Balance: 'gainst the barren crag
She lifts the pastur'd slope; to distant hills
Opposes neighb'ring shades...[1]

In short, Richmond's plan made the best of the good bits, showing off the dramatic rock faces of The Hill, extending the water around the house, and then leaving the road system, the village, Old Park, and Baggeridge Woods to fend for themselves. Richmond's solution has drama, it has variety and contrast.

Little, however, seems to have been done, and Richmond was replaced as a designer by another contemporary of Brown's, William Emes, in 1768, but six years later their client the 1st Viscount died and Brown was immediately commissioned by the 2nd. We do not know how much work he did at this stage, but in a second burst of work from 1780, he was paid at least £1,500, which makes Himley a substantial project.

Brown's treatment of Himley was the opposite of Richmond's. The Hill he clad with "modern foliage," as the historian of Staffordshire, Stebbing Shaw, described it at the time, using sweet chestnuts and other trees, so that the bare rock cannot be seen from the house. The water around the house he culverted to carry it to a new lake that partly drowned the old village; the villagers were rehoused round the corner (and their new houses were admired for their comfort). This freed Brown to landscape the valley

above: Brown's plan for Himley (detail showing the house, the Hill, and the lake).
opposite: A sequence of ponds, itself medieval in origin, falls down the valley from the medieval Baggeridge Woods.

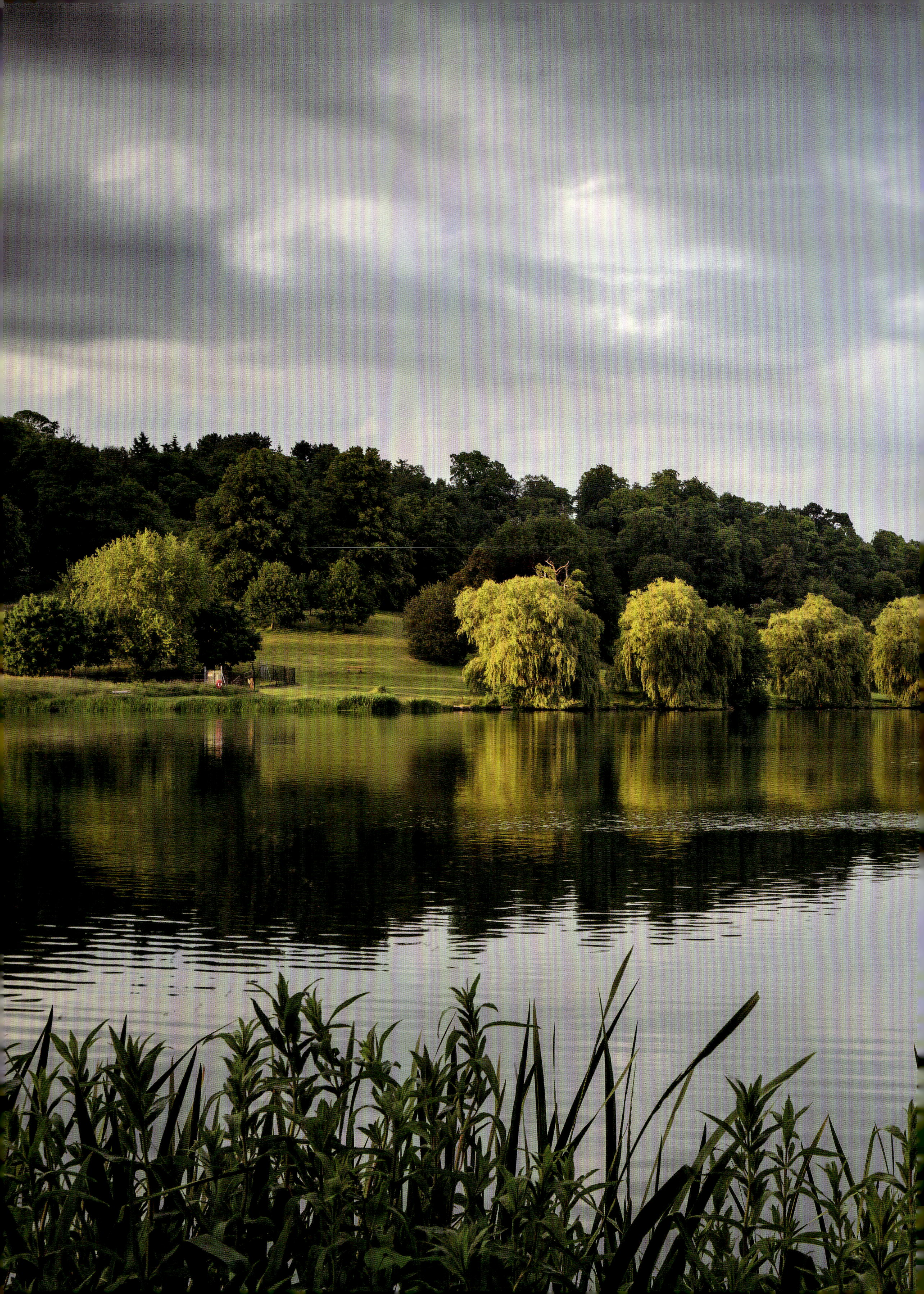

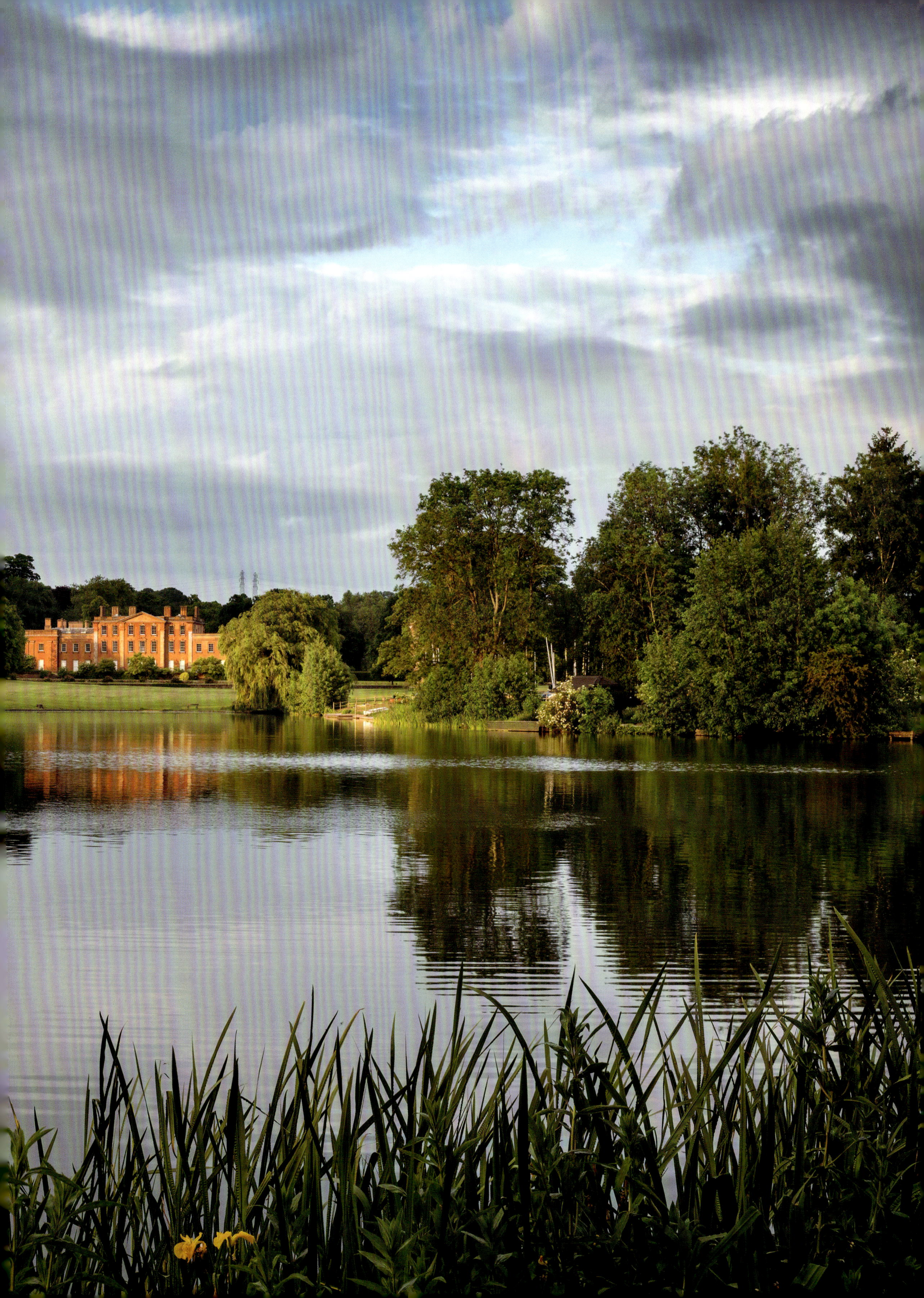

between house and lake into a long grass slope, or glacis, and to move the Dudley-Himley road, so making a longer approach to the house; the new road he proposed to bring into the design by planting an avenue along it, between his new entrance and Himley village.

He then adopted Richmond's idea of a circuit walk around The Hill, but added to it narrow walks with steps and caves cut into the rock, all at a very small scale, and the top of The Hill itself, now hidden from the house by planting, became the new focal center of the landscape, with its views out to the woods and over Old Park. Brown went on to extend Piper's Hill—a spur off The Hill running toward his new lake. This could now carry a drive from the house to the top of The Hill, offering the iconic view of the house from the west, as well as views out to the west, to the "borrowed" landscape of Ward's neighbors.

Brown also re-emparked Old Park, making use of existing hedgerow trees where he could and planting it with further single trees and clumps, of which the largest was at a high point in the middle—a location and a planting he was to deploy again at Moccas Court.

It is interesting to consider why he took these steps. In a very obvious way, moving the roads and village secured a setting for the house from every point of the compass, but underlying that and more impressive is Brown's restraint.

It had long been agreed with the poet Alexander Pope that "all the beauties of gardening might be comprehended in one word, variety."[2] The aesthetic pleasures of variety seem at one with the idea of a garden as an Eden, all-inclusive and endlessly

previous pages: The classic view of the house from the far side of the lake with The Hill to the left.
above: In places at the foot of The Hill the rock is exposed and left sheer and plain; quarries fascinated Brown.
opposite: A woodland sweet chestnut on The Hill.

222 · CAPABILITY BROWN

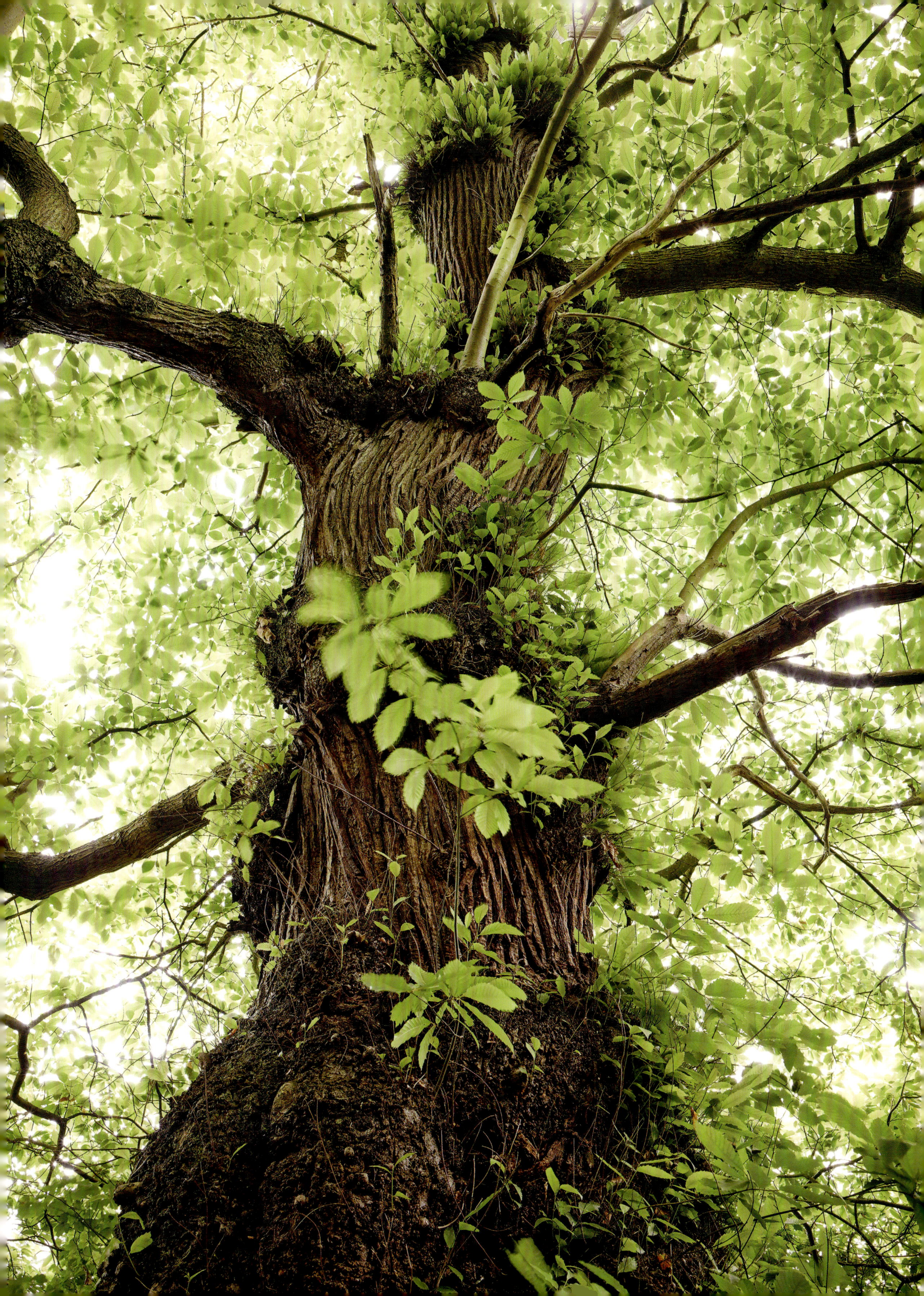

entertaining. So in Brown's day, too, no one ever doubted that "ground is seldom beautiful or natural without *variety*."[3]

However, variety is just what Brown's landscapes were deemed to lack. In the eyes of his critics, they were "in their nature closely allied to monotony."[4] Of course, all Brown's landscapes have variety, but what Himley also has is harmony, which might be described as producing variety without violent or sudden contrast. The latter was also admired in Brown's day, so Horace Walpole thought that William Kent used sometimes to allow "the rudest waste to add its foil to the richest theatre,"[5] and, as we have seen, Brown's friend William Mason recommended contrast with his appreciation of the pleasurable effect that "broken rocks and rugged grounds" could have "when introduced near an extent of lawn."

However, Mason's friend and correspondent, William Gilpin dismissed contrast as unnatural: "Nature... seldom passes abruptly from one mode of scenery to another,"[6] and he was right. Contrast is not just unnatural but is often unhelpful in landscape, and Gilpin's argument explains a number of ideas in Brown's design that otherwise seem quirky. He and his allies preferred harmony and unity to contrast because they produced grandeur, whether in planting (much as he liked the apple blossom, William Shenstone felt that "the prospect would be really grander, did it consist of simple foliage"),[7] or in topography, of which the philosopher Joseph

above: The steps at Himley recall Brown's picturesque treatment of the cascades at Bowood, Blenheim, and Harewood.

Addison wrote "there is generally in Nature something more Grand and August, than what we meet with in the Curiosities of Art."[8] Likewise, an excess of variety, no matter what it cost, cheapened the design, "subject[ing] us to insurmountable toil," as the philosopher Alexander Gerard put it.[9] So in Joseph Cradock's *Village Memoirs*, Mr. Massem, despite his daily purchases of ground and his "Obelisks, Statues, Gazebos, Terminations, and a Laurel-belt," was likely to produce nothing but "an *Olio*, a *Christmas Pie*, a *Solomon Grundy*, or perhaps a *Fool's Coat*,"[10] and William Shenstone, with typical insight, commented that "Islands give beauty, if the water be adequate; but lessen grandeur through variety."[11]

In fact, it is apparent from the progress of his work that, notwithstanding this consensus of approval for variety, Brown had recognized its limitations and saw a reciprocal relationship between contrast and variety on the one hand, and grandeur on the other. Contrast meant both the frantic search for "originality"—meaning "something different"—and the dissolution of grandeur, as William Combe believed: "Where Nature is grand, improve her grandeur, not by adding extraneous decorations, but by removing obstructions. Where a scene is, in itself, lovely, very little is necessary to give it all due advantage, which undergoes no variety of cultivation."[12]

Of all Brown's designs Himley cries out for interpretation along these lines: the view from the house to the lake, even when roughened today by the

above: There were two caves on the Hill; this one was designed with a long view out over the parkland.

below: At the top of Piper's Hill there is a levelled viewpoint that takes in the hall and the lake. A Brownian tunnel runs under the hill and has a view of the hall as perfect as the view through the Lion Bridge at Burghley.

tennis courts and cars of the country park, is nigh-on perfect, with the smooth tump of the artificial Piper's Hill closing the right-hand side. Brown planted over The Hill and lost the contrast, because for him the grandeur of nature was the more enduring quality in landscape. The rock is still there, of course, but it is only from the walks, steps, and caves of his pleasure ground, not from the house itself, that it is to be enjoyed.

The gradation that we find at Himley may be more sophisticated than the linear form that we find at Burghley and Petworth, but gradation remained a leading determinant in the distribution of the components of the Brownian estate into the final phase of his career with Milton Abbey. The abiding impression that we take from Himley is of the understated assurance that true grandeur brings. It is a house that is entirely comfortable in its setting and at peace with itself.

226 · CAPABILITY BROWN

above: The clump that climbs to the top of the hill is beautifully placed
to give a sense of movement. If it had been planted on the crown, *a few yards to the right,*
the scene would be transformed.

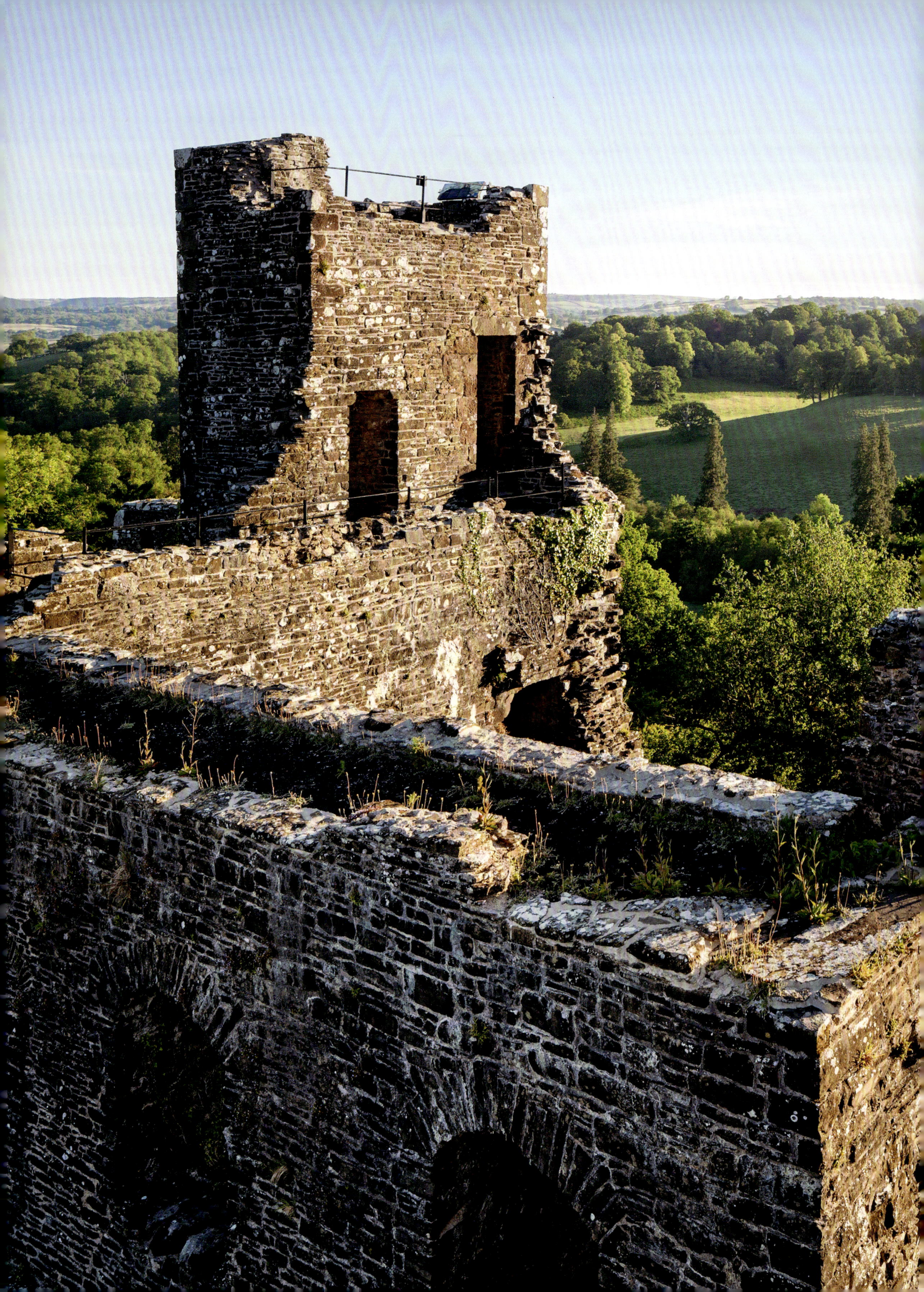

DINEFWR

— CARMARTHENSHIRE —
FROM 1775

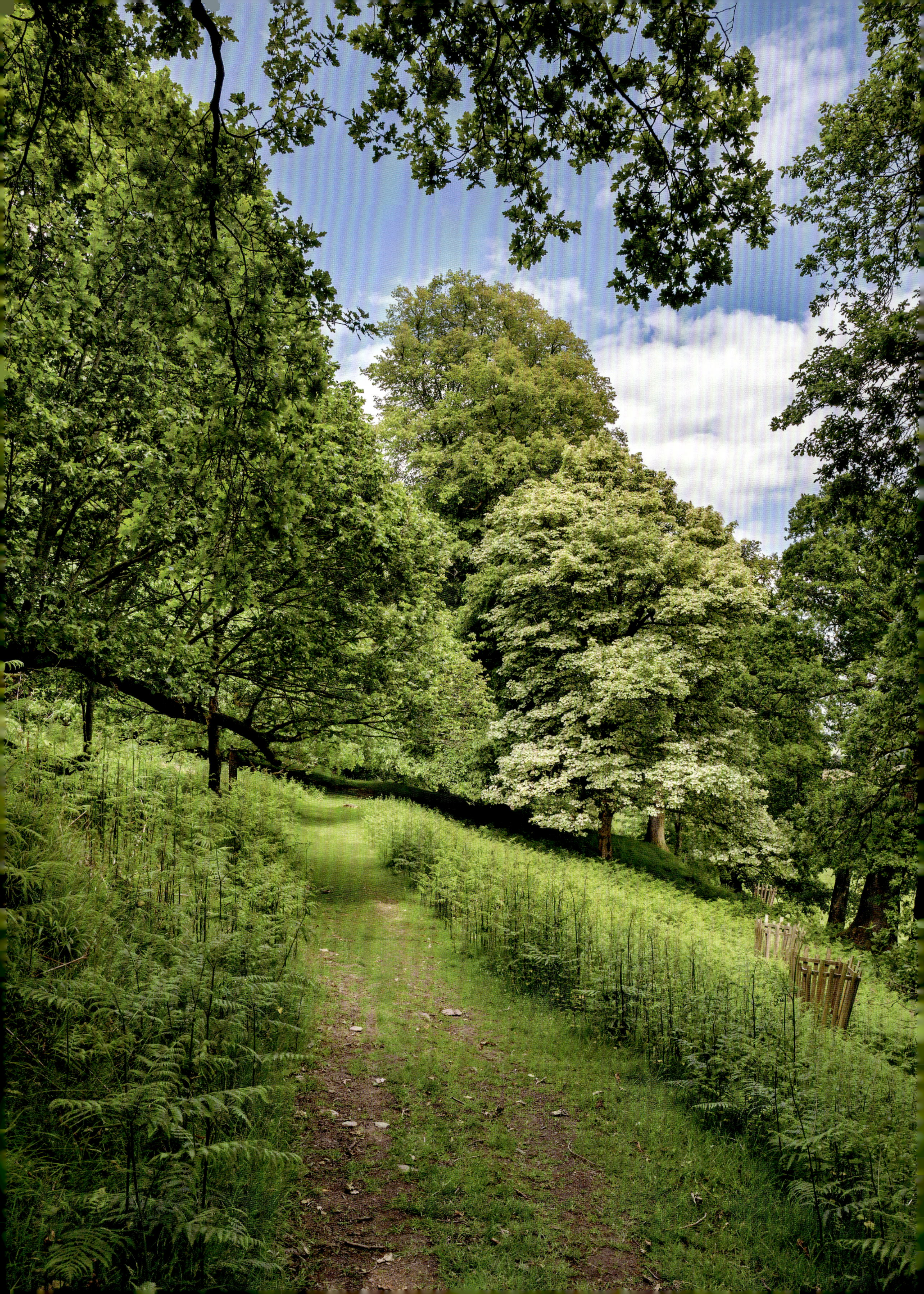

— CHAPTER THIRTEEN —

DINEFWR

Brown made his visit to West Wales in August 1775. He was on a long tour of his commissions in the West Midlands, traveling first to Oakley, Shropshire, then to Dinefwr, and on to Eywood, Herefordshire, and Fisherwick, Staffordshire. Nonetheless, the fresh enthusiasm with which he responded to Dinefwr gives an indication of the capabilities he saw there: "I wish my journey may prove to be of use to the Place, which if it should, it will be very flattering to me." It had a great medieval castle, picturesquely ruined, tangled old trees, a dramatically varied topography falling to the River Towy, and plenty of land—in his own words: "Nature has been truly bountiful and Art has done no harm." This succinct description is borne out by the excited comments of his acquaintance William Gilpin, who had visited Dinefwr five years earlier:

The castle stands upon a bold eminence, incircled with wood: but Mr Rice... has long disused it as a mansion; & has built a very handsome modern house in his park... What particularly recommends the place is the beautiful variety of ground about it. Of all the places I ever saw, I remember none which abounded with so many beauties of the kind. Every part of it is in motion, some in gentle, some in agitated motion; & each swell and valley is peculiar to itself so totally void of art (as indeed, I suppose the whole to be natural), so agreably blended with the ground about it, that perhaps no place could afford a painter a more pleasing study for the inequalities of an unbroken surface... The beautiful views, which this place affords, are numerous wherever the old castle appears, and it appears almost everywhere, a scene purely picturesque is generally presented. The ground is so beautifully disposed, that it is almost impossible to have a bad composition: & yet no pains seem to have been taken to introduce any view. Indeed if any art has been used in this whole piece of scenery, it is exquisitely hid.[1]

This was a landscape of high quality. Dynamically varied and articulated by a superb series of set-piece views, it had an ambition and scale to rank with Milton Abbey. In response, Brown produced a design that was both radical and properly respectful to the

previous pages: Dinefwr Castle floats above the trees—like Milton's Eden "embosom'd high in tufted trees."
opposite: Brown's walk at Dinefwr.

character of the place. His paid commission was for designs for the kitchen garden and for a new entrance, but in practice his proposals covered the whole area of parkland. These proposals read as part of a continuing process that had begun thirteen years earlier with the marriage of his client the Rt. Hon. George Rice to Cecil Talbot and that had been steadily bringing a new aesthetic to the parkland. Brown's advice boils down to making the parkland flow more easily by felling trees that were separating one part from another, by removing the remaining walls within it, and by refashioning the routes through the parkland and fixing on places to stop and take in the view: "a single tree with a Bench round it… the Large Ash with a white Bench.—A room… in the Circular Tower of the Castle."

A number of viewpoints like these were made and are survived by level platforms on the sloping ground. In fact, his contribution at Dinefwr might be regarded as a return to the fixed-point views that Brown created at Stowe, Wotton, and Petworth at the beginning of his career, but here, as at Milton, the views are deliberately casual. There is none of the careful geometry that one finds at Stowe and Wotton. Everything appears to happen dynamically, and one can see the restlessness that Brown brought to the design in the clumps attributed to his hand at Pen lan-fawr, where they fall across the contour, "off the shoulder" of the hills. The same willful asymmetry is to be found in the arrangement of clumps off the east front. Although we know that Brown had considered the views from the house, in particular the

above and opposite: The house at Dinefwr, Newton House, was rebuilt in the nineteenth century.
overleaf: Ring counts suggest that some of the planting in these "off-the-shoulder" clumps may predate Brown, unless he planted the trees as large specimens.

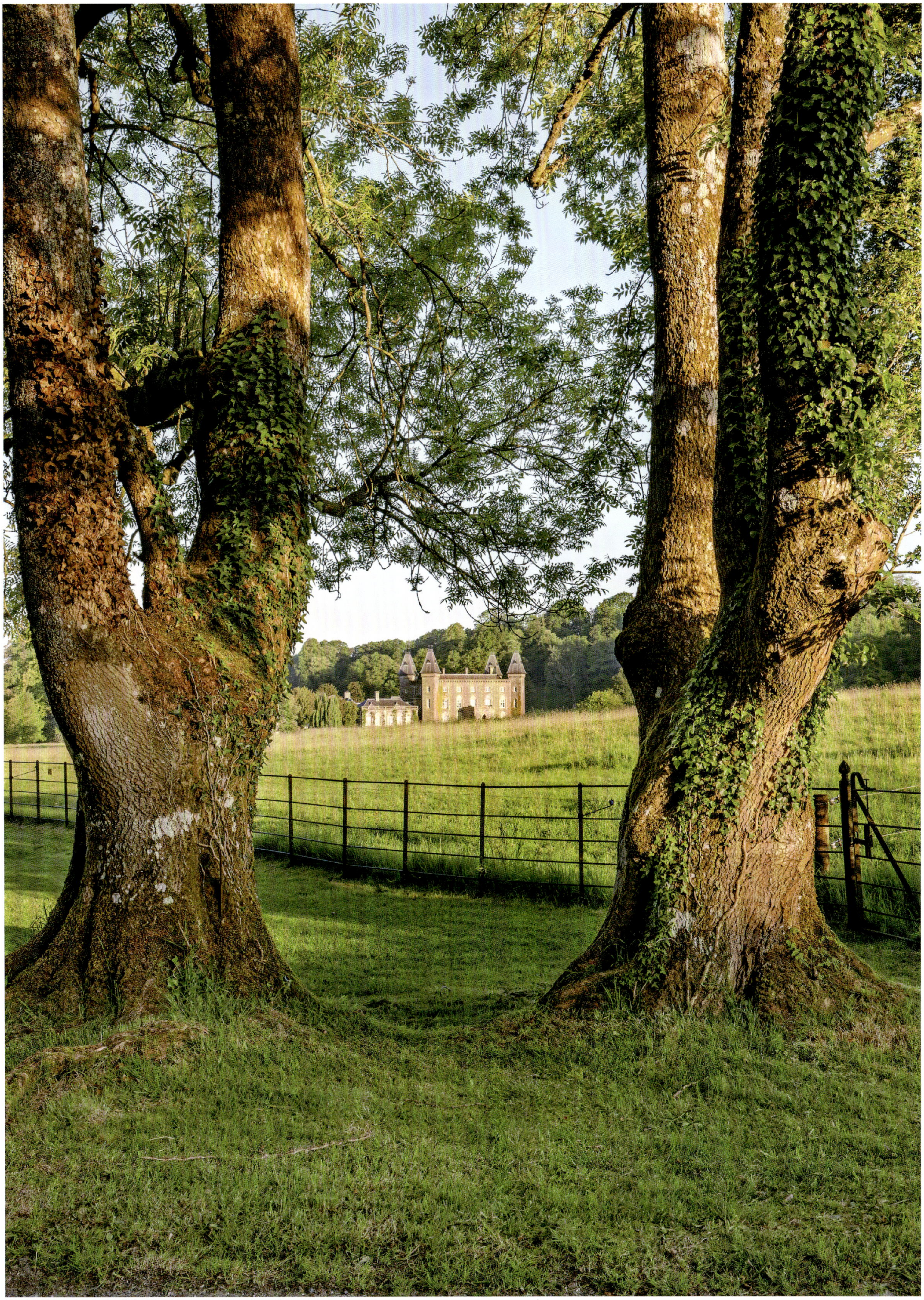

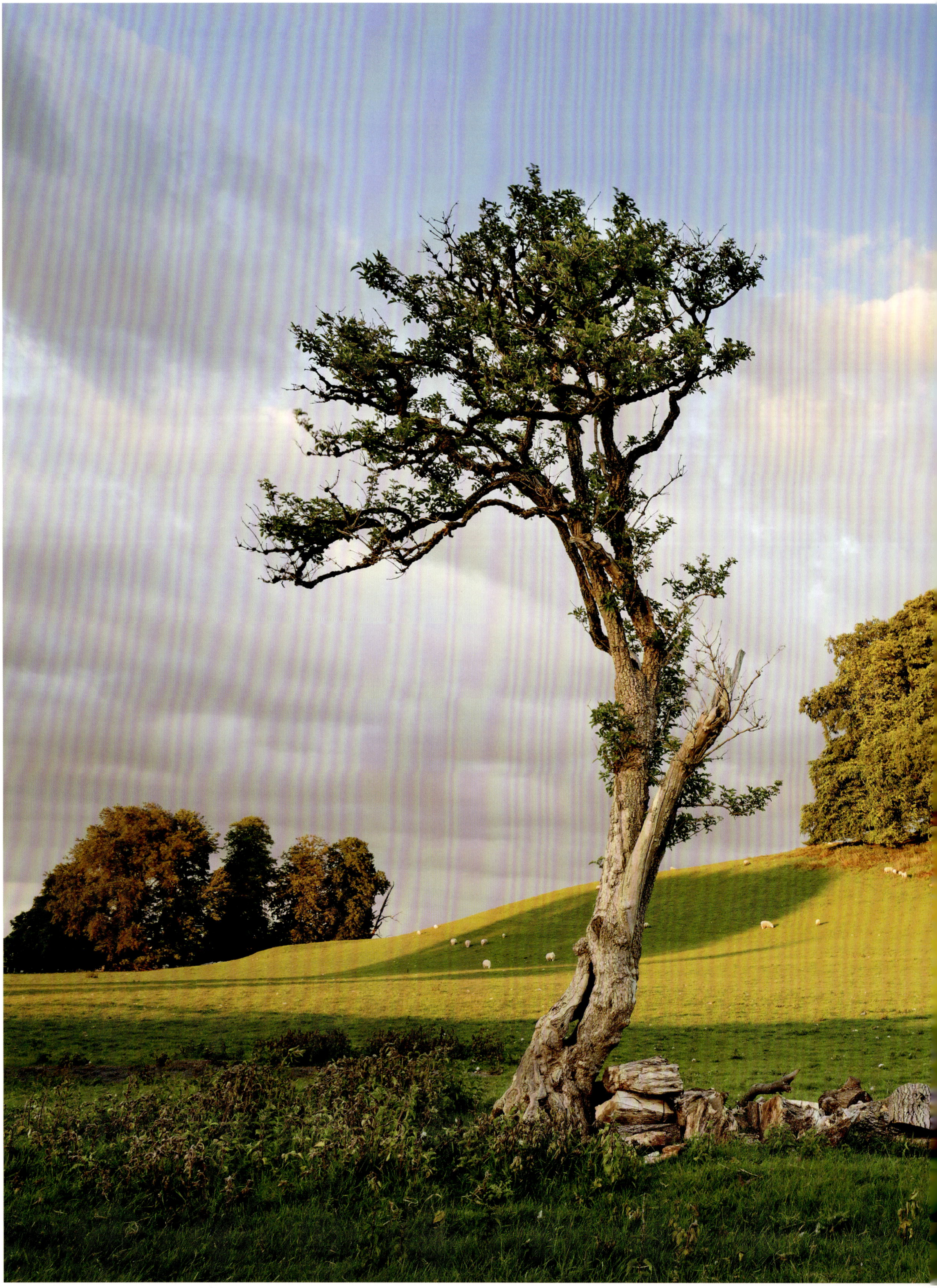

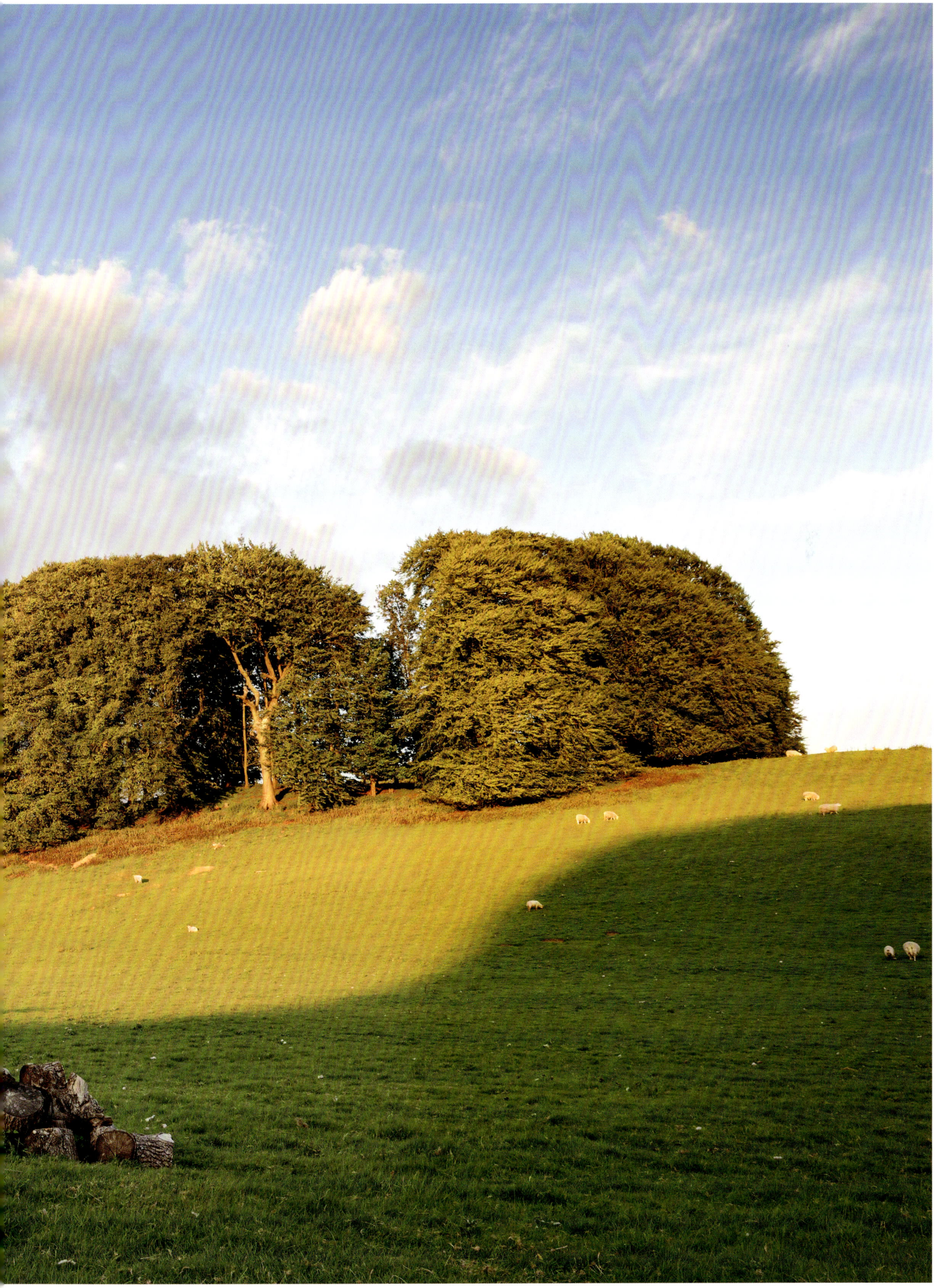

view past the walled garden and off into the distance, the house looks out on parkland that appears to have nothing to do with it. His interest seems to have been moving toward the texture of landscape and the "picturesque," the landscape style that evolved in reaction to Brown's. This was a new and remarkably prescient departure for Brown, and it was carried out consistently over the landscape.

Parkland walks, for example, are not uncommon in Brown's work: one runs west of Burghley House, over the Lion Bridge, and on to the Kennels there. But Brown's walk at Dinefwr was an altogether longer circuit of more than three miles (five kilometers) around the periphery of the parkland. Although it was a patchwork of new and older routes, it was essentially a walk rather than a drive—some of its Brownian sections are less than six feet wide and too narrow for a carriage. One might ask why so much work

above: The view from the front of the house is of an extensive piece of level ground, broken by large clumps.

above: *The valley that runs into the deer park off the back of
the house has a beautifully Brownian form. There is a complete contrast
with the view from the front.*

right: Brown's Walk can still be readily followed for most of its length. It ran around the perimeter of the park before cutting through it to follow the valley past an old quarry that had been turned into a pleasure ground.

was put into constructing a walk in the first place. It may have been to ensure that the ground underfoot stayed dry in wet weather, but Brown's walks tend to read as though the designer wanted people to take a very particular route through the parkland (in this case a route that favored views out of the parkland, as ridings do) and had in mind a sequencing of effects or "diversions" (Llandeilo Bridge, the church at Llandyfesant, the castle, the Heronry, the Walled Garden, and Newton Farm, the new lodge that he recommended) spaced more or less evenly around the circuit. What is surprising about this, however, is that although the French philosopher Jean-Jacques Rousseau had used walking as a way of getting close to himself and to nature ("what is needed is neither absolute rest nor too much agitation, but a uniform and moderated movement having neither jolts nor lapses"), the idea was not to take root in Britain for another twenty years, when it was adopted by the lake poets and by Brown's fiercest critics, the champions of the picturesque—both Uvedale Price and Richard Payne Knight laid out long walks through their landscapes.

The picture at Dinefwr is obscure because within thirty years of Brown's visit a subsequent campaign of planting very much in the picturesque style had taken place. However, one might reasonably regard his Dinefwr as a triumph of the riding (which might be described as the use of roads to show off a landscape rather than to change it), and as one of our earliest essays in the picturesque, which, paradoxically, with its admiration for rough unpolished scenery, is usually taken as the antithesis of Brown's aesthetic.

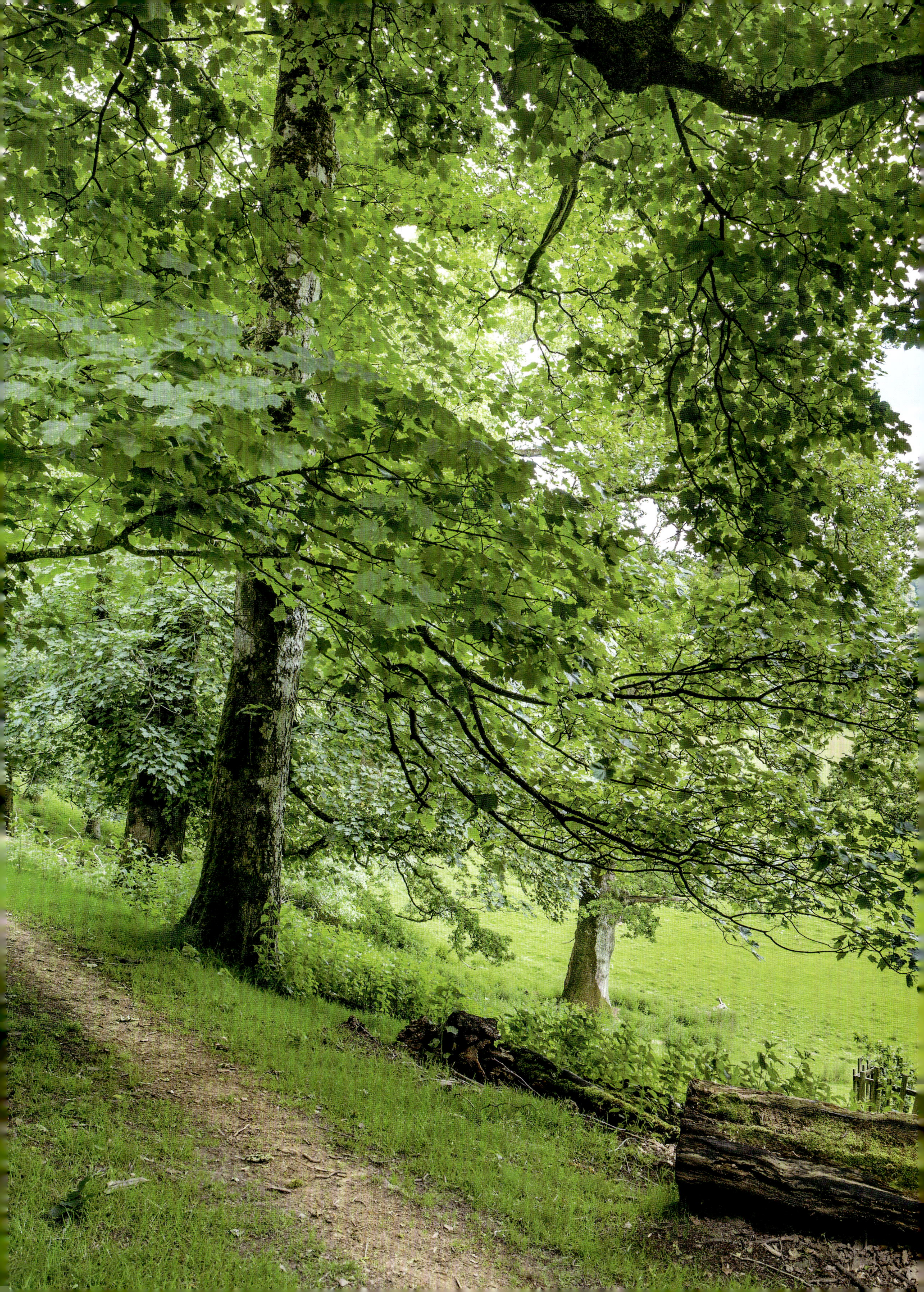

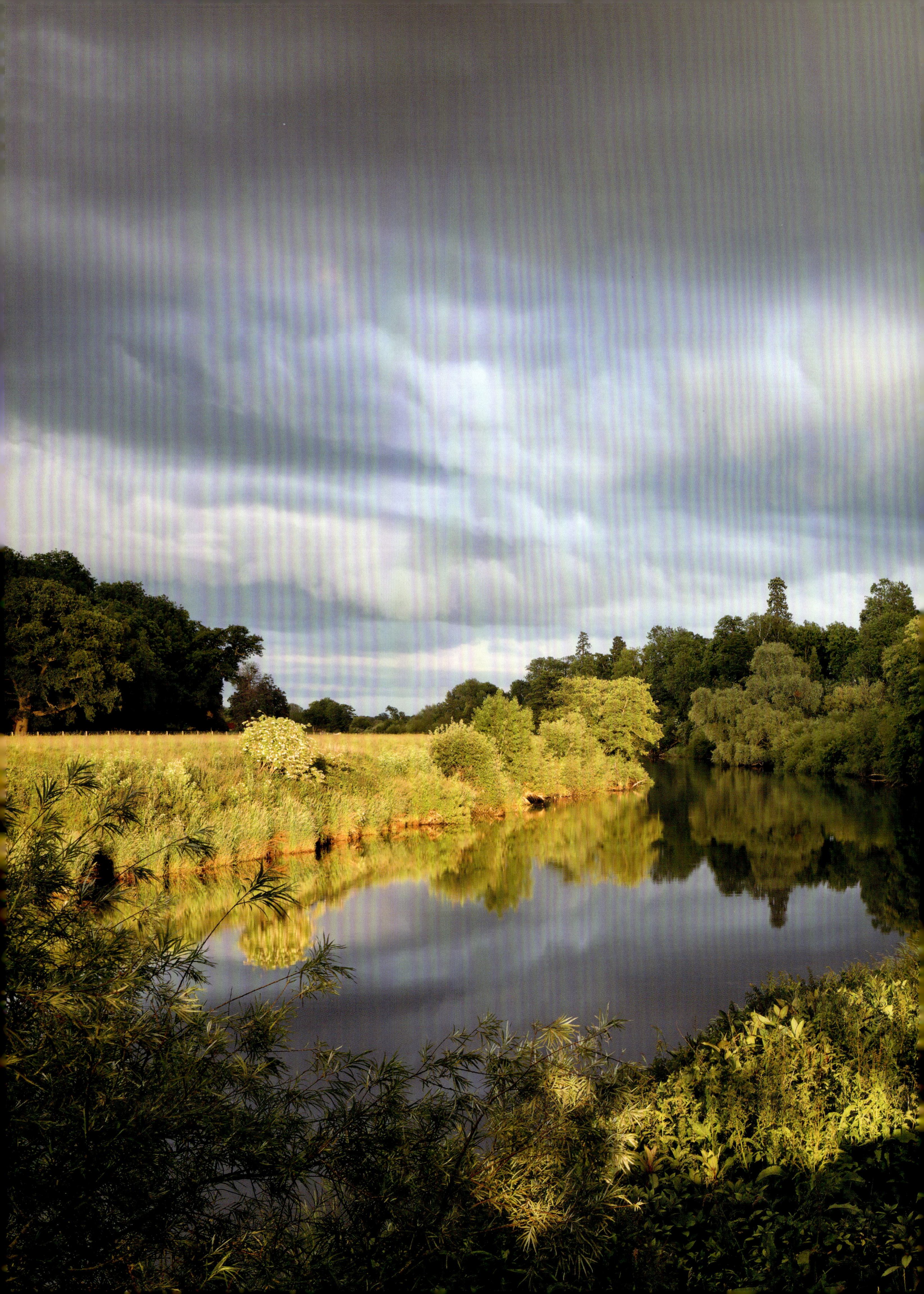

MOCCAS COURT

— HEREFORDSHIRE —
FROM 1778

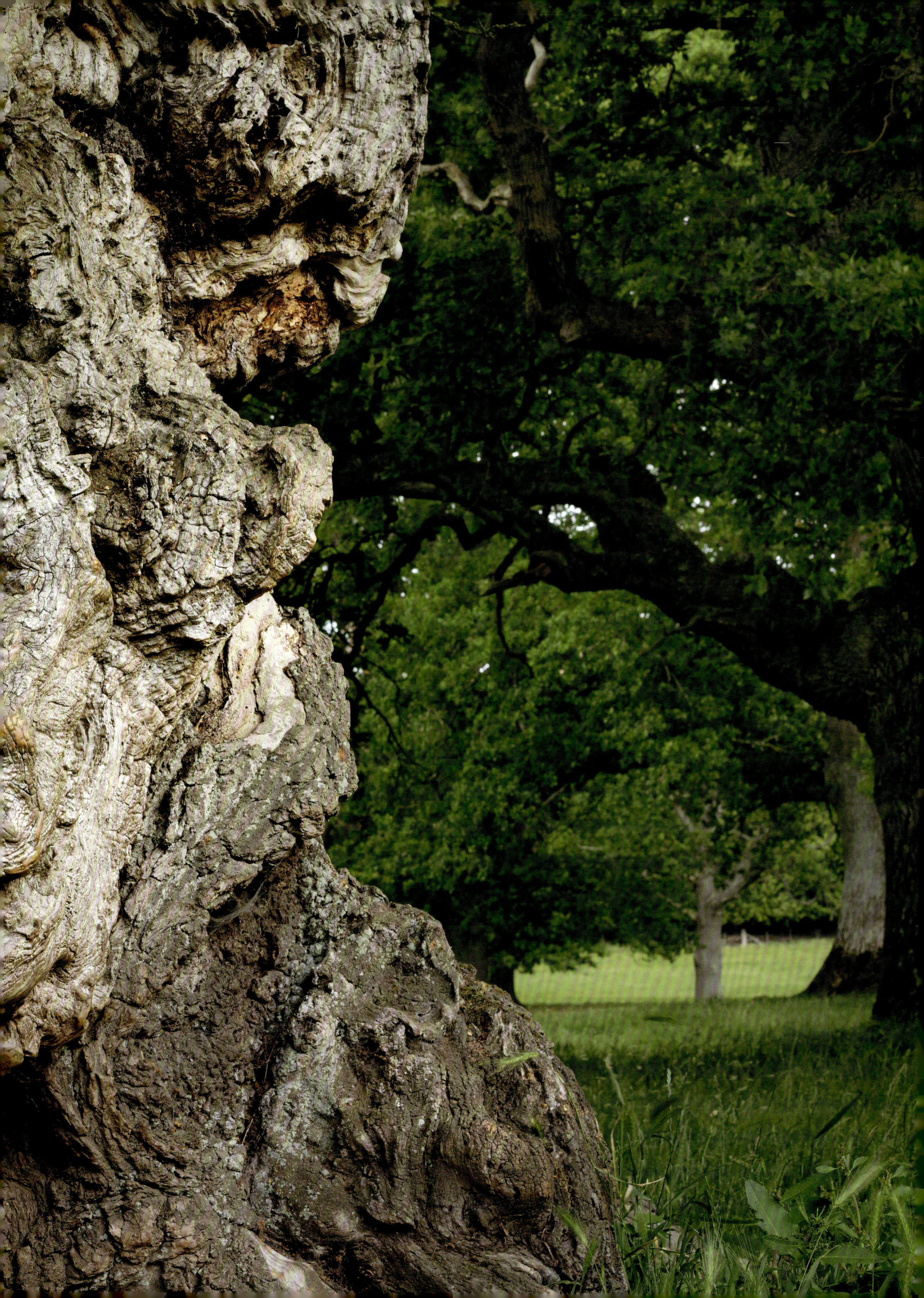

— CHAPTER FOURTEEN —

MOCCAS COURT

The trajectory of Brown's career might be described as a move from Whig (the creation of private exclusive kingdoms, like Stowe, for the new aristocracy of the Glorious Revolution) to Tory (inclusive landscapes like Milton with a benevolent and paternal landlord long-established at its center). Whatever one may think of this theory, the fact is that Moccas Court must be described as an inclusive rag-bag of a landscape, and it was a fiefdom of old-school Toryism. The Cornewalls were proud to trace their lineage back to King John, and their estate at Moccas had been built up by Velters Cornewall (1697–1768), Member of Parliament for Herefordshire for forty-six years, a staunch supporter of his county and its farmers, and an opponent of Lord Bute's Cider Bill of 1763, which would have placed four shillings duty on every hogshead that the farmers produced.

Velters' Moccas was that admired icon of Toryism, the working farm. So the poet John Lockman (1698–1771) wrote of the "hedges trim," the "full-fed beeves," the orchard and the River Wye which "strays through banks of flower fields" around the house, as well as the "craggy cliff" of Brobury Scar on the north bank of the river, and the "brambly steep" of the deer park and its famous ancient oaks rising to the south, with a view of "territory wild and vast... the Welsh Alps."

When Velters' heir and Brown's client, Sir George Cornewall, inherited in 1768, a modest yew walk ran from the old house; but any further ornamentation was stopped by the farmland, arable, pasture, and meadow, and besides the deer park and the earthwork known as Moccas Castle, there were only field names (Little Park, Great Paddock, and Warren) to suggest any grand design in the past history of the place.

Notwithstanding the simplicity of the setting, the Cornewalls were sufficiently aware of their station to be very interested in horses. Velters had a stud of at least forty saleable stallions and mares in 1755,[1] and Sir George kept at least seventeen horses for his own use, besides horses for the farm and for racing. In fact, he began building his new stables to accommodate them in 1782, and he would have needed at least 100 acres of good grass to feed them.

previous pages: The construction of Moccas Court began in 1775 to designs by Antony Keck. It has a bay facing out over the River Wye to take in long reaches of the water. opposite: Moccas has long been famous for the ancient oaks and sweet chestnuts in its deer park.

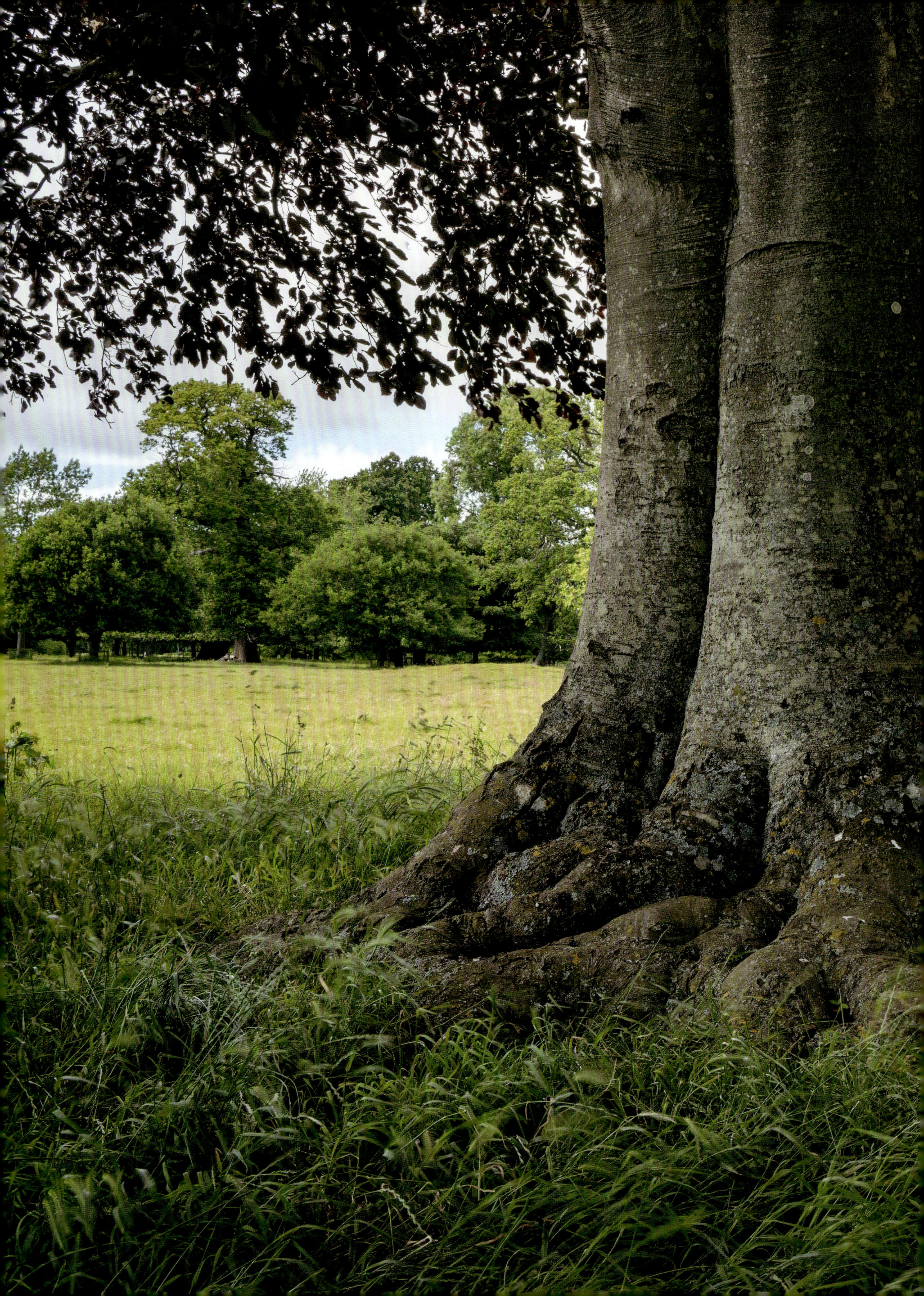

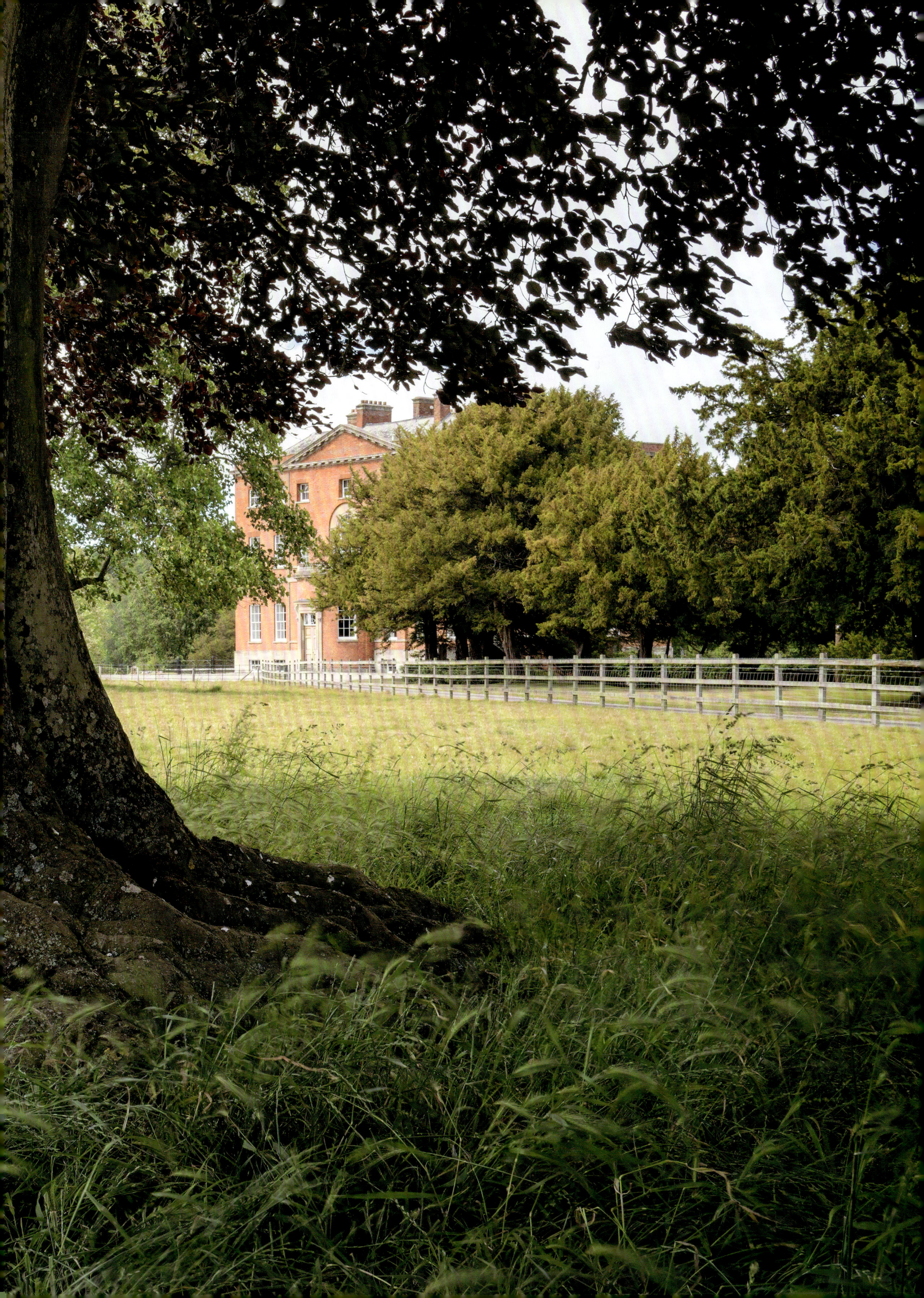

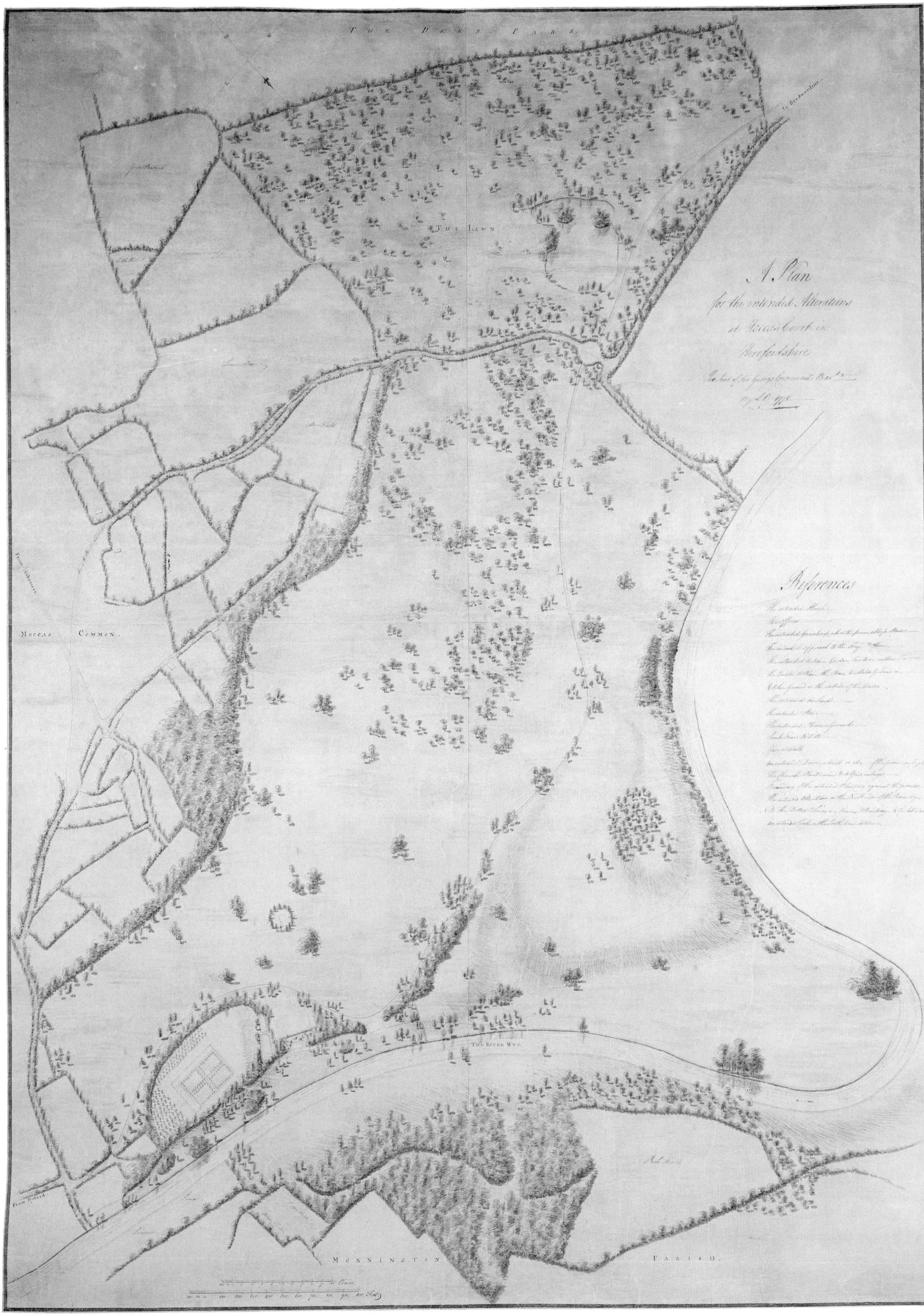
THE DEER PARK
THE LAWN
A Plan
for the intended Alterations
at Moccas Court in
Herefordshire
The Seat of Sir George Cornewall Bart
References
MOCCAS COMMON
THE RIVER WYE
MONNINGTON PARISH

The combination of an ancient family, a need for grass, and a well-run farm all suited Brown's interests at this stage in his career, but at Moccas he had the additional challenge of making some connection between the house in its rich lowland riverside setting and a deer park of unknown antiquity, grown over with ancient oaks and chestnuts, up above in Dorstone parish.

As is so often the case, the records we have for Brown at Moccas are at best ambiguous. We know from Sir George Cornewall's own account that Brown visited in 1778, and billed Sir George for a journey and plans for which he was paid exactly £100 in 1781.

One of these plans survives, covering the land between Moccas Court and the deer park, but we have no notion of the number of others that he might have produced, the length of the visit, or why he was not paid for three years. However, so far as we know, Brown always charged round-number sums when his involvement was limited to the provision of plans and a visit. On this occasion Brown's surveyor, John Spyers, was not needed, but by comparison the plans for Belvoir Castle, made in 1779 and also costing £100, included a survey by Spyers and Brown's master plan, with a reduced version of the same bound into an album of a dozen or so plans and elevations for the proposed new house. Moccas was therefore an ambitious commission, even if the work was to be carried out by Sir George's own men under instruction from the estate owner himself.

previous pages: The landscaping around the house remains plain and simple.
opposite and above: Brown's surviving plan for Moccas only shows the land as far as the deer park. It is characteristic of the relaxed form of his late style that parkland can be indistinguishable from farmland.

MOCCAS COURT · 247

248 · CAPABILITY BROWN

In order to connect the house and the deer park, Brown first realigned the west approach so that it could also serve as a drive to the park. In fact, it seems likely that he extended it through the deer park, up to the Dorstone Ridge, past the lodge (now Lodge Farm) and down into the Golden Valley to the south, more than two miles away.

It is typical of a late work such as Moccas that Brown had no inclination to bring deer up to the house, and instead reconciled the management and look of the land between the house and the park by building on the planting that was already there, incorporating the old wood pasture in Little Park and bulking up hedgerows so as to make a walk from the house to the Cold Bath in Dog Kennel Plantation and on to the cascade at the south end of Depple Wood (both features were built at this time and may have been suggested by him). Again it is typical of his late work that there was no great pleasure ground by the house, instead he planned to make one on Brobury Scar on the north side of the river, with its dramatic view across the river to the house, and another in Depple Wood, where the walk runs beside the river and was so enjoyed a hundred years later by the diarist, Francis Kilvert.

Looking south from the house, the view was neatly divided by the narrow Brick Kiln Wood (planted in 1787 directly in front of the house), with a distant view on one side to the mound of "Moccas Castle" (which then had a building on it) and on the other to the Great Paddock, where the horses were kept on show.

Various other small additions were made—a clump to screen the old warrener's lodge on the high

left: The Wye from Moccas Court, with Brobury Scar on the rising ground of the far bank.

below: From the crags of Brobury Scar on the north bank of the River Wye, Sandby's scene is one of pastoral farmland.

ground in the Warren; and as the ground fell toward the river, a mixture of species was added to vary the walk between Dog Kennel Wood and Depple Wood and set off the fine views across the Wye to the Scar. However, an undated watercolor by Paul Sandby taken from Brobury Scar seems to show the effect of Brown's proposals: the Cold Bath, put up at some time after 1772, old hedges removed, new planting on the Scar, and field boundaries simplified. Moccas church is hidden by the trees, as at Stowe, and sheep are grazing, watched over by a shepherd, closer to the river. The ideas suggest a real reluctance to impose ideas on the landscape rather than respond to its genius loci—and hence a return to the *ferme ornée*, where incidents are linked by a series of walks through the fields.

The result is not actually coherent, but it does incidentally point up the persuasiveness of Brown's cartography. His plans were plain, not highly colored or ornamented for display, but they were surprisingly unspecific—there are no working drawings with measured levels and detail. The vigor in the scribbled pen strokes does, however, contrive to impart

right: The deer park, on the high ground above the house, is the glory of Moccas.

250 · CAPABILITY BROWN

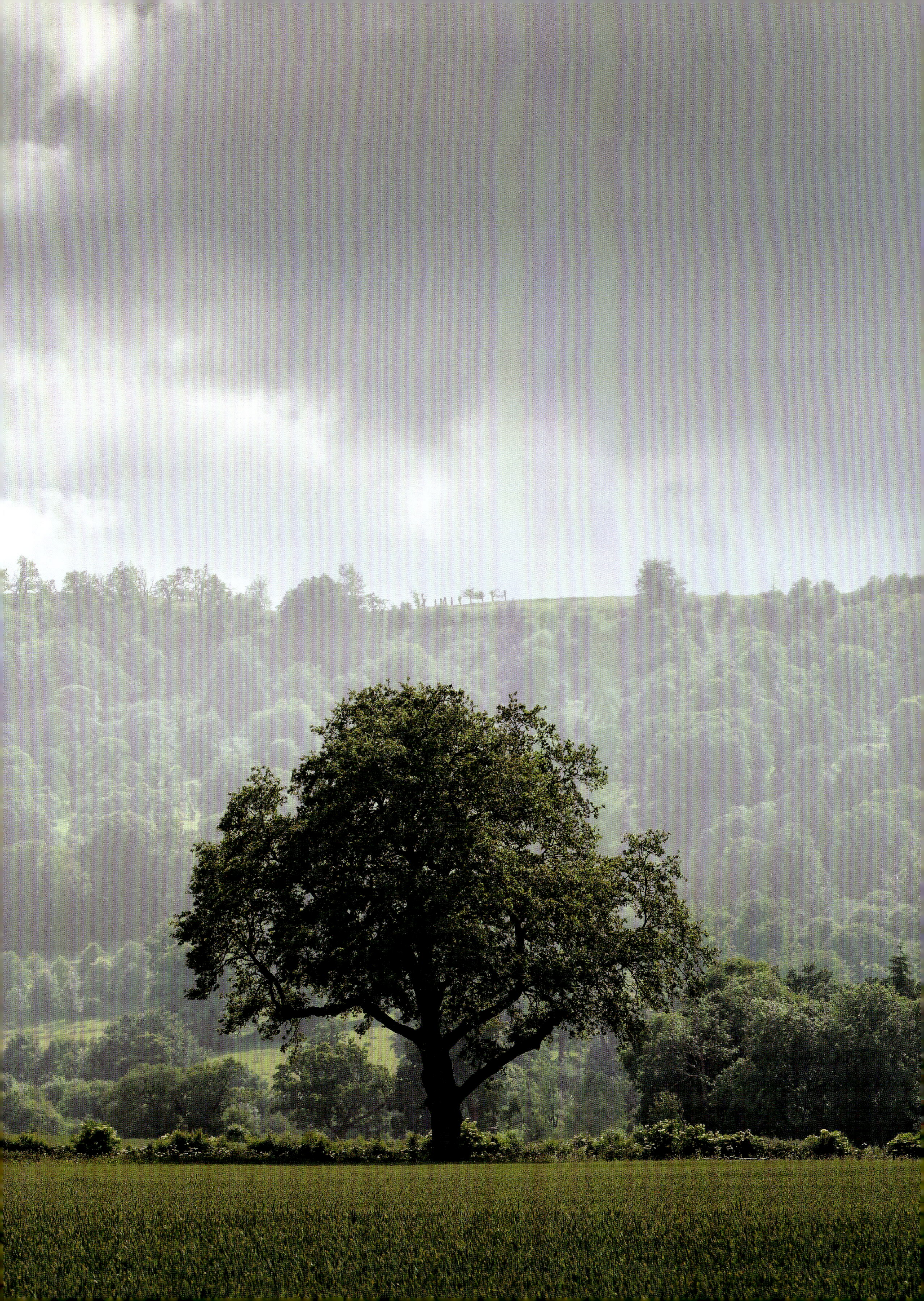

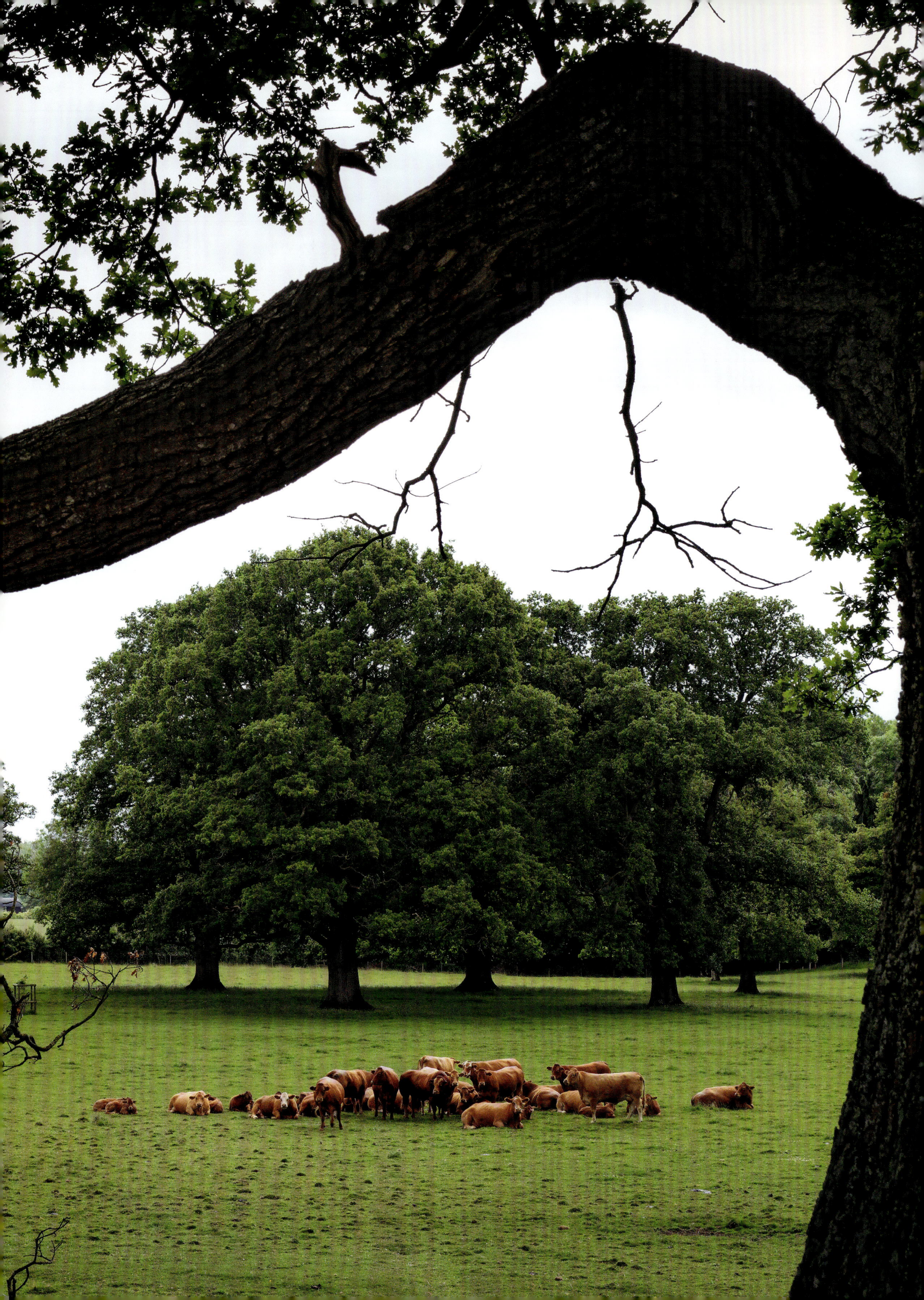

an overall coherence and the authority of a designer who was quite certain of what he was doing. At the same time, his plans might reassure his client that really very little needed to be done to bring out the underlying and essential character of the country. They were simple enough for an owner to carry in his or her head for years. So Brown's ideas for Moccas continued to bear fruit into the nineteenth century, albeit modified by the influence of Sir George's friends (and Brown's enemies)—the Herefordshire squires, Uvedale Price and Richard Payne Knight. Indeed, the oak avenue planted by Sir Gilbert Lewis in 1841 in Little Park effectively links the home ground around Moccas Court to the rougher deer park in the same, thoroughly Brownian fashion as the ridings at Wakefield Lodge.

opposite: The oak clump in the Warren was proposed on Brown's plan.
top: The Oak Avenue.
above: The church is modest and is concealed by planting in most views.

MOCCAS COURT · 253

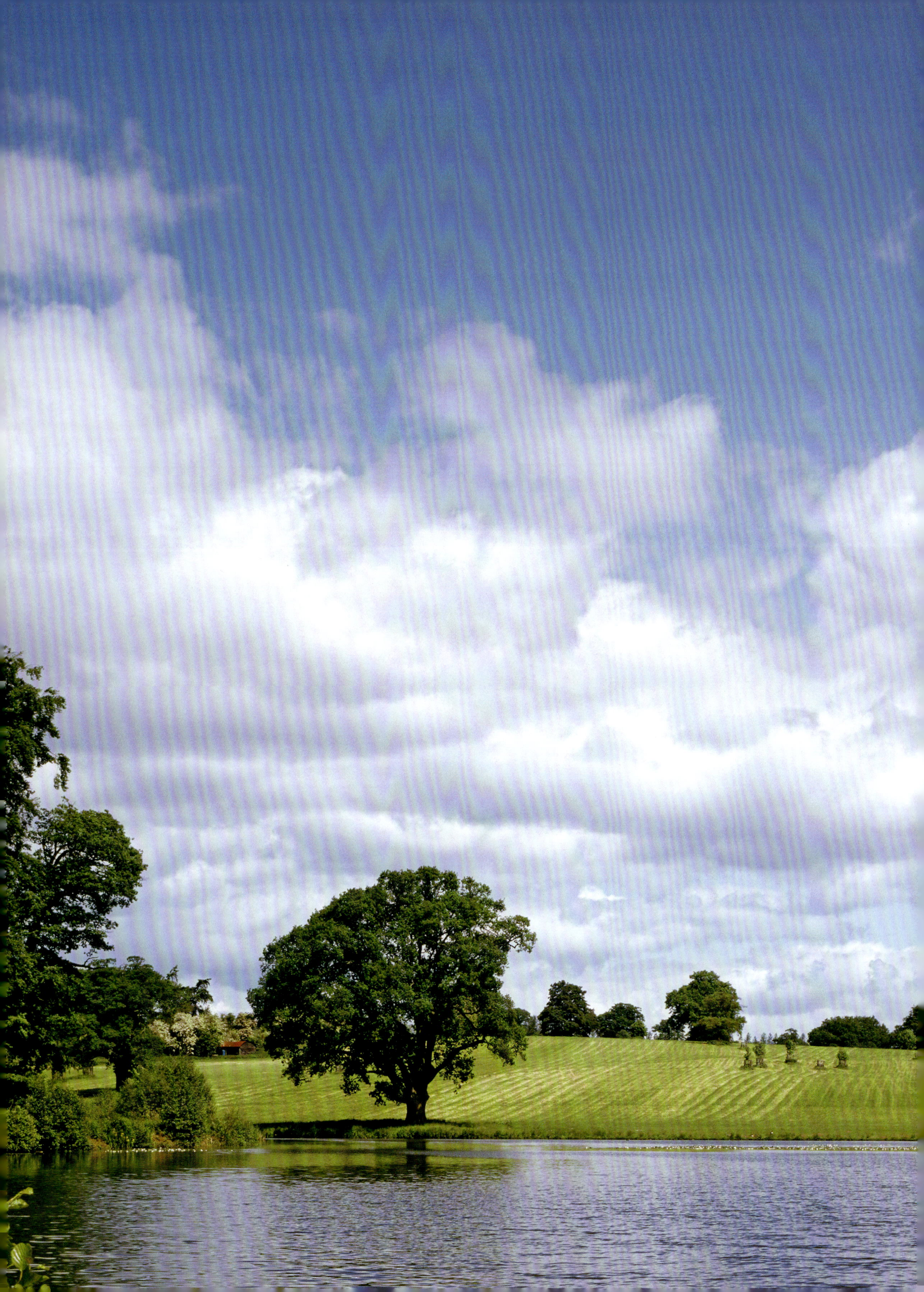

BERRINGTON HALL
— HEREFORDSHIRE —
FROM 1781

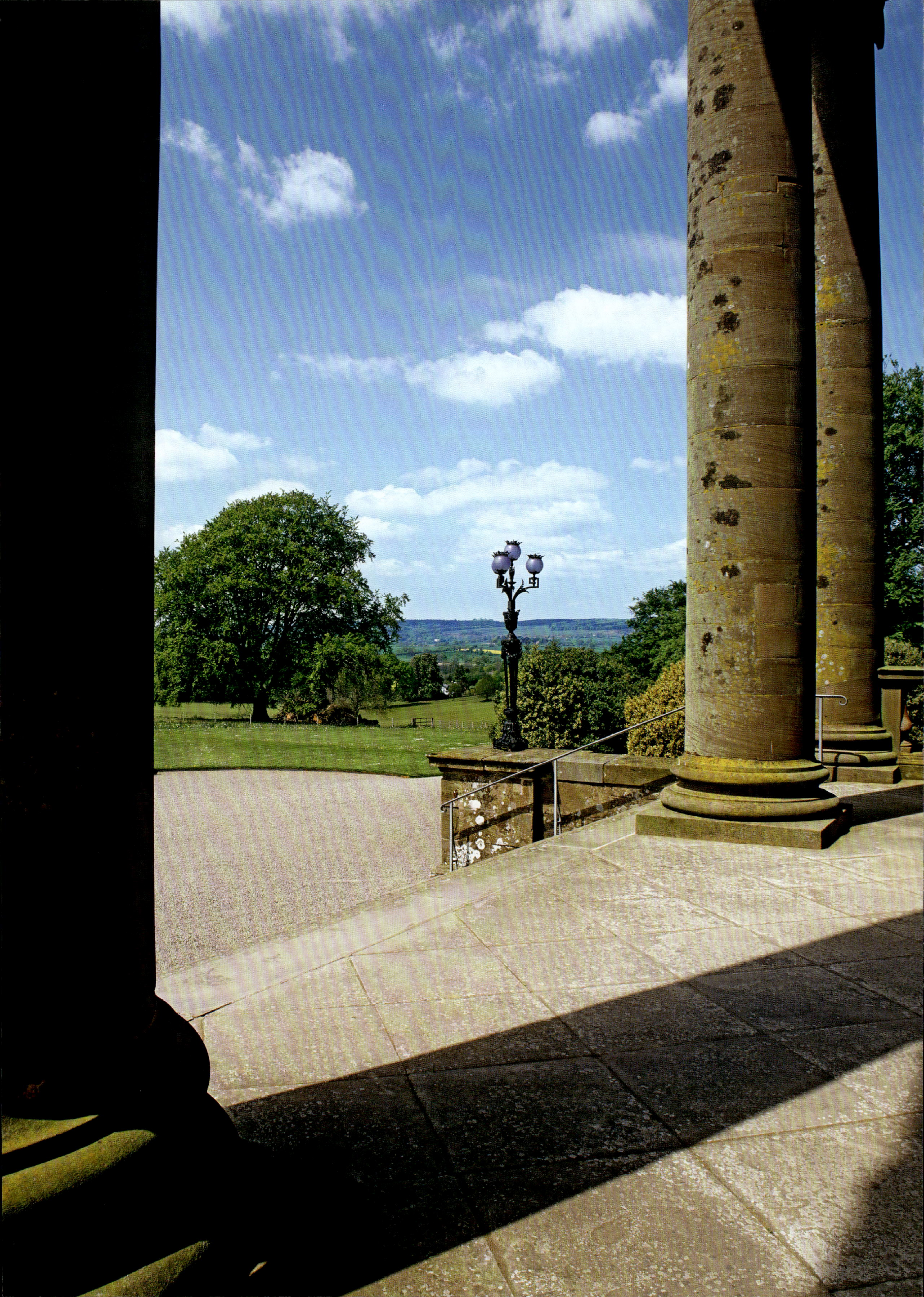

— CHAPTER FIFTEEN —

BERRINGTON HALL

At first sight Berrington does not look like a landscape of troubling complexity: there is a house, grass runs down from it to a lake, there are scatterings of trees and a belt of woodland surrounds the whole, and the Stockton and Moreton Ridings, rather than running out loosely into the countryside, wrap around the whole like string around a parcel. It was a late work, and if this is a summation of Brown's achievement, then it all seems rather anticlimactic.

Hitherto this book has tried to resolve or else smooth away many contending ideas in order to present a digestible narrative, but Brown's work is complex, and it is fitting to end with a landscape that demonstrates that complexity, and a design that belies its apparent simplicity and might reasonably be described as willfully perverse, chaotic, and obscure.

The estate that Brown had to work on had been assembled by a businessman, Thomas Harley, largely from common fields owned by the Cornewalls of Moccas Court. Brown's accounts record payments of £1,600 for Berrington, where he worked from 1781 until he died, with the commission incomplete in 1783. This large sum will have included payments for the house, designed by Brown's son-in-law, Henry Holland. We cannot therefore judge from it how much money was to be spent on the landscape, nor do we have his landscape proposals. Furthermore, his foreman, Christian Sanderson, continued to work there after Brown's death, and as with Blenheim and Weston, it is not possible to distinguish Brown's own work from anything that may have been done by his foreman after him. These are handicaps, but they should not blind us to the omnipresence of Brown and Brownian thinking in the landscape.

The starting point has to be the relationship between the house and the water.

Brown's lake is perched on a slope that falls away toward the west. The fall is concealed by extensive tree planting on the Moreton Ride below the dam. The water is divided into two parts by a large island. On the east side of the island there is a broad channel, running from the house and having the character of a river which looks as though it might take its lazy way south, out of the parkland and toward Leominster.

previous pages: In the view of the house from the far side of the lake, Berrington seems entirely conventional.
opposite: The ground falls north of the house before rising again to Kings Hall Hill.

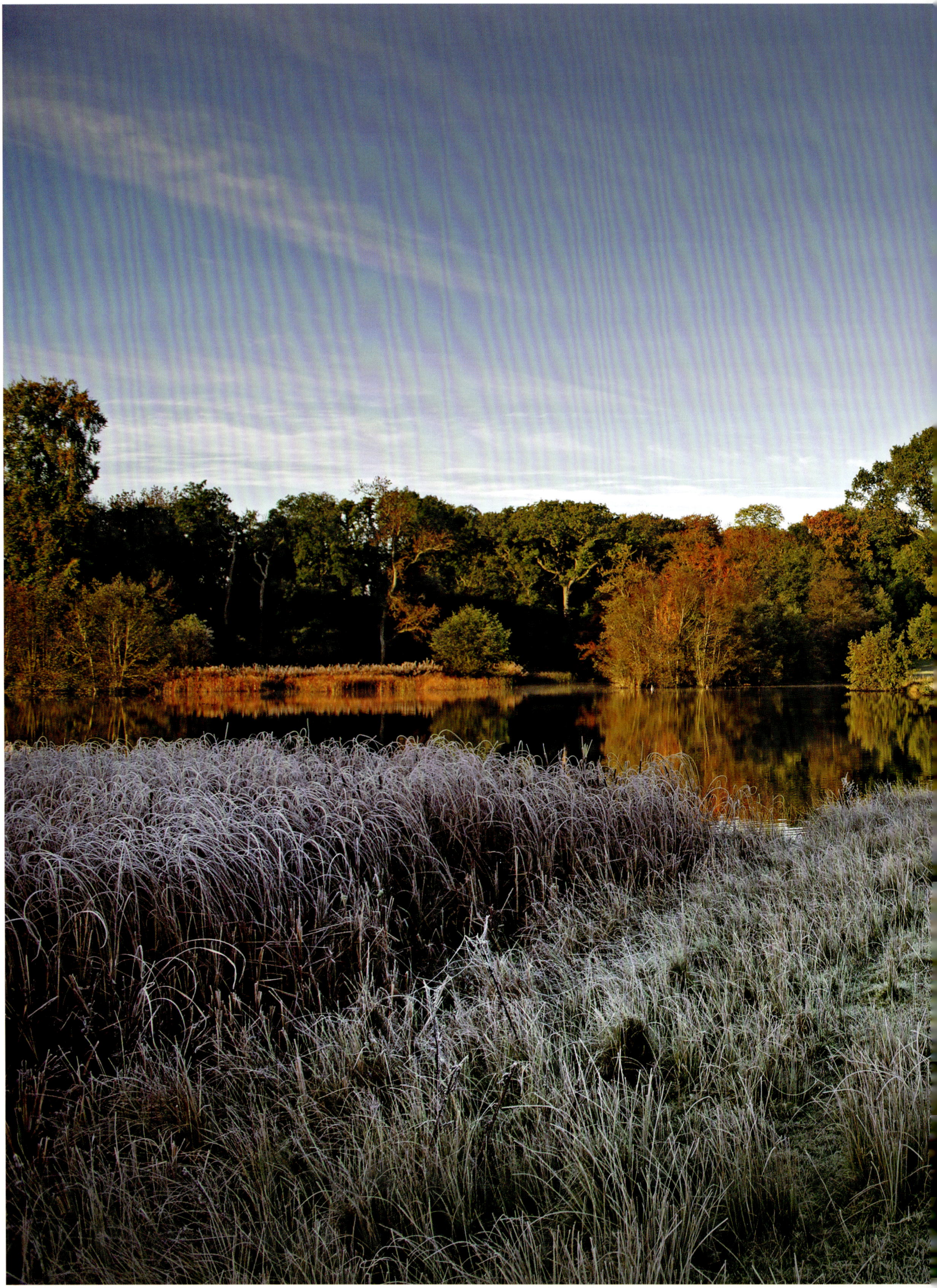

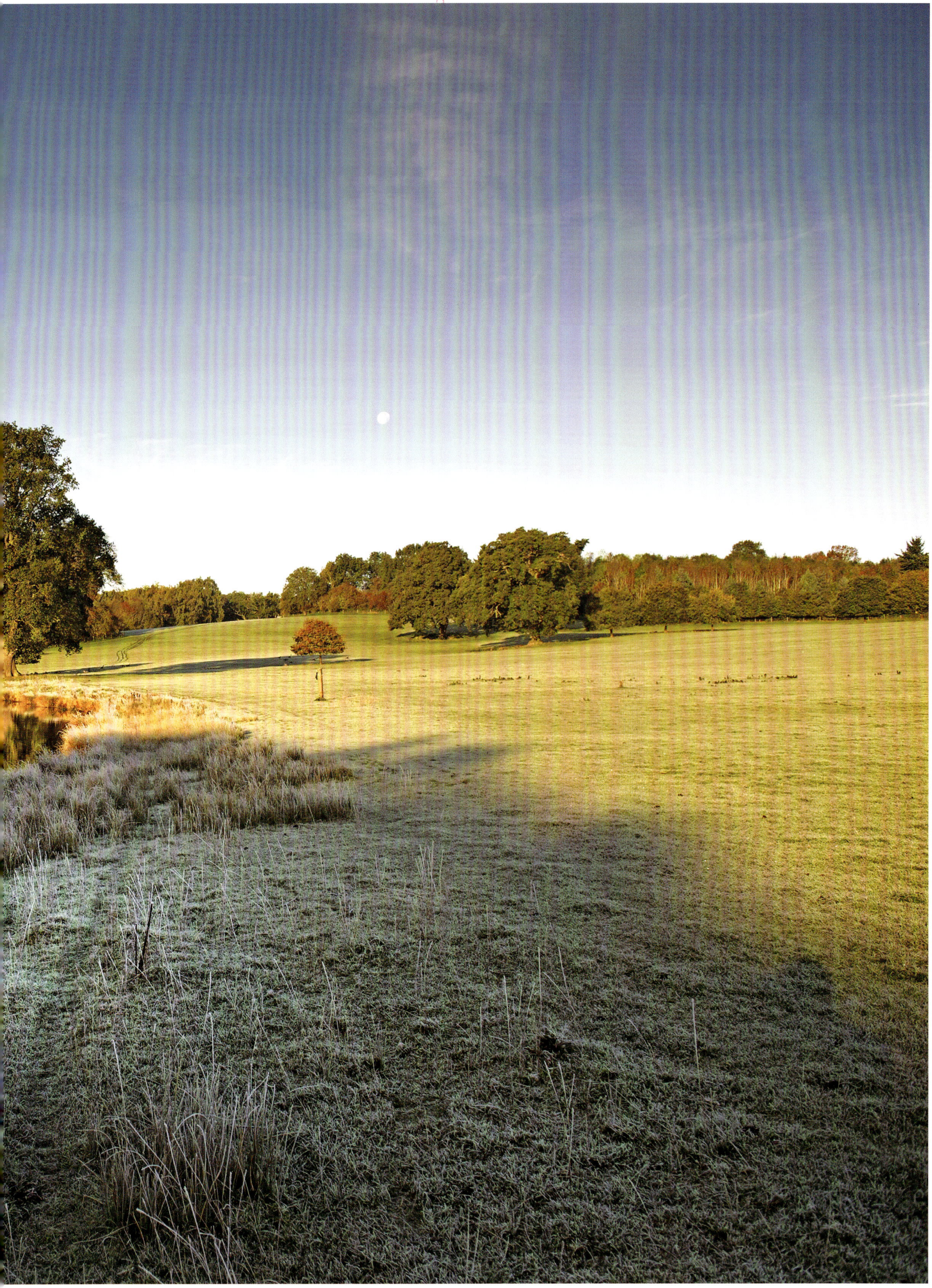

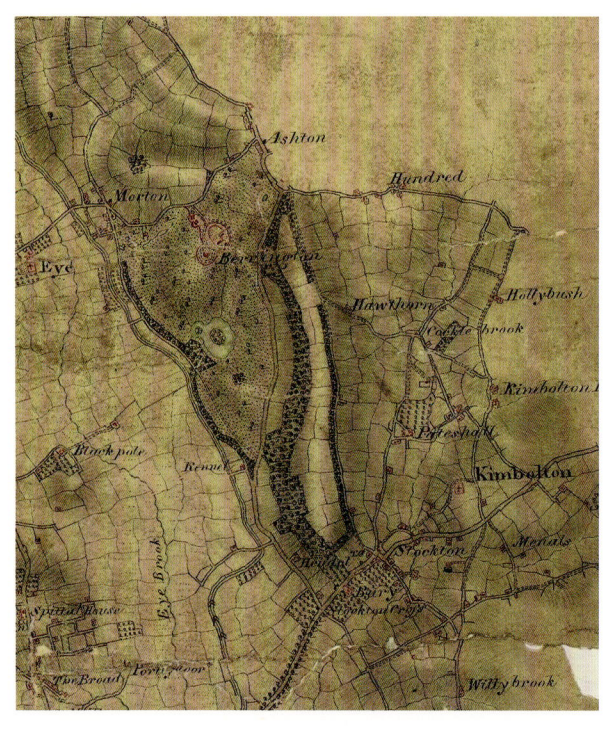

This relatively minor stretch of the water is in full view from the saloon, with Long Wood hanging heavily from the hill on its east side. However, the main body of the water is on the west side of the island. It has been increased in size since Brown's time, but even so, it is still not readily visible from the house: the library window, which overlooks it, is, and always has been, blind. In short, Brown wanted to ensure that the main lake, although his biggest single expenditure in the landscape, would not be visible from the house.

Then there is the trunk road (A49) from Ludlow to Leominster. Brown is conventionally regarded as shutting the public out of his parks by means of belts of woodland, but here the road is raised up into full view on a terrace, so making the landscape and the house more conspicuous to travelers, and vice versa.

Then, one notices the curious incoherence of the

previous pages: The strip of the lake that runs down the east side of the island might have been painted by Claude Lorrain himself. In the view from the saloon it is convincingly riverlike.
above: The Ordnance Survey Drawing of 1815 shows the completed design.

260 · CAPABILITY BROWN

design. It does not hang together. The northeast corner of the landscape, against Ashton, has no bearing on the rest; there is a pretty valley, but it doesn't connect. In the same way the southern section of the parkland, beyond the lake, merges aimlessly into the countryside beyond, nor can one distinguish deer park from parkland.

Then there is the more or less entire absence of a pleasure ground, replaced by an enormous kitchen garden, the walls of which are in full view as one passes from the Triumphal Arch to the house. On top of that comes the location and orientation of the house itself. This was designed by Henry Holland, no doubt working to Brown's instruction, as his father-in-law was the senior partner in their relationship. The house is austere and square and the Triumphal Arch (1778–1781) also by Holland does nothing to aggrandise it, as the Corinthian Arch does the house at Stowe, nor does it figure directly in any obviously composed view. In fact, the principal (London) approach has to turn through a right angle to pass it. The site of the house itself is hardly more understandable. It would be easy to think of other locations that might have been chosen in preference only a few years later—Repton at Luscombe Castle in 1799 chose a site halfway down a steep combe, much more dramatic and sheltered. Brown likewise might have chosen a site halfway down the west-facing valley, to the northwest of the present house. From Brown's site the house looks straight out to the west, away from the pleasure ground, such as it is, away from the approaches, which run into its east side, away from the lake, and toward a broad-backed hill that effectively divides the view in this direction into two. In its position, the house also divides the landscape and does much to obstruct the coherence of the whole.

opposite above: The kitchen garden has walls with rounded corners,
which strengthen the impression of a walled town in this view from Windy Bank.
above: The view from the lake up to the house.

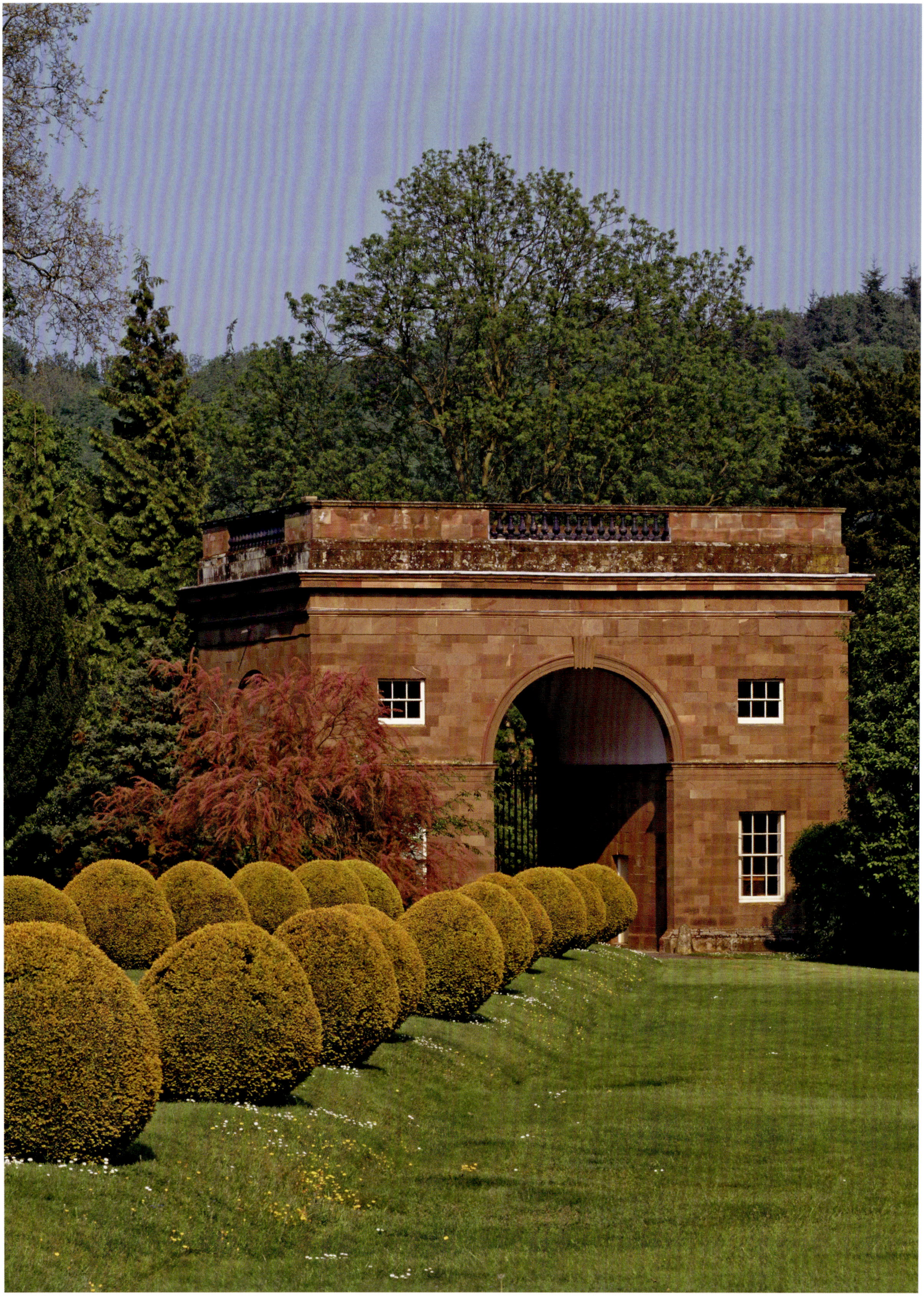

If we are to understand this design, the place to begin is on Windy Bank, east of the Triumphal Arch. A Brownian grass approach runs up to this hill from Ashton and then descends in tight curves to the house. At the crown of the hill, there is an artificial knoll. The earthwork and the winding approach testify to the importance of this hilltop in the mind of the landscaper, and it does offer an excellent prospect with wide and distant views west to Radnor Forest and beyond, but at our feet a melée of masonry: the kitchen garden, stables, midden and rick yards, courts, the Triumphal Arch, and the house itself are laid out chaotically before us—chimneys, roofs, and all, in the guise of an Italian hill town that one might see in the background of a landscape by Claude Lorrain, planted at the head of its own valley, which runs south to the lake. This approach must have been intended to startle, for it is so far removed from the stripped down architecture of the west and south fronts. In this composition, the curved walls of the kitchen garden become the walls of a town, and the Triumphal Arch becomes its gate.

Next comes his treatment of the public road. No one who visits a series of Brown's landscapes in succession could possibly believe that he aimed to conceal them from the public. At Kirkharle and Wallington, at Chatsworth, he manipulated the roads to bring the traffic on them into view at a point where he could take advantage of the animation this provided to a scene, and he had also learned that by raising a road on a terrace he could conceal its surface. The paradox is that Brown is conventionally regarded as having isolated his houses and parks. It was generally accepted that the enclosure of common

above: Once outside the walled garden, the pleasure ground is simple in the extreme.
opposite: The Triumphal Arch at Berrington offers an oblique view to the hall, far removed from the splendor of Stowe.

BERRINGTON HALL · 263

fields would increase the acreage of grassland and that that would force people off the land, and it was also accepted that the creation of parkland was part of that process. So Oliver Goldsmith could write:

> ... *the man of wealth and pride*
> *Takes up a space that many poor supplied;*
> *Space for his lake, his park's extended bounds,*
> *Space for his horses, equipage, and hounds.*[1]

In practice there is no evidence that the creation of country houses and parks reduced rural populations (it did tend to replace an independent tenantry with a dependant servant class, but that is the story of Milton Abbas). This imaginative misperception allowed the appearance of seclusion (planting a belt of trees around a park) to be mistaken for actual seclusion (in fact, the A49 trunk road runs right through the middle of the parkland at Berrington).

This is a step beyond Brown's design for Weston, where a view to the south is to be had from a number of different points in the pleasure ground, and while each is different, all reinforce the simple picture of lowland parkland in champaign country rising to the distant eminence of Tong Knoll.

Great landscapes elicit more from the imagination of the viewer and visitor than one might expect, and it is a striking fact that when asked if the main body of the water was visible from the state rooms, all the staff at Berrington said that it was. Their imaginations had deceived them.

Brown's Berrington relies upon our engaged imaginations. He had learned that he did not have to position every viewpoint in a technically perfect manner, as he did in his early work at Stowe and Wotton. He had discovered that he could make a view that could be properly seen only from the middle of the front, work for a whole parade of rooms. In the prospect from Windy Bank, he could make an austere neo-classical house seem like a small town, and he could make a landscape appear secluded, while putting it on display. The same understanding applies to his treatment of the water. He could make people believe that the house and lake were intervisible by juxtaposing them across the slopes of grass, while actually offering from the house only the river-like strip of water east of the island. He could present the idea of a park with a house set into the middle of the grass, and far from noticing that at Berrington the parkland is actually divided and incoherent, people might welcome the surprise of its odd corners in a landscape that was in their imaginations so simple.

The layout at Berrington has a careless air, as though by accepting the role of the imagination Brown had learned to relax, but there is also here for the first time an intimation of changes to come. The turnpike revolution had reached Herefordshire early, and with it, ridings were no longer needed as private roads. The Stockton Riding does offer extensive views out to the east, which are denied to the house and parkland, but both it and the Moreton are diminished remainders of Brown's ridings of the 1750s and 60s. They provide a circuit for exercise and access to the ancient castle site at Ashton, but the landscaping has receded from them, to concentrate again on the parkland, even if that, following the general trend of Brown's work, is as much a farm as it is a park.

above: The main road from Leominster to Ludlow runs through the parkland, its surface concealed by terracing and earthworks.
opposite: The walled garden at Berrington is the most conspicuous part of the pleasure ground.

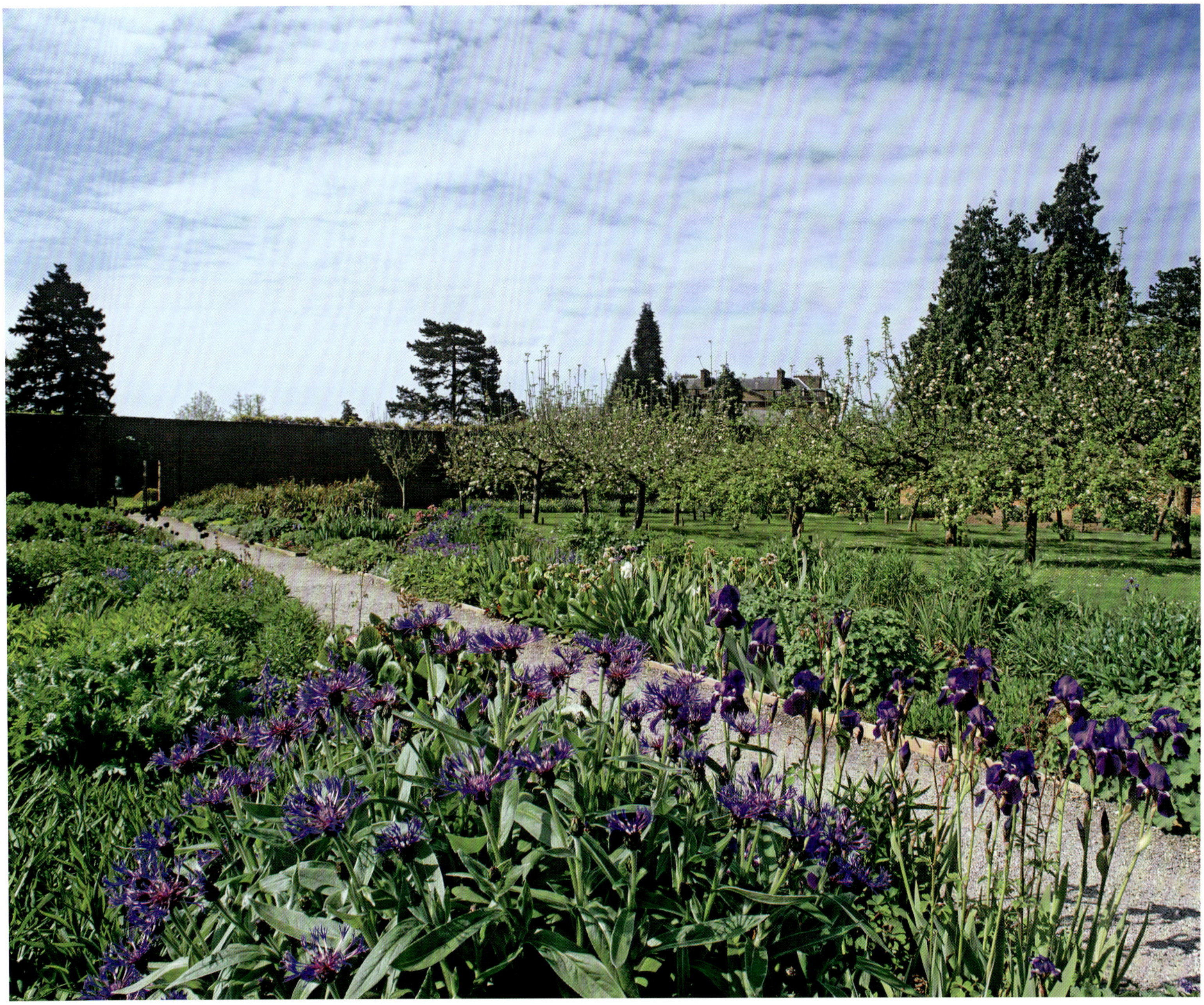

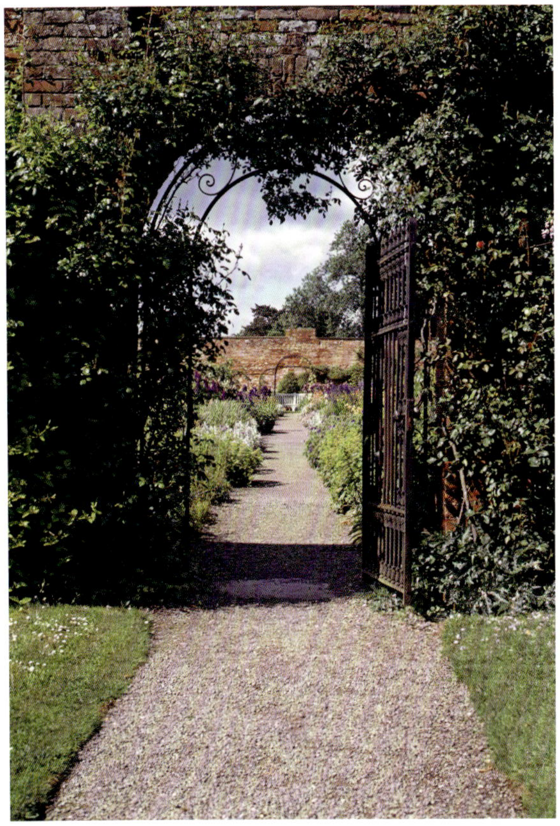

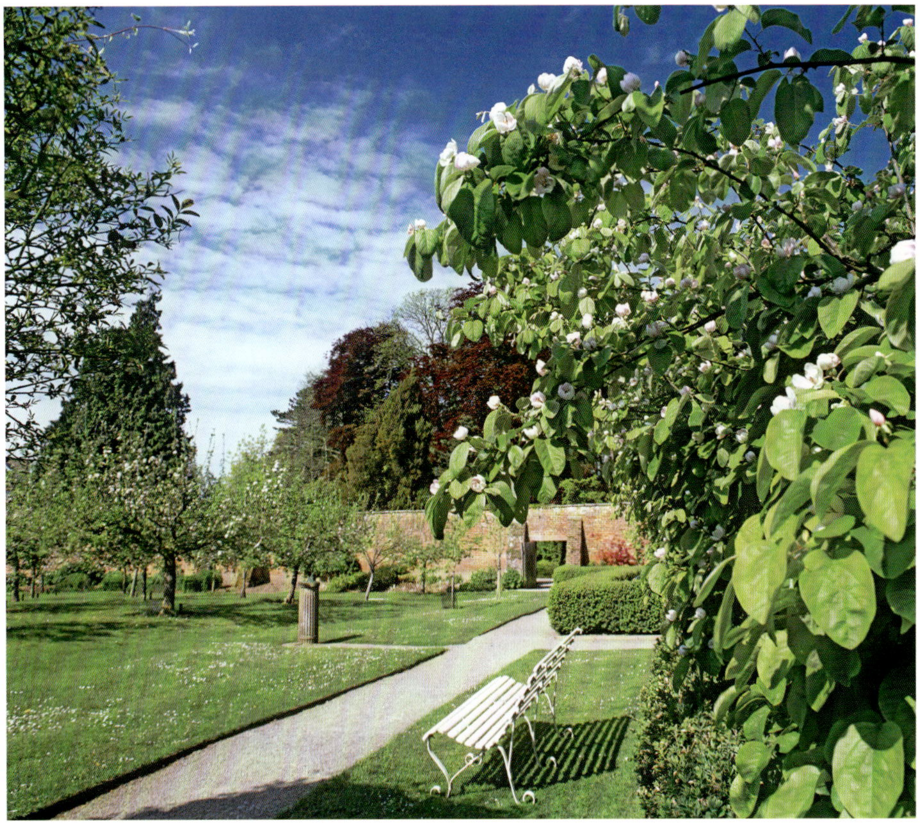

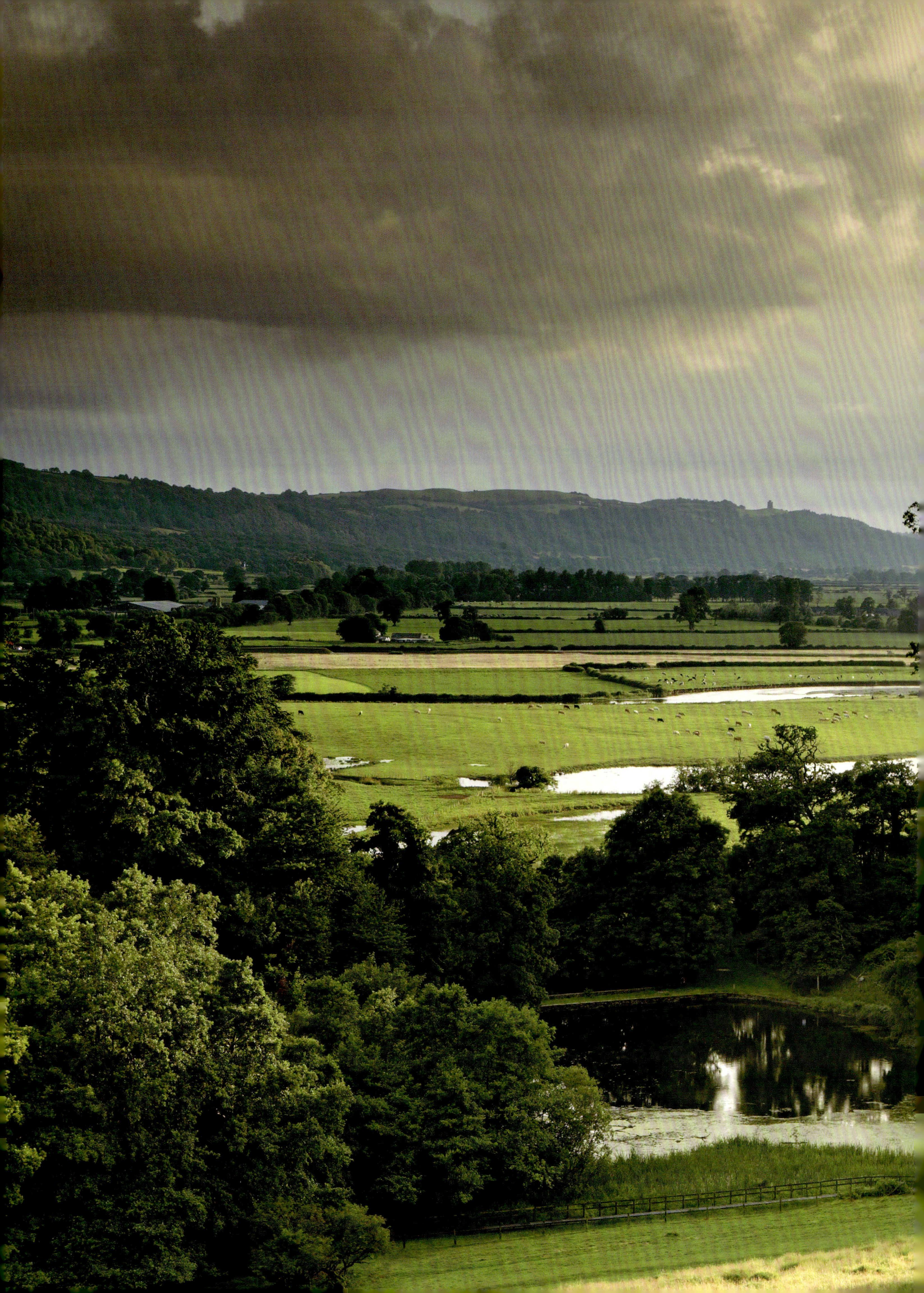

TO CONCLUDE

— CAPABILITY BROWN —
1716–1783

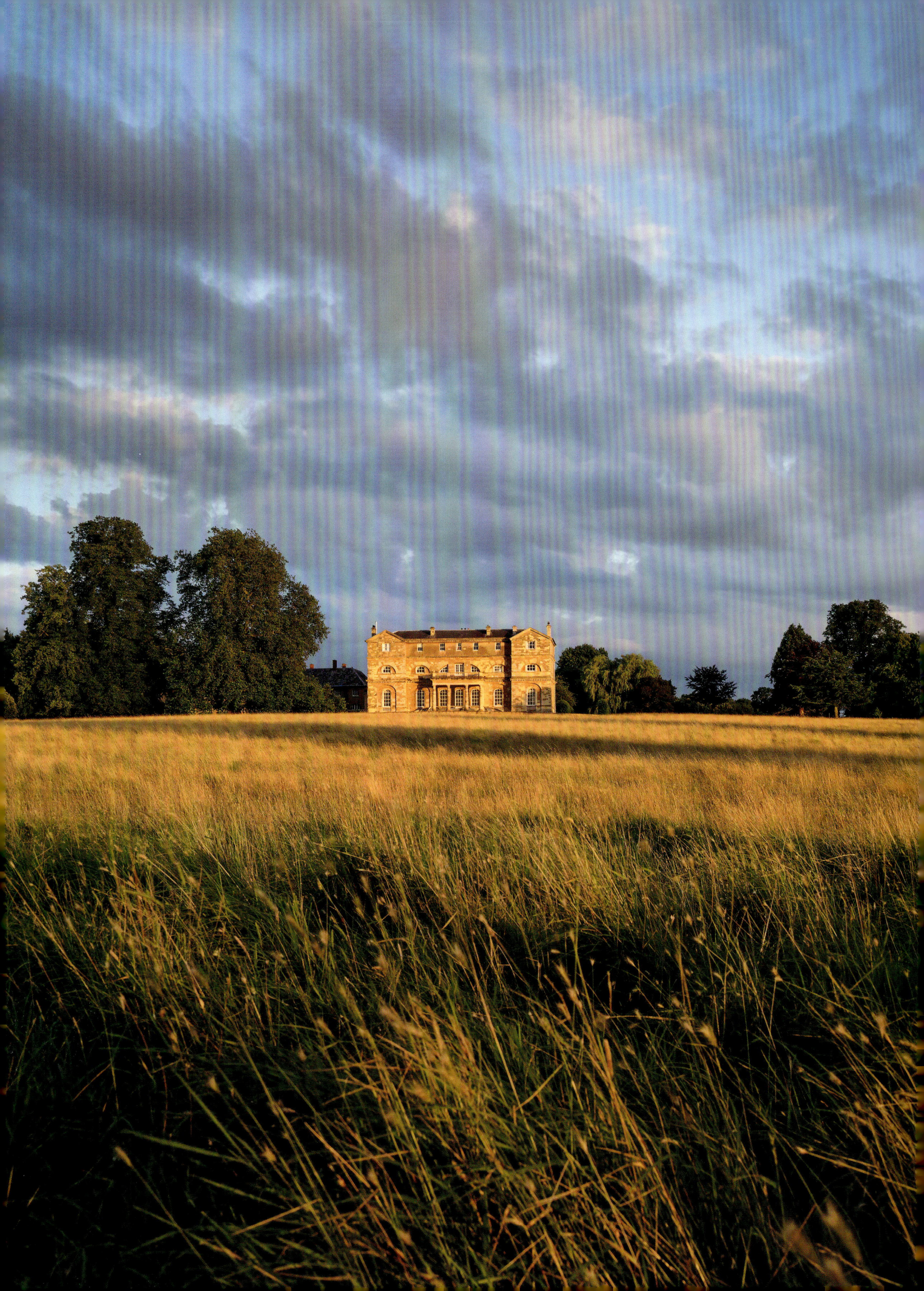

TO CONCLUDE

It would not be appropriate to end a book which is so consciously speculative with a set of answers, like a teacher's edition of a mathematical text. The process of writing has been more akin to sorting the stockroom of a cotton mill. From it I now bring forth some bolts of cloth, I lay them on the counter one after another, side by side, folded and uncut. See what you think. I have found these helpful in my own attempts to understand England and Brown. I do not want to select between them. I leave the cutting shears on the counter.

I

Capability Brown was the right man at the right time. A harmless enough idea of the journalist and philosopher, Joseph Addison—that natural beauty could be judged like a picture—generated some pretty thoughts in the middle of the eighteenth century from architects and designers such as William Kent, Thomas Wright, Thomas Robins, and their like, about making gardens for fairies, Druids, and Knights of yore that still pretended to work as farms. This notion was shortly followed by a mania for farming and Brown rose with that, persuading his clients that they could make economic working units which could also be judged as if they were classically conceived paintings, with a beauty that was true to the native character of England.

II

After his death the same intellectual quest for the physical and irreducible core of England's geography generated a new picturesque belief in the untouched natural world as perfectly beautiful. This unhappily harmonized with Jacobinist support for the primacy of the unmediated "natural" feeling of the individual—a political principle so revolutionary that it made the Lichfield poet Anna Seward shiver in her boots ("may the people, amongst whom I live, be withheld by stronger repellants than their own virtue, from invading my property and shedding my blood!"[1]), and sufficiently effective in France to bring to an end the general consensus in England on the merits of alteration that had attended Brown during his life.

previous pages: The views out from the high ground of the park at Dinefwr take in the meanders of the River Towy and Paxton's Tower, high up on the far side of the valley.
opposite: It is pleasing to think that at Wakefield Lodge Brown completed the work of his master, William Kent.

III

There are elements of Brown's work that we have nonetheless learned to be thankful for: the absence of exotic trees and shrubs from the countryside; the special value placed on ordinariness and the everyday that Constable expressed; a recognition of lowland England as beautiful, despite its undramatic nature and topography; a recognition of the value of human life and human pursuits, however ordinary; a recognition, arising not just from Brown's late work, but from the outset at Wakefield Lodge, that it need take only a little to make something great; the attribution of a particular value to things that are old. These prescriptions of the cultural framework of England are acquired rather than inherent, and many cultures have grown fruitfully from an entirely different stock. Brown made them real and so made them English.

IV

With this perception, we might explain the movement from George Virtue's description of Chatsworth, Derbyshire, as a jewel framed by its wild, mountainous setting at the beginning of the century to Repton's praise for the jeweled foreground of Cobham Hall, Kent, as a frame to the wilder picture of the parkland beyond.[2] If parkland could represent an aboriginal Englishness, being of English make, underpinned by English agriculture, its place would be at the center of the picture.

V

Two scholars, Jay Appleton and Oliver Rackham, have independently found similarities between English parkland and savannah.[3] However true their insight, this is not necessarily because some unconscious psychological desire drove men to make parks that represented the terrain of the Stone Age, or landscapes that accurately reflected a hunter-gatherer instinct to find beauty and comfort in defensible places of retreat (pleasure ground) coupled with open ground which gave no cover to marauding enemies (parkland). If, in consciously trying to reproduce what it regarded as the ancient countryside of England, the eighteenth century stripped all the indications of human interference out of the view (fences and hedges, arable land, foreign trees), the result would be open ground studded by such native trees as had been growing in the hedges but still had a natural habit—that is to say, parkland, or savannah.

VI

Claude Lorrain's paintings offered to England, one hundred years after his death, a vision of the eighteenth century as the country's second golden age, and of Brown as its midwife, bringing into being a confident national psyche conceived after successive victories over France. Brown's parkland is remarkable in that while it was an engine of agricultural change, it had the appearance and associations of a prelapsarian England. Hence the removal of pollards and ploughland, because they were emblems of labor; hence the removal of hunting; and hence the extraordinary role of hay in parkland, because grass provides abundantly and in its harvest, rather than recognize the laborers' effort, it is easy to celebrate the generosity of the planet.

opposite: The Town Pool at Weston Park.

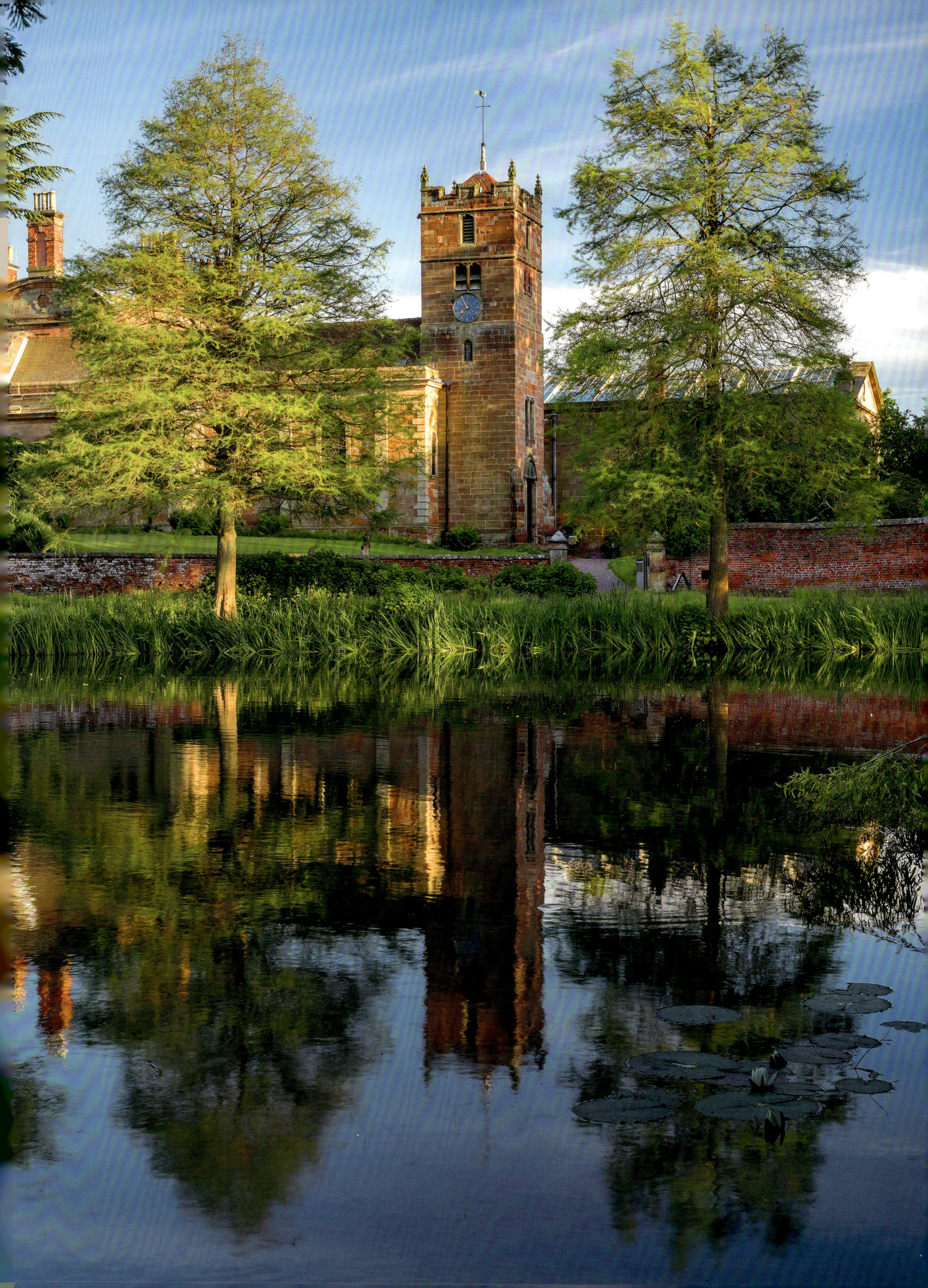

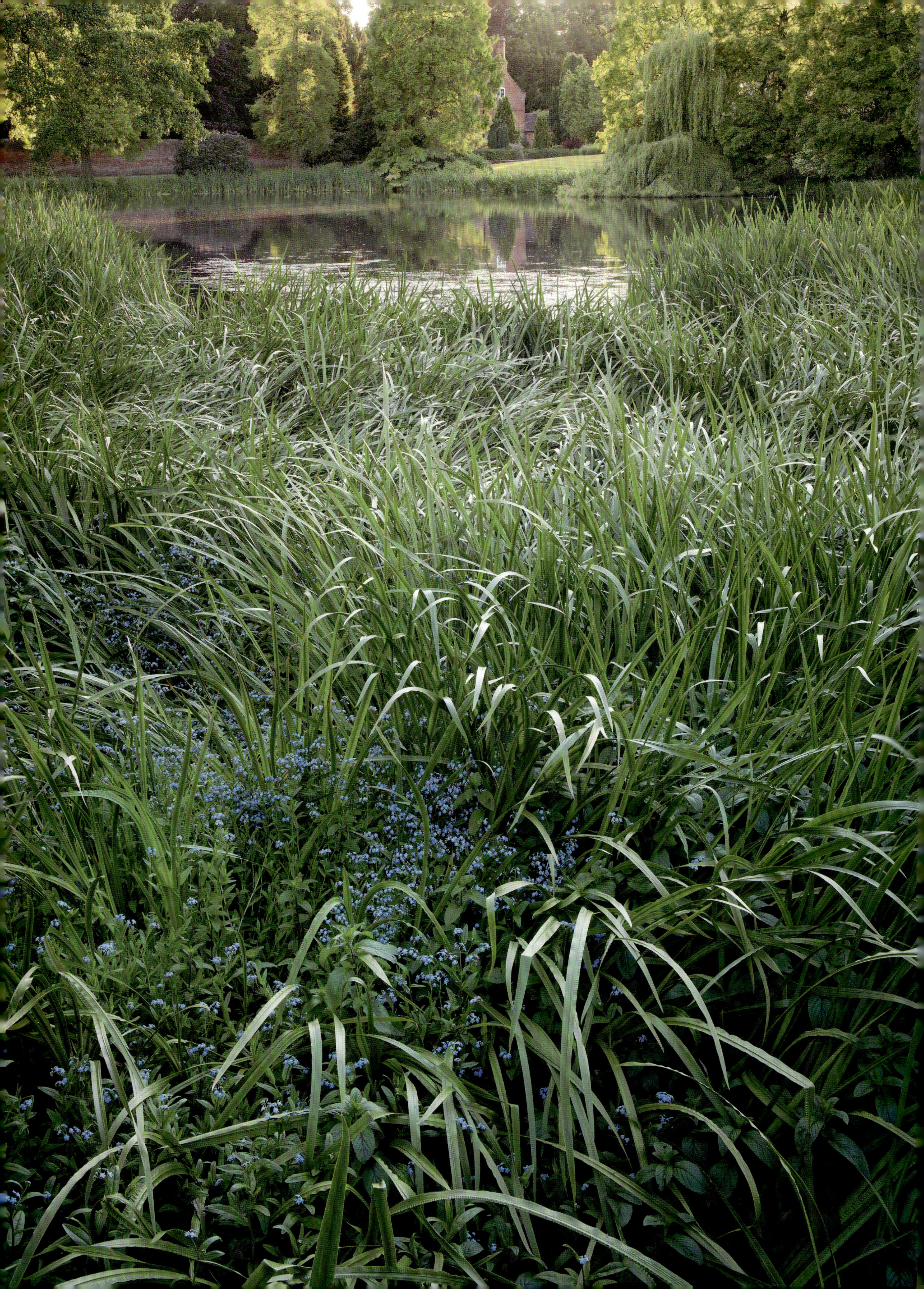

VII

The contempt of Sir Richard Payne Knight and Uvedale Price and their associates in the picturesque movement for Brown's work was also an attempt to take credit for what he had done and to take ownership of it. But they were too late; the horse had already left the stable. In his later work, Brown had far outreached their capacity to imagine what landscape could effect.

VIII

The relaxed appearance of the English landscape style and the need to cement the Constitutional Settlement into the fabric of national life fused the English landscape to the politics of liberty. An absolute ruler such as the Empress Catherine of Russia might don the trappings of English landscape to disguise herself as a monarch of the enlightenment, but Brown's landscapes were actually liberal: the views from the servants' offices at Blenheim were as good as those from the staterooms.

IX

Brown developed the tradition of reference that he had learned at Stowe: classical architecture might refer to Athenian democracy and the Roman republic; Gothic to pre-Roman forebears of English liberty. But he brought this tradition of emblematic design to its natural conclusion. Ancient liberties could be reestablished on the native soil of England, and to capture, distill, and express the conditions in which they would thrive became a driving force of his work. As he incorporated real villages into his design, his idealized England and England itself became one.

X

Brown's work may have been sought after because his contemporaries saw it as putting into one harness their twin projects of the reclamation of ancient England and improved agriculture. Hence his work at Burghley, Lincolnshire, "where I have had twenty-five years' pleasure in restoring the monument of a great minister of a great Queen."[4] The intention of his work was restorative—an idea that Repton was to make explicit eight years after Brown's death: "By the ill judged interference of Art it is become no easy task to display the natural beauties of the place to the best advantage, since in proportion to the mighty efforts which have been used to distort nature, will be the Labour of restoring her original charms."[5]

XI

Brown's authority was such as fleetingly to establish the overriding importance of landscape in place-making and an architecture that would begin with an understanding of the spirit of the place, the genius loci. Such was Brown's influence that his projects were often continued and completed after his death, not just at Moccas, but at Highclere, at Belvoir Castle, at Berrington—even after 1794, when his archcritics, Uvedale Price and Richard Payne Knight of the picturesque movement, published their sustained critical attacks on his work and character.

XII

Brown's influence seeped step by step into the consciousness of the American landscape architect Frederick Law Olmsted. Central Park in Manhattan (1858–1861) tries so hard; its three-dimensional

opposite: Weston Park.

surround buffers the park from 59th Street with great rock outcrops and hillocks, tunnels, bridges, bridges on tunnels, and rides, drives, and walks over them, plaiting the edge, weaving the perimeter. Its leveled green heart is itself full of diversions. It is great: the rocks, which attract idlers and tolerate no end of traffic, have turned out to be an unimaginable success—the rise from the street, up from under a bridge, rising into what was sunlit pasture, now sports fields—but this is more Paxton than Brown. It is trying so hard that it induces magic by way of sleight of hand. Compare that with Prospect Park (1865–1873), a park that sits in Brooklyn like a gift so wonderful that the good citizens did not dare to change it. The smoothed grass of the Long Meadow, the lawns, the ease of it, the rolling folds of the ground, the trees that lightly scarf the park—Prospect is a considerable step from Central toward a true understanding of Brownian design. Then comes Boston (1875–1892), built around the idea of a long parkway, running through the city to Franklin Park, whose only buildings were to be small thatched shelters with "the general aspect of the simplest style of English rural cottages," providing a separate narrative for the city alongside that of the grids of its streets. What is there that could not be found in the ridings of Wallington, Belvoir Castle, or Petworth?

XIII

The current enthusiasm for connecting areas of nature conservation value with the kind of wild corridors that Brown established with his ridings is an appreciation of the need to take in wider, grander horizons if we are to understand and improve our environment—that sense of scale, that drive toward a single unifying vision for landscape, is Brown's.

XIV

It has taken two hundred years for Brown's trees to become sufficiently mature for us to be able to take in his achievement. In 2016, three hundred years after his birth, we should be able to come to judgment on it.

XV

Last, but by no means least, there has to be humor. Brown's designs may elude us just because they were so witty, lightly mocking existing practice—the ha-ha is most obviously a joke, and it is a joke that Brown played with. Others include the Great Stare (i.e., Stair) at Milton Abbey, the self-aware practice of avenue patching, the planting of clumps to look like hills, and vice versa. If one chooses not to recognize the joke and instead to take the landscape literally, then one will get a very different reading of it. Brown's landscapes, however, can accommodate innumerable different readings; their munificence makes them great; the rhythm of their geometry and the many layers of meaning that Brown compressed into simple forms make them great poetry.

opposite: The woodland at Moccas.

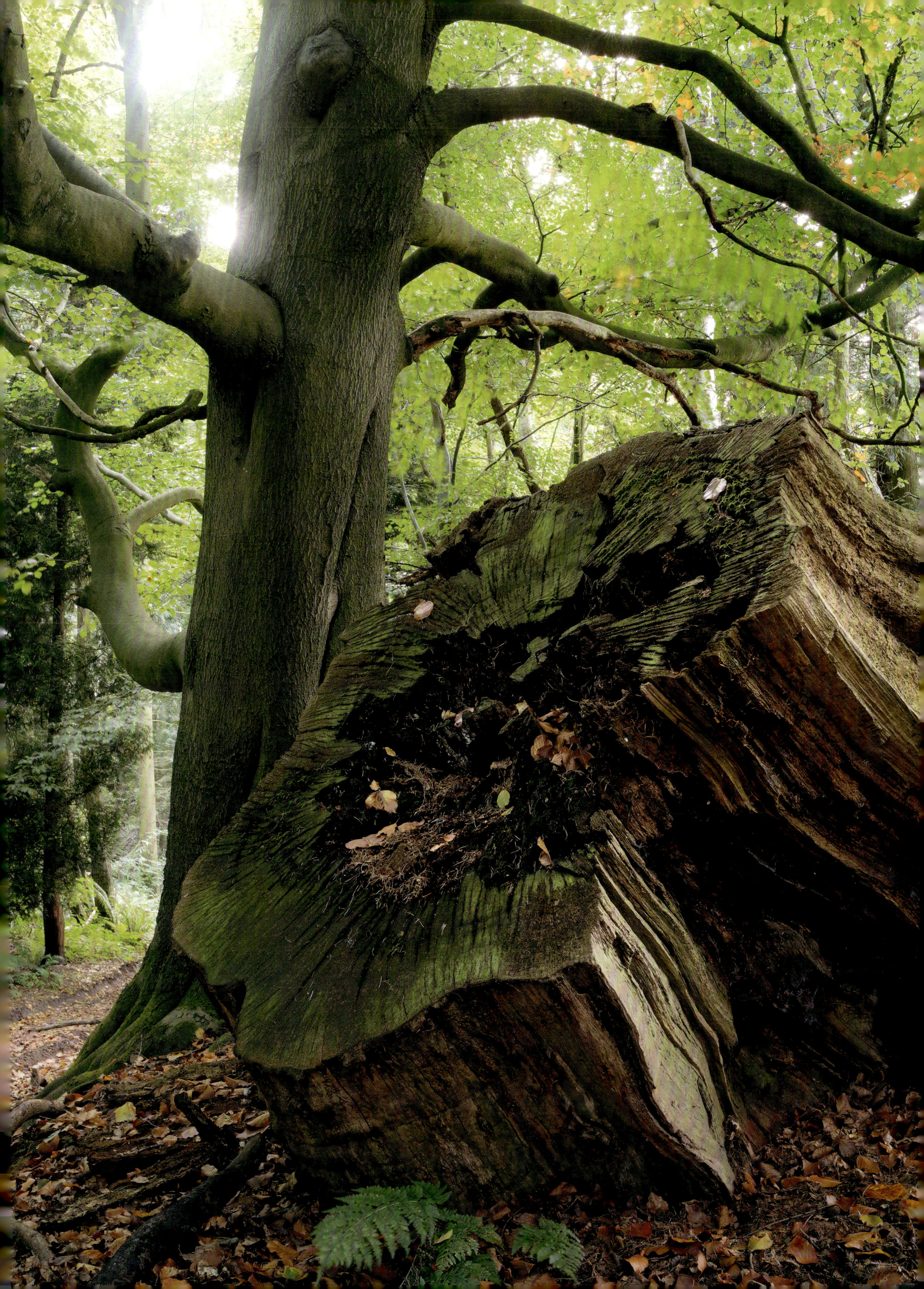

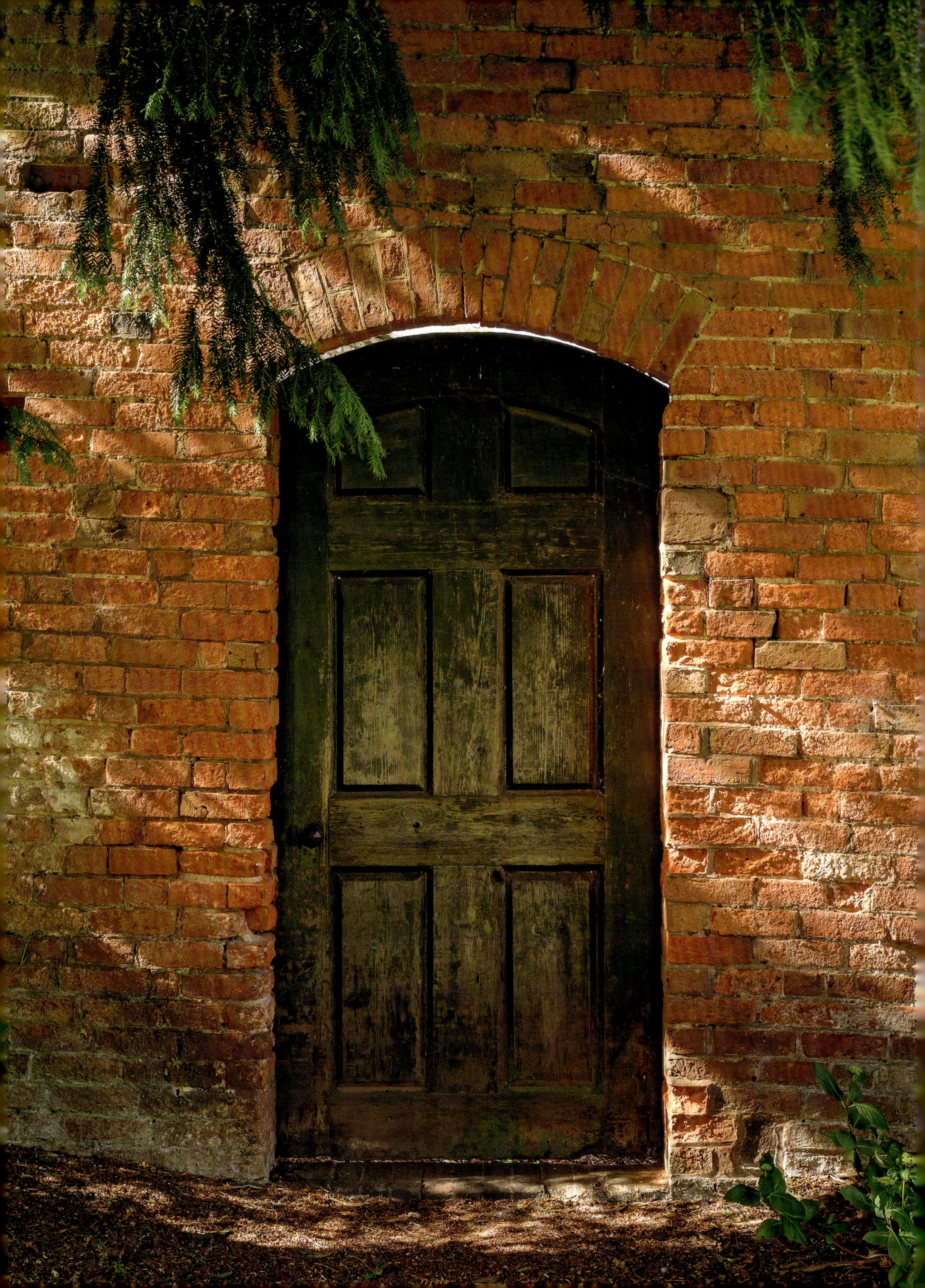

NOTES

INTRODUCTION

1. *The Poems of Mr. Gray to which are prefixed Memoirs of his Life and Writings by W. Mason*, Dublin, 1776, Vol. II, pp. 177–8 (Thomas Gray to William Taylor Howe, 10 September 1763).
2. Rev. William Gilpin, *Tour to the Highlands*, 1776, Bodleian MS Eng. Misc. e. 489, f. 17.
3. Maggie Keswick, *The Chinese Garden*, London, 1978, p. 18.

KIRKHARLE AND WALLINGTON

1. Sir Lambton Loraine, *Pedigree and Memoirs of the Family of Loraine, of Kirkharle*, London, 1902, p. 125.
2. Samuel Johnson, *Dictionary*.
3. Joseph Addison, *The Spectator*, No. 414, 25 June 1712.

STOWE

1. Rev. William Gilpin, *A Dialogue upon the Gardens of the Right Honourable the Lord Viscount Cobham at Stow in Buckinghamshire*, London, 1748, pp. 44–5.
2. Ibid., p. 57.
3. Thomas Whately, *Observations on Modern Gardening Illustrated by Descriptions*, London, 1770, pp. 222–3.
4. *The letters of Mrs. Elizabeth Montagu with some of the letters of her correspondents*, London, 1809, Vol. II, pp. 302–3.
5. Arthur Young, *The Farmer's Tour through the East of England*, London, 1771, Vol. I, pp. 36–7.
6. *Letters of the Late Lord Lyttelton*, London, 1780, p. 30 [the author was actually William Combe, the satirist].
7. Gilpin, pp. 24–5.
8. Whately, p. 175.
9. Stowe papers, Huntington Library.
10. Letterbook of Jemima, Marchioness Grey, 1748, Bedfordshire Record Office, L30/9a/1. ff. 164–175.
11. William Marshall, *Planting and Rural Ornament*, London, 1803, Vol. I, p. 304.
12. Whately, pp. 244–5.

WOTTON HOUSE

1. Thomas Whately, *Observations on Modern Gardening Illustrated by Descriptions*, London, 1770, p. 204.
2. Sir William Chambers, *A Dissertation on Oriental Gardening*, London, 1773.
3. Edmund Burke, *A Philosophical Enquiry into the Sublime and Beautiful*, London, 1757, p. 183.
4. Whately, p. 210.

WAKEFIELD LODGE

1. National Monuments Record Centre, NBR file 61889, p. 4.
2. R. Hewlings, 'Wakefield Lodge and Other Houses of the Second Duke of Grafton,' *Georgian Group Journal*, 1993, pp. 45–6.
3. *The Travels through England of Dr. Richard Pococke*, ed. James Joel Cartwright, London, 1888, Vol. I, p. 72.
4. *An American Quaker in the British Isles: The Travel Journals of Jabez Maud Fisher, 1775–1779*, ed. Kenneth Morgan, New York, 1992, p. 153.
5. Horace Walpole, 'A History of the Modern Taste in Gardening,' in *Anecdotes of Painting in England*, London, 1838, Vol. I, p. 121.
6. George Baker, *The History and Antiquities of the County of Northampton (1836–41)*, London, 1841, Vol. II, p. 230.
7. WSRO 10 WS/24, 25.
8. Notes extracted from the estate papers at Northampton Record Office.
9. Arthur Young, *Annals of Agriculture and Other Useful Arts*, London, 1791, Vol. XVI, p. 522.

PETWORTH HOUSE

1. Thomas Whately, *Observations on Modern Gardening Illustrated by Descriptions*, London, 1770, pp. 160, 164–5, 190.
2. Ibid., pp. 158, 161, 227.
3. *Horace Walpole's Correspondence*, ed. W. S. Lewis, New Haven, 1941, Vol. IX, pp. 96, 155, 201.
4. *Gentleman's Magazine*, December 1757.
5. Whately, pp. 157–9, 227–8.
6. James Dugdale, *The New British Traveller and Modern Panorama of England and Wales*, London, 1819, Vol. IV, p. 370.
7. Lewis, Vol. I, p. 133; Isabel Chase, *Horace Walpole, Gardenist: An Edition of Walpole's 'The History of the Modern Taste in Gardening,'* Princeton, 1943, p. 27.
8. West Sussex Record Office, Petworth papers, 6623; Brown's first contract (May 1753), Item 5: "to finish the parterre in front of the Green House."
9. Brown's plan for Petworth, feature 12.
10. Chase, p. 36.

BURGHLEY HOUSE

1. *The Harcourt Papers*, ed. E. H. Harcourt, Oxford, 1880, Vol. VIII, p. 266.
2. William Mason, *The Works of William Mason, M. A.*, London, 1811, pp. 387–8.
3. Stephen Switzer, *Ichnographia rustica*, London, 1718, Vol. I, pp. xxxvi, 272.
4. John Parnell, 'Journal of a Tour thro' England and Wales,' 1770, London School of Economics Collections, Misc. 38, Vol. III, fol. 97.
5. Forrest's Tours, British Library, Add. Mss. 42232 [c. 1774], f. 55.
6. John Horn, *A History or Description, General and Circumstantial, of Burghley House*, London, 1797, p. 189.
7. Joseph Spence, *Anecdotes, Observations and Characters of Books and Men*, ed. James M. Osborn, Oxford, 1966, Vol. I, p. 427.
8. Forrest's Tours, British Library, Add. Mss. 42232 [c. 1774], f. 55.
9. Correspondence of Henry Hoare with Lord Ailesbury, 15 December 1763, Hoare's Bank, Wiltshire CRO 9/35/165, f. 2406.
10. Rev. William Gilpin, *Practical Hints on Landscape Gardening*, London, 1835, pp. 130–131.
11. Thomas Ruggles, *Annals of Agriculture*, London, 1787, Vol. VIII, p. 167.
12. Horn, p. 192.
13. Rev. William Gilpin, *Observations on several parts of Great Britain: particularly the Highlands of Scotland; relative chiefly to*

opposite: The garden gate at Weston.

picturesque beauty, made in the year 1776, London, 1808, Vol. I, pp. 3-4.
14. Horn, p. 192.
15. Forrest's Tours, British Library, Add. Mss. 42232 [c. 1774], f. 55, f. 55v.
16. Rev. William Gilpin, *Observations on several parts of Great Britain: particularly the Highlands of Scotland; relative chiefly to picturesque beauty, made in the year 1776*, London, 1808, Vol. I, pp. 3-4.

CHATSWORTH

1. *Horace Walpole's Journal of Visits to Country Seats &c*, ed. Paget Toynbee, 1928, Walpole Society, Vol. XVI, pp. 28-9.
2. Edward Knight, 'Notes of various gardens, houses, bridges, market crosses etc.,' 1759-1761, Kidderminster Public Library.
3. Toynbee, p. 65.
4. George Vertue, 'Tour with Lord Oxford 1727,' British Library Add. 70437, f. 17v.
5. Charles Cotton, *The Wonders of the Peake*, London, 1681.
6. Humphry Repton, red book for Oulton (March 1810).
7. Humphry Repton, *Sketches and Hints on Landscape Gardening*, 1795; republished in *Landscape Gardening and Landscape Architecture of the late Humphry Repton, Esq.*, ed. J. C. Loudon, London and Edinburgh, 1840, p. 91.
8. Humphry Repton, *An Inquiry into the Changes of Taste in Landscape Gardening*, 1806; republished in *Landscape Gardening and Landscape Architecture of the late Humphry Repton, Esq.*, ed. J. C. Loudon, London and Edinburgh, 1840, p. 349.
9. Extracts from Repton's red books for Babworth (April 1790) and Kenwood (20 May and 1 July 1793).
10. *The Sporting Magazine*, 1796, Vol. VII, p. 92.
11. Chatsworth, p. 72.
12. *The Torrington Diaries*, ed. Cecil Bruyn Andrewes, 1934-8, Vol. II, p. 37.

BLENHEIM PALACE

1. Prince Ludwig von Pückler-Muskau, *Tour in England, Ireland and France, in the Years 1828 and 1829*, Zurich, 1940, p. 100.
2. Jeri Bapasola, *The Finest View in England: The Landscape Gardens at Blenheim Palace*, Woodstock, 2009.
3. Henry Slatter, *A New Guide to Blenheim Palace*, Oxford, 1835, p. 14.
4. Samuel Heinrich Spiker, *Travels through England, Wales & Scotland in the year 1816*, London, 1820, Vol. I, p. 36.
5. *The Torrington Diaries*, ed. Cecil Bruyn Andrewes, 1934-8, Vol. III, p. 159 (5 July 1792).
6. Rev. William Mavor, *New Description of Blenheim... to which is prefixed, Blenheim, a Poem*, London, 1789, pp. 39-40.
7. Helen Sard Hughes, *The Gentle Hertford, her life and letters*, New York, 1940, p. 214 (3 July 1742).
8. British Library Add. MS 15541, f. 100.
9. British Library ND, letters of Mrs. Montagu (1757 from King's Weston).
10. J. Dawson, *The Holkham Guide*, Burnham, 1817, pp. 144-145.
11. Mavor, p. 146.
12. Richard Payne Knight, *The Landscape*, London, 1795, Part III, l. 27(n).
13. Bodleian MS Eng. Misc. e. 488 (1) Rev. William Gilpin, 'Tour through Cumberland and Westmoreland,' 1772, Vol. I, f. 21v.
14. Uvedale Price, *Essays on the Picturesque*, London, 1810, Vol. I, Part 2, pp. 322-323; and J. Nichols, *Literary Illustrations*, Vol. I, p. 134 (10 September 1768).
15. Andrewes, Vol. I, p. 326 (14 August 1787), and Vol. III, p. 159 (5 July 1792).
16. Mavor, pp. 92-95, 128-129.

BROADLANDS

1. Thomas Hale, *A Compleat Book of Husbandry*, London, 1756, p. 102.
2. William Humphrey Marshall, *The Rural Economy of the Midland Counties*, London, 1790, Vol. I, p. 279.
3. Uvedale Price, *Essays on the Picturesque*, London, 1810, Vol. I, pp. 304-305.
4. William Marshall, *Planting and Rural Ornament*, London, 1803, Vol. I, p. 305.
5. H. Avray Tipping, 'Broadlands I,' *Country Life*, 31 March 1923, p. 440.
6. SUA BRII/16/9, 15 August 1791.
7. Thomas Gray, *Mr Gray's Journal 1769*, Carlisle, 1803, p. 24.
8. Uvedale Price, *Supplement to my Essay on the Picturesque*, London, 1794.
9. Humphry Repton, red book for Woburn (January 1805).
10. *Vide*, S. H. Grimm's picture of the Kitchen Garden at King's Weston, P. R. Kaye collection, British Library.
11. Hervey, cit. Charles Marshall, *An Introduction to the Knowledge and Practice of Gardening*, London, 1796, p. 5.
12. Humphry Repton, red book for Cobham (December 1790).
13. Richard Fenton, *A Tour in Quest of Genealogy through several parts of Wales, Somersetshire, and Wiltshire in a Series of Letters*, London, 1811, p. 164.
14. Humphry Repton, *Fragments on the theory and practice of landscape gardening*, 1816; republished in *Landscape Gardening and Landscape Architecture of the late Humphry Repton, Esq.*, ed. J. C. Loudon, London and Edinburgh, 1840, p. 550.

WESTON PARK

1. William Marshall, *Planting and Rural Ornament*, London, 1803, Vol. I, p. 338.
2. Lemercher de Longpré, Charles Baron d'Haussez, *Great Britain in 1833*, London, 1833, Vol. I, p. 63.
3. Terence M. Russell, Ann-Marie Thornton, *Gardens and Landscapes in the Encyclopaedie of Diderot and d'Alembert*, Aldershot, 1999, Vol. I, p. 366.
4. Kew PRO30/8/62, f. 103 (24 September 1765).
5. *The Letters of William Shenstone*, ed. Marjorie Williams, Oxford, 1939, p. 400 (to Richard Jago, 16 June 1754).
6. Marshall, Vol. I, pp. 258, 281-282.
7. *Diary of a Tour in 1732 through parts of England, Wales, Ireland and Scotland made by John Loveday of Caversham*, ed. John Edward Taylor Loveday, Edinburgh, 1890, p. 10.
8. Richard Fenton, *A Tour in Quest of Genealogy through several parts of Wales, Somersetshire, and Wiltshire in a Series of Letters*, London, 1811, pp. 24-5.

MILTON ABBEY

1. *The Correspondence of William Pitt*, ed. Wm. Stanhope Taylor and John Henry Pringle, London, 1839, Vol. IV, p. 430 (1777).
2. Thomas Whately, *Observations on Modern Gardening Illustrated by Descriptions*, London, 1770, p. 230.
3. Humphry Repton, *Sketches and Hints on Landscape Gardening*, 1795; republished in *Landscape Gardening and Landscape Architecture of the late Humphry Repton, Esq.*, ed. J. C. Loudon, London and Edinburgh, 1840, p. 53.
4. *The Journals and Letters of Fanny Burney (Madame d'Arblay)*, ed. Joyce Hemlow, Oxford, 1972, Vol. I, pp. 23–24.
5. Whately, p. 174.
6. Arthur Young, *The Farmer's Tour through the East of England*, London, 1771, Vol. III, p. 369.
7. William George Maton, *Observations relative chiefly to the natural history, picturesque scenery and antiquities of the western counties of England*, London, 1797, pp. 332–333.
8. Rev. William Gilpin, *A Dialogue upon the Gardens of the Right Honourable the Lord Viscount Cobham at Stow in Buckinghamshire*, London, 1748, p. 52.
9. Evelyn Philip Shirley, *Some Account of English Deer Parks*, London, 1867.

HIMLEY HALL

1. William Mason, *The English Garden: A Poem*, York, 1783, Book II, ll. 98–105.
2. Joseph Spence, *Anecdotes, Observations and Characters of Books and Men*, ed. James M. Osborn, Oxford, 1966, Vol. I, p. 251, Item 604.
3. Thomas Whately, *Observations on Modern Gardening Illustrated by Descriptions*, London, 1770, p. 15.
4. Uvedale Price, *Essays on the Picturesque*, London, 1810, Vol. I, p. 292.
5. Isabel Chase, *Horace Walpole, Gardenist: An Edition of Walpole's 'The History of the Modern Taste in Gardening,'* Princeton, 1943, p. 26.
6. Rev. William Gilpin, *Remarks on Forest Scenery*, London, 1791, Vol. I, p. 184.
7. William Shenstone, 'Unconnected thoughts on Gardening,' *The Works*, London, 1769, Vol. II, pp. 145–6.
8. Joseph Addison, *The Spectator*, No. 414, 25 June 1712.
9. Alexander Gerard, *An Essay on Taste* (reprint of 1780 edition), Gainesville, Florida, 1963, p. 33.
10. Joseph Cradock, *Village Memoirs*, London, 1775, pp. 74–75.
11. Shenstone, p. 141.
12. *Letters of the Late Lord Lyttelton*, London, 1780, Letter the Twentieth, pp. 32–33 [the author was actually William Combe, the satirist].

DINEFWR

1. Bodleian MS Eng. Misc. e. 486 (5), Rev. William Gilpin, 'Pict. View &c through Monmouthsh. & Carmarth,' 1770.

MOCCAS COURT

1. *Berrow's Worcester Journal* (18 September 1755).

BERRINGTON HALL

1. Oliver Goldsmith, *The Deserted Village*, London, 1770.

CONCLUSION

1. *Letters of Anna Seward*, ed. Archibald Constable, Edinburgh, 1811, Vol. IV, p. 10 (to J. Johnson, 20 September 1794).
2. Humphry Repton, *Fragments on the theory and practice of landscape gardening*, 1816; republished in *Landscape Gardening and Landscape Architecture of the late Humphry Repton, Esq.*, ed. J. C. Loudon, London and Edinburgh, 1840, p. 419.
3. See for example Oliver Rackham, 'Savannah in Europe,' in Kirby and Watkins, *The Ecological History of European Forests*, Wallingford, 1998, p. 3; Jay Appleton, *The Experience of Landscape*, Chichester, 1996, p. 68.
4. *The Harcourt Papers*, ed. E. H. Harcourt, Oxford, 1880, Vol. VIII, p. 266 (Brown to Lord Harcourt, 27 August 1778).
5. Humphry Repton, red Book for Thoresby (October 1791).

ACKNOWLEDGMENTS

To the good fortune of my children, to Tomas, Sam, Tobias, Laurie, and Eliza, unbowed and unbrowned, I dedicate this book, and to Gilly, Queen of the Hive, but for whom I would still be muttering to myself in the compost heap.

My editor, Jacob Lehman, with his photographers—particularly Joe Cornish, Richard Bryant, and Andrew Lawson—and our designer, Robert Dalrymple, have refashioned this book into something more beautiful than I could ever have imagined. To them the credit for anything that is good in it is due.

But I would also like to thank the owners and managers of the fifteen landscapes that have been the subject of this book for their enthusiasm and help, as well as Nick Owen and the rest of my colleagues, those who have worked with me at Debois for the last thirty years.

Then I have been supported more widely by my friends Hal Moggridge and Steffie Shields. They have stood beside me throughout this great fight to have Capability Brown's tercentenary celebrated in style. He was a great man who deserves our respect.

Finally I would like to acknowledge the other landscape architects who have devoted themselves to working on historic landscapes and who have freely shared with me their knowledge and advice. It has all been great fun.

PHOTOGRAPHIC CREDITS

Photographs on pages 38–53, 153, 228–239, 254–259 and 261–265 © National Trust Images; pages 126–135 and 138–141 © 2016 Richard Bryant; pages 132, 136 (above), 137 (below), 153 (below), 180–181, and 260 © John Phibbs; pages 132 (by Paul Barker), 136 and 137 (by Simon Watkinson), and 139 (below, by Matthew Bullen) © Devonshire Collection, Chatsworth; pages 142–143 and 148–150 courtesy of the Blenheim Palace Picture Library; pages 144, 147, 151 (above), 152, and 153 (above) © Andrew Lawson.

Plans, maps, and paintings: page 16 courtesy of the Royal Commission on the Historical Monuments of England; page 30 courtesy of John and Kitty Anderson; page 56 courtesy of the Huntington Library, San Marino, California; pages 12 and 111 courtesy of the Burghley House Collection; pages 136 and 137 © Devonshire Collection, Chatsworth; pages 146 and 151 courtesy of the Blenheim Palace Picture Library; page 172 courtesy of the Broadlands Estates; page 197 courtesy of the Dorset History Centre; page 219 courtesy of the Himley Park Estate and Dudley Metropolitan Borough Council; page 246 courtesy of the Getty Center for the History of Arts and the Humanities; page 250 courtesy of the owners; page 260 courtesy of John Phibbs.